Essential Facebook® Development

Essential Facebook® Development

Build Successful Applications for the Facebook Platform

John Maver
Cappy Popp

Addison-Wesley

Upper Saddle River, NJ • Boston • Indianapolis • San Francisco
New York • Toronto • Montreal • London • Munich • Paris • Madrid
Cape Town • Sydney • Tokyo • Singapore • Mexico City

The publisher offers excellent discounts on this book when ordered in quantity for bulk purchases or special sales, which may include electronic versions and/or custom covers and content particular to your business, training goals, marketing focus, and branding interests. For more information, please contact

U.S. Corporate and Government Sales
(800) 382-3419
corpsales@pearsontechgroup.com

For sales outside the United States, please contact

International Sales
international@pearson.com

Visit us on the Web: informit.com/aw

Library of Congress Cataloging-in-Publication Data:

Maver, John, 1972-
Essential Facebook development : build successful applications for the Facebook platform / John Maver, Cappy Popp.
p. cm.
Includes bibliographical references and index.
ISBN 978-0-321-63798-7 (pbk. : alk. paper) 1. Facebook (Electronic resource) 2. Online social networks. 3. Social networks—Computer network resources. 4. Web sites—Design. I. Popp, Cappy, 1970- II. Title.
HM742.M38 2010
006.7'54—dc22

009035432

ISBN-13: 978-0-321-63798-7
ISBN-10: 0-321-63798-4
Text printed in the United States on recycled paper at R.R. Donnelley in Crawfordsville, Indiana.
First printing November 2009

Editor-in-Chief
Mark Taub

Acquisitions Editor
Trina MacDonald

Development Editor
Michael Thurston

Managing Editor
Kristy Hart

Project Editor
Jovana San Nicolas-Shirley

Copy Editor
Sheri Cain

Indexer
Publishing Works Inc.

Proofreader
Apostrophe Editing Services

Technical Reviewers
Jerry Ablan
Joseph Annuzzi, Jr.
Benjamin Schupak

Publishing Coordinator
Olivia Basegio

Cover Designer
Gary Adair

Compositor
Jake McFarland

❖

This book is dedicated to those who aren't afraid to dive in and figure out how things really work.

❖

Contents at Glance

Table of Contents

Part II: Developing Applications

Preface

Currently, Facebook has more than 250 million active users and more than 350,000 active applications; both are growing rapidly. Facebook continues to roll out massive changes to its development platform, rendering previous best practices obsolete. To date, few definitive developer resources explain how to effectively use the new platform features.

However, just knowing the technical aspects of how to build a Facebook application does not guarantee that it will succeed. It is important to understand what makes applications work on Facebook, how to measure their progress, and how to make the changes that maximize their potential for success. This book is not only an up-to-date reference that discusses the latest features of the Facebook Platform, but it also addresses the entire process of creating applications from inception to deployment and beyond.

Who This Book Is For

This book is for intermediate developers who are comfortable with PHP, MySQL, and the major technologies of the web: HTML, JavaScript, and Cascading Style Sheets (CSS). Readers should also be knowledgeable about setting up and configuring a web server, such as Apache or Internet Information Services (IIS).

No prior experience with Facebook development is required, although some familiarity with the Facebook website as a user is assumed. To be a good developer for a platform, it helps to understand it from a user's perspective.

This book helps readers understand what makes a good Facebook application, how to use the core technologies of the Facebook Platform to create it, and the best practices to deploy, monitor, and tune it.

How This Book Is Structured

This book is divided into five main parts:

- Part I, "Introduction to Facebook Applications," overviews the architecture, integration points, and technologies of the Facebook Platform. It explains what makes a successful Facebook application, using examples of proven applications. Debugging tools and techniques are reviewed as they apply to Facebook development. It also provides a quick reference to the key points of the Facebook Terms of Use as they apply to developers.

- Part II, "Developing Applications," goes through creating an application from beginning to end, using a sample application called Compliments. Each chapter in this part builds upon the prior chapter, starting with creating the application infrastructure and adding support for profiles, canvas pages, messaging, and Facebook JavaScript (FBJS).
- Part III, "Integrating Facebook into an External Website," introduces the Facebook JavaScript Client Library and Facebook Connect, which are two technologies for integrating Facebook functionality into external websites and IFrames within the Facebook Platform.
- Part IV, "Post Launch," details some best practices for spreading, measuring application success, and increasing performance.
- Part V, "Appendices," lists commonly referenced URLs in Appendix A and discusses upcoming beta features in Appendix B.

Contacting the Authors

If you have any questions or comments about this book, send us an email at *essentialfacebook@thoughtlabs.com*. You can also visit this book's website, *www.essentialfacebook.com*, for updates, downloadable code examples, and news on the ever-changing Facebook Platform.

Acknowledgments

Writing a book requires a lot of hard work, but not just from the authors. To create this masterpiece, we had an amazing team assisting us:

Trina MacDonald, our acquisitions editor, made sure that everything happened successfully, dealing with all the hiccups along the way. She was essential as a guide for two first-time authors in navigating all the challenges of completing this work.

Joseph Annuzzi, Jr., Jerry Ablan, and Ben Schupak, our technical editors, went through our text, code, and screenshots with a fine-tooth comb, testing everything and adding their own knowledge and experience to make the book even better.

Michael Thurston, our development editor, slogged through many revisions of all of our chapters, refining the text and creating consistency. He helped make our book easy to read and a pleasure to behold.

Olivia Basegio, our assistant editor, worked behind the scenes to keep all of our documents and revisions flowing smoothly between us and our editors.

We thank the entire team for all of their hard work, patience, and abilities. This book could have never been written without them.

—John Maver and Cappy Popp

About the Authors

John Maver has been involved with the Facebook, Bebo, and MySpace platforms from the time they were released, and he has written several successful applications. He has been a speaker at conferences and webinars about Facebook development and was the Featured Developer for the Bebo platform in the spring of 2008. As cofounder and Principal of Thought Labs, John has worked with small businesses and Fortune 100 companies to find the right goals, strategies, and implementations for their social media campaigns. Prior to specializing in social media, John spent ten years leading software-development teams and building award-winning software-debugging products. You can connect with John on Facebook at *www.facebook.com/jmaver* or Twitter at @jmaver.

Cappy Popp frequently speaks about Facebook and other topics at conferences such as GSP East, MITX, Social Media Business School, and others. He has been developing popular applications for Facebook and other social networking platforms since they launched. Cappy also cofounded Thought Labs, where he's implemented many thriving social media solutions for clients of all sizes, from small businesses to some of the world's largest companies.

In addition to "budding author," Cappy has enjoyed many careers, including executive chef, principal software engineer of award-winning debugging tools, and flourishing entrepreneur. Alright, he's still working on that last one.... In his comically fleeting spare time, he is a die-hard foodie with a passion for ethnic cuisine. You can find Cappy on Facebook at *www.facebook.com/cappypopp* or Twitter at @cappypopp.

About the Authors

I

Introduction to Facebook Applications

1

Facebook Applications: The Basics

Facebook currently has more than 250 million active users.

Think about that for a minute. If Facebook were a country, its population would make it the world's fourth largest. It would be larger than Russia, Brazil, Japan, Mexico, or any European nation. It ranks in the top ten most visited websites by the entire world's top Internet research firms. It handles billions of page views per month. Facebook provides some extremely compelling statistics.

General Growth

- More than 250 million active users.
- More than two-thirds of Facebook users are outside of college.
- The fastest growing demographic is people 35 years and older.

User Engagement

- An average user has 120 friends on the site.
- More than 5 billion minutes are spent on Facebook each day.
- More than 30 million users update their statuses at least once a day.
- More than 8 million users become Fans of Facebook pages each day.

Applications

- More than 900 million photos are uploaded to the site each month.
- More than 10 million videos are uploaded each month.
- More than 1 billion pieces of content (web links, news stories, blog posts, notes, photos, and so on) are shared each week.
- More than 2.5 million events are created each month.
- More than 45 million active user groups exist on the site.

International Growth

- More than 50 translations are available on the site, with more than 50 in development.
- More than 70 percent of Facebook users are located outside the United States.

Platform

- More than 1,000,000 developers and entrepreneurs from more than 180 countries.
- More than 350,000 applications are currently available from the Facebook Application Directory.
- More than 5,000 applications have more than 10,000 or more monthly active users.
- Every month, more than 70 percent of Facebook users engage with Platform applications.

The Facebook ecosystem is frequently referred to in terms of a social graph. In this graph, each Facebook user represents a node, and that user's friend relationships represent the edges between these nodes. All these nodes and edges together comprise the social graph. Scientists have studied social graphs for decades, and there is a wealth of available information about them.

One of the most important hypotheses of social networks, especially as they relate to Facebook, is the "small world phenomenon"—the basis for the well-known phrase "six degrees of separation"—which states that there are generally only a few social relationships separating any two arbitrary people in the world. The power of this idea can be clearly seen when you look at this in terms of Facebook's social graph of 250 million nodes. The potential for a single Facebook user to interact with any other in Facebook's closed system is much greater than it would be in an open environment, like the web.

Facebook's Platform gives you direct access to its social graph and the data contained within it, so it's no surprise that the interest in creating Facebook applications has exploded. This book takes you through the necessary steps to get your application built in the best way possible to maximize your chances of getting your application to spread successfully.

Environment and Integration Points

So, you use Facebook. You understand how it works. Perhaps you post photos, comment on your friends' Walls, update your status, and install applications. But, where can an application actually integrate into Facebook's interface? This section provides those answers. Some of these integration points are actually hosted on Facebook's servers, and some are hosted on the application's servers, such as an application's profile presence. The parts of an application that are hosted on your own servers are known as *canvas pages*. It's important to realize that there are important restrictions placed on the Facebook-hosted portions of an application. We overview the integration points in this chapter and give more detailed descriptions in Part II, "Developing Applications."

Profiles

The Facebook profile is the main entry point for Facebook users. To be statistically valid, social graphs require that their nodes (or users) are unique, and Facebook ensures this—or at least mitigates it—in its Statement of Rights and Responsibilities by requiring that each account be backed by a single physical person. Each account is supposed to represent a user's real-world identity. The Profile is where that identity is displayed for a given user.

Applications can integrate with Facebook in multiple locations within its user interface, including the profile. As far as the Facebook Profile goes, there are several places applications can integrate, which are discussed in the following sections.

Profile Boxes

A user's profile is comprised of many sections:

- The Wall and Info tabs share a common left column of application profile boxes.
- The Boxes tab hosts two columns of application profile boxes.
- The Application tabs are full-screen-width application profile boxes.
- The Feed Wall lists activities carried out on Facebook by a user and his friends.

In Facebook, you can reach the profile by clicking the Profile link at the top of any page while you're logged in. The user can allow an application to display a box on the left side of his profile when the Wall or Info tab is selected, or he can allow a box to be placed on his Boxes tab. At least one application must be installed to have the Boxes tab appear on the profile. The size of these boxes is limited by both height and width, if they are placed on the Wall or Info tabs and by width on the Boxes tab. Note that an application cannot place anything on a user's profile without his express permission. (This is covered in Chapter 8, "Updating the Profile.")

Wall, Info, and Boxes Tabs

The Wall and Info tabs share a common left navigation area, which is shown in Figure 1.1. A user can place up to five application profile boxes in this region, and they all must be placed below the Friends section. These boxes are limited in both width and height, so the content they display is crucial. It needs to get users' attention, encourage interaction, and provide a call to action (to get new users to install the application, for example) all within a small space.

Boxes can be placed on the left side of a user's profile by using a special tag that Facebook provides. This tag displays an Add to Profile button to encourage users to install a profile box for an application. This is the only direct means for an application to install a profile box directly to the Wall and Info tabs. Profile boxes can also be relocated here from the Boxes tab.

The Boxes tab is made up of two columns: a wide one on the left and a narrow one on the right. There is no limit to their height, but there are width limits for each column. Users can drag profile boxes from one side to the other, so applications need to handle being rendered well in each or provide a message stating that they cannot be shown in a given column. The dragging behavior cannot be disabled. All content found on the tabs in the Facebook profile is cached and accessed from Facebook's web servers.

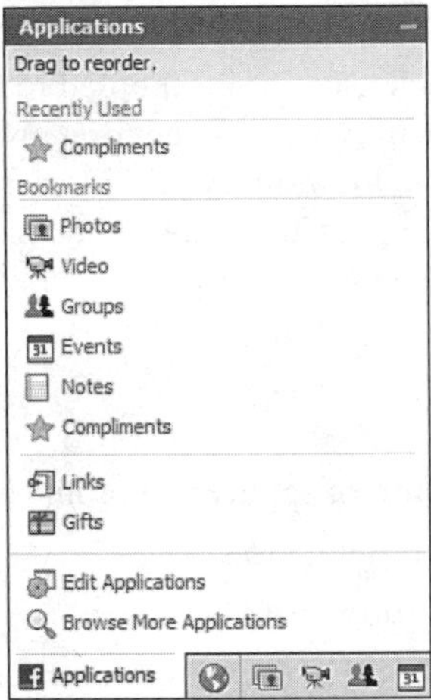

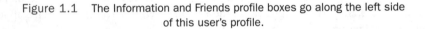

Figure 1.1 The Information and Friends profile boxes go along the left side of this user's profile.

When Facebook first launched the F8 Platform in May 2007, applications had nearly free reign to display whatever they liked, including showing different content to non-application users on behalf of and without a user's consent. Application developers tried every trick in the book to get people to spread and install their applications using any and all loopholes in the Facebook Terms of Service.

Since then, Facebook made many changes to close those loopholes, the largest of which was the new profile redesign (launched in July 2008), which relegated all existing application profile boxes to the Boxes tab. Application developers were less than enthusiastic at first; however, the change certainly cleaned up the profile and, with the creation of the Feed, made it more focused on what users were doing rather than what applications they had installed.

It's more difficult to make successful applications today than it was when Facebook first launched. To be popular and successful—and especially have a profile presence—applications must now be engaging, have powerful messaging in place, and have a high potential for reuse.

Applications Menu

The Applications menu is one of the main places where a user can go to launch an application after she has installed it. This menu is located on the lower-left side of the Facebook interface. Any Windows or Linux user will find the menu idiom easy to understand. It allows a user to access her recently used applications, see applications she has bookmarked, edit global application settings, and search for new applications from the Facebook Application Directory.

As shown in Figure 1.2, the first six bookmarked applications are shown in the Bookmarks section. All other bookmarked applications are shown below this line. Recently used applications are the four most recently used nonbookmarked applications. Interestingly, there does not appear to be a limit to the size of this menu: If you bookmark dozens of applications, your menu will become so long that it will scroll past the top of the browser window. Notice the link for an application named Compliments. This application will be developed throughout this book.

Figure 1.2 Facebook Applications menu

Bookmarks

Bookmarks are simply saved links to applications you've visited on Facebook. They show up in three places in the Facebook profile. You can choose six that are visible both along the lower status area of the interface as nice little icons and on your Home page on the right side of your profile. All other bookmarks are visible both on the Applications menu and by clicking More below your top six bookmarks on your Home page.

There are a couple of ways to add a new bookmark for an application. You can click the Bookmark <Application Name> button to the right of the bookmarked application icons in the status area when you're on that application's canvas page (see Figure 1.3).

You can also check the appropriate checkbox in the Bookmarks tab of the application's settings dialog from the Application Settings page (see Figure 1.4).

Figure 1.3 You can bookmark an application while using it by clicking the Bookmark link that Facebook adds to the bottom of the page.

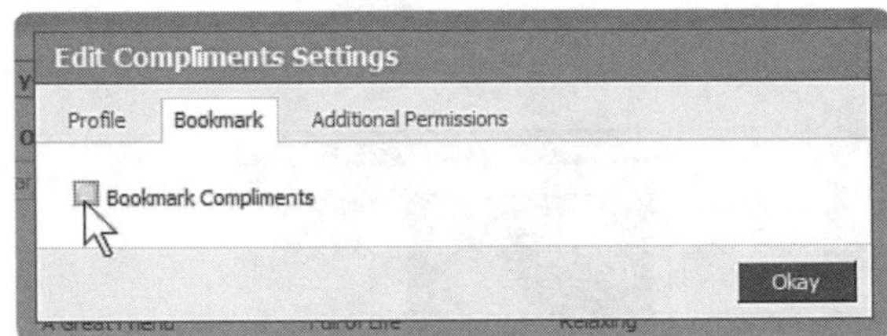

Figure 1.4 Bookmarking an application using Application Settings

Bookmarks are critical in Facebook. Why? If a user installs an application but does not bookmark it, use it within a month, or install it on her profile, that application is only accessible to her via the Application Settings page. Few users ever visit this page or even know it exists. Recently, Facebook added the Edit Applications link to the Applications menu shown in Figure 1.2 to make finding it somewhat easier, but the important thing to realize is that getting users to bookmark your application really affects how often they will use it. You can get application users to bookmark your application simply by asking them to do so within the application itself. Unfortunately, there is currently no way to automatically bookmark an application.

Application Tabs

Application tabs give your application more room on the profile. A user can add up to 18 additional application tabs (the Wall and Info tabs are required and cannot be moved,) four of which can be visible at once, and 14 more as links stored in the drop-down menu to the right of the tab strip. Basically, it gives your application nearly the entire width of the Facebook user interface to show content, but it has some limitations on what information it receives and what you can display, as Chapter 8 discusses. Also, as with profile boxes, your users must specifically take steps to add an application tab. But, if you have a lot of content to display and it's engaging enough, this is a great place to show it off. Plus, you get the added bonus of the application name showing across the tab bar in your users' profile. Figure 1.5 shows a great example of a well-designed application tab from the popular Flixster Movies application. Note how the application's name, "Movies," shows up in the profile and how the content spans nearly the entire page width.

Figure 1.5 The Flixster Movies application tab wisely uses the space it's given.

Application Info Sections

Applications can add discrete sections of content to the Info tab of your users' profiles. The Info tab contains personal information about a user: his contact information, activities, favorite books, movies, and the like, as well as his education and work information. Application data added here needs to follow the structured format of the data Facebook adds here. These sections are interesting because users can edit them themselves. Applications are sent the data after an application user saves it and are then responsible for formatting it appropriately for display. Application users must explicitly choose to place application content in an info section. As with the application profile boxes found on the Wall and Info tabs, Facebook provides a special Add to Info button that applications can use to allow users to do so. It looks nearly identical to the Add to Profile button (discussed previously). There is no other way for an application to add an info section.

Two types of info sections can be created by applications. First, text-only sections are just that. The data is all unformatted text, of which approximately five lines are shown before Facebook adds a See More link to display the remainder. Object info sections can display more structured information. They consist of a single title field and an array of other data, such as links, images, and descriptions. Figure 1.6 shows an example of an application-provided info section. This one is from Facebook's Smiley sample application.

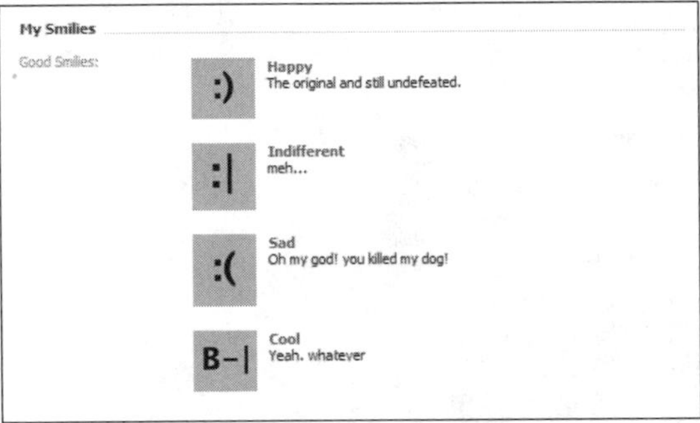

Figure 1.6 Application info section added by Facebook's Smiley sample application

Publisher

Found at the top of both the Home page and the profile, the Publisher has become a principal means for applications to allow users to directly post and share content to their own and their friends' Feeds. Applications can provide custom Publisher integration that allows them to push rich media content to these Feeds. Application users must choose to use an application's Publisher, but after they do, it shows up more prominently in their or their friends' profiles, making it all the more likely that they will use it again. Users can also use the Publisher on their friends' profiles.

When a user clicks the Publisher box, it expands inline to show all the options that user has for publishing content. Facebook always shows the Publisher options from Facebook's own default applications (Link, Photos, and Videos), followed by those provided by applications. Application Publisher options are sorted by the time of their last use.

The more engaging the content an application Publisher creates, the more it involves the application users' friends, which increases the chances that they will interact with it and install your application. Ensure that your content sparks a response from them, interests them, or calls them to take some action. Publishers can be intricate. Figure 1.7 shows the Facebook Photo Publisher. Note how it offers several different options for getting content into Facebook.

Feed

Besides the profile, the Feed is the other major way applications can integrate into Facebook. The Feed is the beating heart of Facebook's social graph, and it's what binds users together. It contains all the activity you and your friends are involved in on Facebook. These activities are collectively known as *stories*. Stories can be posted from within

Facebook, imported from external websites and applications, or created by applications within Facebook.

Figure 1.7 Facebook Photo Publisher allows users to upload or create new photos to share on Facebook.

Two major pieces to the Feed exist: the Feed Wall and the stream. Facebook recently renamed the Home Page News Feed to the stream after it made its update in real time; these terms are interchangeable, and you will come across both while developing applications. The Feed Wall appears on your profile and is populated by information about actions you take on Facebook. The stream is comprised of stories published by your friends on Facebook. It's found on every Facebook user's Home page. Making sure your application uses them to their maximum potential is critical to making your application succeed.

Feed Wall

The Feed Wall is the first tab on your profile. It is a combination of what used to be the Facebook Wall and Mini-Feed. It contains all the recent stories added by a user via a Publisher, a Feed form, or imported through some other means. It also contains stories in which a user participated, even if she did not add the story herself, such as being tagged in a photo.

In the old version of Facebook, the Wall contained stories published by a user's friends, and the Mini-Feed contained stories published by the user. To get that same functionality today, you simply have to filter the Feed Wall using the links provided at the top of the Feed Wall page. For example, in Figure 1.8, the user could make the Feed Wall behave like the old Facebook Wall by clicking Just Friends to filter the Feed to show only content created by his friends. Clicking Just John makes it behave like the old Mini-Feed in that it would only show content directly created by that user.

Stream

The second part of the Feed is known as the stream. It's found on the Home page and is one of the major sources for spreading an application virally, because every piece of content a user publishes via the Publisher—through an application or manually—automatically appears on all that user's friends' streams. The stream also contains all posts made by a user's friends. In the past, Facebook used secret algorithms to determine what content made it into the stream from the stories published on a user's Feed Wall; however, now, all content published by a user via a Publisher or application, and all that user's friends' content, is automatically sent to the stream.

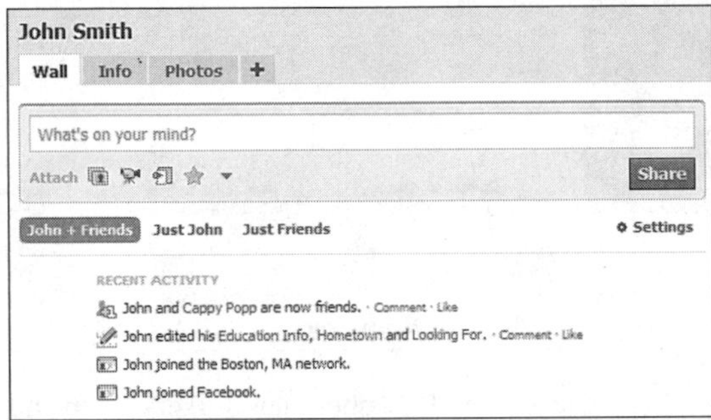

Figure 1.8 My Feed Wall

As previously discussed, applications can provide a custom Publisher, which directly publishes content to the Feed. However, application users must manually post stories to the Feed using a Publisher. Applications can also automatically post stories to the Feed via the Facebook application programming interface (API) or through the use of Feed forms, which Chapter 9, "Feed Stories, Feed Forms, and Templates," covers. In this case, application users do not have to manually publish any content. Stories come in two sizes—one line and short—and each size has specific benefits and shortcomings.

One Line Stories

One line stories are just that: a single line of text. They cannot contain anything else, such as images, videos, audio, or other media. These stories are only visible on a user's Wall on her profile and never in the stream. One line stories are important, however, because the user does not have to allow any special privileges for an application to publish them on her behalf.

The changes Facebook made to the Home page in March 2009 seriously affected the power of these stories. First, one line stories can no longer be published to the stream. This means that, to see them, a user must visit a friend's profile. Also, Facebook no longer aggregates similar one line stories from an application. If five application users generate the same one line story within a short time period, Facebook used to combine them and include all five of these users in a single story, which generally increased that story's potential for engagement and, therefore, its reach in the social graph. For example, instead of, "Cappy took the brainless quiz and got a new high score," published multiple times for different users, you'd see, "Cappy, Peter, Paul, and Mary took the brainless quiz and got a new high score."

Facebook used private algorithms to determine which stories were important enough to be included in the stream. Not all of them made the cut, and aggregation greatly increased a story's chances of inclusion. Facebook still uses this technique to combine automatically published stories in the Highlights section of the Home page. With these changes in place, one line stories have lost some of their punch. They are unique in that they do not require a user's permission to be sent, so they are still worth understanding.

Short Stories

Short stories have no limitations on where they are published. They are always published to the user's Wall Feed and the stream of a user and his friends, depending on their origin. They can contain photos, videos, Flash, or other rich media. They cannot, however, be published without express user consent. Applications must prompt a user to allow an application to publish these types of stories or provide a Publisher to allow users to directly create them. Short stories are more interesting from a content perspective and are, therefore, more effective in helping applications to spread throughout the social graph. But, applications have to convince users of their worth in order for them to invest in allowing these types of stories to be published on their behalf.

You might wonder why you would ever provide a Publisher or Feed form when you can use the API to post all the Feed stories you want. Obviously, for an application to spread quickly, getting stories into the stream is extremely important. Remember, one line stories are the only ones that don't require anything more than authorizing an application to be created; however, their reach is limited to the profile and the Highlights section of the Home page, and applications can send only a limited amount of them per user, per day. Also, all stories published automatically by the Facebook API—no matter their size—are only visible on the user's Wall, never the stream. It's critical that applications master the capability to convince users to create short-form stories so that they reach the wider audience exposed by the stream.

User engagement increases story value—period. Story value is directly related to how useful, interesting, and relevant its content is for those that read it. Getting more detailed and useful content from your application into the stream requires that you learn about and capitalize on all the features Facebook offers to get your messaging published. At the moment, short stories are the only way to get content in the stream. Plus, giving users multiple options for publishing application content greatly increases the chances of it spreading.

Sharing

Social media is based on the concept of sharing content, and Facebook has a built-in sharing system that applications can use. Shared content can either be posted to a user's profile or directly sent to users via a Facebook email message. Users can provide comments on all content they share to further personalize the process. Links to resources are the most easily shared, but sharing embeddable rich content is critical. Facebook users do not have to leave Facebook to view or use it, which ensures a greater potential for its consumption. Applications integrate with the sharing system through a special "sharing" control that Facebook provides. Figure 1.9 shows the Share dialog in action.

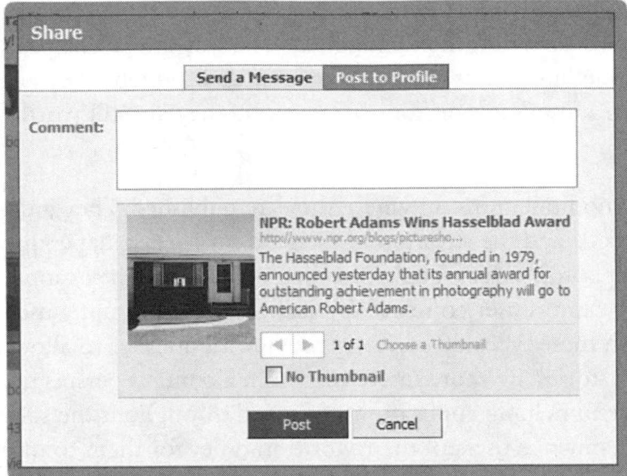

Figure 1.9 Facebook users can share content on Facebook either by directly publishing it to their profiles or by sending it to other users via a Facebook email message.

Photos

Facebook has quickly become one of the biggest photo sharing and storage archives on the web. Several terabytes of photos are uploaded to Facebook every day, and hundreds of thousands of images are served per second. Applications can integrate with this system by allowing users to upload photos, create photo albums, and tag photos. There are also Facebook Markup Language (FBML) controls to allow the rendering of Facebook photos within an application.

Notes

Notes are basically rich text documents that can be created or imported into Facebook. Notes can be created, edited, and deleted by applications via the Facebook API. Users can tag their friends in Notes, which is an operation that results in a Feed story being generated. The most frequent use of the Notes application is as a Really Simple Syndication (RSS) aggregator for a single RSS feed. If an application generates a lot of content, Notes are a great way to get that content into the stream.

Messages, Notifications, and Requests

Facebook provides applications with the capability to send both private messages and notifications. Private messages are just that, and they are equivalent to email. To reduce spamming and abuse, Facebook requires applications to request users to grant special permissions to allow them to send private messages, and these are never sent to their Facebook message

Inbox. Instead, they are sent to the email address the recipient of the message used when she set up her Facebook account.

Notifications are public and are most often used by applications to notify a user and her friends of some action taken within that application. Notifications are stored on the Notifications tab on the Facebook Inbox page, which can be accessed from the Inbox link at the top of the Facebook user interface, as shown in Figure 1.10. An application can send two types of notifications. User-to-user notifications are sent on behalf of one user directly to another. User-to-user notifications can be sent from an application user to the friends of the user, whether they use the application. Using notifications to alert non-application users is, of course, a critical way to get an application to spread. Notifications can also be sent to other application users, even if the sending user is not their friend. Application-to-user notifications are sent from the application to users and generally announce something related to the application in general, such as a new feature, a critical bug fix, or a milestone. To limit abuse of notifications, Facebook strictly enforces the number of notifications that an application can send per user, per day.

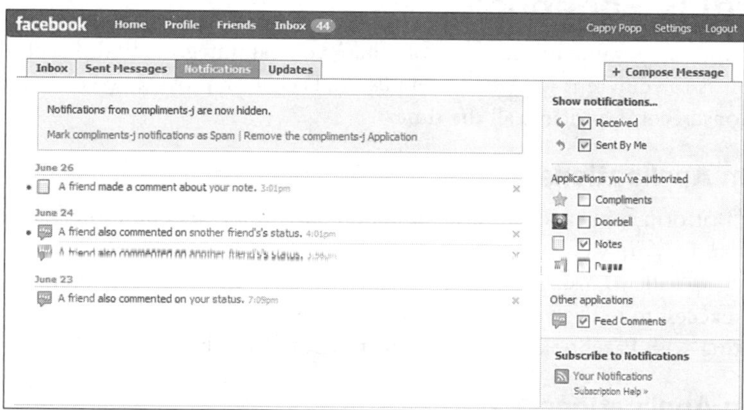

Figure 1.10 Facebook routes notifications to a Notifications tab in the Inbox

Requests and invitations are basically identical—the only difference is their names. These allow applications to send messaging to users that requires them to perform some action, whether it be to use an application, respond to an application-generated event, or take some specific step using an application. Requests have been abused by applications, causing Facebook to corral them in a special page only visible by clicking links from a user's Home page, as shown in Figure 1.11. This move cuts the vast quantities of these types of messages being sent to users. Even so, requests are still an important part of any developer's toolkit for making a successful application.

Figure 1.11 All of a user's requests and invitations are listed on the Requests page, which is accessible from a user's Home page.

Extending Facebook

Now that you know some of the basics of where you can integrate with Facebook, this section covers the different ways to accomplish it. Facebook provides several options, and more options become available all the time.

Platform Applications

Facebook Platform applications can be just about anything. The common features they share are that they are web applications hosted outside of Facebook. Users don't need to do anything specific to install applications—they just need to authorize them to give an application access to their personal information. This is, by far, the most popular method of integrating with Facebook, and it's the main focus of this book.

Desktop Applications

You can also create applications that integrate with Facebook externally. For example, the Firefox Facebook extension provides a lot of functionality of Facebook from within the Firefox browser, while not requiring the user to be on the Facebook site. External applications require special privileges to allow users to remain logged into Facebook indefinitely on their behalf. A popular Twitter desktop client has recently added functionality to set Facebook status messages using this feature.

Public Profiles

Public Profiles—formerly known as Facebook Pages or Facebook Fan Pages—create Facebook presences for companies, celebrities, or brands, and were introduced to add to the functionality offered by Facebook Groups. In March 2009, Facebook significantly changed Public Profiles to make them more like normal user profiles. They differ from user profiles in that there usually is not a single user that backs them, but a set of administrators. Because Public Profiles don't directly map to single users, they don't have friends; they have Fans. When a user becomes a Fan of a Public Profile, he signs up for updates from that Public Profile that get published to his stream. Public Profiles can also host custom applications. Public Profiles provide one of the most important horizons for application growth as businesses and brands enter the Facebook ecosystem more rapidly.

Facebook Connect

Facebook has dubbed Facebook Connect as the "next evolution of the Facebook Platform." It allows developers to integrate Facebook into their own external sites. This technology allows a Facebook user to take his social graph with him across the web. Sites that implement Facebook Connect allow a user to log into them with his Facebook credentials (see Figure 1.12). Once logged in, that site has access to the Facebook details for that user and gives that site access to the Facebook API. This is incredibly powerful because it allows external sites access to the Facebook social graph without having to live within the Facebook user interface or have any of their content hosted on Facebook servers. It's even making its way onto mobile devices. Facebook released Facebook Connect for Apple's iPhone and iPod Touch, which gives the enormously popular iPhone applications a direct way to access Facebook. Facebook Connect is discussed in Chapter 13, "Facebook Connect."

Figure 1.12 Logging into an external site with Facebook Connect

Facebook Platform Core Components

Along with its rich API, Facebook provides several components that allow application developers to easily replicate the look and feel of Facebook within their application and get access to all the data in the social graph. These components are based on existing well-known web development languages like HTML, JavaScript, and SQL to make it easier for developers to be productive quickly.

FBML

As previously mentioned, FBML is an acronym for Facebook Markup Language. FBML is a tag-based language based on HTML. It provides many of the tags supported by that language and provides a large set of Facebook user interface and programmatic primitives. FBML is automatically parsed and translated into HTML, Cascading Style Sheets (CSS), and JavaScript code by Facebook servers when a request for an application page that contains it is detected. FBML gives developers access to controls that allow applications to look like they were developed as part of Facebook.

When an application is created, the developer must choose whether that application will support FBML. It is always suggested that developers new to Facebook applications use FBML unless they have a specific need for a technology that does not allow it. For example, if your application uses third-party JavaScript libraries that are over 64K in size, you cannot use FBML; you must use an IFrame-based application instead.

FBJS

FBJS is Facebook's version of JavaScript. It supports most of the DOM-based manipulation methods that developers are comfortable with and the familiar events, functions, anonymous closures, and properties. It differs from JavaScript in several important ways. First, its syntax is slightly different, primarily to protect Facebook itself from malicious JavaScript code. Next, many DOM properties used in normal JavaScript are replaced by `get/set` property methods. Finally, some widely-used event handlers are not available that are widely used in normal client-side JavaScript.

For example, Facebook does not allow use of the ubiquitous `onload()` event handler to execute code when a web page loads. In all but a few locations, a user must take a physical action on the page (set focus to a control, click a mouse button, hit a key) before FBJS can execute. To further protect itself, Facebook wraps all FBJS in what's called the *sandbox*. To accomplish this, Facebook prepends all FBJS variables, function names, and function parameters with a special string that ensures that no FBJS code conflicts with or can override any existing JavaScript code that might be on the page.

FQL

FQL stands for Facebook Query Language, and it should be familiar to anyone with basic SQL experience. It offers a host of SQL-like features and language elements that allow applications to directly query Facebook's internal data tables. Not all SQL's syntax is supported, but primitives, such as `SELECT`, `WHERE`, `ORDER BY`, and `LIMIT`, clauses are. FQL is powerful in that it accesses and returns the same data provided by many of the Facebook API calls; however, it allows applications to have Facebook filter that data before it's returned to the client, which potentially speeds up page loading and response times.

Many times, applications need to call API methods whose input depends on the result of a previous API call. A great example is demonstrated with getting the names of a user's friends. Using the Facebook API, an application must first call the `friends.get()` method and then pass the result directly back into another API call, `users.getInfo()`. To get the same result in FQL requires one API call, which results in one less round trip to the Facebook servers. FQL can also be "preloaded" for all the pages in an application. This is incredibly useful if an application needs similar Facebook data on every page.

XFBML and the Facebook JavaScript Client Library

Applications based on IFrames and external sites that use Facebook Connect do not have access to FBML and, therefore, don't get access to a lot of the precanned Facebook controls and widgets it provides. Facebook provided XFBML to address this problem, as well as the Facebook JavaScript Client Library to give developers access to more of the features provided by FBML. Not all the FBML tags are supported, but many of the most popular ones are and, in most cases, behave exactly like their FBML counterparts. Applications that use XFBML must render their pages using strict XHTML and must load the Facebook JavaScript Client Library to get access to its features.

Summary

This chapter provided an overview of some of the ways in which Facebook Platform applications can integrate with Facebook, as well as some of the technologies available to make the process easier. Here are the key points to remember:

- Facebook provides several points within its interface for applications to integrate. Facebook profiles and Feed are the most important.
- Developers can interact with the Facebook Platform internally via Facebook applications and pages, and externally via desktop applications and Facebook Connect.
- Facebook provides several technologies that not only allow applications easy access to the data within the social graph, but also give applications the capability to easily match the "look and feel" of the Facebook user interface.

2

Making Great Applications

There are more than 350,000 applications in the Facebook Application Directory, and more than 70 percent of Facebook users engage with them each month. However, only around 5,000 of those applications have 10,000 or more monthly active users. The success of an application can be short lived, so making it near the top doesn't mean that an application will stay there.

What separates the top applications from the rest? In some cases, it is just luck, combined with effective use of the various integration points. However, the applications with staying power tend to exhibit the same quality; they deliver actual value to users. That value can be quick fun, better interaction with friends, or a new way for users to express themselves. Great applications focus on providing value and continuously improving themselves in response to user feedback and Facebook changes.

Although there have been many good applications, there have been a lot of bad [illegible] applications that try to trick users, are difficult to use, or that create huge amounts of spam. This has caused some user backlash and, as a result, Facebook encourages developers to start creating high-quality applications. It created a set of Guiding Principles (described in the section, "Facebook's Guiding Principles") and several programs to verify and reward great applications, which are covered in Chapter 5, "Facebook Terms of Service and Application Programs."

Begin with a Plan

Before you create an application, it is important to understand what your goals are and how you plan to implement them. This section provides the key areas on which to focus.

Objectives

Why are you building this application? Is it to make money, promote or integrate an external brand, show off a new technology or service, or are you building it for yourself? Knowing the objectives will help you understand what metrics to employ to track your success, what areas to focus on in development and in responding to user feedback, and what areas of Facebook communication to focus on. Just like in life, if you don't have any goals, it is difficult to score.

Target Audience

Who do you want to use this application? Facebook has many different demographics, and choosing to focus on one or more of these affects how you develop your application. For example, an application that requires a long attention span is unlikely to succeed if it targets high-school and college students. Instead, focus on providing quick value and communication to fit their usage patterns.

It might also make sense to create applications that are location-specific. An application that centers on Turkish culture might be wildly successful in Turkey and achieve your objectives, even if it isn't popular in the United States.

Of course, after launching the application, an unexpected demographic might dominate the user base. This is a great opportunity to reevaluate both objectives and focus to continue to grow and improve the application.

Value Proposition

Why will users want this application? So many choose to ignore this question and produce applications that gather dust, regardless of how good they look or how much time was spent developing them. Users aren't looking to help you spread your application; they just want something out of it, especially if you ask them to authorize the application instead of just visit it.

Spend the time to really think about what users will get out of your application. The Facebook Guiding Principles and the application profiles shown later in this chapter can help with this process. Remember, one of the best values you can offer your users is a simple-to-use interface.

Competitive Advantage

Why is your application better than your competition's? Make sure to look through the Facebook Application Directory to find applications that offer similar functionality. Read through the forums and Wall posts on each competitor's application About page to find out what users like and don't like about them. You don't have to provide everything for everyone or even match your competitors' features, but you need to provide them with a good reason to use your application.

Involving the User

How will users interact with your application? Facebook applications were once all about having a great profile presence and sending invitations. Now, they focus on creating Feed stories, and profile boxes are not as important. Make sure that your application is designed from the start to use the integration points to your advantage. Use Feed forms to create short stories from inside your application and the Publisher to let users interact from their

Home page or profile. Applications can also integrate with Facebook Chat for real-time communication.

You also need to plan the workflows for how users will engage with the application. Try to refine long sequences of actions—some users will give up at each step. Also, plan to build in A/B testing and metrics for a solid understanding of what is working and what isn't.

Iterating

How will your application respond to feedback? Most applications do best when they create something good enough quickly and then release updates as they gather usage data. It's a good idea to have a set of plans for future releases, but recognize that responding to user feedback can result in the application taking a completely different track than what it started with.

Having clearly defined goals up front helps you decide when to make a set of changes and when to stay the course. It is possible that the users you first acquire are not the ones you were expecting, and the feedback they give might lead you down a path that's inconsistent with your objectives.

Planning for Growth

Do you have a scalability plan? As discussed in the introduction to this chapter, most applications are not successful, so chances are likely that you won't need to allocate dozens of servers at the start. However, doing some planning can prevent you from repeating the experience of the iLike application's founders after their user count dramatically increased—driving around in a truck trying to find more servers for the data center.

Chapter 16, "Improving Application Performance and Workflow," goes over some scalability tips, but you need to design the system up front to use multiple servers. Think about how you can use Facebook's own servers to help take on some of the burden. Also, choose a host that supports autoscaling and pricing based on actual usage, rather than paying by the month.

Facebook's Guiding Principles

Facebook has laid out a set of Guiding Principles to help developers understand how to make successful applications. Most of these seem like common sense, but you can easily find applications that don't follow any of these guidelines and suffer the consequences of low user count, bad reviews, and short lifetimes. Not every application has to offer all these things, but the better an application is at incorporating them, the better its chances are of getting and keeping users.

Make Them Meaningful

As previously discussed, applications need to provide users with some value. That value must be apparent to get users to authorize it, and they must continue to see value to keep it on their profile, allow it into their stream, invite their friends, or simply keep using it.

The following sections discuss the types of value recommended by Facebook's Guiding Principles.

Enable Social Activities

The most powerful feature of Facebook is the social graph. Harnessing the information from a user's friends allows applications to help them connect in new ways or more easily, or just learn more about each other. Some good examples of applications that use Social Activities are iLike, which helps music Fans create and share playlists, and Movies, which uses quizzes to identify similar movie tastes with friends.

Be Useful

Applications must strive to do more than allow users to "throw sheep" at each other. They need to help users easily organize things on a scale that just isn't possible outside of Facebook. Applications like We're Related enable users to quickly build their family trees, whereas users of Cities I've Visited can mark their travels and create reviews to share with everyone.

Allow Users to Express Themselves

Users can fill out their profile info, update their statuses, and upload photos and videos using Facebook's built-in applications. However, many more possibilities exist to allow users to share more about themselves and create content. Sports applications, like Boston Red Sox Fans, allow users to show off their sports affiliations by starting Waves. (Lil) Green Patch lets users demonstrate their support for the environment by building a Green Patch with their friends.

Engage Users' Attention

Applications need to be interesting enough that users will want to use them more than once, even for short periods of time. Social games, like Texas HoldEm and Scrabble, enable users to play against each other. SuperPoke, with its large variety of pokes, has people constantly sending things back and forth.

Make Them Trustworthy

Reading stories about people losing out on jobs because of pictures they shared on Facebook might make you think that privacy isn't that important to Facebook users. Based on the reaction to the last changes Facebook made to its Terms of Use, users really care about it. (Chapter 5 covers this.) They also want applications to work as they expect, both in the interface and in the messages it sends on their behalf.

Secure User Privacy

Facebook users put a lot of trust in applications to treat their data carefully; applications have access to information that some of their friends can't see! Users expect that the same privacy settings they have set in Facebook will be mirrored in the applications they use.

Therefore, Facebook requires users to take specific actions to allow applications to get detailed user information, send emails, and access their data when the user isn't online. However, applications must keep user data secure and private without Facebook forcing them to do so.

Be Respectful of Users

Most applications want their user base to grow, and Facebook provides many methods to let users tell their friends about an application. This creates a temptation to use all the available methods at all opportunities. However, users don't want to be spammers—they want to pass on only information that they think their friends will find interesting. Applications end up being proxies for these users, so the applications must use these communication channels carefully and with content that users would find acceptable.

Have Transparent Functionality

When a user clicks a button or accesses an application, he expects a certain behavior. Applications must not trick users with something else, such as an OK button that secretly sends messages to all of their friends without their permission or creates News stories about actions they never took. Applications that abuse a user's trust will be uninstalled, reviled, and can be suspended by Facebook, as Chapter 5 outlines.

Make Them Well Designed

Well-designed applications are a pleasure to use. Their easy-to-use interfaces consistently deliver the results that users expect.

Build Clean Interfaces

The best looking application in the world will fail if it is too difficult to use. Sometimes, even one difficult step in a workflow is enough to doom an application to failure. When an application is intuitive, users can quickly navigate it, use all the available functionality, and are likely to come back. Design workflows up front and test them after launching to make sure that they function as both you and users expect. Look at top applications for interface patterns that work well and have gone through many iterations in response to user feedback.

Respond Quickly

When applications take a long time to respond to user actions, one of two things will happen: The user will get tired of waiting and give up, or Facebook will display a timeout page saying that something is wrong with the application. In either case, the user didn't get what she expected and, if it continues to happen, she will stop using the application. Use the Insights tool for your application to look at the response times and timeouts, and work to fix these as soon as possible. It is important to identify performance issues early in the cycle, before scalability becomes a real crisis.

Work Reliably

Great applications have great quality. Functionality should be tested before and after deployment to make sure that everything works. When things do go wrong, the developer needs to work to resolve the problems quickly and communicate the results or status with affected users. Users appreciate applications that respect their time and trust.

Examples of Great Applications

This section covers some of the many applications that exhibit the principles discussed in this chapter. The Causes application is one of the official Facebook Great Apps program winners. Graffiti is a great way to express and communicate with friends and LivingSocial has been one of the best users of the new stream functionality.

LivingSocial

LivingSocial (*http://apps.facebook.com/facebookshelf/*) lets users keep track of what they are using, how they feel about it, and get recommendations by looking at what their friends are doing. It supports several common categories, such as movies, books, games, and beer. The majority of the application's value is based on a user's friends using it—the more friends that create reviews or say which books they are reading, the more useful content is available to a user. Figure 2.1 shows how LivingSocial helps users find new books to read.

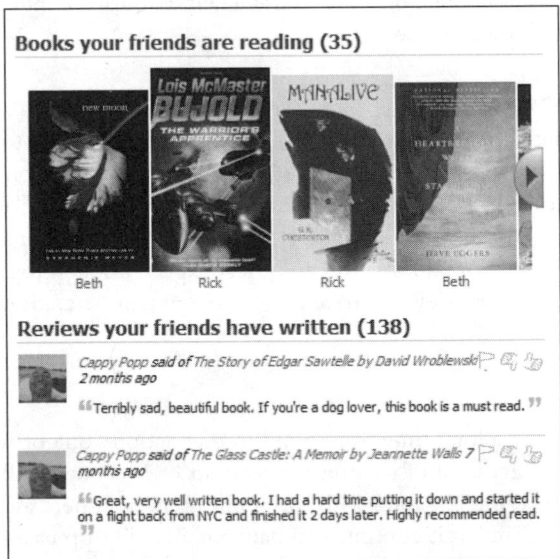

Figure 2.1 The LivingSocial application displays book reviews from friends.

LivingSocial also makes effective use of the stream, letting users pick their Top 5 favorites in a given category and publishing a news story about it. These stories provide value, because friends can learn about new items, give their opinion, or create their own Top 5. Figure 2.2 shows an example of a news story from LivingSocial.

Figure 2.2 The LivingSocial application creates news stories displaying users' Top 5 picks for a category.

As a result of these News stories, LivingSocial has rocketed to the top, becoming the largest Facebook application ever, based on monthly active users. This demonstrates the importance of keeping up with changes in the Facebook Platform, such as the one from profile boxes to the stream.

Causes

Causes (*http://apps.facebook.com/causes/*) allows users to create communities around issues and nonprofits that matter to them, and easily recruit members and donations to join them in support. This application is a great example of providing value: It significantly lowers the costs of acquiring new supporters compared to traditional marketing methods. It also allows anyone to participate, with over one million registered nonprofits from which to choose. Figure 2.3 shows the impact one user has had on her favorite causes.

Users not only get to help the causes they care about, but they also get social recognition for doing it. This is a great example of how applications can let users demonstrate their associations to their friends.

Graffiti

Graffiti (*http://apps.facebook.com/graffitiwall/*) enables an entirely new way of expression by letting users hand draw pictures and send them to their friends. This might seem insignificant at first, but after you marvel at the absolutely stunning entries in the drawing contents or see how users create birthday messages for each other, you will understand how important self-expression can be. Figure 2.4 shows a few of the top creations for the current week.

Graffiti has been around since the Facebook Platform launch, and it has stood the test of time. However, it has not yet embraced the new importance of using the News Feed as the primary application communication channel. It will be interesting to see how the application decides to take advantage of it.

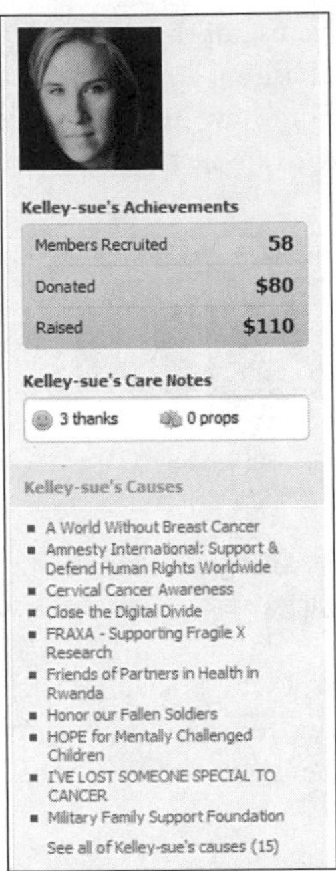

Figure 2.3 The Causes application displays each user's total impact.

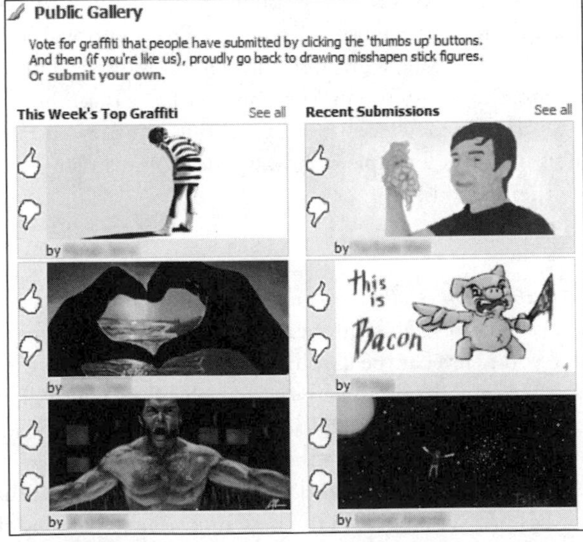

Figure 2.4 Users create amazingly detailed images using the Graffiti application

Summary

You now know what makes a great application, and you have a basis for creating your own. Here are some key points:

- Make sure you understand what you are building and why before you start your application. Have clear objectives and know who your users are.
- Early on, focus on providing value for users and make sure that the user workflows are well designed and simple to perform.
- Plan for success by designing for scalability at the beginning.
- Iterate rapidly in response to user feedback, but make sure that the user demographic giving the feedback aligns with your objectives.
- Build applications that connect users, provide real value, and allow them to connect in new or more in depth ways.
- Respect user privacy and trust by keeping users' data safe and only sending communications they expect.
- Test application functionality before deploying, respond quickly to issues, and provide a fast and reliable experience.
- Make your applications simple to use and intuitive.
- Use other successful applications to understand what works well on Facebook.

3

Platform Architecture Overview

With such a large number of active users, Facebook has enormous demands on its infrastructure. Facebook also has a vibrant application community and needs to provide a fast and reliable interface for developers to use. To accomplish this, Facebook has embraced many open source technologies and contributed many improvements back into the community.

This chapter describes how the Facebook Platform works: the servers and software it runs on and the mechanisms that developers can use to interact with it.

Facebook's Internal Servers

According to Facebook, it is the second most-trafficked PHP-based website in the world, one of the largest users of the MySQL database, and the largest user of memcached, which is a high performance caching system. Facebook has also invented many of its own technologies and released some of them as open source projects. This section discusses the Facebook infrastructure and the details of its technologies.

Servers

Facebook uses multicore Fedora and Red Hat Enterprise Linux servers. Facebook has reported that it has 10,000 web servers, 1,800 MySQL servers, and 805 memcached servers. Currently, it does not use a storage area network (SAN); instead, it relies on a large number of hard drives in RAID 10 configuration. (RAID 10 is a hard-drive storage technology that allows both increased performance and data loss protection.)

The servers supply over 28 terabytes (TB) of memory and process 200,000 User Datagram Protocol (UDP) requests per second. This is based on Facebook's customization of its server software, improving significantly on the 50,000 requests per second offered by the stock versions.

Technologies

Facebook uses a customized Linux, Apache, MySQL, PHP (LAMP) stack. For many of these technologies, Facebook has released enhancements back to the community. Facebook has also opened up some of its own internal technologies. Here are brief descriptions of the major technologies:

- **Apache HTTP server** (*http://httpd.apache.org/*) is the #1 web server used on the Internet. The Apache Software Foundation manages it, and users from around the world constantly update it.
- **PHP** (*www.php.net/*) is an extremely popular, C-like scripting language that is primarily used for dynamic web development. (Currently, it's installed on more than 20 million websites and runs on more than one million web servers.) PHP code is executed on the server and can be embedded within existing HTML or be used to generate dynamic HTML that is sent to a client's browser. It currently provides the user interface code for not only Facebook, but also Wikipedia, Yahoo!, YouTube, and others. Primarily an interpreted language, it benefits from third-party optimizers, which can dramatically increase its performance.

  Facebook has contributed to an optimizer extension for PHP, called the Alternative PHP Cache (APC) (*http://pecl.php.net/package/APC/*). APC caches the base executable constructs parsed from raw PHP, called opcodes, so that that PHP doesn't have to reinterpret them each time the page executes. This extension, and others like it, can really affect the performance of PHP sites.
- **MySQL** (*www.mysql.com/*) is the world's most popular open source database. It is fast, reliable, and easy to operate. Many of the most popular websites on the Internet use it.
- **Memcached** (*http://danga.com/memcached/*) is a high-performance, distributed memory object caching system for databases. Originally created for LiveJournal.com, Facebook uses it to improve the performance of its many MySQL databases.

  Facebook has significantly contributed to the memcached project, boosting its performance and adding functionality.
- **Facebook Open Platform** (*http://developers.facebook.com/fbopen/*) is a snapshot of the infrastructure that makes up the Facebook Platform. It includes an implementation of the Facebook application programming interface (API), Facebook Markup Language (FBML) parser, Facebook Query Language (FQL) parser, Facebook JavaScript (FBJS), and a test harness and several common API utility methods and FBML tags.
- **Thrift** (*http://developers.facebook.com/thrift/*) is a Facebook-created framework for creating scalable cross-language services. Thrift lets developers create definition files with datatypes and interfaces, and it generates client and server code from those

definitions in C++, Java, Python, PHP, and Ruby. Facebook uses Thrift in its Search, Mobile, Posts, Notes, Feed, and the Developer Platform.

- **Scribe** (*http://developers.facebook.com/scribe/*), also developed by Facebook, is a scalable and robust server used to parse and collect server logs from a large number of servers in real time. Scribe was built using Thrift. Scribe is based on a multi-instance architecture: There can be many concurrent Scribe servers and clients active at once in a system. If a Scribe server goes down, clients write logs locally until the server comes back up. Facebook runs Scribe on thousands of its servers to deliver billions of messages a day.

Facebook's External REST Interface

Facebook exposes an interface to application developers based on Representational State Transfer (REST). REST is an architectural style that uses Hypertext Transfer Protocol (HTTP). This section discusses how REST works and then describes how Facebook expects developers to use it.

Using REST on the Web

The majority of the web uses HTTP and, therefore, REST implementations can take advantage of the many features that the web offers, such as interoperability, scalability, security, and standard URLs. REST deals with everything as resources, addressed using standard URIs.

The basic tenets of REST are as follows:

- **URIs are resources.** (Example: *http://server.com/person/john/*) REST is stateless on the server: The state is contained on the client and is passed to the server as part of the URI. For example, a user might get a list of restaurants in Massachusetts by going to *http://server.com/restaurants/ma/*. She might then click one of the resulting restaurant names (Mangia, for example) to get more information, resulting in the URL *http://server.com/restaurants/ma/mangia/*. This process continues as the user narrows her search, and it might eventually include additional information as query parameters, such as *http://server.com/restaurants/ma/mangia/?search=pizza*, to find what types of pizza Mangia serves.
- **HTTP verbs are the methods.** (Example: `GET`, `POST`, `PUT`, and `DELETE`) In general, `GET` should be a read-only, repeatable operation to return resource information. This allows servers to easily cache and scale. `POST`, `PUT`, and `DELETE` change the resource.
- **Content-type describes how the data is exchanged.** (Example: `Content-type=application/xml` sent in the HTTP header) Responses from the server should be XHTML, XML, or JavaScript Object Notation (JSON). Clients of the service should know which to expect and handle it accordingly.

- **Status codes are the result.** (Example: 200 is OK; 400 is a bad request.) Having a defined set of returned status codes is important. Table 3.1 lists the standard ones, which are recognized as part of HTTP/1.1.

Table 3.1 **Common Status Codes**

Code	Meaning
2xx	**Success**
200	OK.
201	Created.
3xx	**Redirection**
301	Moved permanently to another address.
302	Moved temporarily to another address.
304	Not modified, use the local cache.
4xx	**Client Error**
400	Bad request, the syntax was bad.
401	Unauthorized, authentication must be used.
403	Forbidden, the user doesn't have rights.
404	Not Found, the URL doesn't exist.
405	Method not allowed, the wrong verb was used.
5xx	**Server Errors**
500	Internal Server Error, something bad on the server.

Implementing REST in Facebook

Facebook provides a REST-like implementation for its API. It's not pure REST, because individual resources (methods, objects) are not given unique URIs. For example, to get a list of friends of the current user using a REST API, you might expect to use a `GET` request to retrieve it from a collection URI (perhaps *http://api.facebook.com/users/*). Then, the client code could use one of these user identifiers returned from this query to access specific data of a single user, again using a dedicated URI (for example, *http://api.facebook.com/users/uid100*).

Instead, Facebook implements the interface for its API by using a single endpoint, to which you must supply all the data needed for the request in `POST` (default) or `GET` parameters. It's effectively a remote procedure call (RPC) over HTTP-style interface. Each

API call has its own set of parameters, and Facebook requires that the application also pass identifying information and a security hash to ensure that the calls are legitimate.

For example, to manually call the Facebook API function `friends.getAppUsers()`, which returns a list of friends of the current user who are also users of your application, you can use a URL like this one:

```
http://api.facebook.com/restserver.php?method=facebook.friends.getAppUsers&session_
➥key=XXXXXXXXXXXXXXXXX&api_key=XXXXXXXXXXXXXXXXXX&call_id=1234557716.362&v=1.0
➥&sig=XXXXXXXXXXXXXXXXXXX
```

Fortunately, Facebook and the developer community provide wrappers for many languages that make calling the Facebook API as simple as a function call, allowing you to use this instead:

```
$facebook = new Facebook($app_apikey, $app_secretkey);
$result = $facebook->api_client->friends_getAppUsers();
```

Later, this chapter describes the available client libraries that wrap the API. However, because Facebook uses a standard REST interface, almost any language with web capabilities can use the API.

Overview of the Facebook API

The Facebook API is grouped into numerous functional areas, each of which focuses on a different aspect of the Platform. Facebook consistently modifies them as new features are added, security issues are addressed, or behaviors become deprecated or obsolete. This section broadly covers these areas, because many API methods are discussed in detail throughout this book. APIs that are in beta—meaning that they are still in development, not supported by Facebook, possibly unstable, and subject to change at any time are also called out.

Permissions API

The permissions API contains methods that control overall application management. There are methods to manage applications' developer settings, retrieve application Facebook metrics, ban specific users, and get application public information. These methods also help automate application configuration and setup on different servers.

Authorization API

Used for desktop or external Facebook applications, the authorization API handles session management and login information. For internal Facebook web applications—on which this book primarily focuses—these methods are not often used, except for those that handle oversight of application extended permissions, which Chapter 6, "The Basics of Creating Applications," covers.

Batching API

Communicating with a remote server via HTTP or any protocol is expensive in terms of an application's response time and latency. Usually, this is the slowest part of a web application: waiting for the data requested from some remote source to be returned. Facebook applications are no exception. Because applications must always make API calls to a remote Facebook server, the batching API was created to allow them to bundle up to 20 calls and make a single call to Facebook instead of several individual ones. This saves significant amounts of an application's time. Facebook also allows these calls to be made sequentially or in parallel, depending on the application's needs.

Comments API (Beta)

Comments are a relatively new addition to the API. When Facebook rolled out the new stream-based model, it added the ability for users to comment on individual Feed stories. This part of the API allows applications to get, create, and remove these comments programmatically.

Data Store API (Beta)

Nearly every non-trivial Facebook application requires some sort of database or scalable application-specific storage to manage application state and offline caching of data. When Facebook Platform first launched, using an external database, like MySQL, for this purpose was a developer's only real option. Facebook then provided its own solution that allowed data to be stored on its servers. The data store API allows for the creation and use of tables, objects, and associations between them. According to Facebook, it can handle tens of millions of records with little performance degradation.

Although interesting in concept, the data store API is somewhat difficult and esoteric to use and debug. Currently, it is unsupported, and parts of it work sporadically. It's also been in beta for almost two years. Facebook is aware of this issue, but is not giving an estimate as to when it will be fully functional. So, if you decide to use this API, be careful; these methods are in beta and subject to change at any time at Facebook's discretion! It's recommended that you use your own database instead.

Events API

One of the powerful features of Facebook is its rich event system, which allows users to create events with built-in RSVP features, event-specific media, and export capabilities. The events API allows applications to manage events on its users' behalf, although this requires extra permissions for an application to do so.

FBML API

The FBML API is a varied mix of methods that allow developers to create custom FBML tags, refresh cached images, upload localized strings for internationalization purposes, and do high-performance updates of cached profile box FBML. Custom FBML tags can be registered with Facebook and be made public so that other developers can use them in their own applications.

Feed API

As mentioned in Chapter 1, "Facebook Applications: The Basics," the heart of Facebook is the Feed and the stream that arises from it. Chapters 9 and 10 cover the feed API comprehensively, so this section doesn't cover it in depth. The Feed API basically allows applications to register templates for the stories they publish to the stream and to directly publish these stories programmatically.

FQL API

FQL allows developers to access the same information provided by API methods, but by using a SQL-like query language. Note that many of Facebook's API methods use FQL internally to access the data they return or need. Therefore, it's in a programmer's best interest to understand FQL, because, in many cases, it's more efficient to use a FQL query than an equivalent API call. The API has just two methods: one to allow a single query and one to do multiple dependent queries in sequence. The latter capability was recently added. Unfortunately, you cannot use it to preload FQL, which is something that's discussed in Chapter 16, "Improving Application Performance and Workflow."

Links API

The links API allows applications to give its users the ability to post links to their Walls directly from the application. Users must opt in to allow applications to perform this behavior. These API calls work in a similar fashion as the ubiquitous Facebook Share button (found throughout the site).

User Management API

Probably the most frequently used set of APIs in the Facebook Platform, the user management APIs provide applications direct access to the users in the social graph. (We grouped these together under the heading user management; Facebook has no such term for them.) These APIs contain all the methods for getting users' friends, individual user's information, verifying if specific users have authorized an application, and organizing lists of friends. Most of these methods are used throughout this book.

When looking at the Facebook API documentation on its Wiki, the methods that start with "users" or "friends" fall in this category. This is a mature API, and most of the methods within it have been part of the Platform API since its launch.

Notes API (Beta)

Facebook Notes are rich text documents that can be created within Facebook. Recently, Facebook added support to allow users to create, edit, and delete them from within an application. Like many other powerful features offered by Facebook, this requires a user to grant the application special permissions to allow its use.

Messaging API

Messaging is another category we created to group API methods with similar behaviors. This grouping contains API methods to allow applications to send Facebook notifications and email (via the notification APIs), update users' Facebook status (via the status APIs), and send LiveMessages. LiveMessages are new to Facebook. You use them to send messages to a particular user's browser via FBJS. They are extremely useful in applications that have sequential or turn-based semantics, such as games.

Pages API

Pages API methods allow developers to get specific information about Facebook Public Profiles. Facebook Public Profiles were once known as Facebook Pages or Facebook Fan Pages, but with their recent redesign, they behave and look like normal user profiles. These APIs, however, still use the term "pages" when referring to them. They return information about whether a logged-in user is an administrator of the Public Profile, if he is a Fan (remember, Fans are like friends, but are specific to Public Profiles), and whether a specific application has been added to the profile.

Photo and Video API

Being one of the largest photo- and video-sharing sites on the web, Facebook provides a set of APIs for developers to manage these assets from within their applications. Photo and video API methods allow users to upload, create albums, and retrieve tagged user information, among other things. Many of these methods also require extended permissions for applications to use them.

Profile API

The profile API methods manage users' application profile boxes, application tabs, or info sections (custom content found on the Info tab of a user's profile.) Chapter 8, "Updating the Profile," uses all of them, so they are discussed there.

Open Stream API (Beta)

The newest addition to the Facebook API is the Open Stream API. As Chapter 9, "Feed Stories, Feed Forms, and Templates," shows, publishing content to the stream is currently a somewhat complex and detailed process. With Facebook's switch to the real-time streaming update model, it realized that it needed to provide developers a new way to access the Feed than what's provided today. Not only that, Facebook wanted to provide developers access to the stream from outside Facebook, whether it be on an external website, a mobile application, or a desktop application. This is the future of developer access to the heart of Facebook's information flow. Because this is such a new feature and subject to constant changes (sometimes several changes per week), this book doesn't cover it in detail; by the time this book publishes, that information would probably be outdated. Check this book's website for more information; it will have updated content when this feature is more concrete.

The new API allows applications to read content from the stream, publish their own content, and manage comments and ratings for individual Feed stories.

Facebook JavaScript Client Library

The Facebook JavaScript Client Library was created to let applications use the Facebook API on the client rather than the server. This means that a Facebook application can run anywhere JavaScript can, not just inside Facebook. Facebook Connect builds on this library to offer additional functionality for external websites, such as logging in with Facebook credentials and publishing news stories.

Websites that use this library have access to most of the Facebook API and a subset of FBML, called XFBML. After the page loads and initializes the Facebook JavaScript Client Library, it's allowed to call API functions and use XFBML. XFBML can either be displayed inline on the page or dynamically created via the library.

Listing 3.1 shows an example script block that displays the picture of the viewing Facebook user.

Listing 3.1 **Displaying the User with XFBML**

```
<script
  src="http://static.ak.connect.facebook.com/js/api_lib/v0.4/FeatureLoader.js.php"
  type="text/javascript">
</script>

<div id='container'></div>
<script type="text/javascript">
// Load XFBML support
FB_RequireFeatures(['XFBML'], function(){
  FB.Facebook.init(api_key, location_of_receiver_file);
  var api = FB.Facebook.apiClient;
  // require user to login
  api.requireLogin(function(exception){
```

Listing 3.1 **Continued**

```
    // Get the user's id from the API
    var uid =  api.get_session().uid;
    // Create an XFBML profile picture for this user and update the DOM
       var container = document.getElementById('container');
    container.innerHTML = '<fb:profile-pic uid="'+uid+'"/>';
    FB.XFBML.Host.parseDomTree();
  });
});
</script>
```

Chapter 12, "Facebook JavaScript Client Library," discusses this library in detail.

Facebook Mobile Support

Facebook provides basic mobile integration for most mobile phones and a richer experience for the iPhone (by using the Facebook Connect for iPhone library). For non-iPhones, the integration points are a presence on *http://m.facebook.com*—Facebook's mobile website—and the use of Facebook's Short Message Service (SMS, or text messaging) service.

Applications on the mobile Facebook website use a subset of FBML to create mobile profile and canvas pages. When Facebook detects a mobile browser, a special `fb_sig_mobile` parameter is passed to the application as a `POST` variable. The application can then return FBML enclosed in special `<fb:mobile>` tags for display. Mock AJAX and FBJS are not available in the mobile version of FBML.

After a user adds the application, she has to go to the Settings page on *http://m.facebook.com* and enable the application to show up on her mobile profile. After it's enabled, the application shows up on the mobile profile under Boxes.

> **Note**
>
> At the present time, mobile Facebook site integration is not stable. Facebook has stated in the forums that it is working on enhancing its mobile integration.

Facebook's SMS lets applications send and receive SMS notifications. Users must first allow this feature by enabling the SMS extended permission in the application. Then, the application can send them an SMS. An application can check whether a user has set permissions by calling the `sms.canSend()` API function.

Applications can send a single user an SMS notification or start an SMS conversation, depending on the parameters to the API call. An application might use the conversational style for handling information requests that get more specific. The user can reply to the SMS or follow a link inside of it to the application's mobile Facebook Page.

Users can also send an SMS to the application via the Facebook shortcode 32665 by using the format `"app_canvas_name <query>"`. The Facebook application is passed some extra `POST` parameters with the ID of the user and the message.

The handler code might look similar to Listing 3.2.

Listing 3.2 **Handling an SMS Response**

```
if (isset($_POST['fb_sig_sms'])) {
  // Get the received SMS information
  $user = $_POST['fb_sig_user'];
  $message = $_POST['fb_sig_message'];
  $sessionID = $_POST['fb_sig_sms_sid'];

  // Process the message

  // Send back a response
  $response = "Thanks for your message - $message";
  $sessionID = $facebook->api_client->sms_send($userID, $response, $sessionID, 0);
}
```

Strangely, the API wrapper code for handling SMS calls is not part of the PHP client library. Add the functions in Listing 3.3 to your application to extend the wrapper to include SMS functionality.

Listing 3.3 **`sms_canSend()` and `sms_send()` Functions**

```
/**
* Checks to see if the user has enabled SMS for the application
* @param int $uid  Optional: The user id to check
*   A null parameter will default to the session user.
* @return 0 for success or an error code
*/
public function sms_canSend($uid) {
    return $this->call_method('facebook.sms.canSend', array('uid' => $uid));
}

/**
* Sends a text message to the user
* @param int $uid  Optional: The user id to send the message to
*   A null parameter will default to the session user.
* @param string $message:  The content of the message to send
* @param int $session_id:  The session id for the current conversation
*   A null parameter signifies a new conversation. This value is returned
*   from this function or as a REQUEST variable when an SMS is received
*   by the application
* @param bool $req_session:  Whether the message is part of a conversation
*   A false value signifies a a single text message. Any replies to it will be
*   received with no information about the outgoing message
* @return 0 for success if req_session is false or the session id if req_session
*    is true. Returns an error code otherwise
*/
```

Listing 3.3 **Continued**

```
public function sms_send($uid, $message, $session_id = null, $req_session =
➥ false) {
    return $this->call_method('facebook.sms.send', array('uid' => $uid,
                              'message' => $message, 'session_id' => $session_id,
                              'req_session' => $req_session));
}
```

Facebook Connect for the iPhone allows iPhone developers to include an Xcode project into their applications. Information about Xcode and developing for the iPhone can be found in *The iPhone Developer's Cookbook* by Erica Sadun. General concepts for this library are the same as the overall Facebook Connect Library, which is detailed in Chapter 13, "Facebook Connect." iPhone applications will be able to access the Facebook Platform API to get user information, set a status, create a news story, and get friend information. This is a great opportunity to bring a rich social experience to a great mobile platform.

Library Support

As previously discussed, manually calling the Facebook REST API is possible but takes work. Facebook provides and officially supports two wrapper libraries to help with this, and the developer community has created wrappers for many other languages.

Official Libraries

Facebook updates its libraries somewhat frequently, and these changes are preannounced on the developer blog. Often, API methods can be deprecated but still function correctly until a cutoff date. This means that older applications do not necessarily have to be updated to always use the latest version of the library, but developers still must be aware of cutoff dates. The officially supported libraries are as follows:

- **PHP 5.** The most widely used by developers. Most examples and Developer forum posts reference the use of this library.
- **JavaScript Client Library.** Although it's not as complete as the PHP library, this library forms the basis of Facebook Connect and will be expanded as time goes on.
- **Facebook Connect for iPhone.** Written in Objective-C, which is the iPhone's primary development language, this library provides services and primitives to make it easier for iPhone developers to allow their applications to connect to Facebook from the handset.
- **ActionScript 3.0.** Supported by Adobe, this library allows Adobe Flash, Flex, and Air applications to directly call the Facebook API.
- **Force.com for Facebook.** Supported by Salesforce.com, this library allows developers on the Salesforce.com platform to integrate Facebook into their custom Salesforce platform applications.

Unofficial or Third-Party Supported Libraries

The Facebook Platform developer community maintains the following client libraries. Facebook does not officially support them. Many of them are active, whereas others are more of a proof of concept. The current unofficial libraries are as follows:

- .NET Facebook API Client (supported by SocialCash.com)
- Android
- ASP.NET
- ASP (VBScript)
- Cocoa
- ColdFusion
- C++
- C#
- D
- Emacs Lisp
- Erlang
- Google Web Toolkit
- Java
- Lisp
- Perl
- Python
- Ruby on Rails
- Smalltalk
- Tcl
- VB.NET
- Windows Mobile

Application Architecture

Every Facebook application must have the same basic architecture to interoperate with the Platform. Facebook provides a Facebook Developer application to allow developers to make new applications and fill in the details where they are hosted. Each application is issued some identifying keys, and developers are required to enter URLs for how users and Facebook access the application.

Facebook does not actually host developer's applications. It acts as a proxy instead so that when the user visits the Canvas Page URL, Facebook creates an outer frame and then calls the application's Canvas Callback URL to get information to display. The workflows later in this chapter detail how this information gets rendered.

Chapter 6 details how to build the application architecture. This section overviews how an application interacts with the Facebook Platform.

Secret Keys

When an application is created using the Facebook Developer application, it is given a public and private key pair. The public key is called the *API key*, and the private key is called the *Secret key*. This key pair verifies that all calls made to the Facebook API are from that application. It is important that developers protect their Secret keys and report their loss if they are ever compromised. Otherwise, anyone can start making calls masquerading as that application, modifying or even deleting user data.

Canvas Page URL

The Canvas Page URL is the location on Facebook that users visit to get to the application. It is in the format *http://apps.facebook.com/yourcanvasurl*. It has to be unique, unlike the Application Name. For example, two applications might be called SuperQuiz, but only one can have *http://apps.facebook.com/superquiz*. The other application has to use something else, like *http://apps.facebook.com/superquiz-2*.

In general, it isn't a great idea to have the same name as another application. At the launch of the Facebook Platform, squatters quickly registered applications with many common names, attempting a land grab similar to what happened in the early days of the web. Since then, the level of squatting seems to have died down, and the ability to have duplicate application names reduced the value of having a specific URL.

Canvas Callback URL

The Canvas Callback URL is the location on your server where your application resides. Facebook calls this URL when it needs to display an application page, when a user adds or removes the application, and when it needs to update its cache.

The server hosting the Canvas Callback URL can handle the callbacks using whatever web server or language the developer deems appropriate. Facebook passes a set of data as `POST` variables to the Canvas Callback URL, containing information about the viewing user, the session, and the application. The server can manually process these or use one of the API wrapper libraries to do it.

Canvas Page Workflow

Every time a user goes to an application canvas page, Facebook calls the application's Canvas Callback URL. Applications have to decide if they will have FBML or IFrame-based canvas pages. (Chapter 7, "Building the Canvas," discusses the benefits of each.) The biggest difference between FBML and IFrame canvas pages is that applications that produce FBML must have Facebook render their content before displaying it. This is so that Facebook can turn each FBML control into its HTML and JavaScript equivalents. IFrame-based canvas pages just show their content directly but cannot use FBML. They can show XFBML using the Facebook JavaScript Client Library, however (discussed in Chapter 12).

Figure 3.1 and Figure 3.2 show the workflows for how Facebook interacts with an application's canvas page. They also show how an application can send content for Facebook to display in the user's profile box. Chapter 7 discusses canvas pages.

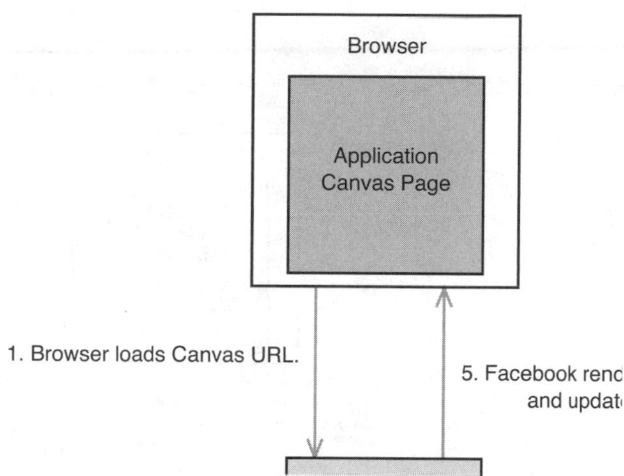

Figure 3.1 Workflow for displaying an FBML application canvas page

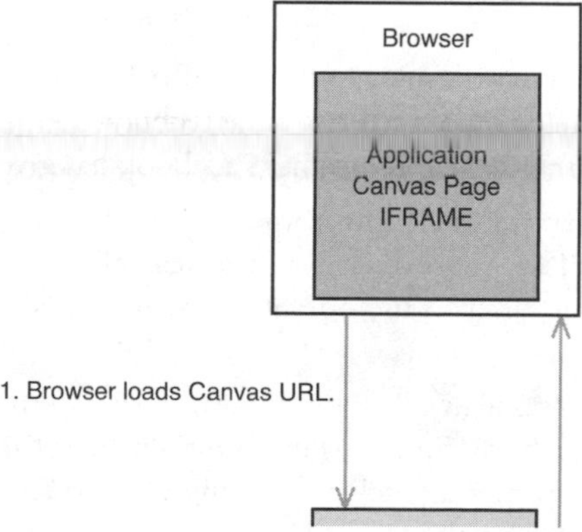

Figure 3.2 Workflow for displaying an IFrame application canvas page

Profile Box Workflow

To speed up profile load times, Facebook caches application profile box content. This content is set by the application ahead of time and can be updated either by sending new content using the `profile.setFBML()` API method or by asking Facebook to update portions of its cache `<fb:ref>` functionality. Chapter 8 covers profile boxes in depth.

Figure 3.3 shows the workflow for how Facebook interacts with an application profile box page.

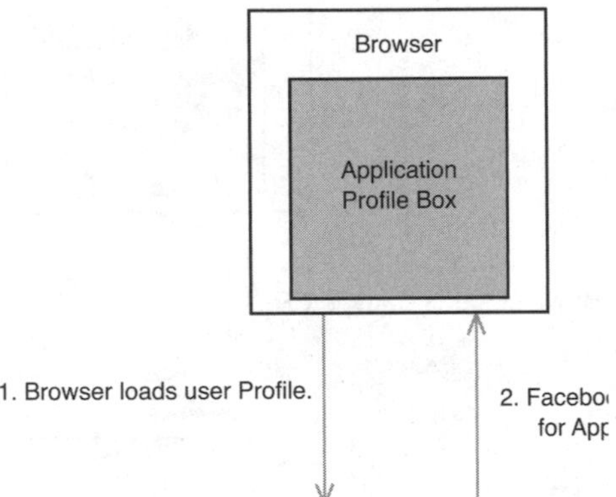

Figure 3.3 Workflow for displaying the application profile box

Summary

This chapter described how the Facebook Platform works, from its underlying technologies to how it communicates with applications. Here are some key points:

- Facebook uses open source technologies to allow the Facebook Platform to handle the large user base. Developers can use the same technologies for their own applications and benefit from the contributions that Facebook has given to the community.
- Using REST allows services to benefit from the strengths of the web, and this is what the Facebook API uses. Although you can manually create a call to the REST server, it is much easier to use one of the many available Facebook API client libraries.
- The Facebook JavaScript Client Library is the way that external websites can use the API to integrate Facebook functionality into their sites. Facebook Connect builds on this, adding capabilities, such as allowing users to log into external sites using their Facebook credentials.

- Facebook provides mobile integration via SMS processing, mobile Facebook website integration, and a special Facebook Connect for the iPhone library. These allow application developers to embrace the gigantic mobile user base.
- Applications have two unique URLs: the Canvas Page URL that users go to and the Canvas Callback URL with which the Facebook Platform communicates. Applications and Facebook use key pairs to verify that the communication is valid.

4

Platform Developer Tools

A variety of developer tools are useful for Facebook development and application debugging. This chapter shows you how to use some of the most common ones. Some of these tools are provided by Facebook, whereas others are freely available browser add-ons or external tools.

Facebook Provided Tools

Facebook provides some free online developer tools (at *http://developers.facebook.com/tools.php*) for testing calls and responses from the Facebook REST application programming interface (API), rendering sample Facebook Markup Language (FBML) in different contexts (for example, on the profile or the Boxes tab), and managing Feed templates for specific applications. Facebook also provides a setting in its PHP client library, which can help diagnose common problems. Finally, Facebook allows developers to create special test accounts to exercise multiuser functionality of applications.

API Test Console

The API Test Console is an indispensable tool that allows developers to test calls to and responses from many of the most used Facebook API methods in the context of any of their applications. You can pass in various parameters, change the response format to different types, validate callbacks if the method supports them, and see what the API will produce without having to write code for all the testing infrastructure.

Figure 4.1 shows a sample API test for the `friends.areFriends()` API method.

As you can see in Figure 4.1, the API Test Console offers a number of fields that developers can use to modify the data sent to Facebook for each call. Each of these fields and their use is described in the following section. Many fields are added dynamically, depending on the API method selected in the Method field. For example, the default API method that's selected when you open the tool is `friends.get()`. Facebook provides a field for its single parameter `flid` below the method drop-down field. If you switch the API to `friends.areFriends()`, you notice that two completely different fields appear for entering the two parameters that this API expects.

Figure 4.1 The Facebook API Test Console allows developers to call many Facebook API methods in the context of a specific application.

User ID

To use the API Test Console, you must be logged into Facebook, and the User ID field holds your Facebook user ID. The API calls are done on your behalf, which means that all of your normal privacy constraints are still in effect. Unfortunately, this field can only be changed by logging into Facebook as another user.

Application

Application is from where the calls will be coming. You can use the generic Test Console value (if you don't have a preference) or choose any of your other applications. This important feature allows you to test APIs that are application-specific. For example, to verify that Facebook is correctly caching the contents of an application's profile box, you can call the `profile.setFBML()` and `profile.getFBML()` methods. This first sets the contents of the profile box, which, as discussed in Chapter 1, "Facebook Applications: The Basics," are cached on Facebook's servers. The second returns you the FBML contents of the profile box currently cached by Facebook. This is more efficient than doing this manually by using your application.

Response Format

You can change the type of result that is displayed to XML, JSON, or PHP. The API actually only returns XML or JSON, but the PHP format is what the PHP Client Library would convert the response to. Here are the response variations for the API function `friends.areFriends()`:

XML

```
<?xml version="1.0" encoding="UTF-8"?>

<friends_areFriends_response xmlns="http://api.facebook.com/1.0/"
xmlns:xsi="http://www.w3.org/2001/XMLSchema-instance"
xsi:schemaLocation="http://api.facebook.com/1.0/
http://api.facebook.com/1.0/facebook.xsd" list="true">

  <friend_info>
    <uid1>698700806</uid1>
    <uid2>714497440</uid2>
    <are_friends>1</are_friends>
  </friend_info>
</friends_areFriends_response>
```

JSON

```
[{"uid1":698700806,"uid2":714497440,"are_friends":true}]
```

Facebook PHP Client

```
Array
(
  [0] => Array
    (
      [uid1] => 698700806
      [uid2] => 714497440
      [are_friends] => 1
    )
)
```

Callback

The Callback field is the name of a function to call with the response as an argument. It works only when the response format is set to JSON or XML. In the test console, it simply displays the response as the sole argument to the function name you supply. (See the sidebar for more information about JSONP.) Here is the JSON result of the `friends.areFriends()` call when a callback is specified:

```
mycallback();
```

JSONP

JSON with padding (JSONP) is a technique that allows developers to use code from different domains to create engaging web applications without duplicating tons of code. Clients dynamically create a `<script>` tag with its `src` attribute set to a JSONP-enabled web service they want to call, appending a query parameter, such as a callback function name. For example:

```
// dynamically created script tag pointing to JSONP enabled web service
<script src='http://example.com/getdata?callback=handleData' />
```

The web service returns the data as a parameter to the callback function, which gets executed back on the client:

```
handleData( {"data" : "value" });
```

This simple technique allows developers to build engaging web-based applications using code from multiple domains. Many well-known JavaScript libraries and websites now handle JSONP requests. There are downsides to it, of course. Take security, for example: Because the data is sent in plain URL-encoded text, never use JSONP to send sensitive data.

Unfortunately, FBJS does not allow the creation of dynamic `<script>` blocks, so you cannot use this technique on FBML-based canvas pages, profiles, or application tabs. You must use the FBJS AJAX methods instead. The previous technique would work on an IFrame-based canvas page or on an external site.

Method

Method is the Facebook API function that you want to test. Below it are fields for any parameters the method might require. A documentation link brings up the wiki page for that method. After you click the Call Method button, the code for that call using the Facebook PHP client library is generated for you in the box at the top right, so you can paste it into your code. For example, if you tried the `friends.areFriends()` API method with appropriate parameters, the following code line appears:

```
$facebook->api_client->friends_areFriends(698700806,714497440);
```

You can also test FQL queries here by selecting the `fql.query()` method and entering your FQL into the query field. FQL was introduced in Chapter 1 and is discussed in detail in Chapter 16, "Improving Application Performance and Workflow."

FBML Test Console

FBML can be used in many contexts, such as the canvas, profile boxes, Feeds, Notifications, Email, and application tabs. FBML must be rendered into HTML by Facebook before being displayed, so developers can not test it locally. This console lets developers enter FBML and see how it would be rendered in any of the allowed display locations. It can be especially useful for the profile box, where the same code can be rendered completely differently, depending on the display context. Additionally, it gives great insight into what FBML tags can be used in which locations in the Facebook user interface. The console notifies users if certain tags are not supported on the profile, for example. Figure 4.2 shows some FBML being rendered for the profile.

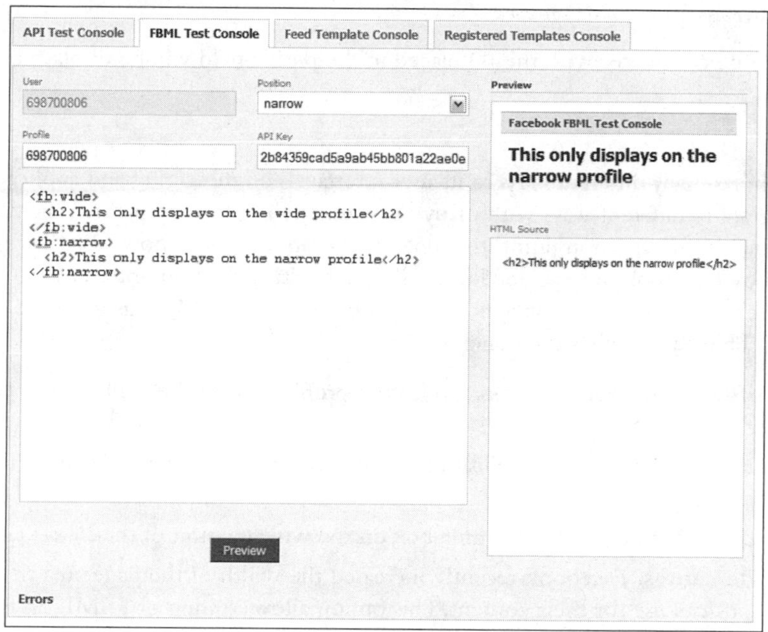

Figure 4.2 FBML Test Console

In Figure 4.2, the FBML code on the left contains a section for the narrow profile marked `<fb:narrow>` and a section for the wide profile marked `<fb:wide>`. The Position field is currently set to narrow, and that is what the Preview box displays. By changing the drop-down field for Position from narrow to wide, the `<fb:wide>` section is rendered instead. More information about the profile types is given in Chapter 8, "Updating the Profile."

Like the API Test Console, the FBML Test Console provides numerous fields that a developer can use to customize the behavior and output of the code rendered by it. The following section covers these fields.

User

The User field behaves exactly like the User ID field from the API Test Console. It is the Facebook user ID of the currently logged in Facebook user. FBML rendering is done on his behalf, which means that all the normal privacy constraints for what that user can see are still in effect. This field can only be changed by logging into Facebook as another user. However, unlike the API Test Console, the FBML Test Console still works if no user is currently logged in to Facebook, but the viewing user is treated as a non-friend of the profile owner.

Profile

Profile is the Facebook user ID of the profile owner. The FBML is rendered as if it were on that user's profile. That makes a difference if the FBML contained something like this:

```
hello <fb:name uid='profileowner'/>
```

The name of the user with the ID placed in the profile field will be displayed.

Position

Facebook has many different parts to its user interface, and messaging and applications can integrate in different ways with many of them. The Position drop-down field lists a great number of integration points that developers can use to test how FBML would be rendered by Facebook in a specific location. This is critical for testing because, in many cases, Facebook only allows a specific subset of FBML and HTML tags for some of the locations. This list describes each one:

- **Profile main.** Represents an application profile box on the Wall or Info tab of a user's profile.
- **Narrow.** Represents an application profile box on the narrow column of the Boxes tab.
- **Wide.** Tests an application profile box on the wide column of the Boxes tab.
- **Wide canvas.** Facebook recently increased the width of the page area that applications can use for their content. This option allows testing of FBML on the new wider canvas pages.
- **Canvas.** Tests application canvas pages that have not been converted to the new, wider format.
- **Email.** Tests application-generated email. Chapter 10, "Publisher, Notifications, and Requests," covers this in detail.
- **Notification.** Helpful for testing application notifications (of both types: user-to-user and application-to-user).
- **Request.** Tests invitations and requests, which have restricted sets of the FBML they can use. Chapter 10 covers these in detail.
- **Feed title.** Tests titles of Feed stories.
- **Feed body.** Tests the bodies of Feed short stories. (One line stories do not have bodies.)
- **Feed full.** Deprecated; do not use. Facebook removed the full Feed story type a while ago and, as of this writing, this artifact has not been removed.
- **Mobile.** Useful for testing rendering of mobile profile content.
- **Tab.** Tests application content as it would appear on an application tab.

API Key

This is the API key of the application to use for the rendering call. There is no reason to change the default value. If you use an invalid API key, the test console uses its default value instead.

FBML Textbox

The FBML textbox is where a user can enter the actual raw FBML he wants to see rendered. Any valid HTML, inline CSS styles, and FBJS are accepted.

Preview

The top Preview box shows the rendered FBML in the context of the viewing user, the profile owner, and the display context. Firefox users can inspect and tweak the results with the Firebug extension and then modify the original FBML with the changes.

HTML Source

The HTML Source area shows the HTML code that Facebook created from the FBML supplied by the user. This is a great place to learn how the Facebook FBML controls work. Notice that, in many cases, HTML is not the only code rendered for a specific FBML tag. Depending on the tag, a lot of JavaScript for handling Facebook internal tracking, dynamic control behavior, and more, can also be rendered. For example, if a user typed the FBML `<fb:name uid='714497440' />` in the FBML box and chose Canvas from the Position drop-down field, Facebook outputs the code shown in Listing 4.1 in the HTML Source field. The details of how it works and the types it mentions are internal to Facebook and are beyond the scope of this discussion; however, viewing it gives you a sense of how a seemingly simple tag can be turned into a good deal of code after Facebook processes it.

Listing 4.1 **Facebook Generated Code for `<fb:name>`**

```
<a
  href="http://www.facebook.com/profile.php?id=714497440"
  onclick="(new Image()).src =
&#039;/ajax/ct.php?app_id=2353941073&action_type=3&post_form_id=cf23e5
3a9d27bdb66fbd180d634b754f&position=3&&#039; + Math.random();
return true;">
  Cappy Popp
</a>
<script type="text/javascript">
onloadRegister(function() {
  if (window.Env) {
    Env["nctrlid"]="932a2f05b698419c1033d2dca78201dc";
  }
});
onloadRegister(function() {
  if (window.Env) {
```

Listing 4.1 **Continued**

```
    Env["nctrlnid"]="";
  }
});
onloadRegister(function() {
  if (window.NectarPhotosLog) {
    Arbiter.subscribe(NectarPhotosLog.NECTAR_LOG, NectarPhotosLog.arbiterHandler);
    onbeforeunloadRegister(function() {
      Arbiter.inform(NectarPhotosLog.NECTAR_LOG, {"flush" : true});
    }, false);
  }
});
</script>
```

Feed Template Console

Feed Templates are discussed in Chapter 9, "Feed Stories, Feed Forms, and Templates." They are the basis for creating Feed stories that appear on a user's Home page and Wall. They can be registered in code, but this Test Console allows developers to use a wizard interface to not only allow them to register their templates, but also to see how the stories will look when Facebook renders them to the Stream.

Figure 4.3 shows the last page of the Feed Template wizard. The key points to understand about this wizard are

- The actor is the user who takes the action that produces the story. You can't change the actor. Feed stories are always about the actions taken by a specific user. In the wizard, the actor is represented by `{*actor*}` (called a token), and the value is the user ID of the logged-in developer using the console. When the real story is actually generated using this template, the actor is replaced with the application user.
- The wizard generates a random set of friends to put in the stories as the `{*target*}` token. You can't change this until the last screen of the wizard. When the real story is actually generated using this template, the application can specify the story targets.
- The Sample Template Data contains JSON-encoded data used to replace custom tokens in the template. For example, a one line template might be `{*actor*} {*action*} a friend today`. The corresponding Sample Template Data entry would be `{"action":"smiled at"}`. All tokens in the template, except for the `{*actor*}` and `{*target*}` tokens, which are reserved by Facebook, must have corresponding valid JSON values in the template data.
- You can skip any step; nothing is saved until the Register template bundle is clicked on the last page of the wizard. Anything that is saved can always be removed on the Registered Templates Console tab or through the API.

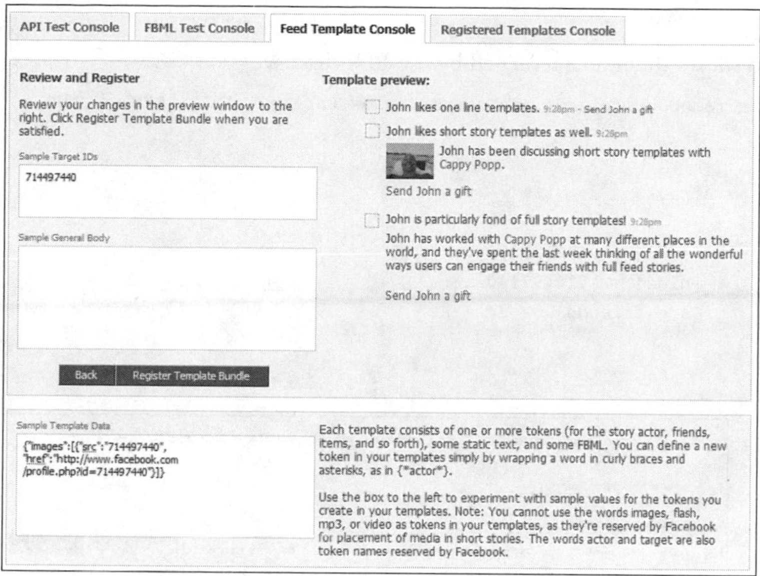

Figure 4.3 Feed Template Console

Registered Templates Console

The Registered Templates Console simply allows developers to see which Feed template bundles have been registered for an application and delete them.

In Figure 4.4, two bundles have been registered for the My Smiley application, each with a one line, short, and full story template. Clicking Deactivate beside one of the bundles permanently deletes that template bundle. Developers can also see the unique IDs each bundle has, and they use this in their application code to submit a Feed story or programmatically delete the bundle.

Facebook Debugging Support

Facebook's PHP API client library helpfully shows the input and output of all API calls, if you set the following before creating the Facebook object in your code:

```
$GLOBALS['facebook_config']['debug'] = true;
$fb = new Facebook($_appApiKey, $_appSecret);
$fb->api_client->friends_areFriends(698700806,714497440);
```

This creates a section at the top of the canvas page, which shows the parameters passed to the API function:

```
1: Called facebook.friends.areFriends, show Params | XML | SXML | PHP
Array
(
    [uids1] => 698700806
    [uids2] => 714497440
```

```
)
```

It also shows the results returned by the PHP library:

```
1: Called facebook.friends.areFriends, show Params | XML | SXML | PHP
Array
(
    [0] => Array
        (
            [uid1] => 698700806
            [uid2] => 714497440
            [are_friends] => 1
        )
)
```

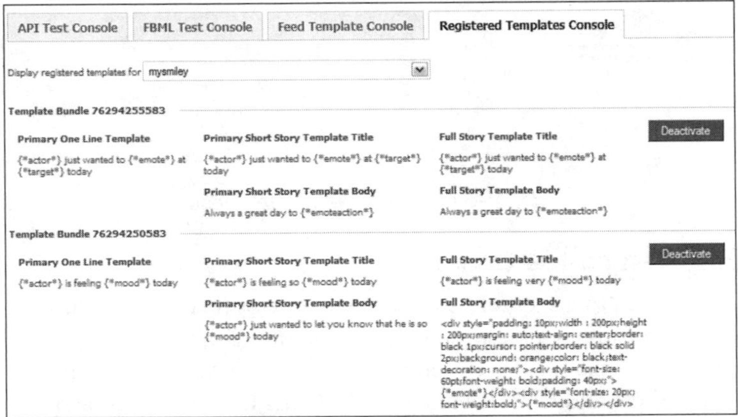

Figure 4.4 Registered Templates Console

Enabling Facebook debug output is great for tracing and debugging Facebook API calls. It can not be used in some cases. For example, Feed forms, which Chapter 9 covers, fail if Facebook debugging output is turned on. In general, however, it a useful tool for developers. Remember to set `$GLOBALS['facebook_config']['debug']` to `false` before releasing any code that uses it.

Another useful feature that Facebook provides developers is the output of the unfiltered FBML for an application's canvas page before Facebook parses it. This is extremely helpful in diagnosing user-interface problems in an application caused by a missing closing tag or misplaced quote. Only developers of the application have access to this feature, and it will never be shown to nondevelopers of an application. Listing 4.2 shows the first few lines of output for a sample application that's introduced later—called Compliments—when a developer views the source of its canvas page rendered in a browser.

Listing 4.2 **Facebook Provides Developers with the Unparsed FBML It Gets Before It Parses It**

```
<!DOCTYPE html PUBLIC "-//W3C//DTD XHTML 1.0 Strict//EN"
   "http://www.w3.org/TR/xhtml1/DTD/xhtml1-strict.dtd">
<html xmlns="http://www.w3.org/1999/xhtml" xml:lang="en" lang="en" id="facebook">
 <!—Rendering the page using the following FBML retrieved from
http://example.com/compliments/
You are seeing this because you are a developer of the application and this
information may be useful to you in debugging.  The FBML will not be shown to
other users visiting this page. (dashes were replaced with underscores):
    <link rel='stylesheet' type='text/css'
      href='http://example.com/compliments/css/reset.css?v=1243795325' />
    <link rel='stylesheet' type='text/css'
      href='http://example.com/compliments/css/main.css?v=1245995552' />
    <script
      src='http://example.com/compliments/js/fbjs.js?v=1246592479'>
    </script>
    <fb:title>Send a Compliment</fb:title> <!—  rest of document elided — >
```

Developer Test Accounts

Often, developers need multiple accounts to test their application's functionality; however, Facebook's Terms of Service require all accounts to represent real people. Therefore, Facebook has provided a way for developers to create multiple accounts for testing purposes, but unfortunately, these accounts have significant limitations.

To create a Test account, developers need to create a new Facebook account and visit *www.facebook.com/developers/become_test_account.php*. This page lets you convert an account into a test account. You can reverse this change later by removing the account from the Facebook Platform Developer Test Accounts Network.

Test accounts have the following limitations:

- They cannot access the Facebook Developer application. This means that you cannot use test accounts to administer applications that are set to developer access only (Sandbox mode). Unfortunately, testing before releasing an application is important. The end of this section covers a simple workaround for this.
- They cannot interact with "real" users, only other test users. They can't be friends with, send messages to, or even see real users, even if they both are using the same application. You end up creating a bunch of test accounts so that they can interact in your application. If you require testing with hundreds of friends, you have to create hundreds of test accounts. If you know other Facebook developers, your test accounts can interact with their test accounts, so you can access a larger pool.

Facebook has said that, in the future, it might enhance test accounts by automatically creating a large number of friends for them. That would certainly make it easier than having to create them all yourself.

As previously mentioned, test accounts cannot access the Facebook Developer application, so you cannot give test accounts access to sandboxed applications. However, you can list them as developers of an application *before* you visit the test account conversion page. After they are developers of the application, you can convert them, and they have full access to it, even in Sandbox mode.

Browser Debugging Tools

Many of the modern browsers have extensions that allow client-side debugging of JavaScript, HTML and CSS, as well as monitoring and modifying network traffic. Sadly, Internet Explorer 6 is still very common and has the fewest and least developed set of tools. Firefox, Safari, and Internet Explorer 8 all have much better debugging support. This section discusses Firebug in detail and gives some brief descriptions of the other common ones.

Firebug Add-On for Firefox

Firebug (*http://getfirebug.com*) is an add-on to Firefox that revolutionized the browser-development experience. For Facebook development, the key features are JavaScript debugging, inspection, and modification of HTML and CSS, network monitoring, and the console.

JavaScript Debugging

The JavaScript debugger supports breakpoints, stepping in and out of code, a watch window, logging, and profiling. For general usage, Firebug provides a set of tutorial videos and advanced documentation on its website. This section provides some tips for debugging JavaScript on Facebook. Figure 4.5 shows the Firebug Script Debugger.

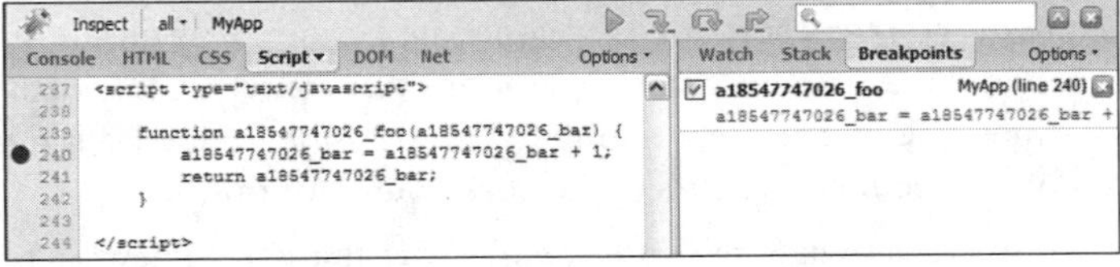

Figure 4.5 Firebug Script Debugger

When trying to debug JavaScript on a Facebook FBML canvas page, it is important to understand what Facebook does to that JavaScript during rendering. First, all variables and functions are renamed with a prefix of a*XXX*, where *XXX* is the application ID assigned when creating the application. So, as Figure 4.5 shows,

```
function foo(bar) {
    bar = bar + 1;
```

```
    return bar;
}
```

is rendered as follows:

```
function a18547747026_foo(a18547747026_bar) {
    a18547747026_bar = a18547747026_bar + 1;
    return a18547747026_bar;
}
```

Facebook does this to all JavaScript that it encounters outside of IFrames. The process is called *sandboxing*, and it's a security measure. First, it's used for namespacing: It ensures that none of the JavaScript provided by a third party running on a page in the Facebook user interface will have name conflicts with any of the JavaScript that Facebook uses. Second, sandboxing allows Facebook to restrict third-party JavaScript to a well-defined subset of what is available to "real" JavaScript. It removes many common functions (such as `eval()`, `alert()`, many DOM manipulation functions, and more). The resulting subset of JavaScript that developers can use is called Facebook JavaScript (FBJS).

Facebook puts a copy of the original page source at the top of the page in a comment and the modified source at the bottom. When trying to set breakpoints in your JavaScript functions, always make sure that you use the lower, modified source. Firebug nicely marks the line numbers that can have breakpoints in green.

In a profile box or application tab, Facebook takes all of your functions, renames them, and sticks them inside JavaScript `eval()` calls passed to `onLoadRegister()`:

```
onloadRegister(function() {eval_global("app_9209742358.pending_bootstraps.push
(\"\\n function a9209742358_foo(a9209742358_bar) { \\n a9209742358_
bar = a9209742358_bar + 1;
\\n return a9209742358_bar;\\n }\\n \");");});
```

You can't set breakpoints on these lines. Instead, Firebug has a great feature that turns executed `eval()` code into its own entire virtual script file. So, execute your function once, and then you can select it from the script list, set breakpoints, and execute it again. Notice the virtual script created by Firebug in Figure 4.6; it's the name above the Script tab.

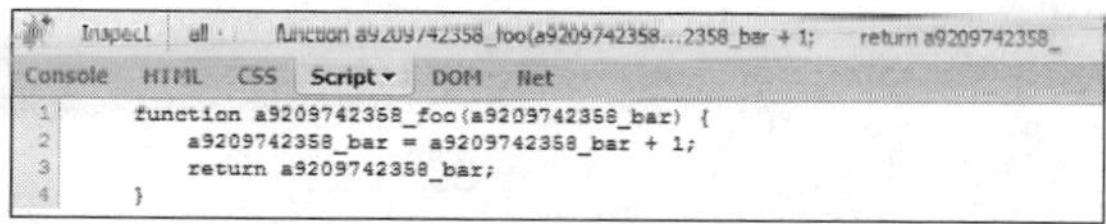

Figure 4.6 Debugging JavaScript on the profile

HTML and CSS Inspection and Modification

When building your application, getting it to look just right can be difficult, especially because parts of it are first being rendered by Facebook. Firebug lets you view every DOM element and all the styles that have been applied to it. You can even modify the styles on the fly or edit the HTML for the page. This is a great way to fine-tune your application user interface quickly, and when satisfied, copy the changes back into your code.

Figure 4.7 shows the margin style for an HTML `<div>`. To modify this, simply click and change the number on the Style section or use the up and down arrow keys to change the value. You can even right-click and add new properties. The web page automatically updates with each change so that you can see the results.

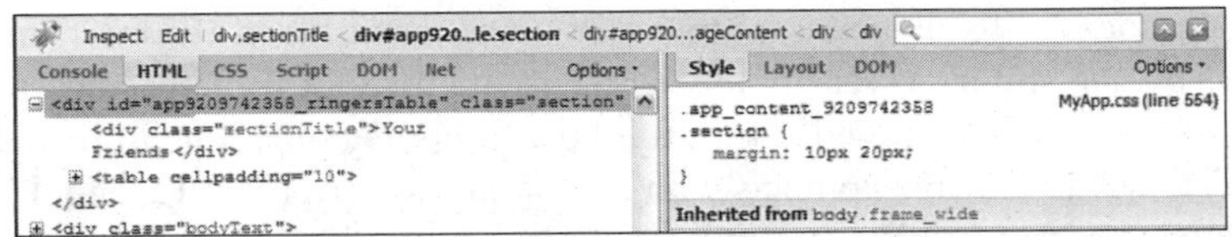

Figure 4.7 Modifying CSS styles directly

You can also click the HTML or CSS tabs and directly edit the HTML and style sheets. This lets you add new elements or CSS selectors or modify existing ones.

Network Monitoring

Firebug lets you see all the network traffic that occurs in the process of displaying your page. You can see what images, CSS files, and JavaScript files get loaded and how long the load time is for each file. You won't see any of the API calls done when the page loads, but any AJAX calls or Form posts your client-side code does shows up. For each of these, you can examine the HTTP headers, variables, and response. This can be invaluable in debugging asynchronous code, like AJAX calls, when they aren't working as expected.

Figure 4.8 shows an AJAX call from a Facebook canvas page. In this case, a link was clicked that used the FBJS AJAX capability to pass a set of `POST` data back to the application. When this happens, an item appears in the Net tab called `POST fbjs_ajax_proxy.php`. Clicking the POST tab shows the variables passed to the call, and the response shows the return payload.

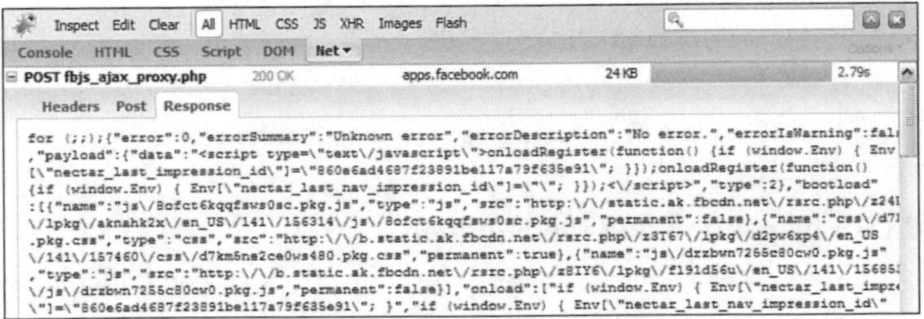

Figure 4.8 Firebug Network Monitoring tab

Console

Firebug has a Console view that displays error messages, logging output, and supports a variety of typed commands to dump data. It even has a built-in JavaScript profiler to work out the slow parts of your client-side code. Figure 4.9 shows a manual HTML dump of an element on the page using the following command line:

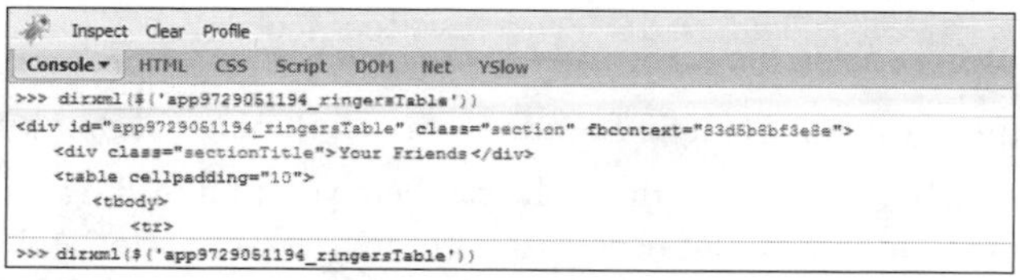

Figure 4.9 Firebug Console

```
dirxml($('app9729051194_ringersTable'))
```

Firebug provides a rich set of APIs that can be used in its Console or directly in your JavaScript code. For example, the Console logger can be accessed from inside your page's JavaScript by inserting a call to the `console.log()` function provided by Firebug; however, this code fails if the page is loaded in a browser without Firebug installed. If you use Firebug logging often, it makes sense to create a logging wrapper function that checks if the Console object and log functions are available and do nothing if it isn't Firefox. A rudimentary example in FBJS is shown in Listing 4.3.

Listing 4.3 Simple Browser-Agnostic JavaScript `log()` Function to Wrap Firebug's `console.log()` Function

```
var log = function(content) {
  if( console &&
      console instanceof Object &&
      console.log &&
      typeof console.log === 'function') {
       console.log(content);
  }
}
```

You can now use the `console.log()` function in your Facebook code; if Firebug is not installed or you are running on a browser that does not support it, the function has no effect, save some miniscule processing hits for calling it. A more complete implementation checks for other features offered by the Firebug API and handles them similarly. To find out more about the different functionality and APIs available in Firebug, visit *http://getfirebug.com/docs.html*.

Web Developer Add-On for Firefox

The Web Developer add-on (*http://chrispederick.com/work/web-developer/*)places a lot of useful functionality right on the toolbar, such as validation, inspection, and manipulation. Figure 4.10 shows the many options available in the toolbar.

Figure 4.10 Web Developer Toolbar

Here are some of the most helpful features when developing Facebook applications:

- **Disable Cache.** Turning off the cache can help you find loading issues with external resources and let you test new versions of images, JavaScript, and CSS files. This is extremely helpful when you debug caching issues with Facebook for images or Profile content.
- **Convert Form Methods.** This lets you change POSTs to GETs for any form on the page, which allows you to find problems with the data being sent easily in the address bar.
- **Outline.** Use this to put borders around all page HTML elements or just those of a certain type. This helps you quickly find the cause of layout issues.
- **Resize.** You can easily test your browser in a variety of common sizes without having to reset your desktop resolution. This can help you solve difficult CSS positioning problems.

YSlow Add-On for Firefox

The Yahoo Developer Network has some amazing articles and videos on best practices; in fact it has an entire Exceptional Performance team that focuses solely on researching how to improve web performance. The YSlow add-on for Firefox (*http://developer.yahoo.com/yslow/*) adds another tab into Firebug and uses those best practices to analyze your Facebook application's performance.

Figure 4.11 shows the Performance view for YSlow. The overall grade for the page being analyzed is shown, along with a grade for each rule. You can expand any rule to find out what is behind the grade or click the rule to go to a web page with more information about how to improve that particular rule.

The YSlow Stats view analyzes the page content loaded, showing the total download size and calls when the browser cache is empty and again after the cache is enabled. You can drill in further to see the cost of each file loaded on the Components view. This helps make sure that your web server is properly set up to do cache management for the different file types.

This tool is most useful for canvas pages, because Facebook already caches profile boxes and application tabs. When looking at an analysis of your canvas page, you have to ignore the Facebook-specific files—there really isn't anything you can do to improve their load times.

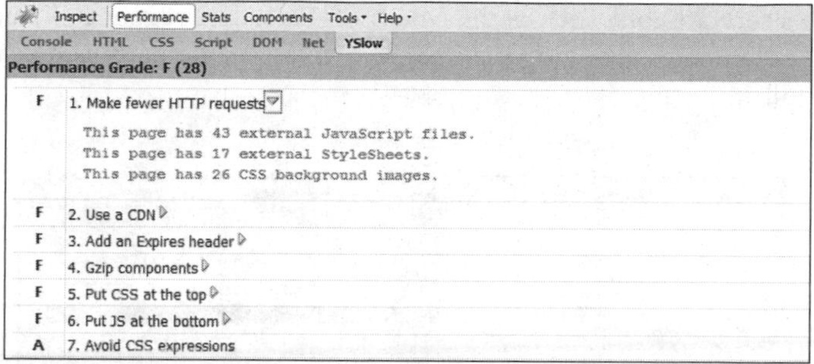

Figure 4.11 YSlow Performance tab

Firebug Lite Extension for Internet Explorer 6 and 7

Although Internet Explorer 6 and 7 don't have an integrated tool like Firebug, Firebug Lite (*http://getfirebug.com/lite.html*) provides a limited feature set—basically, the Console and read-only views of HTML, CSS, JavaScript, and the Network Monitor. By including a JavaScript file on the page or by dragging the Firebug Lite bookmarklet onto it, you get a window that looks similar to the full Firebug window. Figure 4.12 shows the Firebug Lite HTML view.

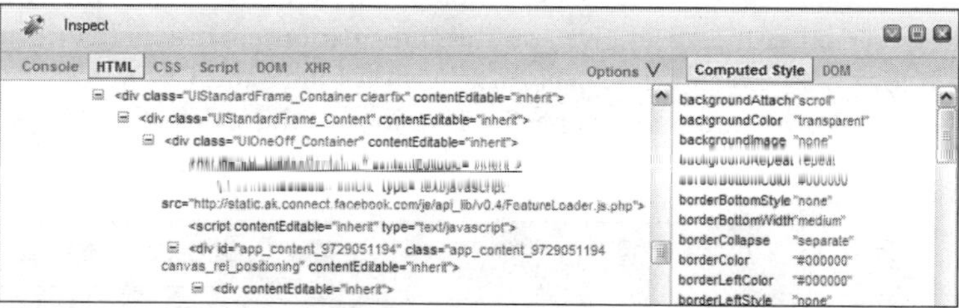

Figure 4.12 Firebug Lite HTML view

Although you can't change anything, you still have access to the Console logging and dumping commands and have the ability to inspect elements on the page.

IE Developer Toolbar for Internet Explorer 6 and 7

Microsoft provides the Internet Explorer Developer Toolbar as a download for Internet Explorer 6 and 7. You can find it at *www.microsoft.com/downloadS/details.aspx?familyid=E59C3964-672D-4511-BB3E-2D5E1DB91038&displaylang=en*. It combines a lot of the utilities in the Web Developer add-on for Firefox with the inspection capabilities of Firebug. It allows you to inspect elements, see their styles, and override them with new values. It does not have an integrated script debugger; for that, you must use a separate tool, such as the Microsoft Script Debugger or Visual Studio. Figure 4.13 demonstrates changing the margin style for an element using the Developer Toolbar.

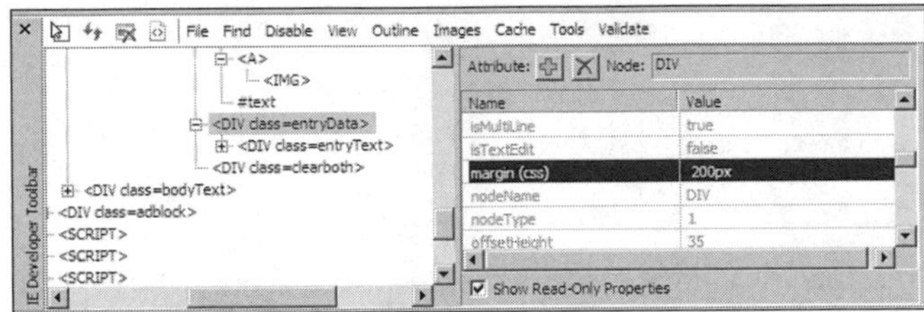

Figure 4.13 Internet Explorer Developer Toolbar for IE 6 and 7

Debugger Tools for Internet Explorer 8

With the release of Internet Explorer 8, Microsoft included a full developer toolset on par with Firebug. In fact, aside from a few name changes, it looks very much like Firebug. You can inspect and modify HTML and CSS on the fly, and debug and profile JavaScript right inside the browser. Finally, developing websites that work across browsers is much simpler. The only thing missing is built-in network-monitoring support. The Internet Explorer team said that it had to make trade-offs in order to ship, and that feature didn't quite make it. However, other free tools give you this information, such as Fiddler (*www.fiddler2.com*) on Windows or Paros and (*www.parosproxy.org*) on Linux and OS X.

Figure 4.14 shows using the Developer Tools to inspect the styles of an HTML element.

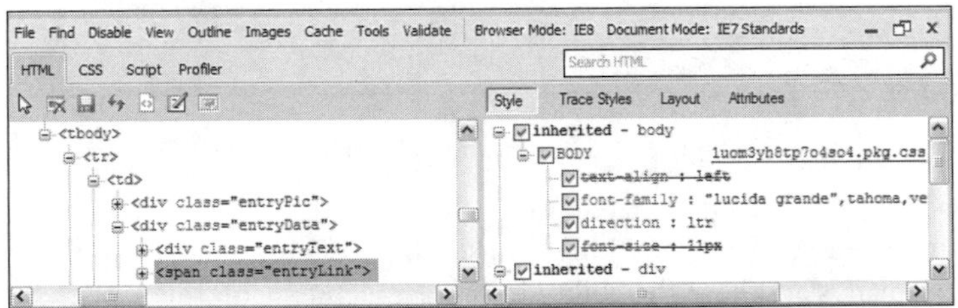

Figure 4.14 Developer Tools for Internet Explorer 8

Summary

This chapter reviewed the tools that Facebook provides to test features of the platform and various extensions for browsers that make debugging easier. Here are some key points:

- The API Test Console allows you to try API calls from the context of your application without having to actually run your application.

- The FBML Test Console can be the quickest way to test, render, and tweak FBML for profile boxes or application tabs without having your application do all the round trips.
- The Feed Template Console provides a wizard to generate Feed template bundles and the Registered Templates Console lets you remove template bundles that have been previously registered.
- Firebug is a browser extension for Firefox that is invaluable for diagnosing problems with HTML, CSS, or JavaScript. It allows quick editing of just about everything on the page. Firebug Lite provides some of this functionality for Internet Explorer.
- Internet Explorer's developer toolset has been lagging behind Firebug until the release of the Developer Tools, which was integrated into Internet Explorer 8. These new tools include JavaScript debugging, but sadly, they do not help fix problems in Internet Explorer 6.

5

Facebook Terms of Service and Application Programs

Facebook has to be careful with what it allows users and developers to do to make the service usable and enjoyable by all. It also wants applications to be as well developed and beneficial as possible. To meet these goals, Facebook created a number of documents that describe the rules and three programs that help encourage better applications.

Facebook Terms of Service

Every website has rules for what it deems acceptable behavior. On Facebook, these rules are detailed in a set of documents that each user and developer must agree to interact with the website and the Platform. Over time, as users and developers have tested these limits, the rules have changed and expanded. For developers, some of the biggest changes came as a result of some applications spamming users or tricking them into actions that they didn't intend. Users became upset, and that affected how they viewed all applications. The updated guidelines helped to soothe the backlash. In some ways, the new rules have also limited the extremely rapid growth that applications experienced at the launch of the platform. However, it is still possible for good applications that follow the rules to succeed.

It is important that every developer read through all these documents at least once and then verify each of their application's features to ensure compliance. These documents are updated several times a year, so check them every once in a while and follow the Facebook developer blog for notices about updates. Note that Facebook can change its terms and its services at any time without giving notice.

Each document is listed in this section, along with the most important points.

User Guidelines

All Facebook users must comply with Facebook's Statement of Rights and Responsibilities, which are derived from the Facebook Principles. Developers must ensure that their applications do not cause users to violate these terms.

Facebook Principles

The Facebook Principles document describes the overall goals that Facebook has for its website and development platform. The Statement of Rights and Responsibilities derives from these principles:

- **Freedom to Share and Connect.** People should be able to share anything and connect with anyone as long as both agree.
- **Ownership and Control of Information.** People own their information and can share it on Facebook. They can control who can see it via privacy controls and can remove it from Facebook.
- **Free Flow of Information.** People should be able to see everything that others have shared with them quickly and easily.
- **Fundamental Equality.** Individuals, advertisers, developers, and organizations should all have a single set of principles, rights, and responsibilities that apply to them.
- **Social Value.** People should be able to build reputations, and their accounts will only be removed if they violate the Statement of Rights and Responsibilities.
- **Open Platforms and Standards.** Programming interfaces and specifications for sharing and accessing information should be made available to everyone.
- **Fundamental Service.** People should be able to use Facebook for free to connect and share, regardless of how active they are.
- **Common Welfare.** The Statement of Rights and Responsibilities document should be based on these Principles.
- **Transparent Process.** Facebook should make information about its plans and policies available and use a town-hall process to amend the Principles and the Statement of Rights and Responsibilities.
- **One World.** Everyone in the world should be able to use Facebook.

Statement of Rights and Responsibilities

The Statement of Rights and Responsibilities (*www.facebook.com/terms.php*) are the rules that all users must agree to when they sign up for Facebook. The latest update is as of May 1, 2009.

Here are the key points for users:

- **Privacy.** User privacy is very important to Facebook. It is documented in the Facebook Privacy Policy, which is described in more detail in the section, "Privacy Policy."

- **Content.** Users own the content and information they post on Facebook and can control how this information is shared via privacy and application settings. Facebook can use this content until it is deleted by the user. Any information collected from users must be by their consent and have an accompanying privacy policy.
- **Prohibited Content.** Facebook will not verify all content, but can ask users to remove it if it violates these terms. This content cannot include the following:
    - Other people's contact and financial information, intellectual property without permission, or information that is fraudulent.
    - Alcohol-related or other mature content on pages that have not set appropriate age restrictions.
    - Pornography, graphic violence, or anything that Facebook might consider offensive.

- **Safety.** Users must interact appropriately and lawfully. Users are not allowed to scrape the Facebook site or harvest information without consent. They cannot intimidate, harass, or spam other users. They cannot use their profiles to show ads, run contests, or sell products.
- **Accounts.** All user accounts must be accurate and current and be created only for and by that user. All users must be over the age of 13, live in a country not embargoed by the U.S, and not be convicted sex offenders or on the U.S. Treasury Departments list of Specially Designated Nationals.
- **Rights.** Facebook tries to protect user and property rights. If Facebook removes suspect content, it can be appealed. Users can also claim their own intellectual property. No one can use Facebook's trademarks (Facebook, Facebook and F logos, FB, Face, Poke, Wall and the shortcode 32665) without permission.
- **Termination.** Facebook can terminate or suspend access to an account or delete a profile at any time without notice.

Evolving Terms of Service

In February 2009, Facebook updated its Terms of Use to state that it has the legal right to display archives of user's uploaded photos, messages, and other content after they terminate their Facebook account. The rationale was that services in general work like that; when someone sends someone else an email and then deletes their account, the email doesn't disappear from the recipient's inbox.

A big media frenzy developed, and Facebook founder Mark Zuckerberg wrote two blog posts in response. In the first, he described how Facebook tries to walk the fine line between allowing maximum sharing of content and maximum control. He stated that this area would continue to be a big focus for Facebook, but that sometimes, it would make mistakes. In the second post, he said that Facebook was going to revert the Terms back to the previous version and, to help develop the next version, he would ask for user input in creating the documents for the Facebook Bill of Rights and Responsibilities.

Users' comments were reviewed and the two documents, Facebook Principles and the Statements of Rights and Responsibilities, were released.

Privacy Policy

Facebook's Privacy Policy (*www.facebook.com/policy.php*) governs all activity on its website and, by default, all the activity of third-party applications that run within it. Developers are responsible for complying with this privacy policy or replacing it with a privacy policy of their own that is at least as stringent. The latest update is as of November 26, 2008.

The Facebook Privacy Policy is based around two major principles:

- Users need to control their personal information: what they put in their profile, posts, pictures, and what other users can see via privacy settings.
- Users should have access to information that others want to share and this should be as easy as possible.

To enable this, Facebook is a licensee of TRUSTe (*www.truste.org*), which is an organization that reviews privacy policies and practices. For international users, Facebook also participates in the EU Safe Harbor Framework (*www.export.gov/safeharbor/*), which creates a standard set of rules for the EU member countries.

Facebook collects any information that users enter on their profile or post as content. It also collects the browser and IP address of its users, along with information about how a user interacts with the website.

Facebook can display this information to other users based on the owning user's privacy settings, display it in search results inside and outside of Facebook, and use it as an aggregate for statistics and personalizing ads and promotions. Service providers for Facebook might have access to the information, but they are governed by strict contracts on how they can use it. Facebook also limits search-engine access to a small portion of user information.

Changes to a user's profile information are effective immediately, replacing existing representations of that information; however, information that they have shared with others, such as email or comments, can still be displayed.

Developer Guidelines

Developers are specifically governed by the Statement of Rights and Responsibilities and the Platform Guidelines, which is part of the Facebook Platform Documentation wiki.

Statement of Rights and Responsibilities

Facebook wants developers to create great applications; it also wants to protect its users. The Statement of Rights and Responsibilities contains a section related to applications on the Platform or using Facebook Connect. The latest update is as of May 1, 2009.

Here are the key points of this document for developers:

- **Responsibility.** Developers are responsible for their applications and must ensure that it meets the requirements of the Platform Guidelines.

- **Customer Service.** Your application must provide an email address for customers to use for application support. Users should be able to easily remove or disconnect from your application.
- **Data.** Users must know how you will use their data. Any data usage must comply with their privacy settings unless they give consent for other uses. If the user removes the application or disconnects, you must delete their Facebook data.
- **API.** Developers can use the API, code, and tools provided by Facebook, but only for their applications. Developers cannot resell these items.
- **Copyright Policy.** Applications must comply with the Digital Millennium Copyright Act and have a policy for removing content and repeat offenders. Applications must also comply with the Video Privacy Protection Act and must obtain explicit consent from users before allowing them to share videos.
- **Ownership.** Facebook can display application content in streams, profiles, and other locations. Facebook can also display ads or other content around any part of your application that appears inside the Facebook website frame. Facebook can analyze your application's content and data for its own purposes. Facebook can create applications that are similar to or compete with yours.
- **Publicity.** Developers can use Facebook logos and issue press releases as outlined in the Platform Guidelines. You cannot misrepresent your relationship with Facebook. Facebook might issue press releases about its relationship with you.

Platform Guidelines

Platform Guidelines (*http://wiki.developers.facebook.com/index.php/Platform_Guidelines*) cover the details of how applications should interact with users and the Facebook Platform. Most are common sense: Your application should be a good citizen of Facebook. The latest update is as of May 19, 2009:

- **Content.** Applications cannot have content or ads with nudity, sexual terms or content, obscene or libelous content, anti-religious or hate speech, or terrorism that infringes on the rights of others. They cannot promote or enable the sale of tobacco, ammunition, firearms, or content from uncertified pharmacies. It cannot display alcoholic beverages unless the application follows the exception procedures detailed in the Platform Policy. The application cannot enable or promote gambling.
- **Functionality.** Applications cannot collect Facebook usernames or passwords, automatically log into Facebook, or impersonate another Facebook user. They cannot distribute unauthorized or copyrighted content or trick users to download viruses or Trojans. They cannot circumvent a user's Facebook privacy settings.
- **Advertising and Marketing.** Applications cannot show advertising or web search on anything on Facebook except their canvas pages. Marketing must follow spam laws and user preferences for opt-in or opt-out.

- **Prohibited Application Actions.** Applications cannot do any of the following:
  - Force users to invite friends in order to use the application or create a forced loop of invitation dialogs if the user presses the skip or cancel button.
  - Have profile boxes or canvas pages that go outside of their physical size constraints.
  - Trade reviews or try to "game" the posting of reviews.
  - Try to confuse or mislead users.
  - Pool notifications or news stories between applications to work around notification limits or to trick users into installing another application.
  - Use another user's session key instead of the active user.

- **Application Response to User Actions.** When a user takes an action, applications must respond in a way that complies with the following:
  - Users must not be surprised by the outcome of actions they take.
  - Applications must not let users trigger actions that apply to multiple people with one click. Users must manually select recipients, rather than have them be autoselected by the application.
  - Notifications, news stories, and other output of the application must correspond to actions that the user has actually taken, and they must be done within 12 hours of the action.

- **Feed Policy.** When an application creates a feed story, it should be an interesting action or something that the user wants to share. It needs to also meet the following guidelines:
  - It should be triggered by a significant action the user took.
  - It should be accurate, and `user_message` should only be filled out with content generated by the user.
  - It should not contain information that a user would expect to be private.
  - It should be published immediately, unless explicitly delayed by the user.
  - All calls to action should be done as action links instead of as part of the story.
  - Information cannot be presented for the first time to the user with a Feed form.
  - Publishing a story cannot be incentivized.

- **Info Tabs.** Updated content can be placed on the Info tab in response to user actions. It cannot be autogenerated without the user's consent each time.
- **Application Integration Points Policy.** Applications cannot incent users to add or use an integration point, or prompt users to add integration points that don't relate to the user's current context.
- **Application Tab Policy.** Application tabs can only contain content for that application and cannot include advertising or promote other applications. They cannot

display different content to different viewers except based on demographic restrictions or to the profile owner.

- **Publisher Policy.** The Publisher cannot show any advertising or promote other applications. Applications cannot incent the user to use the Publisher. The Publisher's output should be what the user expects.
- **Notifications Policy.** Notifications sent by the application must meet these conditions:
  - User-to-user notifications must be sent within one hour of the first action that triggered it and should be expected to be sent.
  - Application-to-user notifications should be from the application and not the user. They must also be about either more than one user or more than one action. They must be sent a maximum of one week after the earliest trigger and must contain the date of that trigger.
- **Storable Data Policy.** Applications are only allowed to store a small set of IDs. Everything else, such as usernames or interests, can only be cached for 24 hours. Facebook wants applications to get user's data directly from Facebook's API. Here is the storable Facebook data:
  - User ID
  - Primary Network ID
  - Event ID
  - Group ID
  - Photo ID
  - Photo Album ID
  - Friend List ID
  - Marketplace Listing ID
  - Facebook Page ID
  - Proxied Email Address ID
  - Number of Notes written by a user
  - Last update time of a user's profile
- **UI Elements Policy.** Applications cannot use graphics that look like pieces of web functionality, such as ads with pictures of HTML drop downs, with the intent to mislead users into clicking them. They cannot display pop-ups or pop-unders. Profiles cannot automatically play audio, video, or interactive content unless that content is first clicked to activate it.
- **Escalation Policy.** Facebook has escalation procedures for non-compliance with these Guidelines. The procedures do not have to be done in sequence. The procedures are as follows:

- **Notice of Concern.** Your application is under review for some content or functionality. You can voluntarily modify it to comply and prevent escalation.
- **Request for Action.** Facebook requests that specific changes to the application be made. Developers can voluntarily make these changes.
- **Notice of Violation.** Facebook has determined that the application is violating some of the terms. A time limit for mandatory compliance will be given, along with the possibility of Facebook suspending or restricting your application.
- **Notice of Restriction or Moratorium.** Your application has been restricted or suspended for some period of time because of violations.
- **Notice of Suspension.** Facebook has temporarily removed your application from Facebook.
- **Notice of Termination.** Facebook has permanently removed your application from Facebook.
- **File Sharing.** If your application allows users to post, view, listen, or download content, your application must also
    - Host a page with the copyright policy similar to *http://developers.facebook.com/samplecopyright.php* and have a link to this on each page that allows users to view or upload content.
    - Register a designated agent for copyright-infringement claims with the U.S. Copyright Office. This costs $80. (More information is at *www.copyright.gov/onlinesp/agent.pdf*.)
    - Add this statement to each page on which users can view the content: "By making any content available through this application, you represent and warrant that you own all rights necessary to properly do so."

- **Facebook Connect Policy.** These policies govern websites that use Facebook Connection functionality:
- **Connecting.** The site must use the official Facebook Connect button, and it must have as much prominence as any other login mechanism. Users must be able to log out. When logged in, the user's profile picture overlaid with the Facebook favicon and their name must be shown. Only the Connected website can use the user's data.
- **Friends.** When showing lists of friends where some of those friends are from Facebook, the website must show this by using the word Facebook or the Facebook favicon. If the website uses Friend Linking, it must also allow searching by email address or contact importer.
- **PR Policy.** You can publicize your application by talking to the press, but you cannot do a press release without prior written consent from Facebook. The PR website at *http://wiki.developers.facebook.com/index.php/Developer_PR_Policy* provides examples of specific language you can use in discussing the Facebook Platform.

- **Verified App Badge.** If your application has been verified by Facebook, you can display the official badge online or in print, but you cannot alter it. It must be clear that your brand is responsible for the application and not Facebook.

Facebook Application Programs

After an avalanche of applications that were banal, tricked users, or were of overall low quality, Facebook launched two programs to spur development of better caliber applications.

Application Verification Program

This optional program vets applications against a set of criteria to let users know that they can trust these applications to be well behaved and provide a good user experience. The cost for this program is $375/year for businesses and $175/year for students and nonprofits.

Benefits

Applications that pass verification get the following benefits:

- **Higher limits** on user communication from inside the application
- **Better visibility** in the News Feed
- **Badges** on the application's About page and in the Application Directory
- **Special offers**, such as a $100 advertising credit and discounts on Facebook events, like F8
- **Early access** to new Platform features
- **Feedback and data** from Facebook to help improve their applications even further

Criteria

All application criteria use the Terms of Service and other documents as a baseline. They must also follow the Guiding Principles for trustworthiness (laid out in Chapter 2, "Making Great Applications"). The rest of the criteria are:

- **Communication.** Do any emails, requests, notifications, and News Feed stories result from expected and non-forced user actions? Is the content of the communication well written and useful to the recipient? If message attachments are provided by the application, do they work as the user expects?
- **Display.** Do the profile boxes, application info sections, and application tabs show information and share compelling and user-focused information?
- **Content.** Does the application provide a mechanism to report inappropriate user-generated content and respond to it effectively?

Application Process

To apply, developers register their intent, and then wait for an email that they have been accepted to submit their application. Then, they fill out a form with information about their business, what data they collect from users, screenshots of the application, and the method of payment for the application fee.

If the application does not pass verification for minor violations, the developers are notified and given a chance to fix the problems. If more serious issues exist, the application must fix them and wait for a period of three months before re-applying.

Applications that pass verification are eligible for the Great Apps program, but they must continue to follow policy guidelines. If violations occur, the verified status is revoked.

fbFund

To encourage the development of higher quality and utility applications and to jump start the new development team, Facebook developed the fbFund. The fbFund has $10 million dollars in capital and is administered by Accel Partners and The Founders Fund.

Each funding round is different. The first focused on the best applications in general, the second on best utilization of the new profile integration points, and the current one is about the best use of Facebook Connect.

During the second round, 25 finalists were picked, and each received $25,000 in funding. The Top 5 applications were picked by popular vote and given $225,000.

The current round will select up to 50 winners for the first round, after which several of them will become finalists and be awarded $100,000 and spend the summer in an Incubator program run by Dave McClure.

Benefits

Winners of the fbFund receive numerous benefits:

- **Funding** of between $25,000 to $100,000
- **Mentorship** from Facebook executives and other entrepreneurs and attendance at the Incubator program
- **Marketing** in the form of promotion at Facebook events and on the Developer Events

Criteria

The fbFund winners are chosen based on a number of criteria, but overall, Facebook is more interested in smart people with great ideas who can execute rather than formal business plans. Some previous winners state that single-person startups are less likely to win.

The formal criteria are as follows:

- **Originality of Concept.** Is the application a new concept?
- **Market.** Does the application meet market needs in general or of a specific target?
- **Social/Useful.** Does the application allow people to interact with each other, and does it have real value to users?
- **Expressive.** Can users share more information through the application?
- **Intuitive.** Is the application easy to use?

- **Potential.** Can the application grow and be monetized?
- **Team.** Is the team behind the application driven and can it execute?

To receive funding and participate in the Incubator program, companies must move to Silicon Valley and be incorporated in the U.S., preferably as a Delaware C Corporation.

Application and Voting Process

Applicants fill out a form on the Facebook Developer website that describes their company, team, and application. There is careful attention to the credentials of each team member, because the fbFund isn't funding just the application, but the developers behind it.

At the end of the application, developers must provide an executive summary, a presentation deck, and an elevator pitch. Round 1 winner LuckyCal recommends the following practices:

- Do the elevator pitch as a video, preferably with both a view of the head of the person talking and usage of the key parts of the application.
- In the presentation deck, break down plans for how the money from funding will be used and how the application will make money.
- Make sure that your presentation shows why the application is worth funding; don't make the investors guess.

After submitting the form, applications must wait until the finalists are announced. If an application is not funded, developers receive an email stating this, but without specific details about why the application was not chosen. Applications are invited to apply again during the next round.

When the finalists are announced, the winners are decided by popular vote. The top winners receive larger funding amounts and access to the Incubator program.

Funded Company Examples

Here is a sampling of the winners of the first two rounds of funding:

Round 1

- **Goalcamp:Challenge.** Users create and join challenges, such as running 50 miles and compete against their friends.
- **ConnectedWedding.** Users can plan their wedding and create a wedding web page.
- **CourseFeed.** Notifies students when new homework assignments are posted and lets them share notes and plan study groups with other users.
- **Hotberry.** A framework for users to create their own games on Facebook.
- **J2Play.** Enables applications to add cross-network social features, including mobile support.
- **LuckyCal.** A calendar that integrates Facebook events with external events automatically found based on the user's interests.
- **MyListo.** Users share product reviews with their friends and can search for reviews by how close their friendship is with the reviewer.

- **Podclass.** A way to enable companies to offer their course materials and students to access them inside Facebook.
- **Trazzler.** Helps users decide where to go by determining their Travel Personality and lets them view trips that their friends took.
- **Zimride Carpool.** Users can enter their location and destination, and the application will notify them with available carpool candidates.

Round 2

- **GroupCard.** Friends sign a group ecard for an occasion, including messages, photos, audio, and gifts.
- **Kontagent.** A metrics platform for Facebook applications that provides detailed insights into application usage and virality.
- **Mousehunt.** An incredibly popular game where users work as teams to hunt mice in an infested kingdom.
- **Weddingbook.** Couples share their wedding plans with friends, and users can talk with other engaged couples in the application community.
- **Wildfire.** Companies use a simple framework to create branded promotions and contests that use Facebook's viral features.

Summary

This chapter reviewed the important points of the many Facebook Terms of Service documents. It also described the application programs that Facebook offers to developers. Here are some key points:

- Most of Facebook's policies are common sense and easy to follow. They keep the application environment from harming users and prevent "bad" applications from bringing down the good ones.
- Review Facebook's policies while designing your application and, every so often, make sure that your application is still in compliance with any changes.
- Although it's optional, the Application Verification Program provides a solid checklist by which all applications should abide. The benefit of increased exposure and communication limits might be valuable enough to developers to compensate for its fee.
- The fbFund offers developers a great chance to earn recognition and cash, but it requires a good idea, a solid team, and the ability to execute. Developers need to be mindful of the need to move to Silicon Valley if they win.

II

Developing Applications

6

The Basics of Creating Applications

This chapter covers the basics of creating and configuring a new Facebook application. First, we cover the many configuration settings provided by the Facebook Developer application and how they should be set for a new application. Next, we create the basic PHP skeleton of a Facebook application and introduce some of the functionality provided by Facebook Markup Language (FBML) and the official Facebook PHP client library. Then, we discuss how applications are authorized by users and how Facebook authenticates applications. Finally, Facebook sessions, signatures, and the data Facebook sends to an application's canvas page are covered.

In this chapter, you set up and create a sample application, Compliments. This application, which you will develop over the next several chapters, allows Facebook users to send compliments to their Facebook friends using all the integration points that Facebook provides.

Setting Up the Environment

The first thing you need to do is download the Facebook PHP client library from Facebook from its public source control repository: *http://svn.facebook.com/svnroot/platform/clients/packages/facebook-platform.tar.gz*. You'll need to extract the files from the downloaded archive using your favorite archiving tool.

The PHP client library is comprised of three files. The first, `facebook_api_restlib.php`, contains the implementation of the `FacebookRestClient` class that encapsulates the raw, low-level HTTP access of the Facebook REST-API. The second file, `facebook.php`, provides an implementation of the `Facebook` class, which encapsulates Facebook web application behavior. The third file, `facebook_desktop.php`, provides the `FacebookDesktop` class to do the same for Facebook desktop applications. Both `facebook.php` and `facebook_desktop.php` include `facebookapi_php5_restlib.php` internally, so you never have to include it directly in your application code to access the Facebook API from PHP.

Next, you need to set up a web server to host your application. For the rest of this book, we refer to your web server in URLs, such as *http://example.com*. For the purposes of creating this application, it might be simplest to run on a local server. There are also many hosting companies that specialize in Facebook application hosting. Here are the steps to set up everything:

1. First, create a new directory on your web server for your application. Create a new directory called Compliments to hold your application files. This directory will be known as the application's root directory. Next, create a new virtual directory, which maps to this physical directory. Restart your web server.
2. Now, install the Facebook PHP client library on your web server by extracting it to a location that the application can reference. If you plan on writing multiple Facebook applications, you can either extract one copy of the PHP client library for each new application or use one global copy that will be referenced by all of your applications. We suggest the former because it limits compatibility errors that can arise if you update the library, and it breaks a feature in use by one of your older applications. To do this, extract the files to a new directory inside the compliments directory called `fblib`. The path to the facebook.php file should now be `/compliments/fblib/facebook.php`.
3. Next, create the first file of your new Facebook application. In the `compliments` directory create a new file called `index.php`. Put the following line in this file:

   ```
   <?php phpinfo(); ?>
   ```

4. To verify that your web server and new application are correctly set up, make sure that you can access the `index.php` file from your web server. Browse to the location of this new file using your favorite browser by typing *http://example.com/compliments/index.php* in the browser's address bar. You should now see the screen fill with information about the currently installed version of PHP. Check your server's error logs for information if you cannot see the page or if your browser gives you an error.
5. Finally, create a new MySQL database for the application called `compliments`. For security purposes, it's good practice to create a new application-specific user for this database. Ensure the user you choose for the Compliments application is granted the `SELECT`, `ALTER`, `UPDATE`, `INSERT`, and `DELETE` privileges for the new database. Note this new user's username and password. You won't be using the database in this chapter, but you need it for Chapter 7, "Building the Canvas."

Using the Developer Application

The Facebook Developer application allows you to create new Facebook applications and manage existing applications. To start the process of creating the Compliments application, you need to add the Facebook Developer application to your Facebook account.

Log in to Facebook and go to *www.facebook.com/developers*. Click Allow to authorize the Facebook Developer application (see Figure 6.1).

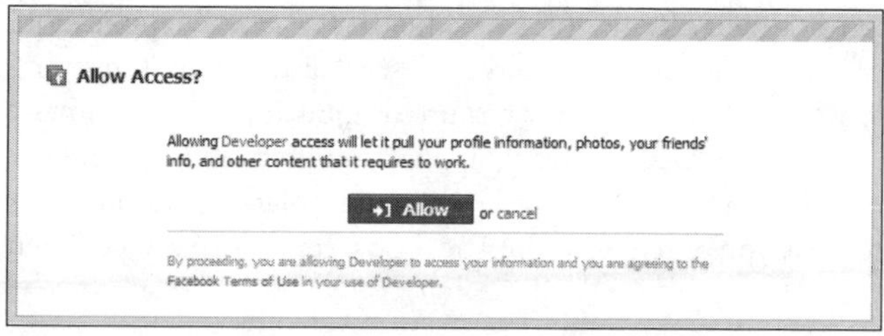

Figure 6.1 Authorizing the Facebook Developer application

After you install the Developer application, you are taken to its canvas page. Click the Set Up New Application button in the top right of the page. Figure 6.2 shows its location.

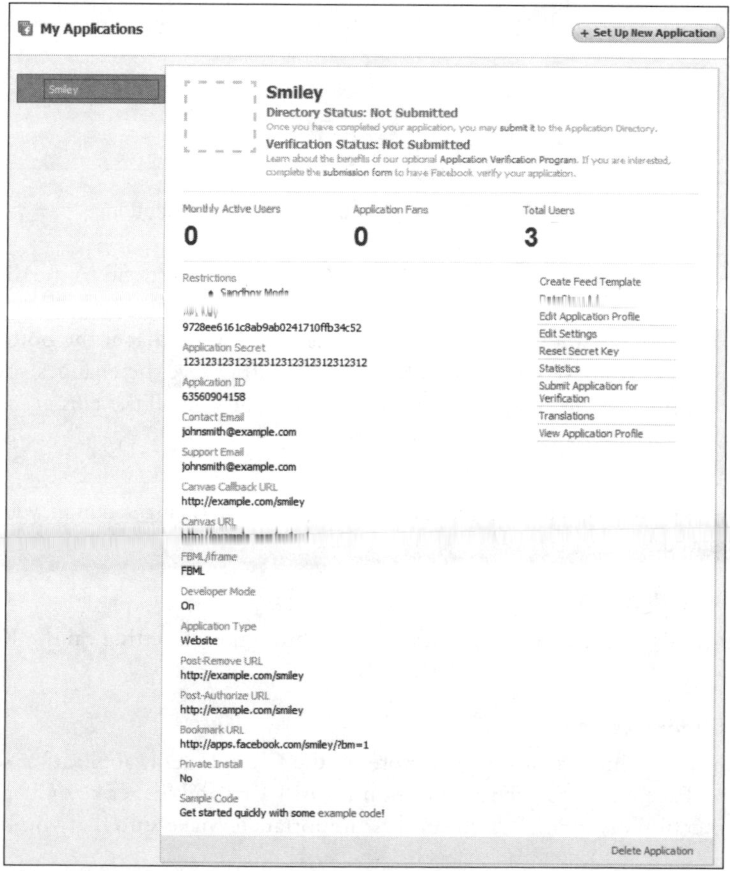

Figure 6.2 Creating a new application with the Developer application

The next screen, shown in Figure 6.3, prompts you to name your new application. Facebook does not allow application names to be longer than 50 characters, and it also requires that the names do not contain the following words: face, poke, or wall. The name also must not be too much like any of the names of the default applications that Facebook provides, such as Photos, Videos, and Notes. As discussed in Chapter 2, "Making Great Applications," Facebook does not require unique application names, but it does require that the Canvas Page URL for each application be unique. (More on that later.) For now, enter the name Compliments in the Application Name field, and check the radio button that states that you agree with the Facebook Terms of Service. Then, click Save Changes.

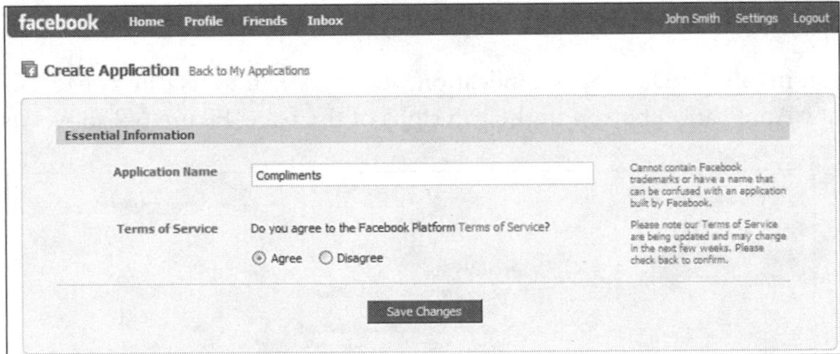

Figure 6.3 Naming the Compliments application

Notice the tabs along the left side of Figure 6.4. These correspond to the different groups of settings for the Compliments application. The following sections cover each of these tabs and the relevant settings for Compliments. Be aware that at the bottom of each of these tab pages is a Save Changes button. You can either save the changes you made to each page before clicking another tab or click it after you edit all the tabs.

> **Warning**
>
> If you browse away from this page without clicking the Save Changes button, your changes are not saved.

Basic Settings Tab

Using Figure 6.4 as a reference, this section goes through each setting on the Basic Settings tab.

Essential Information

The first and most important things to note on the Compliments application settings page are the Facebook-provided Application ID, API Key, and Secret key. Chapter 3, "Platform Architecture Overview," discusses their importance. Make sure that you keep these values safe.

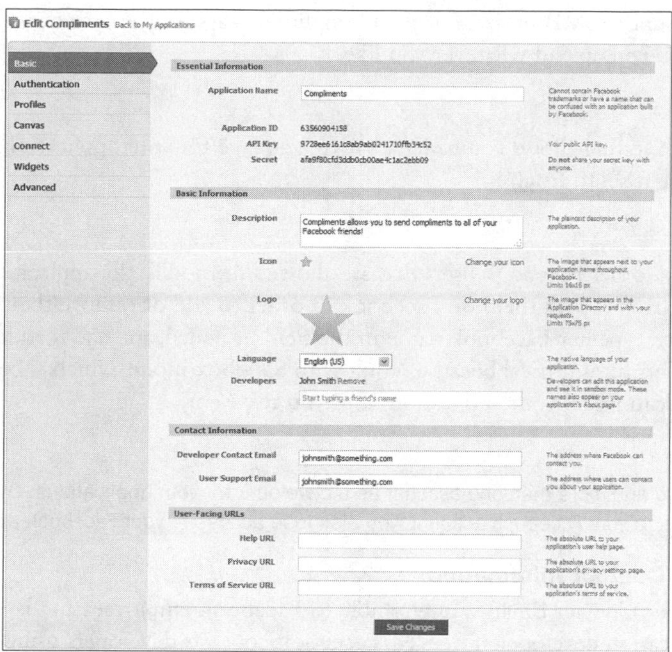

Figure 6.4 Compliments application's Basic Settings tab

Application Description

The Application Description field is displayed in the Facebook Application Directory (which Chapter 14, "Measuring Application Success," covers) and is shown to new users before they add or authorize the application. It's limited to 250 characters and must be plain text. You don't need to worry about setting this field at the moment. The application is not going to be added to the Application Directory until it is complete. For now, it's only going to be installable by people you specify.

Application Icon and Logo

Application icons are used in the following areas: the Applications menu, Application Settings pages, and in the Allow Access authorization dialog. Icons are limited to 16×16 pixels in size. Many times, the application icon will not be rendered on a white background, so Facebook recommends that developers use transparent GIF images for all application icons. PNG images also allow transparency, but they are not supported by all browsers (notably Internet Explorer 6).

The application logo is shown, obviously, in the Application Directory. It has a maximum size of 75×75 pixels and can be in GIF, JPG, or PNG format. If either of these images is larger than their allowed dimensions, they are automatically resized to fit and converted to GIF format. Image files you upload to Facebook for either the icon or the logo must be under 5MB in size. For the Compliments application, we chose a gold star image, but you can upload whatever you like.

Language

The Language setting allows you to set a native language for your application. For Compliments, leave it set to English.

Developers

Developers are other Facebook users that are allowed to modify the application settings. You must be friends with them on Facebook in order to add or remove them. To add a new developer, type her Facebook name in the field provided, and she is added to the Developer list. This list is critical because, along with Sandbox mode, which is covered later, it restricts who can install your application until you release it.

> **Tip**
>
> Always try to add more than one account as a developer for your applications. Otherwise, if you lose access to your Facebook account, you also lose access to your Facebook applications.

Application Contact Information

The Developer Contact Email is only visible to Facebook employees and is used to contact the application developer, if needed. Facebook contacts developers using this address, usually if an application has complaints against it or violates the Facebook Terms of Service. The User Support Email is available to your application's users when they want to contact you from your application's Help or About pages. Both of these addresses are required and default to the email address the application creator used when signing up for Facebook. Both can be changed if desired, but leave them as their default values for Compliments.

User-Facing URLs

The Help, Privacy, and Terms of Service URLs can give custom URLs for application-specific help, privacy, and Terms of Service, if desired. For Compliments, leave these fields blank. If you set the Terms of Service URL, users will be prompted to accept your custom Terms of Service before they authorize the application. This is important in cases where legal liability might be involved. If you don't provide URLs for these, the Facebook Help, Privacy, and Terms of Service pages are used.

Authentication Settings Tab

The Authentication Settings tab, shown in Figure 6.5, controls what kind of profile an application can be installed on and whether the application will be notified when users install or uninstall.

Users and Facebook Pages

The first setting in this tab allows the developer to set whether the application is installable to user profiles, Public Profiles, or both. User profiles are normal Facebook user accounts. Public Profiles are the new name for what were once called Facebook Pages and are used by brands, celebrities, or companies that don't map directly to a single user account. To allow an application to be installed on user profiles, check the Users checkbox; to allow an application to be installed on Public Profiles, check the Facebook Pages checkbox. For the Compliments application, leave this set to having just the Users checkbox checked, which means that the application will not be added to Public Profiles.

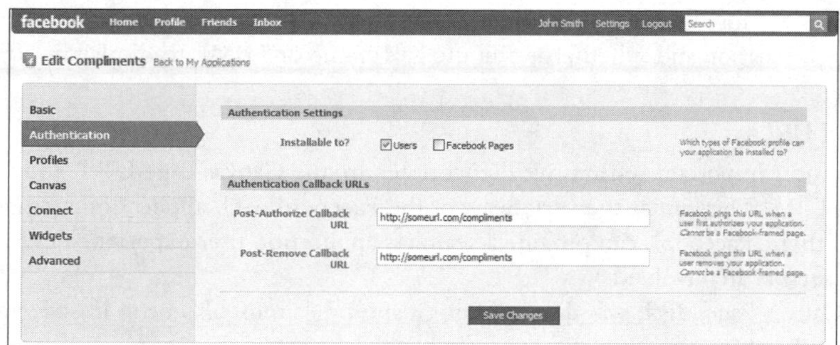

Figure 6.5 Compliments application's Authentication Settings tab

Authentication Callback URLs

The URLs provided in the Authentication Callback fields notify you when a user authorizes or uninstalls your application. They must be URLs that do not point to Facebook servers. Facebook sends a number of parameters to these URLs when it is called to allow the application to handle application authorization and removal appropriately. Note that these URLs are simply pinged, which means that an HTTP request is made to these URLs—the browser is not redirected to them. You cannot execute code that outputs any content for users in response to these notifications, because they will never see it.

The Post-Authorize Callback URL is pinged by Facebook when a user first authorizes an application. After authentication, the user's browser is redirected to the application's default canvas page. The URL is useful if an application creates records of its users in a database or needs to do special processing when a new user authorizes an application. Developers can add GET parameters to this URL, if desired, for even more customization; however, the full URL must be less than 100 characters long. Facebook sends a special POST variable named `fb_sig_authorized` set to a value of 1 when this URL is notified.

The Post-Remove Callback URL is called after a user removes an application. Facebook sends a special POST variable named `fb_sig_uninstall`, also set to a value of 1, when this URL is pinged. As with the previous URL, GET parameters can be added, if desired, but the 100-character limit also applies here.

For Compliments, set both to the URL of your application root on your web server. Figure 6.5 sets them to dummy URLs as examples. Instead of adding custom GET parameters to these URLs, we'll look at the Facebook POST variables to handle the notifications appropriately in Compliments.

Profiles Settings Tab

The Profiles Settings tab contains settings for application profile tabs and profile boxes. The options on this tab are not discussed until Chapter 8, "Updating the Profile." For Compliments, leave all the settings at their defaults.

Canvas Settings Tab

The Canvas Settings tab focuses on the settings for the application's canvas page, including the callback location and whether it will use an IFrame or FBML to display its contents.

Required URLs

The two most important settings we'll encounter are the Canvas Page URL and Canvas Callback URL. They are at the very heart of the Facebook web application architecture. Through them, Facebook can provide a seamless application user experience even though multiple servers are involved.

The Canvas Page URL was discussed in Chapter 3. It must also be at least 7, but not more than 20, characters long and can only contain letters, underscores, or dashes. As Figure 6.6 shows, Facebook lets you know if an application URL is unavailable. Also, at the time of this writing, there is an outstanding bug within Facebook that requires all Canvas Page URLs to be lowercase. For Compliments, choose an available Canvas Page URL that's meaningful to you. We recommend that you use a URL that at least describes your application; however, this is not always possible. Obviously, "compliments" is unavailable, so try a few times to get a URL that works.

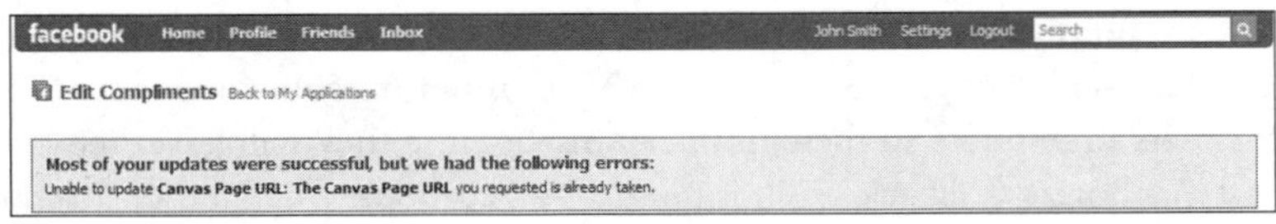

Figure 6.6 Error shown when the Canvas Page URL is already taken.

The Canvas Callback URL points to the application's physical location on your web server where the code for the application exists. This URL cannot be more than 100 characters. For the Compliments application, use the same URL you entered for the Post-Authorize Callback above (the URL of application root on your web server).

> **Caution**
>
> Make sure that you add the trailing slash to your Canvas Callback URL! If you forget it and try to hit a page in the application's root (for example, *http://example.com/compliments/index.php*), you won't find the file, because Facebook appends the file resource to the Canvas Callback URL, resulting in *http://example.com/complimentsindex.php*.

Figure 6.7 shows a completed required URLs example.

Figure 6.7 Required URLs section of Canvas Settings tab

Optional URLs

The Bookmark URL is used in several locations. Figure 6.8 displays the Application menu that appears at the bottom of each Facebook Page. Here, the Bookmark URL is where the user goes when he clicks either the Compliments link in the Bookmark section or the Compliments icon on the toolbar. These locations only appear after a user bookmarks your application. Figure 6.9 displays the Compliments About page for a user who hasn't authorized Compliments. Clicking the Go to Application button takes the user to the location he specified in the Bookmark URL. Figure 6.10 shows the About page for an authorized user, and the Go to This Application link also uses the Bookmark URL location. If the Bookmark URL is not set, all these locations go to the application's Canvas Page URL. Leave the Bookmark URL blank for Compliments to use the default.

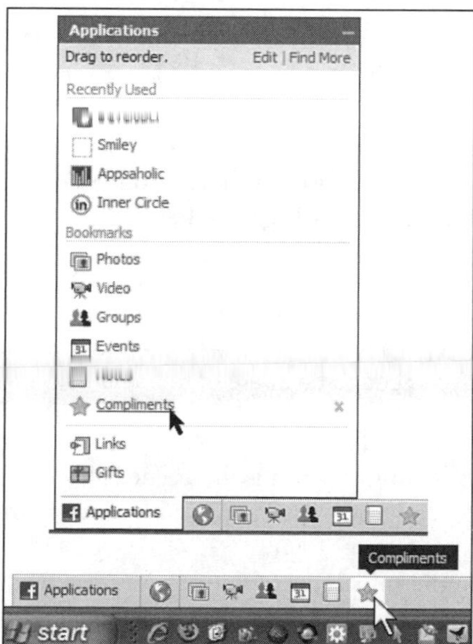

Figure 6.8 Bookmark URL usage in the Facebook Applications menu

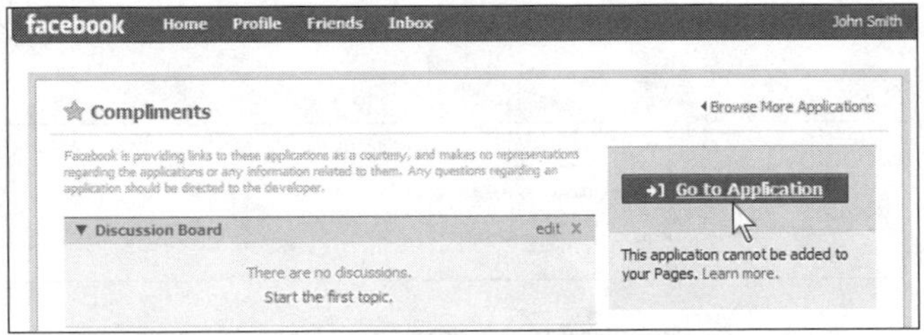

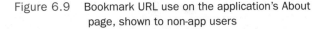

Figure 6.9 Bookmark URL use on the application's About page, shown to non-app users

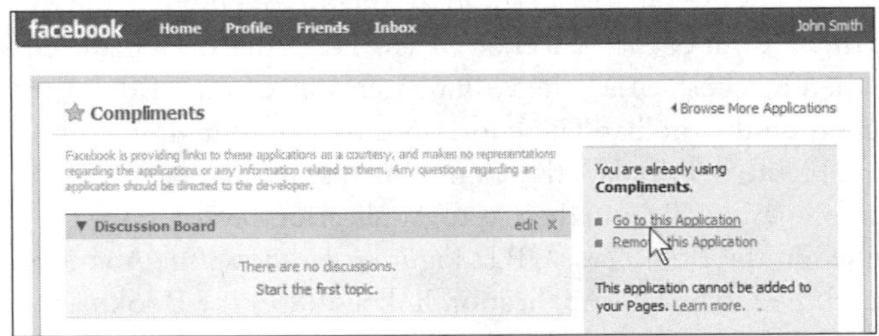

Figure 6.10 Bookmark URL use on the application's About page, shown to app users

The Post-Authorize Redirect URL redirects users who have just authorized your application to a custom landing page. This can be useful if your application needs some initial configuration or data input from the user. Note that Facebook only redirects to this URL in certain circumstances, depending on how the user authorizes the application. (This is discussed in the section, "Application Authorization.") For Compliments, leave it blank because it also defaults to the Canvas Page URL.

> **Note**
>
> Facebook does not provide a Post-Remove Redirect URL. It doesn't on purpose, just to keep an application from trying to engage a user in any way after he has decided to remove it. It's a nice feature for users, but you need to be aware of this when developing an application.

Canvas Settings

The first option in the Canvas Settings section is the Render Method. It lets you choose whether your canvas page will render in FBML or in a custom IFrame. Chapter 7 covers this in detail; for now, just leave it set to FBML.

IFrame Size lets you decide the initial size of your canvas page IFrame, if you chose IFrame as your Render Method. The first option, Smart Size, causes the IFrame rendered on the canvas page to fill all the space it can on the canvas page; however, after it's rendered, it cannot be resized if the content of the IFrame changes. This can be a severe limitation for an application developer if the content of the IFrame changes, as scroll bars will be added to the IFrame if the content overflows the initial space provided. The second option, Resizable, allows you to resize the IFrame as needed. It also requires a static HTML page to allow communication between the canvas page hosted on Facebook and the IFrame along with some JavaScript to implement the resizing logic. For now, leave the option set to Smart Size.

The Canvas Width option is irrelevant. It is used for canvas pages that were designed to work with Facebook's old profile design. Because we're creating a new application, it does not apply. Leave it set to the default, Full Width (760px).

The Quick Transitions option is a feature intended to make canvas pages load much faster than usual. When enabled, Facebook uses AJAX to quickly load your application canvas pages without having to reload the entire Facebook frame that surrounds them, which might take a significant amount of time, especially for FBML applications. To keep things simple at this point, leave it set to Off for now. Feel free to explore its behavior and its impact on your application canvas page load times.

Connect Settings Tab

The Connect Settings tab contains options focused on Facebook Connect. Because Chapter 13, "Facebook Connect," covers this topic, just leave all the settings on this page to the defaults. One section to note is the Template Bundles section, which allows you to quickly add template data for use in Feed forms, calls to the `feed.publishUserAction()` API method, and Feed dialogs. However, the Feed Template Console tool, described in Chapter 4, "Platform Developer Tools," is much easier to use and allows previews of the templates as they would render in the live stream. If you are a pro at writing Facebook Feed templates, feel free to use this section to do so!

Widgets Settings Tab

The Widget Settings tab configures a Facebook widget called the Comments Box. It can be placed on any website or IFrame application and allows people to comment on content outside of Facebook and have these comments published to the stream. These comments can be programmatically accessed, and the box itself can be styled with custom cascading styles sheets (CSS). It is not relevant to this discussion, so leave all the options at their defaults.

Advanced Settings Tab

The Advanced Settings tab allows developers to handle security, enable Developer-only Sandbox mode, and a variety of other settings.

Advanced Settings

In the Advanced Settings section, check the option to enable Sandbox mode. This ensures that only the developers chosen on the Basic Settings tab can see and install the application. This option is disabled when the application is launched, but keeping it restricted to the developers working on it is a wise choice at the outset. Leave the Application Type set to Web, because we are developing a Facebook web application that will run in a browser.

Mobile Integration

The Mobile Integration options enable applications to support sending and receiving SMS messages, as discussed in Chapter 3. You can also link your iPhone application ID with your application, if you are using the Facebook Connect for iPhone library.

Attachments

The Attachments section settings are used if an application wants the capability to attach items to private Facebook messages. For example, the Compliments application could provide some way of allowing a user that had authorized the application to attach a compliment to any message she sends. If we entered the text Attach a Compliment in the Attachment Text field, it would show up in the Compose Message page along the bottom of the Message body field, as shown in Figure 6.11.

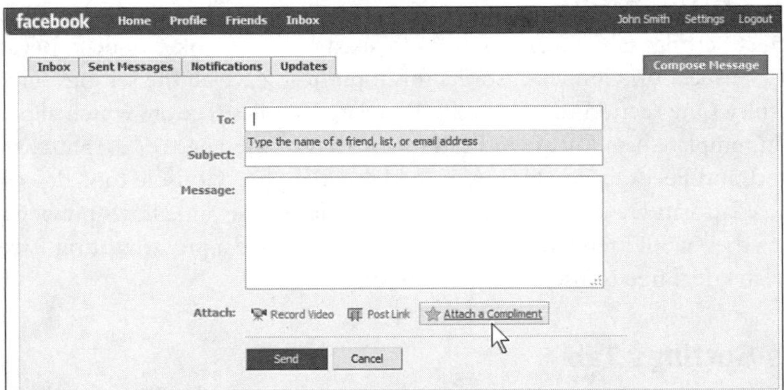

Figure 6.11 Compose Message page showing the application's attachment text

To get the actual page that provides the user interface for uploading the attachment, Facebook uses the value of the Attachment Callback URL field. If a user clicked the Attachment Text link, shown in Figure 6.11, he is redirected to this URL where it's assumed the application presents a page that let him upload some attachment. For example, if the Compliments application wanted to allow users to attach complimentary photos, it could provide a URL to a photo upload page. For Compliments, just leave these fields blank.

Security

The Security section provides two options. The first, the Server Whitelist, allows a developer to specify the specific IP addresses that Facebook can use to communicate with the application. This setting is obviously only valid for Facebook web applications. Requests for the application from any IP addresses not listed here will be automatically blocked.

This is a quick way to protect an application from impersonation attacks in the event its secret key is stolen; however, it also means that it's not possible to test the application using `localhost`.

The second option, the Session Secret Whitelist Exception setting, is only relevant if you use the Server Whitelist and your application is either an IFrame-based or an external application using Facebook Connect. This setting allows the application to sidestep the whitelist restriction so it can call the JavaScript Client Library. Leave this disabled for the moment.

Legal

The Legal section is only relevant if an application sells or rents videos. If so, it must comply with Federal regulations provided by the Video Privacy Protection Act. Leave it set to the default.

Creating the Application Skeleton

We'll now begin coding the Compliments application. We'll start with a simple PHP skeleton that will implement just the basics of integrating with Facebook by handling application authorization and removal. We'll go over each part of it in detail.

From the Developer application, we'll need the API key, Secret key, and Canvas Callback URL. We'll create a file that sets these to constant values that we can include in all the files of the application. Create a new file named `globals.inc` and save it in a subdirectory of your application root directory, named `inc`. In this file, enter the code shown in Listing 6.1, replacing the name, key, and callback URL values with the ones you previously copied.

Listing 6.1 **`globals.inc`: PHP to Set Global Constants**

```
<?php
  require_once dirname(__FILE__).'/../fblib/facebook.php';
  // Facebook API Key
  define('FB_API_KEY', '<fill in your app api key>');

  // Facebook Secret Key
  define('FB_APP_SECRET', '<fill in your app secret key>');

  // Application name
  define('FB_APP_NAME', '<fill in your canvas page url application name>');

  // root URL of application on Facebook
  define('FB_APP_URL', Facebook::get_facebook_url('apps').'/'.FB_APP_NAME);

  // local application root URL
  define('LOCAL_APP_URL', '<fill in your application web root>/'.FB_APP_NAME);
?>
```

This file houses all the constant and global values we will need throughout the Compliments application as it's developed. The first thing we do is reference the Facebook library by including the Facebook PHP Library's web application code, found in `facebook.php`. This allows us to access all the types needed to communicate with Facebook from any page in our application that includes `globals.inc`. Next, we define a set of constants that will be frequently used in the application code. Note that we use the `Facebook::get_facebook_url()` method from the Facebook PHP client library to ensure that we get the Facebook URL defined by the PHP client library rather than hardcoding it.

> **Note**
>
> For ease of explanation and code organization, we place `globals.inc` in a subdirectory of the web server's document root. For security reasons, you would most likely not do this on a production web server. Be sure you secure this and all other files that you do not want to be accessible via a browser using any and all means your web-server software supports!

Next, open the `index.php` file you created in your application's root directory and include the code in Listing 6.2.

Listing 6.2 **`index.php`: Basic Skeleton Application**

```
<?php

    require_once 'inc/globals.inc';

    $facebook = new Facebook(FB_API_KEY, FB_APP_SECRET);
    if( isset( $facebook->fb_params['authorized'] ) ) {
        // do new user initialization
    } else if ( isset($facebook->fb_params['uninstall'] ) ) {
        // do user cleanup
    } else {
        if( ! $facebook->api_client->added ) {
            // handle non-app users by giving them a link to add the application
            echo "<p>Hello, non-app user!</p>
                  <a href='".$facebook->get_add_url()."'>
                    Click here to add this application.</a>";
        } else {
            echo "<p>Hello, app user
                  <fb:name uid='{$facebook->user}' useyou='false' />!</p>";
        }
    }
?>
```

`index.php` is our first application canvas page. Although it's simple, this code accomplishes several complex tasks, including creating an instance of the Facebook object, handling application authorization and removal, and rendering content to both users and non-users of the application.

First, we include the `globals.inc` file created in Listing 6.1. This gives us access to the API key and Secret key. These are important because they are required parameters of the Facebook `class` constructor. Creating an instance of this class grants our application the capability to call the API through the PHP client library. Thankfully, the library handles all the necessary application authentication code that grants this access.

The next block handles the ping that Facebook sends to the Post-Authorize Callback URL we set in the Authentication Settings tab of the Developer application. Currently, this block does nothing, but as the comment in the code suggests, this is where we can do any initialization or setup of a new user that did not require rendering anything to the browser (remember, it's a ping, not a redirection.) For example, we could create a new user account in a database, store the time the application was installed for this user, or do any user-specific application setup that did not require visible output. We use the Facebook class' `fb_params` collection to check if the `fb_sig_authorize POST` variable was sent to the page. This variable is sent when Facebook pings your Post-Authorize Callback URL. We discuss this in the section, "Application Authorization."

We then check for application removal requests. As mentioned previously, Facebook pings the application's Post-Remove Callback URL when a user removes an application. This time, we check for the `fb_sig_uninstall POST` variable. In this block, we would perform any user-specific application cleanup required, like removing a user account from a database, recording the application removal time, or determining how long this user had the application installed. As with the post-authorization code, this code should not try to render anything to the browser, because it will never be seen by the user.

Finally, we handle the actual rendering of the canvas page to both users who have authorized the application and those who have not. This is a critical point to understand: Users do not have to install an application to view canvas page content, and an application needs to provide at least some level of content to all Facebook users, whether or not they have authorized it. In fact, as a best practice, Facebook suggests that you only require a user to authorize your application when it provides enough value to the user to warrant it, as discussed in Chapter 2.

We check the `$facebook->api_client->added` property to determine if the current Facebook user viewing the canvas page has authorized the application. Note that we use the `api_client` property of the Facebook instance to get access to `added`. The `api_client` property wraps an instance of the `FacebookRestClient` class that we mentioned at the beginning of this chapter. If they have not authorized the application, we render a welcome message and a link to the application's authorization page (provided by the `Facebook::get_add_url()` method). Figure 6.12 shows what a user who has not authorized the application sees when he first visits the rudimentary Compliments canvas page. When that user clicks the Click Here to Add This Application link, he is automatically directed to the Compliments application authorization page, shown in Figure 6.13.

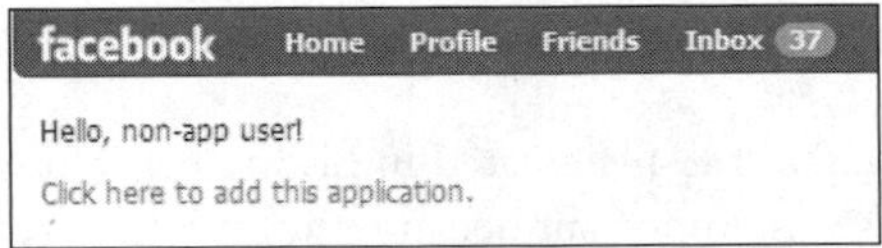

Figure 6.12 Compliments canvas page for non-authorized users

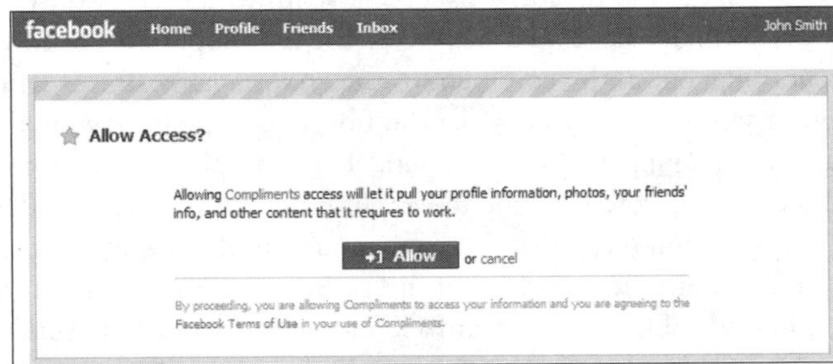

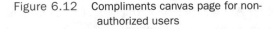

Figure 6.13 Compliments authorization page

If the user clicks the Allow button in the Compliments application authorization page, Facebook first pings the Post-Authorization Callback URL and then redirects the user to the Canvas Callback URL, which causes the last block of code in the `index.php` file to execute. At this point, he has become an authorized application user.

Next, we introduce the first of many FBML tags, `<fb:name/>`. This renders the name of the viewing user, linked to his Facebook profile page. The `useyou='false'` attribute forces Facebook to always render this link with the full name of the viewing user. Otherwise, it renders the pronoun "you" instead of the user's full name. Figure 6.14 shows what our new app user sees.

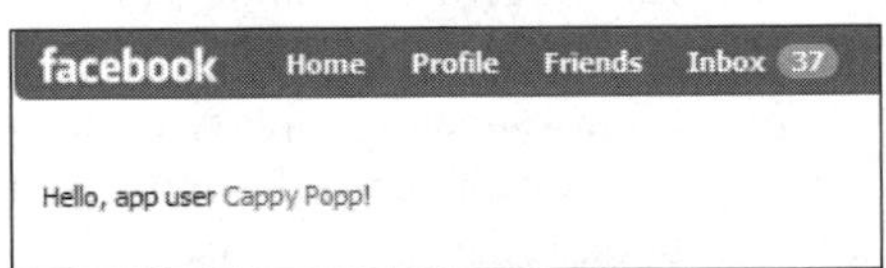

Figure 6.14 Compliments canvas page for authorized users

Application Authorization

Application authorization is somewhat analogous to the concept of installation, but the user does not have to copy any code or software to their machine. Applications do not have to be authorized for a user to interact with them, but by authorizing an application, a user gives it access to more of her personal Facebook data and allows it to perform several actions on her behalf, as the following sections discuss.

Parameters Sent to Applications

Facebook sends numerous parameters to your application's canvas page whenever it's requested. What variables are sent depends on several factors, such as whether the user has authorized the application, whether she is logged into Facebook, or if the canvas page she views is FBML or IFrame-based. Generally, Facebook sends these parameters as HTTP `POST` variables to FBML pages and `GET` variables to IFrame pages, but some exceptions exist.

These parameters are critically important because they not only contain important information, but they also generate a signature used to authenticate the communication between your application and Facebook, as discussed later. The most important parameters Facebook sends to an application canvas page and when are discussed in the following tables. Note that Facebook sends other parameters to application tabs and profiles; these are covered as need be throughout this book. All values are strings. Tables 6.1–6.7 show the parameters sent to pages for each user state.

Table 6.1 **Parameters Always Sent by Facebook**

Parameter	Sample Value	Description
`fb_sig_added`	0 or 1	If 0, the user has not authorized the application.
`fb_sig_locale`	en_US	The user's locale.
`fb_sig_time`	1241624901.1105	The time the request was made as a UNIX timestamp.
`fb_sig_api_key`	12...ef (32 hex characters)	The application's API key.
`fb_sig_app_id`	63560904158	The application's ID.
`fb_sig`	12...ef (32 hex characters)	Authentication signature.

Table 6.2 **Parameters Sent When User Not Logged In and Has Not Authorized Application**

Parameter	Sample Value	Description
`fb_sig_in_canvas`	1	The request was made for an application canvas page.

Table 6.2 **Continued**

Parameter	Sample Value	Description
fb_sig_added	0	The user has not authorized the application.
fb_sig_logged_out_facebook	1	The user is not logged into Facebook.

Table 6.3 **Parameters Sent When User Has Not Authorized Application and Visits Canvas From Outside Link**

Parameter	Sample Value	Description
fb_sig_in_canvas	1	The request was made for an application canvas page.
fb_sig_added	0	The user has not authorized the application.

Table 6.4 **Parameters Sent When User Has Not Authorized Application and Visits Canvas From Inside of Facebook**

Parameter	Sample Value	Description
fb_sig_in_canvas	1	The request was made for an application canvas page.
fb_sig_added	0	The user has not authorized the application.
fb_sig_canvas_user	123456789	The user's ID.
fb_sig_friends	12345,123456, ...	The user's friends' IDs.

Table 6.5 **Parameters Sent to the Post-Authorize Callback URL**

Parameter	Sample Value	Description
fb_sig_authorize	1	User has just authorized the application.
fb_sig_profile_update_time	1241386582	UNIX timestamp of the last time this user's profile was updated.
fb_sig_added	1	The user has authorized the application.

Table 6.5 **Continued**

Parameter	Sample Value	Description
`fb_sig_user`	123456	The user's ID.
`fb_sig_session_key`	2.jKBV2I4Xd6JvIUvKxwFMRQ__.86400.1241546400-1699891100	The valid session key for this user.
`fb_sig_expires`	1241546400	Expiration time of session key as UNIX timestamp.
`fb_sig_ext_perms`	`auto_publish_recent_activity`	Extended permissions granted to the application.

Table 6.6 **Parameters Sent When User Has Authorized Application**

Parameter	Sample Value	Description
`fb_sig_in_canvas`	1	The request was made for an application canvas page.
`fb_sig_added`	1	The user has authorized the application.
`fb_sig_user`	123456789	The user's ID.
`fb_sig_friends`	12345,123456, ...	The user's friends' IDs.
`fb_sig_profile_update_time`	1241386582	UNIX timestamp of the last time this user's profile was updated.
`fb_sig_ext_perms`	`auto_publish_recent_activity`	Extended permissions granted to the application.
`fb_sig_session_key`	2.jKBV2I4Xd6JvIUvKxwFMRQ__.86400.1241546400-1699891100	The valid session key for this user.
`fb_sig_expires`	1241546400	Expiration time of session key as UNIX timestamp.
`auth_token`	12...ef (32 hex characters)	Sent via `GET;` only sent the first time the user visits the canvas page after authorizing an application.

Table 6.6 **Continued**

Parameter	Sample Value	Description
`Installed`	1	Sent via `GET;` only sent the first time the user visits the canvas page after authorizing an application.

Table 6.7 **Parameters Sent to the Post-Remove Callback URL**

Parameter	Sample Value	Description
`fb_sig_uninstall`	1	The user has removed the application.
`fb_sig_added`	0	The user has not authorized the application.
`fb_sig_user`	123456	The user's ID.

The `fb_params` property of the Facebook PHP client library's Facebook class is automatically populated with all the parameters from the current request when you create an instance of the `Facebook` class. This property is actually an associative array keyed by the parameter name without the `'fb_sig_'` prefix. For example, to get the value of the `fb_sig_time` parameter from your canvas page, you might use the following PHP:

```
$facebook = new Facebook('[your API Key]', '[your Secret Key]');
$time = $facebook->fb_params['time'];
```

Generating Signatures

The signature sent to your application in the `fb_sig` parameter verifies that all the calls you make to Facebook actually come from your application, and the calls Facebook makes in return actually come from Facebook. Luckily, Facebook's PHP client library creates the signature for you; however, it's important to understand that the Secret key is used to how they are created to reinforce the importance of keeping your Secret key safe. The easiest way to create the signature is to call the `Facebook` class's `generate_sig()` method, passing it an array of `argument=value pairs` and your Secret key. The code for this method is shown in Listing 6.3.

Listing 6.3 **`Facebook::generate_sig` Method**

```
/*
   * Generate a signature using the application secret key.
```

Listing 6.3 **Continued**

```
   *
   * The only two entities that know your secret key are you and Facebook,
   * according to the Terms of Service. Since nobody else can generate
   * the signature, you can rely on it to verify that the information
   * came from Facebook.
   *
   * @param $params_array   an array of all Facebook-sent parameters,
   *                        NOT INCLUDING the signature itself
   * @param $secret         your app's secret key
   *
   * @return a hash to be checked against the signature provided by Facebook
   */
  public static function generate_sig($params_array, $secret) {
    $str = '';
    // sort the $params array alphabetically by key
    ksort($params_array);
    // Note: make sure that the signature parameter is not already included in
    //       $params_array.
    foreach ($params_array as $k => $v) {
      // build up the signature string
      $str .= "$k=$v";
    }
    // append the app's secret key
    $str .= $secret;

    // CREATE THE SIGNATURE
    return md5($str);
  }
```

You can see that your application's Secret key is appended to the string of argument=value pairs and the entire string is encoded using the PHP `md5()` function. The result of this encoding is the signature passed in `fb_sig` both to and from Facebook. So, it is vitally important to keep this value safe, or anyone with access to it can impersonate your application (or worse). This signature verification process is revisited when we cover communicating with Flash in Chapter 11, "FBJS, Mock AJAX, and Flash."

Before an Application Is Authorized

If a user visits the canvas page of an application that he has not authorized, the page is passed only his Facebook user ID and the user IDs of his Facebook friends. The code on that canvas page is also allowed to call Facebook API methods that do not require a Facebook session key (discussed next.) The list of these methods changes frequently, so you need to consult an individual API method's documentation to see if it requires one. Applications can also use FBML to render links to unauthorized users' profiles and their profile pictures. In turn, unauthorized users can publish data to the stream for an application using a Feed form, and applications can send requests on their behalf using a request form. These are discussed in Chapter 9, "Feed Stories, Feed Forms, and Templates."

After an Application Is Authorized

After a user authorizes an application Facebook creates a new session and passes that application a temporary session key that application can use to access the full Facebook API. Session keys expire in one hour; however, infinite sessions are possible which we'll cover in Chapter 9. The application also gets access to more personal data about the authorized user, it can publish one line Feed stories to the stream without the user's consent, and can send notifications to the user's friends (even if they have not authorized the application) and other application users (even if they are not friends of the user.) The user can also publish stories directly to the stream using the application's Publisher interface, if one is implemented by the application.

How an Application Is Authorized

There are a couple of ways to authorize applications. First, applications that use the Facebook PHP client library can call `require_login()`. This method causes an automatic redirection to Facebook's `login.php`, which causes the application's authorization page to appear. The full URL of the redirection is

```
http://www.facebook.com/login.php?api_key=[your API
Key]&v=1.0&next=http%3A%2F%2F[your web
server]%3A81%2F[appname]%2F%3F_fb_fromhash%[some
hash]&canvas=1
```

After the authorization page appears, Facebook redirects to the Terms of Service URL you provided in the Developer application. Clicking Allow on this page authorizes the application.

Second, HTML link tags, form tags, and the FBML forms can include a special attribute, `requirelogin='1'`. If we modify the code from Listing 6.2 as follows, we can see this process at work:

```
if( ! $facebook->api_client->added ) {
    // handle non-app users by showing
    // them the minimalist AJAX authorization dialog
    echo "<p>Hello, non-app user!</p>
          <a href='#' requirelogin='1'>Click here to authorize the
application</a>";
}
```

This causes a different behavior: When Facebook parses the `<a/>` entity, it sees the `requirelogin='1'` attribute and pops up a dialog using AJAX, shown in Figure 6.15, to allow the user to quickly authorize the application while not redirecting him away from the page that he's currently viewing.

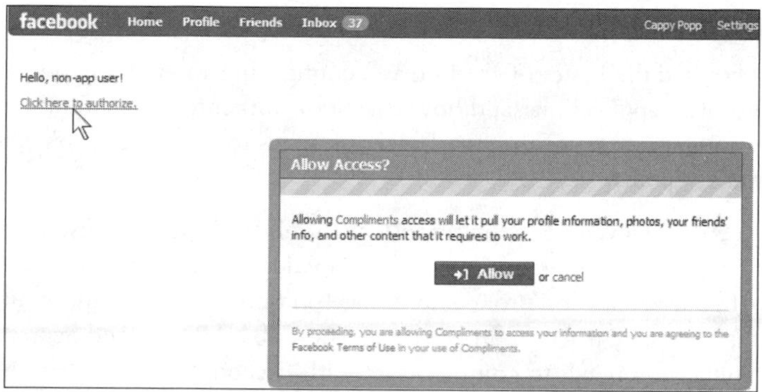

Figure 6.15 AJAX Authorization dialog

This is a much less intrusive and more streamlined way to allow new users to authorize an application, but it has one important drawback. Facebook ignores the Post-Authorize Redirect URL that you specify. So, if you require your newly authorized users to perform some setup tasks immediately that depend on them being redirected to this URL, this authorization method might not work for you.

Finally, applications that do not use Facebook's PHP client library can use FBML to provide the same behavior provided by `require_login()`. If you replace all the code in index.php with the following, you can see how this works (you need to replace the values in brackets with your own):

```
<fb:if-is-app-user>
  [illegible]
<fb:else>
  <fb:redirect url='http://www.facebook.com/login.php?v=1.0&api_key=[your API
 Key]&next=<?php echo(urlencode('http://example.com/<appname>')) ?>&canvas='/>
</fb:else>
</fb:if-is-app-user>
```

Here, we introduce a few new FBML controls. First, `<fb:if-is-app-user/>` allows only the display of the content it encloses if the viewing user has authorized the application. It is essentially the FBML equivalent of the `FacebookRestClient::added` property (discussed earlier). Next, `<fb:else/>` simply acts like the `else` statement in PHP. In this example, it renders its enclosed content if the viewing user has not authorized the application. Finally, we have `<fb:redirect/>`. When Facebook parses this FBML tag, it simply redirects the viewing user's browser to the URL specified by the `url` attribute. So, when Facebook parses this code, it automatically redirects all unauthorized users to Facebook's login page, just like `require_login()` did in the first example.

Summary

This chapter covered the basics of creating and configuring a new Facebook application, how users authorize applications, and how Facebook authenticates them. It also covered Facebook sessions and some of the data Facebook sends to an application's canvas page. Here are some key points:

- The Facebook Developer application is the tool developers can use to create new applications on Facebook. It provides literally dozens of settings, including the URL of your application's root canvas page on both Facebook and your local web server. It is also the place to find an application's ID, API key, and Secret key, which every application needs to communicate with Facebook.
- Applications can present different content to users that have authorized them and to those that have not. Developers must not force users to authorize an application unless it provides them engaging content that requires them to do so. However, authorized users provide the application with access to more information and the ability to perform actions on that user's behalf.
- Applications can be notified when a user authorizes and removes them. Depending on how they were authorized, applications can redirect users that have just authorized them to a specific canvas page. But, applications cannot redirect users after they remove an application, nor can they show them any content after the application has been removed.
- Facebook uses a special signature—built using the parameters passed to the application along with that application's Secret key—to verify that all requests made by an application to Facebook actually come from that application and the calls Facebook makes in return actually come from Facebook.

7

Building the Canvas

This chapter details the differences between using an IFrame and Facebook Markup Language (FBML) for the application canvas page, and then shows you how to create a page of each type connected with tabs by updating the Compliments application.

Choosing Between an FBML and IFrame Canvas

In Chapter 6, "The Basics of Creating Applications," we chose FBML as the canvas page type. This is the easiest way to get started with Facebook application development, because it provides a simple way to display content with the Facebook "look and feel" and full use of the Facebook controls. However, the type of canvas that is right for your application depends on numerous factors.

Learning Curve

FBML pages require learning three things: FBML tags, Facebook JavaScript (FBJS) syntax, and the Facebook application programming interface (API). Facebook provides documentation for the FBML tags, but you have to learn the nuances of each tag. FBJS is a limited form of JavaScript that changes the common DOM manipulation methods to use get and set functions. It can be painful to figure out which subset works and how to get the access that your application needs. The Facebook API is used for both canvas types, although FBML can reduce the number of calls needed.

Until recently, IFrame pages couldn't use the FBML tags. Therefore, their learning curve was limited to standard web technologies of cascading style sheets (CSS), HTML, JavaScript, and the Facebook API. With the release of the Facebook JavaScript Client Library and XFBML, IFrame applications can now use FBML tags on their pages. We go over how to use XFBML in Chapter 12, "Facebook JavaScript Client Library." Overall, the learning curve for an IFrame page is lower than for FBML pages.

One caveat is that profile boxes and applications tabs cannot use IFrames. So, it might end up that you have to learn FBML to produce the functionality you want in those contexts.

Migration of Existing Applications

If you already have an application that you are porting to Facebook, IFrames make this simple. You can reuse your existing HTML and JavaScript rendering, and use the Facebook API to get the data you need. To convert applications to FBML requires rewriting JavaScript as FBJS and removing dependence on any external JavaScript libraries, such as YUI, jQuery, and so on.

Cross-Platform Portability

If you are planning to support multiple platforms, such as an external website or OpenSocial, IFrames provide a common display model. You just change how you get the data for each platform. Other platforms, such as Bebo, have licensed the Facebook Platform and natively support FBML. However, Bebo's implementation isn't always current with Facebook's latest changes, so you probably have to have different display code for each platform.

Look and Feel

Applications that have the Facebook look and feel fit in well with the Platform. That isn't to say that applications shouldn't try to be distinctive, but Facebook users expect applications to work like Facebook. FBML provides the easiest method to do this, giving applications access to the same controls and styles that Facebook itself uses.

IFrame applications can emulate this look and feel by copying the Facebook styles and creating or finding their own Facebook-like controls. We do this later for the `<fb:friend-selector>` control. This can be time-consuming, because most of the Facebook tags don't have publicly downloadable equivalents. XFBML provides some help with this, but not all the tags are natively available. After you build a library of these controls, you can reuse them in other applications.

Performance

FBML pages can be faster than IFrame applications because they can eliminate or reduce the number of API calls needed by using FBML tags, such as `<fb:profile-pic>`. Recently, Facebook added the Chat bar, which has to be created on each full page load. IFrame applications can avoid this on subsequent page loads, because they only have to change the inner IFrame source instead of the entire page.

When an FBML page does an AJAX call, it must pass through a Facebook proxy to parse any returned FBML. IFrame AJAX calls go directly to the callback URL.

With XFBML, IFrame applications can reduce their API calls by using these tags. They can return `<fb:profile-pic>` in their HTML, and the Facebook JavaScript Client Library can convert these tags to the appropriate HTML. Any API calls that the library uses for conversion are batched, and the results are cached. However, this update happens after the page loads and can make the page appear to flash while the DOM is updated with the new HTML.

IFrames that use the Facebook JavaScript Client Library can receive results of preloaded FQL queries and get cached access to the user's friend list that is not passed to the canvas page by default. This helps IFrames catch up with some of FBML's speed advantages.

Testing

Because all FBML must be rendered by Facebook before it is displayed, it can be more difficult to test. Either you copy what you expect the FBML to be to the FBML Test Console or you have to access your page through Facebook. IFrame testing can be much simpler: You can access your page directly on your local server. Of course, in those cases, you might have to emulate the `GET` variables that Facebook passes to IFrame pages to allow your application to function normally.

Preparing the Compliments Canvas Pages

The Compliments application's canvas page allows the user to send a compliment to one of his friends. We create it first in FBML and then as an IFrame; this way, we can go through how each type works. At the end, we add a tab control that lets users navigate between the pages. For ease of reading, we use Compliments as the application name in the Canvas Callback URL, but you should substitute your own application name.

Before we create the canvas pages, we need to do a little preparation: set up the database, add some utility functions, create an external CSS file, and handle versioning for external files.

Database Setup

We created the Compliments database in Chapter 6. For this chapter, we just need one table to store information about the compliments that users send. We need to keep the Facebook user ID for the person sending the compliment, the Facebook user ID for the person he is sending it to, and the type, text, and time of the compliment. Use the create statement in Listing 7.1 to build the table.

Listing 7.1 **Database Table Create Statement**

```
CREATE TABLE  'compliments'.'compliments' (
  'appUserID' int(10) unsigned NOT NULL,
  'targetID' int(10) unsigned NOT NULL,
  'category' varchar(45) COLLATE utf8_unicode_ci NOT NULL,
  'compliment' varchar(300) COLLATE utf8_unicode_ci NOT NULL,
  'complimentTime' datetime NOT NULL,
  PRIMARY KEY ('appUserID','targetID','complimentTime')
) ENGINE=InnoDB DEFAULT CHARSET=utf8 COLLATE=utf8_unicode_ci;
```

We need to update `globals.inc` with information about the database server, database, and the user login and password that we created in Chapter 6. Add the contents of Listing 7.2 to the end of `globals.inc` before the closing `?>`.

Listing 7.2 **globals.inc: Database Constants**

```
// IP or URL of the MySQL database server
define('FB_DB_SERVER', '<your db server>');

// the database schema used for the application
define('FB_DB_SCHEMA', 'compliments');

// database user
define('FB_DB_USER', '<db user>');

// database password
define('FB_DB_PASS', '<db_password>');
```

We use a simple database wrapper class that will handle connections, data translation, and diagnostics. Add the source in Listing 7.3 into a new file called `db.inc` in the `inc` directory. The key things to notice about the DB class is that it automatically creates and destroys database connections with the scope of each instance. All queries go through `execQuery()` that will put any failures into the error log. Finally, `addCompliment()` is the function we use to store the compliment values in the database as they are sent.

Listing 7.3 **db.inc: Database Access Class**

```
<?php
class DB extends mysqli {
  /** Construct - create connection to db */
  public function __construct() {
    parent::__construct(FB_DB_SERVER, FB_DB_USER, FB_DB_PASS, FB_DB_SCHEMA);

    if ($this->connect_error) {
      die('Connect Error (' . $this->connect_errno . ') '.
       $this->connect_error);
    }
  }

  /** Destructor - closes connection to db **/
  function __destruct() {
    parent::close();
  }
  /**  Executes a query and logs errors **/
  private function _execQuery($query) {
    $result = $this->query($query);
    if (!$result) {
        die("<br/>INVALID query: '" . $this->error . "' => $query<br/>");
    }
    return $result;
  }
```

Listing 7.3 **Continued**

```
  /** Adds a compliment into the database **/
  function addCompliment($appUserID, $targetID, $category, $compliment) {
    $appUserID = $this->real_escape_string($appUserID);
    $category = $this->real_escape_string($category);
    $targetID = $this->real_escape_string($targetID);
    $compliment = $this->real_escape_string(htmlspecialchars($compliment));

    $query  = "INSERT INTO compliments ( appUserID, targetID, category,
               compliment, complimentTime ) VALUES ( $appUserID, $targetID,
               '$category', '$compliment', NOW() )";
    $result = $this->_execQuery($query);
  }
}
?>
```

Adding the Utility Functions

We also add a utility function to write information to a custom application log and another that dumps `GET` and `POST` variables received into that log. First, add the two constants in Listing 7.4 to `globals.inc`. They define a log file called `yourapplication_log.txt` in the application root directory. Make sure that this file is writable by your web server.

Listing 7.4 **globals.inc: Logging Constants**

```
// Application root directory
define('LOCAL_APP_DIR', getcwd().'/');

// Application diagnostic log
define('DBG_OUT_FILE', LOCAL_APP_DIR.FB_APP_NAME . '_log.txt');
```

Now, create a new file called `utils.inc` in the `inc` directory, and add the source from Listing 7.5 into it. The first function, `wr()`, writes any string passed in to the log. This is useful for dumping out diagnostic information or trace info. Remember to comment out the `wr()` calls after you are done using them, or your log can quickly become huge. The second function, `dumpRequestVars()`, dumps the `REQUEST` variables that your pages receive from Facebook, your application's AJAX calls, and form `POST`s. This is an easy way to find out what Facebook is passing to your application pages. You can supply this function with a context argument that will be written out at the top of the dump as a label. An easy context would be to pass it `_FILE_` to show the name of the calling file. You can also pass another parameter to disable the display of Facebook specific `REQUEST` variables.

Listing 7.5 **utils.inc: Logging Functions**

```
<?php
/** write test to the diagnostic log **/
function wr($str) {
  $dt = date('j-m-y, h:i:s');
  if (defined('DBG_OUT_FILE')) {
    if (!$file_handle = fopen(DBG_OUT_FILE, "a")) {
      echo "Cannot open file";
    }
    if (!fwrite($file_handle, "($dt): $str\n")) {
      echo "Cannot write to file";
    }
    fclose($file_handle);
  }
}

/** dump out the REQUEST variables to the log  along with optional FB vars**/
function dumpRequestVars( $showFacebookVars = true, $context = NULL ) {
  if (isset($context)) {
    wr("***Dumping vars for $context");
  }
  $requestVars = array('GET' => $_GET,
                       'POST' => $_POST,
                       'COOKIE' => $_COOKIE);
  define('INDENT_HEAD', str_pad('', 4) );
  define('INDENT_DATA', str_pad('', 6));
  define('FB_PREFIX', 'fb_sig_');

  $msg = '';

  $argCount = func_num_args();
  if($argCount > 1) {
    $msg .= ' [';
    for($i = 1, $args = func_get_args(); $i < $argCount - 1; ++$i) {
      $msg .= strval($args[$i]).':';
    }
    $msg .= strval($args[$i]).'] '. PHP_EOL;
  }

  foreach(@$requestVars as $key => $value) {
    $msg .= INDENT_HEAD . "$key length: ". count($value). PHP_EOL;
    foreach($value as $k => $v) {
      if( !$showFacebookVars && 0 === strpos($k, FB_PREFIX)){
        continue;
      }
      $v = isset($v) ? $v : '[null]';
```

Listing 7.5 **Continued**

```
      $msg .= INDENT_DATA . "$k ==> '$v'". PHP_EOL;
    }
  }
  wr($msg);
}
?>
```

Using External CSS Files

Both FBML and IFrames support inline CSS styles, but we will take advantage of browser caching and use an external file instead. Create two new empty files called `main.css` and `ie.css` and put them in a new `css` directory in the application root. The `main.css` will contain the styles for the canvas page as a whole, and `ie.css` will contain overrides specific to Internet Explorer. We will add the styles for each file later in this chapter as we build the canvas functionality.

External CSS files are included the same way in both FBML and IFrame-based canvas pages:

```
<link rel='stylesheet' type='text/css'
 href='http://server.com/compliments/css/main.css' />
```

For FBML pages, Facebook rewrites the URL to be cached on its own servers as well, like this:

```
http://apps.facebook.com/fbml_static_get.php?src=http%3A%2F%2Fserver.com%3A85%2F
compliments%2Fcss%2Fmain.css%3Fv%3D1242598113&appid=195482325614&pv=1&sig=
5a4f20affb0ebb39cac74572d57135f&filetype=css
```

When using any external file, it is important to handle versioning so that the file that is loaded by the browser is the most current one, instead of the old cached version. The simplest way to do this is to append a version identifier to the file, such as `main.css?v=1`. Increasing this number to `main.css?v=2` causes the browser to pull the v2 file instead of using the cached v1 file. It can be difficult to remember to increment this version number each time you change a file. To have this happen automatically use PHP's `filemtime()` function to get the last modified time for a file. You can then append this value to the filename, like this: `main.css?v=1232323251`.

Add the utility function in Listing 7.6 to `utils.inc`. This function takes a path to a file from the application root as an argument, gets the last modified time, and returns a string with the version attached. We use this function in the new canvas page code in the next section.

Listing 7.6 **`utils.inc`: File Version Function**

```
/** return the passed in file with a version appended **/
function getFileVer($filePathFromRoot) {
  $modTime = filemtime(LOCAL_APP_DIR . $filePathFromRoot);
```

Listing 7.6 **Continued**

```
  return "$filePathFromRoot?v=$modTime";
}
```

Defining the Types of Compliments

We are going to allow the users to pick from a predefined set of compliments. Each compliment will consist of a type, a title, and small and large images. For example, the "friend" type of compliment has the title "A Great Friend" and small and large images of a cuddly cat. We define a list of these categories in an array in `globals.inc`. Add the contents of Listing 7.7 to your `globals.inc` file.

Listing 7.7 **`globals.inc`: Compliments Array**

```
$g_categories = array(
   'friend'    => array( "title" => "A Great Friend",
                         "bigimg" => "cat_48.png",
                         "smallimg" =>"cat_24.png"),
   'life'      => array( "title" => "Full of Life",
                         "bigimg" => "parachute_48.png",
                         "smallimg" =>"parachute_24.png"),
   'relaxing' => array( "title" => "Relaxing",
                         "bigimg" => "beach_sit_48.png",
                         "smallimg" =>"beach_sit_24.png"),
   'cook'      => array( "title" => "A Great Cook",
                         "bigimg" => "pan_48.png",
                         "smallimg" =>"pan_24.png"),
   'magic'     => array( "title" => "Magic",
                         "bigimg" => "rabbit_48.png",
                         "smallimg" =>"rabbit_24.png"),
   'driven'    => array( "title" => "Driven",
                         "bigimg" => "single_seater_48.png",
                         "smallimg" =>"single_seater_24.png")
   );
```

Creating the Compliments FBML Canvas Page

Now that all that preparation is done, it is time to create the FBML canvas page. This page will contain a form that allows the user to create a compliment to send to one of their friends.

Dumping the FBML Canvas REQUEST Parameters

We need to include our newly created files and our `dumpRequestVars()` call to `index.php`. The top of that file should now look like Listing 7.8.

Listing 7.8 **`index.php`: Including Support Files**

```
<?php
require_once 'inc/globals.inc';
require_once 'inc/utils.inc';
require_once 'inc/db.inc';

dumpRequestVars(true, basename(__FILE__));
```

Go to your application's Canvas Page URL to allow `dumpRequestVars()` to capture the `REQUEST` variables that Facebook passes your application, and then go to your application's root directory on your web server to verify that the `compliments_log.txt` file was created. It should now contain something like what is shown in Listing 7.9.

Listing 7.9 **Dump of FBML Canvas `REQUEST` Variables**

```
(11-07-09, 10:00:55):  [index.php]
    GET length: 0
    POST length: 16
      fb_sig_in_canvas ==> '1'
      fb_sig_request_method ==> 'GET'
      fb_sig_friends ==> '714497440'
      fb_sig_position_fix ==> '1'
      fb_sig_locale ==> 'en_US'
      fb_sig_in_new_facebook ==> '1'
      fb_sig_time ==> '1247364062.2857'
      fb_sig_added ==> '1'
      fb_sig_profile_update_time ==> '1241522567'
      fb_sig_expires ==> '1247454000'
      fb_sig_user ==> '698700806'
      fb_sig_session_key ==> '2.b_R2hCwU8fJ5ZgrG5R1K_g_.86400.1247454000-698700806'
      fb_sig_ext_perms ==> 'auto_publish_recent_activity'
      fb_sig_api_key ==> '52bcc10ac263e1d0d2645182e01e0c99'
      fb_sig_app_id ==> '195482325614'
      fb_sig ==> '51d7c909fddca1a9bd244d58c88a1207'
    COOKIE length: 0
```

Table 7.1 lists the key variables to note for FBML pages.

Table 7.1 **Key `POST` Variables Passed to FBML Canvases**

Variable	Sample Value	Description
`fb_sig_in_canvas`	1	If this is present, the page is running in an FBML canvas.
`fb_sig_friends`	714497440, 698700806	A comma-separated list of the user's friends—the equivalent of calling the `friends_get()` API function.
`fb_sig_added`	0 or 1	Set to 1 if the user has authorized the application.
`fb_sig_user`	698700806	The Facebook ID of the viewing user.

Adding the Send Compliment Form

To display the Send Compliment form, we need to update the code that handles authorized users. Change the bottom of `index.php` to use a new `renderPage()` function, like this:

```
if (!$facebook->api_client->added) {
  // handle non-app users by giving them a link to add the application
  echo "<p>Hello, non-app user!</p>
    <a href='" . $facebook->get_add_url() . "'>
    Click here to add this application.</a>";
} else {
    renderPage();
}
```

Listing 7.10 shows the `renderPage()`function. Add it to the bottom of `index.php`. We go over it detail next.

Listing 7.10 **`index.php: renderPage()` Function**

```
/** outputs the page content **/
function renderPage() {
  global $facebook;
  global $g_categories;

  // include the external stylesheet and create the header
  $pageOutput = "
    <link rel='stylesheet' type='text/css'
      href='".LOCAL_APP_URL.getFileVer("/css/main.css")."' />
    <!—[if IE]>
    <link rel='stylesheet' type='text/css'
      href='".LOCAL_APP_URL.getFileVer("/css/ie.css")."' />
    <![endif]—>
    <fb:title>Send a Compliment</fb:title>
```

Listing 7.10 **Continued**

```
    <div class='banner'
      style='background: url(".LOCAL_APP_URL."/img/banner.png) no-repeat;' />";

  // Handle the form submit
  if (isset($_POST['submitCompliment'])) {
    $target = isset($_POST['target']) ? $_POST['target'] : "";
    $compliment = isset($_POST['compliment']) ? $_POST['compliment'] : "";
    $category = isset($_POST['category']) ? $_POST['category'] : "";
    if ( strlen($target) == 0 || strlen($compliment) == 0 ||
         strlen($category) == 0 ) {
      // Output the error
      $pageOutput.= "
        <fb:error>
          <fb:message>Sending the Compliment failed!</fb:message>
          Please check that the form is filled out correctly
        </fb:error>";
    } else {
      // Add the compliment to the database
      $db = new DB();
      $db->addCompliment($facebook->user, $target, $category, $compliment );
      // Output the results
      $pageOutput.= "
        <fb:success>
          <fb:message>
            Your Compliment to <fb:name uid='$target' linked='false'/> was sent.
          </fb:message>
          <fb:profile-pic size='square' uid='$target' />
          <img class='categoryImg'
            src='".LOCAL_APP_URL."/img/".$g_categories[$category]['bigimg']."'/>
          <fb:name uid='$target' linked='false'/>
          is <b>{$g_categories[$category]['title']}</b> because \"$compliment\"
        </fb:success>";
    }
  }
  // Show the compliment form
  $pageOutput .= "
    <div id='panel' class='panel'>
      <form method='POST' id='complimentform' >
        <h1>Select one of your friends and enter your compliment.</h1>
        <table id='complimentTable'>
          <tr>
            <td class='label'>Your Friend:</td>
            <td class='content'>
              <fb:friend-selector id='fsel' name='uid' idname='target'/>
            </td>
          </tr>
```

Listing 7.10 **Continued**

```
            <tr>
              <td class='label'>is:</td>
              <td class='content'>";
  foreach( $g_categories as $name => $info ){
    $pageOutput .= "
                <div class='category'>
                    <img class='categoryImg'
                      src='".LOCAL_APP_URL."/img/{$info['bigimg']}'/><br>
                    <span class='categoryTitle'>{$info['title']}</span><br/>
                    <input type='radio' name='category' value='$name' />
                </div>";
  }
  $pageOutput .= "
              </td>
            </tr>
            <tr>
              <td class='label'>because:</td>
              <td class='content'>
                <input class='textInput' name='compliment' />
              </td>
            </tr>
          </table>
          <input class='inputbutton' type='submit' name='submitCompliment'
            value='Send Compliment' />
        </form>
      </div>";

  echo $pageOutput;
}
```

All output from this function is stored in a local variable, `$pageOutput`, which is echoed out at the end of the function. The first thing this function does is include the `main.css` and `ie.css` external CSS files using our versioning function. We build the URL for the file using the `LOCAL_APP_URL` constant defined in `globals.inc`. Notice that this is the Canvas Callback URL on your web server, and not the Canvas Page URL. Make sure that you always use full paths for all URLs on your server, or Facebook ignores them when it parses the page content.

Next, the page title is set to "Send a Compliment" using the `<fb:title>` FBML tag. You have to use this for FBML pages, because they have no access to the `<head>` tags. Facebook automatically prefaces the page title with "<application name> on Facebook | ". A nice banner image with the application name is set for the top of the page.

The form submit handler is next, but before looking at it, skip forward to the "Show the compliment form" comment. The code below that creates the form. The form uses the `<fb:friend-selector>` FBML tag to display an autocomplete control with all the user's friends. This simple tag does a lot of work under the hood, as we see when we try to replicate its functionality in an IFrame. Table 7.2 shows the attributes used for this tag and their descriptions. The compliment types are output as radio buttons, containing the compliment title and picture, and the user can enter a reason for the compliment in a text input.

Table 7.2 **<fb:friend-selector>** Attributes

Attribute Name	Type	Details
`uid`	int	The user whose friends you can select from, defaulting to the logged-in user's ID.
`name`	string	The name of this element on the form, defaulting to `friend_selector_name`.
`idname`	string	The name of a hidden element that is created on the form containing the ID of the selected friend. The name of this element defaults to `friend_selector_id`.
`include_me`	bool	Toggle to include the logged-in user in the list of selectable friends, defaulting to `false`.
`exclude_ids`	array	A comma-separated list of user IDs to exclude from the list of selectable friends.
`include_lists`	bool	Toggle to include a user's friend lists in the selection options, defaulting to `false`.

The form POSTs back to itself, and the handler looks for the target and compliment variables. If any are empty, an error appears with the `<fb:error>` FBML tag, which is one of the three status message tags Facebook provides to match its style. The `<fb:error>` tag renders its content inside a pink box, `<fb:explanation>` renders a white box, and `<fb:success>` renders a yellow box. All three tags support a `<fb:message>` subtag, which renders a bold header.

If no error occurs, the picture and name of the recipient is shown using the `<fb:profile-pic>` and `<fb:name>` tags. Notice how both tags save our page from having to make the API call to `user_getInfo()` to get the data needed for display. We simply pass the user ID, and Facebook does all the work. Table 7.3 shows the attributes for `<fb:profile-pic>`. The callback handler also creates an instance of the DB class and calls `addCompliment()` to put the compliment information in the database for use in later chapters.

Table 7.3 **<fb:profile-pic>** Attributes

Attribute Name	Type	Details
`uid`	int	Required. The ID of the user or Public Profile whose picture is to be displayed. You can also pass `loggedinuser` on a canvas page to use the ID of the currently logged-in user.

Table 7.3 **Continued**

Attribute Name	Type	Details
`size`	string	The size of the image, defaulting to `thumb`. This can be ▪ `thumb` (50px wide) ▪ `small` (100px wide) ▪ `normal` (200px wide) ▪ `square` (50px by 50px) This size is overridden if the `width or height` attributes are set.
–	string	The width to set the image to.
`height`	string	The height to set the image to.
`linked`	bool	Toggle to link the image to the user's profile, defaulting to `true.`
`facebook-logo`	bool	For Facebook Connect, toggle to overlay the Facebook favicon over the image, defaulting to `false.`

The form uses a few CSS styles, so add the contents of Listing 7.11 to the `main.css` and Listing 7.12 to `ie.css`. There is a `clearfix` class added to both files that allows elements to clear their own floats. For more detail on this technique, see *www.darowski.com/tracesofinspiration/2008/11/14/my-favorite-css-techniques/*.

Listing 7.11 **`main.css`: Common Styles**

```
/*General Page styles*/
.banner { height:90px; width:100%; margin: 0 0 10px; }
.panel { text-align:center; background-color:#F7F7F7;
        border-top:1px solid #CCCCCC; padding:10px 0;
        width:100%; }
#complimentTable { width:500px; margin: 5px auto; }
#complimentTable  .label{ width: 100px; vertical-align:middle; }
#complimentTable  .textInput { width: 400px; }
#complimentTable  .inputtext { width:400px; }


.categories { padding-bottom: 5px; }
.category { float:left; width:100px; height:75px; text-align:center;
          margin:8px 15px; }
.category .categoryImg { width:48px; height:48px; }
.category .categoryTitle { height:20px; font-weight:bold; }

.clearfix:after { content: "."; display: block; height: 0; clear: both;
                visibility: hidden; }
```

Listing 7.12 **ie.css: Internet Explorer–Specific Styles**

```
.clearfix { height: 1%; }
```

Give this new FBML canvas page a try in your browser. Make sure that the friend selector works and that submitting the form updates the database and displays the results. The page should look similar to what's shown in Figure 7.1.

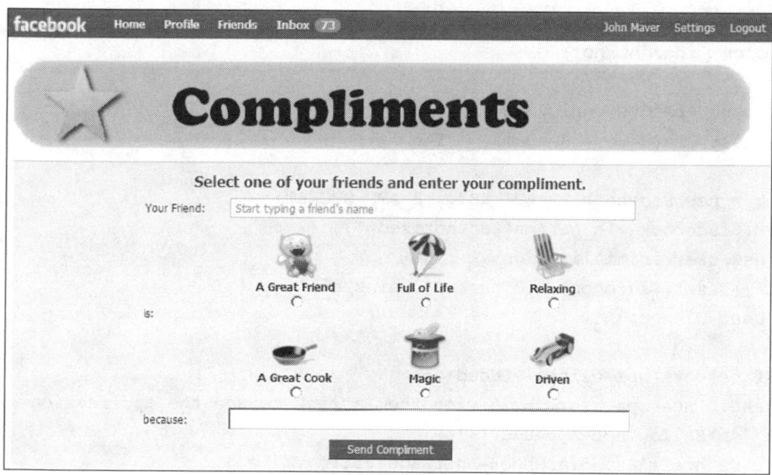

Figure 7.1 Compliments application FBML canvas page

Creating the Compliments IFrame Canvas Page

The FBML page was relatively easy: Facebook did most of the work for us using the FBML tags. The IFrame page has to use the Facebook API and some JavaScript to accomplish the same thing.

Loading the IFrame Canvas Page

There are two ways to get an IFrame page loaded in an application whose type is set to FBML. The best way is to append `fb_force_mode=iframe` to the end of the URL. This causes Facebook to load its outer chrome and create an IFrame with the `src` set to your URL.

The second way is to create an FBML canvas page and use the `<fb:iframe>` tag to create your own IFrame to hold your page. This method is slower, because Facebook must load both your FBML and IFrame canvas pages.

We use the `fb_force_mode` way for the Compliments application.

Adding the Send Compliment Form

Let's create a second page called `index_iframe.php` and put it in your application root. Add the code from Listing 7.13 into this file. It is the same as `index.php`, except for the `renderPage()` function.

Listing 7.13 **`index_iframe.php`: IFrame Canvas Page**

```
<?php
require_once 'inc/globals.inc';
require_once 'inc/utils.inc';
require_once 'inc/db.inc';

// Comment out before deploying
//dumpRequestVars(true, basename(__FILE__));

$facebook = new Facebook(FB_API_KEY, FB_APP_SECRET);
if (isset($facebook->fb_params['authorized'])) {
  // do new user initialization
} else if (isset($facebook->fb_params['uninstall'])) {
  // do user cleanup
} else {
  if (!$facebook->api_client->added) {
    // handle non-app users by giving them a link to add the application
    echo "<p>Hello, non-app user!</p>
          <a href='" . $facebook->get_add_url() . "'>
            Click here to add this application.</a>";
  } else {
    renderPage();
  }
}

/** outputs the page content **/
function renderPage() {
  global $facebook;
  global $g_categories;

  // include the external stylesheet and create the header
  $pageOutput = "
    <!DOCTYPE html PUBLIC '-//W3C//DTD XHTML 1.0 Strict//EN'
      'http://www.w3.org/TR/xhtml1/DTD/xhtml1-strict.dtd'>
    <html xmlns='http://www.w3.org/1999/xhtml' xml:lang='en'>
    <head>
      <title>Send a Compliment</title>
      <link rel='stylesheet' type='text/css'
        href='".LOCAL_APP_URL.getFileVer("/css/main.css")."' />
      <link rel='stylesheet' type='text/css'
```

Listing 7.13 **Continued**

```
        href='".LOCAL_APP_URL.getFileVer("/css/iframe.css")."' />
      <!–[if IE]>
      <link rel='stylesheet' type='text/css'
        href='".LOCAL_APP_URL.getFileVer("/css/ie.css")."' />
      <![endif]–>
      <!– YUI files –>
      <link rel='stylesheet' type='text/css'
href='http://yui.yahooapis.com/combo?2.7.0/build/autocomplete/assets/skins/sam/aut
ocomplete.css'>
      <script type='text/javascript'
src='http://yui.yahooapis.com/combo?2.7.0/build/yahoo-dom-event/yahoo-dom-
event.js&2.7.0/build/datasource/datasource-min.js&2.7.0/build/autocomplete/auto-
complete-
min.js'></script>
    </head>
    <body>
      <div class='banner'
        style='background: url(".LOCAL_APP_URL."/img/banner.png) no-repeat;' >
      </div>
      <div class='tabs clearfix'>
        <ul class='tabList'>
          <li><a href='".FB_APP_URL."/' target='_top'>Send(FBML)</a></li>
          <li class='selected'>
            <a href='".LOCAL_APP_URL."/index_iframe.php?fb_force_mode=iframe&".
              getFBQueryString($_GET) ."' target='iframe_canvas'>Send(IFrame)
            </a>
          </li>
        </ul>
      </div>";

  // Handle the form submit
  if (isset($_POST['submitCompliment'])) {
    $target = isset($_POST['target']) ? $_POST['target'] : "";
    $compliment = isset($_POST['compliment']) ? $_POST['compliment'] : "";
    $category = isset($_POST['category']) ? $_POST['category'] : "";
    if ( strlen($target) == 0 || strlen($compliment) == 0 ||
          strlen($category) == 0 ) {
      // Output the error
      $pageOutput.= "
        <div class='error'>
          <h1>Sending the Compliment failed!</h1>
          <p> Please check that the form is filled out correctly</p>
        </div>";
    } else {
      // Add the compliment to the database
      $db = new DB();
      $db->addCompliment($facebook->user, $target, $category, $compliment );
```

Listing 7.13 **Continued**

```
      // Output the results
      $userInfo = $facebook->api_client->users_getInfo($target,
        array('name', 'pic_square'));
      $pageOutput.= "
        <div class='success'>
          <h1>Your Compliment to {$userInfo[0]['name']} was sent.</h1>
          <img src='".$userInfo[0]['pic_square']."'/>
          <img class='categoryImg'
            src='".LOCAL_APP_URL."/img/{$g_categories[$category]['bigimg']}'/>
            {$userInfo[0]['name']}
            is <b>{$g_categories[$category]['title']}</b> because \"$compliment\"
        </div>";
    }
  }

  // Show the compliment form
  $pageOutput .= "
    <div class='panel'>
      <form method='POST' id='complimentform' >
        <h1>Select one of your friends and enter your compliment.</h1>
        <table id='complimentTable'>
          <tr>
            <td class='label'>Your Friend:</td>
            <td class='content yui-skin-sam'>
              <div id='autocomplete'>
                <input id='name' />
                <div id='result'></div>
              </div>
            </td>
          </tr>
          <tr>
            <td class='label'>is:</td>
            <td class='content'>
              <div class='categories clearfix'>";
  foreach( $g_categories as $name => $info ){
    $pageOutput .= "
                <div class='category'>
                    <img class='categoryImg'
                      src='".LOCAL_APP_URL."/img/".$info['bigimg']."'/><br>
                    <div class='categoryTitle'>{$info['title']}</div>
                    <input type='radio' name='category' value='$name' />
                </div>";
  }
  $pageOutput .= "
              </div>
```

Listing 7.13 **Continued**

```
          </tr>
          <tr>
            <td class='label'>because:</td>
            <td class='content'>
              <input class='textInput' name='compliment'/></td>
          </tr>
        </table>
        <input id='target' name='target' type='hidden'>
        <input id='submitbtn' class='inputbutton' type='submit'
          name='submitCompliment' value='Send Compliment' />
      </form>
    </div>";

  $pageOutput .= getTypeAheadControl();

  $pageOutput .= "
    </body>
    </html>
  ";

    echo $pageOutput;
}

/** returns HTML for the typeahead control**/
function getTypeAheadControl() {
  global $facebook;

  // Create the JavaScript array of friend info
  $friendInfo = $facebook->api_client->users_getInfo(
    $facebook->api_client->friends_get(), array('name', 'uid', 'affiliations'));

  $typeAheadData = array();
  foreach($friendInfo as $friend) {
    $data = array();
    $data[] = $friend['name'];
    $data[] = $friend['uid'];
    $data[] = isset($friend['affiliations'][0]) ?
              "({$friend['affiliations'][0]['name']})" : "";
    $typeAheadData[] = $data;
    unset($data);
  }
  $typeAheadData = json_encode($typeAheadData);

  $output = "
    <script>
      YAHOO.util.Event.onDOMReady(init);
```

Listing 7.13 **Continued**

```
      function init() {
        var dsLocalArray = new YAHOO.util.LocalDataSource($typeAheadData);
        dsLocalArray.responseSchema = {fields:['name', 'uid', 'network']};
        var targetTypeAhead = new YAHOO.widget.AutoComplete('name','result',
                                                                dsLocalArray);

        targetTypeAhead.useShadow = true;
        targetTypeAhead.forceSelection = true
        targetTypeAhead.resultTypeList = false;
        var target = YAHOO.util.Dom.get('target');
        var onSelect = function(sType, aArgs) {
          target.value =  aArgs[2].uid;
        };
        targetTypeAhead.itemSelectEvent.subscribe(onSelect);
        targetTypeAhead.formatResult =
          function(oResultData, sQuery, sResultMatch) {
            var aMarkup = ' \
                <div><em>' + oResultData.name + '</em></div> \
                <div class=\'network\'> \
                  <small>' + oResultData.network + '</small> \
                </div>';
            return (aMarkup);
          }
      }
    </script>
  ";

  return $output;
}
?>
```

Before we go into the details of the function, let's look at what is passed to the page now that it is an IFrame. Clear the contents of your log and load the new page in your browser. Your log should now contain something like what is shown in Listing 7.14.

Listing 7.14 **Dump of IFrame Canvas `POST` and `GET` Variables**

```
(12-07-09, 12:45:47):  [index_iframe.php]
    GET length: 15
      fb_force_mode ==> 'iframe'
      fb_sig_in_iframe ==> '1'
      fb_sig_locale ==> 'en_US'
      fb_sig_in_new_facebook ==> '1'
      fb_sig_time ==> '1247373951.9121'
      fb_sig_added ==> '1'
      fb_sig_profile_update_time ==> '1241522567'
      fb_sig_expires ==> '1247461200'
```

Listing 7.14 **Continued**

```
      fb_sig_user ==> '698700806'
      fb_sig_session_key ==> '2.9sPGpoCtcYN7gRRENVmQ_g__.86400.1247461200-698700806'
      fb_sig_ss ==> 'DLbQloNc714MyBVKce8nlg__'
      fb_sig_ext_perms ==> 'auto_publish_recent_activity'
      fb_sig_api_key ==> '52bcc10ac263e1d0d2645182e01e0c99'
      fb_sig_app_id ==> '195482325614'
      fb_sig ==> 'e256a4605755282ae7637df819fb43a1'
    POST length: 0
    COOKIE length: 4
      52bcc10ac263e1d0d2645182e01e0c99_user ==> '698700806'
      52bcc10ac263e1d0d2645182e01e0c99_session_key ==>
'2.9sPGpoCtcYN7gRRENVmQ_g__.86400.1247461200-698700806'
      52bcc10ac263e1d0d2645182e01e0c99_expires ==> '1247461200'
      52bcc10ac263e1d0d2645182e01e0c99 ==> '7161f5158008087d02c9a6d8161050e6'
```

Notice that these are now `GET` variables instead of `POST` variables. The Facebook PHP client library class handles this for you, putting them all into its `$fb_params` member. The `fb_sig_in_canvas` variable has changed to `fb_sig_in_iframe`. `fb_sig_friends` is no longer passed, so we have to use the API to get this information. Finally, note that Facebook now saves session information as cookies for use by the Facebook JavaScript Client Library and Facebook Connect.

Let's go through the `renderPage()` function. This version includes an additional CSS file with styles for IFrame-specific overrides. Create `iframe.css` in the `css` directory and add the styles from Listing 7.15 into it.

Listing 7.15 **iframe.css: Style Overrides for the IFrame Canvas Page**

```
/*Styles to emulate Facebook*/
body { font-size:11px; font-family:'lucida grande',tahoma,verdana,arial,sans-
serif;}
h1 {font-size:14px; color:#333333; margin:0; padding:0;font-weight:bold;}
td { font-size:11px; text-align:left;}
.inputbutton { background-color:#3B5998;
               border-color:#D9DFEA #0E1F5B #0E1F5B #D9DFEA; border-style:solid;
               border-width:1px; color:#FFFFFF; padding:2px 15px 3px;
               text-align:center; font-size:11px;
}
.error { background-color:#FFEBE8; border:1px solid #DD3C10; margin:0 0 10px;
       padding:10px; }


.success { background-color:#FFF9D7; border:1px solid #E2C822; margin:0 0 10px;
         padding:10px; }


/*IFrame tabs*/
.tabs { padding-left:10px; }
```

Listing 7.15 **Continued**

```
.tabList { list-style-image:none; list-style-position:outside;
           list-style-type:none; margin:0px; padding:0px; }
.tabList li { display:inline; background-color:#F1F1F1; }
.tabList li a { display:inline-block; padding:3px 8px; text-decoration:none;
                color:#000000; background-color:#F1F1F1; font-weight:bold;
                margin:0px -2px; border:1px solid #898989;}
.tabList li a.selected:hover {text-decoration:none;}
.tabList .selected a { background-color:#6D84B4; color:#FFFFFF;}

/*YUI autocomplete*/
#autocomplete { padding-bottom:2em; } /*Add to prevent collapse into next div*/
.yui-skin-sam .yui-ac-content .network { color:#95A5C6; }
.yui-skin-sam .yui-ac-content li{ border-top:1px solid #DDDDDD; padding:3px; }
.yui-skin-sam .yui-ac-content li.yui-ac-highlight { background:#3B5998; }
```

To emulate the `<fb:friend-selector>`, we use the YUI JavaScript libraries. The CSS and JavaScript files are included and referenced from their server. We will go over how we emulate `<fb-friend-selector>` after we discuss the rest of the function.

After the form is submitted and the data is verified, we want to display the results to the user. However, we no longer have access to the FBML tags for name and picture. So, we must call `users_getInfo()`, passing the Facebook user ID of the target and a list of the fields we want—`name` and `picture`. After we have that information, it is simple to show the image and name of the target.

Building the form is more complex. We need to get the names, primary network, and ID for all the user's friends to display in the AutoComplete field. We call `users_getInfo()` again, this time passing the results of a call to `friends_get()` and our list of desired fields. That gives us all the information we need to show the list.

The code for the YUI AutoComplete control is contained in the `getTypeAheadControl()` function. This control requires a `LocalDataSource`, which needs to be initialized with a multidimensional array of our data. We iterate through the data we got back from `users_getInfo()` and create the JavaScript array. The `<div>` with ID `autocomplete` contains the elements the control needs to work. The containing `<td>` has the class `yui_skin_sam`, which enables skinning of the control using the Yahoo CSS file included at the top of the function.

The `<script>` block sets up the YUI control. We write out the JavaScript array as a parameter to the `LocalDataSource` constructor. We describe the data schema and pass that information to the AutoComplete constructor, telling it to display the name field. Two custom function overrides exist. The first overrides the selection event and stores the Facebook user ID for the selected user in the hidden form input `target`. The second does custom HTML formatting for the AutoComplete list, so that we can show the primary network below the username.

As you can see, this required much more work than the FBML version for the same functionality. Thankfully, there are external JavaScript libraries to help with this effort, and the Facebook JavaScript Client Library (which Chapter 12 covers) can allow you to use the FBML controls in your IFrame.

Using Tabs for Multiple Pages

Now that we have two pages, it makes sense to connect them with a standard Facebook tab control. We do this differently for the FBML and IFrame pages, because Facebook provides a nice set of tags for FBML, and we have to roll our own for the IFrame.

Listing 7.16 shows the code for the FBML tabs. Add the lines in bold just after the banner `<div>` in `renderPage()` in `index.php`. The URLs should be located on Facebook instead of on our server.

Listing 7.16 **`index.php`: Tabs for the FBML Canvas Page**

```
<div class='banner'
  style='background: url(".LOCAL_APP_URL."/img/banner.png) no-repeat;' />
<fb:tabs>
  <fb:tab-item href='".FB_APP_URL."/' title='Send(FBML)' selected='true'/>
  <fb:tab-item href='".FB_APP_URL."/index_iframe.php?fb_force_mode=iframe'
    title='Send(IFrame)' />
</fb:tabs>";
```

Listing 7.17 shows how to do the tabs for the IFrame. We don't want to load the entire page again—just the IFrame `src`—to take advantage of the speed increase. We have to pass along all the `fb_sig` variables that our current IFrame was passed to keep the session information intact. Add the lines in bold just after the banner `<div>` in `renderPage()` in `index_iframe.php`. Listing 7.18 contains a new function, `getFBQueryString()`, to put into `utils.inc` that gathers up all the `fb_sig` variables and creates a query string out of them. We then append that to the end of the URL for the IFrame tab.

Listing 7.17 **`index_iframe.php`: Tabs for the IFrame Canvas Page**

```
<div class='banner'
  style='background: url(".LOCAL_APP_URL."/img/banner.png) no-repeat;' >
</div>
<div class='tabs clearfix'>
  <ul class='tabList'>
    <li><a href='".FB_APP_URL."/' target='_top'>Send(FBML)</a></li>
    <li class='selected'>
      <a href='".LOCAL_APP_URL."/index_iframe.php?fb_force_mode=iframe&".
        getFBQueryString($_GET) ."' target='iframe_canvas'>Send(IFrame)
      </a>
    </li>
  </ul>
</div>";
```

Listing 7.18 **utils.inc: getFBQueryString Function**

```
function getFBQueryString($array) {
  $fbParams = array();

  foreach ($array as $key => $value) {
    if (strpos($key, "fb_sig_") === 0) {
      $fbParams[$key] = $value;
    }
  }
  if ( isset($_GET['fb_sig'] )) {
    $fbParams['fb_sig'] = $_GET['fb_sig'];
  }
  $fbQueryString = http_build_query($fbParams);
  return $fbQueryString;
}
```

Test out the IFrame canvas page and the tabs in your browser. The page should look similar to what's shown in Figure 7.2.

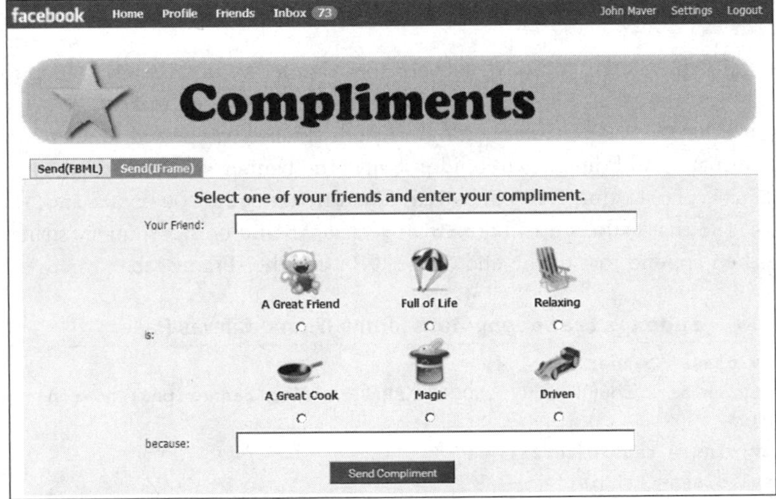

Figure 7.2 Compliments application IFrame canvas page

Summary

This chapter talked about the differences between FBML and IFrame canvas pages and built one of each. Here are some key points:

- FBML canvas pages offer simplicity and access to the Facebook look and feel via FBML tags, but at the cost of more limitations when using JavaScript and other HTML tags.
- IFrame canvas pages are flexible and allow the reuse of existing full-featured content, but they require extra work to emulate the functionality that Facebook users are accustomed to having. The Facebook JavaScript Client Library can enable IFrame canvas pages to incorporate those Facebook-specific tags.
- FBML tags perform a lot of the work for you, replacing API calls to fetch user information, pictures, and more. Using these tags can save development time and make canvas pages load faster.
- The `fb_force_mode` query parameter allows applications to set a canvas page to a specific type, regardless of what the overall application type is set to. This is the best way to mix IFrame canvas pages into an FBML application.
- Using the `<fb:tab>` tag on FBML canvas pages and custom tabs on IFrame canvas pages can make navigating through an application's features intuitive and reduce loading times by only rendering what is needed.

8

Updating the Profile

Although Facebook has shifted to the stream as the source of what a user is doing, the profile still provides a snapshot into who a user is and what she finds important. Applications can supply profile boxes, application tabs, and info sections that add to this information.

This chapter goes over the constraints and benefits of each profile box type and then shows how to create and update them. The Compliments application will be updated to use each profile feature. We also discuss how to use manage the Facebook cache for Facebook Markup Language (FBML) and images.

Profile Boxes

As discussed in Chapter 1, "Facebook Applications: The Basics," there are three kinds of profile boxes: Main, Wide, and Narrow. Main profile boxes appear on the left of the Wall and Info tabs of the profile and they are limited to 184px wide x 250px high. Only four of these profile boxes can appear at a time; as additional boxes are added, the oldest ones are moved to the Boxes tab. Narrow and Wide profile boxes appear on the Boxes tab. The Narrow and Wide designation is for on which side of the page they appear. The left side is Wide, with a width of 380px. The right side is Narrow, with a width of 184px. Both sides have no height limit. Figure 8.1 shows the various profile box sizes.

Users can move a profile box between the Wall and Boxes tabs by clicking the blue pencil in the top-right corner of the profile box and clicking Move to X Tab. Users move a box between the Wide and Narrow sides of the Boxes tab by dragging and dropping it. Content inside a `<fb:narrow>` tag only shows up when the profile box is on the Narrow side, while content in a `<fb:wide>` tag only shows up on the Wide side. A good profile box should support all these locations by displaying content formatted appropriately for the context.

All profile boxes are FBML based. However, Facebook specifically disallows profiles from using IFrames and from anything automatically playing, such as Flash or JavaScript. Users must first interact with the profile content before it can become active.

Profile box content is set by the application using the `profile.setFBML()` application programming interface (API) call. Listing 8.1 shows a sample call. Notice that the Main profile box FBML is passed separately from the Narrow and Wide FBML. The `$markup` and `$profileAction` parameters have been deprecated, so `NULL` should always be passed for these. Table 8.1 shows the parameters of the PHP Client Library's `profile_setFBML()`.

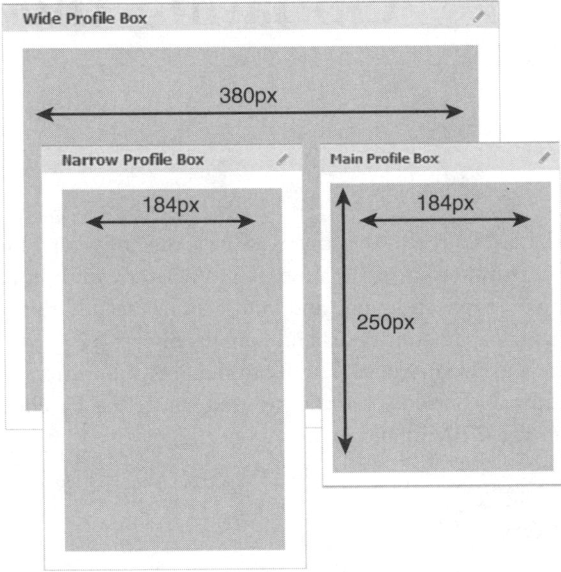

Figure 8.1 Size constraints of the different profile boxes

Table 8.1 **`profile_setFBML()` Parameters**

Parameter Name	Type	Details
`markup`	string	Deprecated. Always pass `NULL`.
`uid`	int	The user ID for the user or Public Profile to update, defaulting to the current user.
`profile`	string	The FBML for the profile box on the Boxes tab.
`profile_action`	string	Deprecated. Always pass `NULL`.
`mobile_profile`	string	The FBML that appears on *http://m.facebook.com*.
`profile_main`	string	The FBML that appears on the Wall tab, called the Main profile box.

Listing 8.1 **Example of Setting the Profile FBML**

```
$markup         = NULL;
$mainFBML       = "Appears on Wall tab";
$profileFBML    = "
  <fb:narrow>Appears on narrow side</fb:narrow>
  <fb:wide>Appears on wide side</fb:wide>";
$mobileFBML     = "
  <fb:mobile>Appears on m.facebook.com</fb:mobile>";
$profileAction  = NULL;

$facebook = new Facebook(FB_API_KEY, FB_APP_SECRET);
$facebook->api_client->profile_setFBML($markup, $appUserID, $profileFBML,
                                       $profileAction, $mobileFBML, $mainFBML);
```

Creating the Compliments Profile Boxes

We will update the Compliments application to use all the profile boxes and then go through each part of the changes. The Compliments profile boxes let viewers send the owner a compliment. When the user clicks the Send button, he is taken to the application canvas page to see that his compliment has been sent. Figures 8.2 and 8.3 show the Main profile and Wide profile boxes.

Figure 8.2 Compliments Main profile box

The first step is to add a call to a new function, `updateProfileBox()`, to `index.php` and `index_iframe.php`. Add the following line just before `renderPage()`:

```
updateProfileBox( $facebook->user );
```

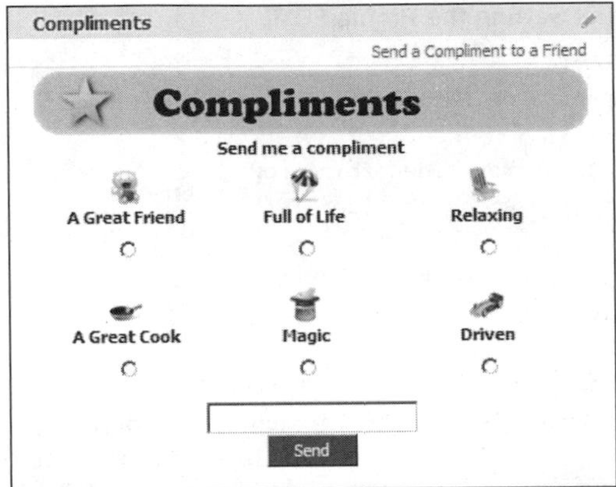

Figure 8.3 Compliments Wide profile box

Defining the Profile Box Utility Functions

Next, create a new file called `profile.inc` in the `inc` directory, and add the source from Listing 8.2 into it. This file contains all the code relating to creating profile content and updating it on Facebook. Add the following line to the top of `index.php` and `index_iframe.php` to include this new file:

```
require_once 'inc/profile.inc';
```

Listing 8.2 **`profile.inc`: Profile Box Utility Functions**

```
<?php
/** Updates the profile box for a user with the latest content for that user **/
function updateProfileBox($appUserID){
  $facebook = new Facebook(FB_API_KEY, FB_APP_SECRET);
  $generatedProfileFBML  = generateProfileBoxFBML($appUserID);
  $profileFBML           = $generatedProfileFBML['profile'];
  $mainFBML              = $generatedProfileFBML['main'];
  try {
    $facebook->api_client->profile_setFBML(NULL, $appUserID, $profileFBML,
      NULL, NULL, $mainFBML);
  } catch (Exception $ex) {
    wr("<Exception: uid: $appUserID - " . $ex->getMessage() . ">" );
    return false;
  }
  return true;
}

 /** Generates the profile box FBML for a user */
function generateProfileBoxFBML($appUserID) {
  global $g_categories;
```

Listing 8.2 **Continued**

```
// include our external stylesheet
$styles = htmlentities(file_get_contents(LOCAL_APP_DIR.'/css/profile.css'),
  true);

$headerBlock = "
  <style>
    $styles
  </style>
  <fb:subtitle>
    <fb:action href='".FB_APP_URL."'>Send a Compliment to a Friend</fb:action>
  </fb:subtitle>";

$categories = "";
foreach( $g_categories as $name => $info ){
  $categories .="
    <div class='category'>
      <img class='categoryImg' title='{$info['title']}'
        src='".LOCAL_APP_URL."/img/".$info['smallimg']."'/><br>
      <div class='categoryTitle'>{$info['title']}</div>
      <input type='radio' name='category' value='$name' />
    </div>";
}

$formBlock = "
  <div class='sendCompliment'>
    <span class='sendTitle'>Send me a compliment</span>
    <form method='POST' id='complimentForm' action='".FB_APP_URL."'>
      <div class='categories'>
        $categories
        <div style='clear:both;'></div>
      </div>
      <input type='hidden' name='target' value='$appUserID'/>
      <input class='textInput' name='compliment'/><br/>
      <input class='inputbutton' type='submit' name='submitCompliment'
        value='Send!'>
    </form>
  </div>";
$wideContent = "
  <fb:wide>
    <div class='wide'>
      <div class='profileContent'>
        <img class='banner' src='".LOCAL_APP_URL."/img/banner_w.png'/>
        $formBlock
      </div>
    </div>
```

Listing 8.2 **Continued**

```
    </fb:wide>";

  $narrowContent = "
    <fb:narrow>
      <div class='narrow'>
        <div class='profileContent'>
          <img class='banner' src='".LOCAL_APP_URL."/img/banner_n.png'/>
          $formBlock
        </div>
      </div>
    </fb:narrow>";

  $mainContent = "
    <div class='main'>
      <div class='profileContent'>
        <img class='banner' src='".LOCAL_APP_URL."/img/banner_n.png'/>
        $formBlock
      </div>
    </div>";

  $profileText['profile'] = $headerBlock . $wideContent . $narrowContent;
  $profileText['main'] =  $headerBlock . $mainContent;
  return $profileText;
}
?>
```

The `updateProfileBox()` function calls `generateProfileBoxFBML()`to create the FBML for the various profile boxes. It then sends that FBML to `profile_setFBML()`, passing `NULL` for the unused parameters. In general, it is a good idea to put calls to the Facebook API inside exception handlers. Sometimes, the Facebook servers can be down for a period of time, and it is better to fail gracefully than have the application die. We display this as an example for this function, but eliminate it in future listings for clarity.

`generateProfileBoxFBML()` creates all the FBML for the profile boxes. The first thing it does is include a style sheet specifically for the profile. Unfortunately, Facebook does not support external style sheets on profiles, so we use PHP to put it into a `<style>` block as part of the FBML.

A header block is created that uses the `<fb:subtitle>` tag. This tag adds text to the top left of the profile box. You might often see this in applications saying Displaying 10 of 100 Items. It takes an optional `seeallurl` parameter that adds a See All link to the top right of the box. `<fb:subtitle>` also supports `<fb:action>` child tags. These add links at the top right of the box for various actions the user can take. Compliments uses this tag to add a Send a Compliment to a Friend link.

Next, we iterate through the `$g_compliments` array to generate the set of radio buttons for compliment categories from which the user can choose. This works the same way as it did on the canvas page, where it is placed into a form block. Notice that the hidden input for the target is set to the profile owner's user ID. When the form is submitted, the user is redirected to the canvas page to see that her compliment was sent successfully. In Chapter 11, "FBJS, Mock AJAX, and Flash," we use Facebook JavaScript (FBJS) to handle this right on the profile box.

Because each profile box context has different size constraints, we create a separate block for Wide, Narrow, and Main. Each block has a `<div>` at the top with a class set for the type of block. We use this class in the style sheet to manage the styling for each set of context. The Narrow and Wide blocks enclose their code in `<fb:narrow>` and **`<fb:wide>`** tags.

An important thing to know about these two tags is that they are not just processing comments, but they create full blocks, as if they were `<div>`s. Listing 8.3 shows an example of how these tags close off blocks of FBML.

Listing 8.3 **Not Using Full Blocks with `<fb:wide>` and `<fb:narrow>`**

```
// Block 1: goal of starting a div with a different header for
// narrow and wide boxes
<fb:narrow>
<div class='header'>
  <img src='narrowheader.jpg'/>
</fb:narrow>
<fb:wide>
<div class='header'>
  <img src='wideheader.jpg'/>
</fb:wide>
</div>

// Block 2: this ends up being the equivalent of
<div class='narrow'>
<div class='header'>
  <img src='narrowheader.jpg'/>
</div>
<div class='wide'>
<div class='header'>
  <img src='wideheader.jpg'/>
</div>
</div>

// Block 3: It must be done like this instead
<div class='header'>
  <fb:narrow>
    <img src='narrowheader.jpg'/>
  </fb:narrow>
  <fb:wide>
    <img src='wideheader.jpg'/>
```

Listing 8.3 **Continued**

```
  </fb:wide>
</div>
```

The first block in Listing 8.3 tries to use the `<fb:narrow>` and `<fb:wide>` tags to display the right header image, just by setting part of the header `<div>`. However, the rendered code ends up working like the second block, where the header `<div>` is closed by the end of the narrow section. The correct way to achieve this is to use code like the third block, which treats the `<fb:narrow>` and `<fb:wide>` tags as complete `<div>` sections.

Styling the Profile Boxes

We need to add the styles for the profile boxes. Create a new file called `profile.css` in the `css` directory and add the source from Listing 8.4 into it. This file sets some base styles for the profile and then uses overrides to correctly display the content for each profile box context.

Listing 8.4 **`profile.css`: Styles for Use in the Profile Boxes**

```
.profileContent { margin-top:-12px; text-align:center;}
.sendCompliment { text-align:center;}
.sendTitle {font-weight: bold;}
#complimentTable  .textInput {width: 200px;}

.categories { padding-bottom: 5px; }
.categoryTitle { height:30px; font-weight:bold; }
.category { float:left; text-align:center; margin:3px; width:43px;
            height:65px; padding:5px; }
.categoryImg { width:24px; height:24px;}

.wide .banner { width:380px; height:45px; }
.wide .category { width:108px; }
.wide .categoryTitle { height:20px;}

.narrow .banner { width:193px; height:23px; }

.main .banner { width:193px; height:23px; }
```

Adding the Profile Boxes

Profile boxes are not automatically created for the user. The user must manually click a Facebook-provided button to add one to her profile. Thankfully, Facebook also provides a way to only display this button if the user hasn't already added the profile box. Figure 8.4 shows what this button looks like.

When a user clicks this button, she is presented with the dialog in Figure 8.5. She can choose the Wall or Boxes tab as destinations for the profile box. If she clicks Add, she's taken to her profile and asked if she wants to Keep or Remove the box. If she chooses No Thanks, the dialog disappears.

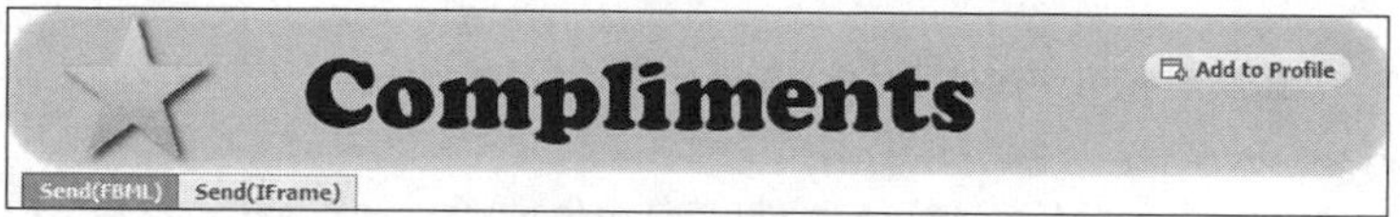

Figure 8.4 Add to Profile button in the Compliments canvas page banner

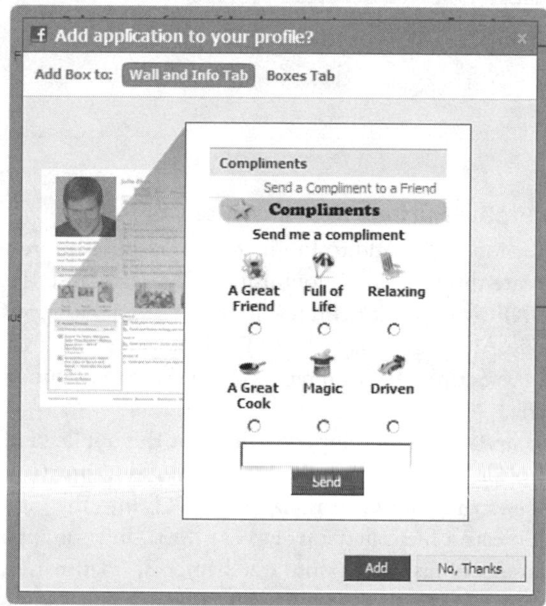

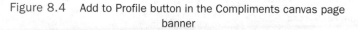

Figure 8.5 Dialog that appears when a user clicks the Add to Profile button

> **Warning**
>
> The Add to Profile button does not appear for a user unless the profile content has already been set using the `profile.setProfileFBML()` API method.

Displaying Add to Profile Buttons in FBML Canvas Pages

Displaying the Add to Profile button is simple for an FBML canvas page. Just add the bold lines in Listing 8.5 to the `renderPage()` function in `index.php`, after the banner in the header block. The `<fb:if-section-not-added section='profile'>` tag tells Facebook to only render the inside FBML if the user hasn't added the profile box yet. This can be useful if your application wants to offer additional text about why the user should add the profile box that would only be shown when the profile box hasn't been added. `<fb:add-section-button section='profile' />` renders the actual button. This is all enclosed in a `<div>` so that we can position it where we want on the page using CSS.

Listing 8.5 **`index.php`: FBML for the Add to Profile Button**

```
<div class='banner'
  style='background: url(".LOCAL_APP_URL."/img/banner.png) no-repeat;' >
  <div id='buttons' class='clearfix' >
    <div id='addbutton'>
      <fb:if-section-not-added section='profile'>
          <fb:add-section-button section='profile' />
      </fb:if-section-not-added>
    </div>
  </div>
</div>
```

Displaying Add to Profile Buttons in IFrame Canvas Pages

Getting an IFrame version of the Add to Profile button requires more work, because there is no way to create this button without using FBML. Because IFrames don't support FBML, we must use XFBML, which requires the Facebook JavaScript Client Library and all the supporting code. Although Chapter 12, "Facebook JavaScript Client Library," discusses the Facebook JavaScript Client Library, we add the basic setup now to enable the Add to Profile button.

The first step is to update the Developer Settings for this application. Go to *www.facebook.com/developers/apps.*php and click the Edit Settings link for Compliments. Go to the Connect tab and enter in your Canvas Callback URL into the Connect URL field and click Save. Next, create a file called `xdreceiver.html` in your application root directory, and add the contents of Listing 8.6 into it. Chapter 3, "Platform Architecture Overview," covered what this file is used for, but as a refresher, it allows the Facebook JavaScript Client Library to work around the browser limitation of communicating between different domains.

Listing 8.6 **`xdreceiver.html`: Cross-Domain Receiver for the Facebook JavaScript Client Library**

```
<!DOCTYPE html PUBLIC "-//W3C//DTD XHTML 1.0 Strict//EN"
  "http://www.w3.org/TR/xhtml1/DTD/xhtml1-strict.dtd">
<html xmlns="http://www.w3.org/1999/xhtml" >
<head>
  <title>Cross-Domain Receiver Page</title>
</head>
<body>
  <script src="http://static.ak.facebook.com/js/api_lib/v0.4/XdCommReceiver.js?2"
   type="text/javascript"></script>
```

Listing 8.6 **Continued**

```
</body>
</html>
```

The Facebook JavaScript Client Library can now communicate with our application. To put the Add to Profile button on the page, we need to create a placeholder `<div>` that the Library can use. Add the following bolded lines to the `renderPage()` function in `index_iframe.php`, after the banner in the header block:

```
<div class='banner'
  style='background: url(".LOCAL_APP_URL."/img/banner.png) no-repeat;' >
  <div id='buttons' class='clearfix' >
    <div id='addbutton'></div>
  </div>
</div>
```

Now, we need to add a script block that loads and initializes the Facebook JavaScript Client Library and tells it to replace the placeholder `<div>` with the Add to Profile button. Add the code in Listing 8.7 to the end of `renderPage()` in `index_iframe.php`, just before the `</body>` tag.

Listing 8.7 **`index_iframe.php`: Using the Facebook JavaScript Client Library to Show the Add to Profile Button**

```
$pageOutput .= "
  <script
    src='http://static.ak.facebook.com/js/api_lib/v0.4/FeatureLoader.js.php'
    type='text/javascript'></script>
  <script type='text/javascript'>
    FB_RequireFeatures(['XFBML'], function() {
        FB.Facebook.init('".FB_API_KEY."', 'xdreceiver.html', null);
        FB.Connect.showAddSectionButton('profile',
          document.getElementById('addbutton'));
        FB.Connect.showAddSectionButton('info',
          document.getElementById('infobutton'));
    });
  </script>
  </body>
  </html>
";
```

This loads the Facebook JavaScript Client Library, requiring that it loads all the necessary parts to display XFBML. It initializes it with the application API key and the location of the `xdreceiver.html` file, relative to the root. It then calls `showAddSectionButton()` with the placeholder `<div>`. As with all XFBML, this code runs on the client, so there might be a slight delay as the library renders the new button HTML. Chapter 12 details how the Facebook JavaScript Client Library works.

It is time to test the profile boxes. Go to your application and click the Add to Profile button on either the FBML or IFrame tab. Click Add, which takes you to your profile. Click Keep to accept the new profile box. Try moving it from the Wall to the Boxes tab and from the Narrow to the Wide side. See how the layout changes with each location.

Application Tabs

Application tabs are a way for applications to display profile content in a much larger space. They behave mostly like profile boxes, but are 760px wide. Application tabs are populated via a callback instead of presetting the content once via `profile.setFBML()`. This callback is used the first time a user goes to that tab on his profile. As long as he is still on his profile, switching back to that tab uses a cached version.

When an application supports an application tab, the user can click the + at the right side of his profile tab list and select it from a list to add the tab. The name of the tab is limited to 11 characters, and it can be different than the application name.

To allow users to add an application tab, you need to update the Developer Settings. Go to the Profiles tab and fill in `Compliments` for the Tab Name and `apptab.php` for the Tab URL. Then, create a new file called `apptab.php` in the application root directory and add the contents of Listing 8.8. This file is the handler for the application tab callback and reuses functionality from `profile.inc` to help generate the FBML.

Listing 8.8 **`apptab.php`: Callback Handler for Displaying the Application Tab**

```
<?php
require_once dirname(__FILE__).'/inc/globals.inc';
require_once dirname(__FILE__).'/inc/db.inc';
require_once dirname(__FILE__).'/inc/utils.inc';
require_once dirname(__FILE__).'/inc/profile.inc';

dumpRequestVars(true, basename(__FILE__));

$facebook = new Facebook(FB_API_KEY, FB_APP_SECRET);
$generatedProfileFBML = generateProfileBoxFBML($facebook->profile_user);
$appTabFBML = $generatedProfileFBML['tab'];
echo $appTabFBML;

?>
```

This code calls the `generateProfileBoxFBML()` function to get the FBML for the tab and then echoes it out. We need to update `profile.inc` with the content of Listing 8.9 to add the tab specific content. Add the `$appTabHeaderBlock` section just after the `$headerBlock` in the file and add the `$tabContent` section after `$mainContent`.

Listing 8.9 **Application Tab Updates for `profile.inc`**

```
$appTabHeaderBlock =  "
<style>
  $styles
</style>
<div class='subtitle'>
  <a href='".FB_APP_URL."'>
    Send a Compliment to a Friend
  </a>
</div>";

$tabContent = "
<div class='tab'>
  <div class='profileContent'>
    <img class='banner' src='".LOCAL_APP_URL."/img/banner.png'/>
    $formBlock
  </div>
</div>";

$profileText['tab'] = $appTabHeaderBlock . $tabContent;
```

Application tabs do not support the `<fb:subtitle>` tag we used for the profile boxes, so we need to manually create the link. We also need a larger banner image, so we will use the same one as the canvas page. Just like the other profile boxes, we enclose the FBML in a `<div>` with the class `tab` so that we can apply custom styles. Add the styles in Listing 8.10 to `profile.css`.

Listing 8.10 **Application Tab Updates for `profile.css`**

```
.tab .banner { width:760px; height:90px; }
.tab .sendTitle {font-size:20px; }
.tab .category { width:108px; }
.tab .categoryTitle { height:15px; }
.tab .textInput { width: 400px; }
.tab .profileContent { text-align:right; margin:0px;}
.subtitle { text-align:right; border-bottom:1px solid #ECEFF5; color:#444444;
          margin:0px 0px 5px 0px; padding:2px 8px; }
```

Test out the tab by going to your profile, clicking the + next to your tabs and selecting Compliments. You should see what is shown in Figure 8.6.

Application Info Sections

Application info sections appear on the user's Info tab on his profile. Info sections come in two formats: Text and Object. Text info sections consist of several text fields and values, while Object info sections can contain images and descriptions. To see a Text info section, look at your own profile's Info tab. All the information that Facebook displays there uses Text info sections.

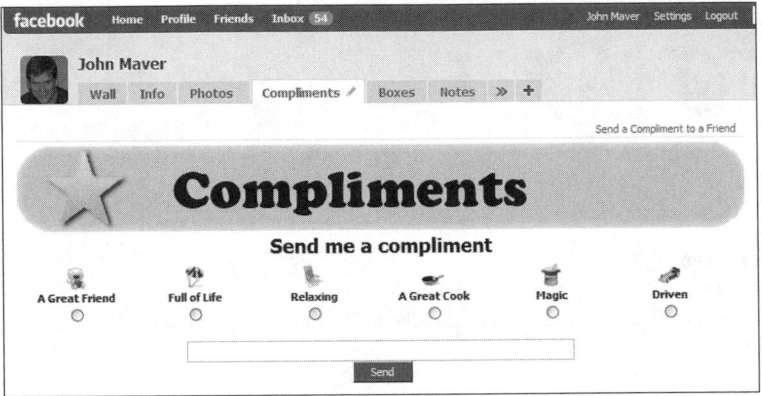

Figure 8.6 Compliments application tab

Applications create these info sections in a similar way to profile content. First, the user must click an Add to Info button in the application. Next, the application must call the `profile.setInfo()` API method, passing in the info section data. This data is then cached until the application calls this API function again. Table 8.2 shows the parameters of the PHP client library's `profile_setInfo()` method.

Table 8.2 **`profile_setInfo()`** Parameters

Parameter Name	Type	Details
`title`	string	Title for the info section.
`type`	int	Either 1 for a Text info section or 5 for an Object info section.
`info_fields`	array	The array of data to put in the info section. Each datum consists of the following: ▪ `field:` Name of the info field. ▪ `info-items array`, with each `info-item` composed of a `label`, `link`, and, optionally, an `image`, `description`, and `sublabel`.
`uid`	int	The user ID adding the info section.

The Compliments application adds an Object info section containing the latest compliments that the user has received. It updates this info section each time the user visits the application. The implementation for this mirrors what we did for the profile boxes. Figure 8.7 shows what the user sees on the Info tab.

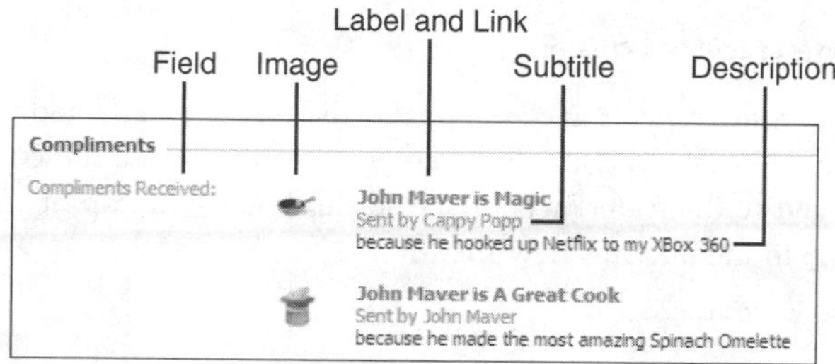

Figure 8.7 Compliments info section with labels for each field of the `info-item`

Getting the Compliments Data

As each user sends a compliment, we store it in the database. We need to get the last five compliments received for our info section, so add the `getComplimentsForUser()` function from Listing 8.11 into `db.inc` to fetch that data. This function returns the result as an associative array keyed by the compliment sender's Facebook user ID.

Listing 8.11 **`db.inc: getComplimentsForUser()`** **Function**

```
/** returns the latest compliments for a user **/
function getComplimentsForUser($appUserID) {
  $appUserID = $this->real_escape_string($appUserID);
  $count = 5;

  $query  = "SELECT DISTINCT * from compliments WHERE targetID = $appUserID
            ORDER BY complimentTime LIMIT $count";
  $result = $this->_execQuery($query);
  $output = array();
  if ( $result ) {
    while ($row = $result->fetch_assoc()) {
      $output[$row['appUserID']] = $row;
    }
    $result->close();
  }
  return $output;
}
```

Creating the Info Section

Now that we have the data, we need to display it. Add a call to a new function, `updateInfoSection()`, to `index.php` and `index_iframe.php`, just after `updateProfileBox()`:

```
updateInfoSection( $facebook->user );
```

Next, create a new file called `info.inc` in the `inc` directory, and add the source from Listing 8.12 into it. This file contains all the code needed to create the content for our info sections and update them on Facebook. Add this line to the top of `index.php` and `index_iframe.php` to include this new file:

```
require_once 'inc/info.inc';
```

Listing 8.12 **`info.inc`: Info Section Utility Functions**

```
<?php
function updateInfoSection($appUserID) {
  global $g_categories;

  $db = new DB();
  $infoData = $db->getComplimentsForUser($appUserID);
  $facebook = new Facebook(FB_API_KEY, FB_APP_SECRET);

  // Get all the complimentor's names from Facebook
  $uids = array_keys($infoData);
  $uids[] = $facebook->user;
  $users = array();
  $userNames = $facebook->api_client->users_getInfo($uids, 'name');
  foreach ($userNames as $user) {
    $users[$user['uid']] = $user['name'];
  }

  // Display the latest compliments received
  $complimentInfoFields = array();
  foreach( $infoData as $compliment ) {
    $complimentInfoFields[] = array(
      'label'=> $users[$compliment["targetID"]].' is '.
        $g_categories[$compliment["category"]]["title"],
      'image' => LOCAL_APP_URL."/img/".
        $g_categories[$compliment["category"]]["bigimg"],
      'sublabel' => 'Sent by '.$users[$compliment["appUserID"]],
      'description'=> 'because '.$compliment["compliment"],
      'link'=> FB_APP_URL );
  }

  $infoFields = array(
```

Listing 8.12 **Continued**

```
    array('field' => 'Compliments Received', 'items' => $complimentInfoFields)
  );

  // Update the info section
  $facebook->api_client->profile_setInfo( 'Compliments', 5, $infoFields,
    $appUserID );
}
?>
```

updateInfoSection() gets the last set of compliments the user has received from the database using getComplimentsForUser(). This is returned as an associative array keyed by user IDs. We need to display the name of each user who sent a compliment. Unfortunately, info sections do not support FBML tags, so we can't use a simple tag, such as <fb:name uid='xxxxxxx' />, to do the work for us. Instead, we call users_getInfo() to get the names for each sender, passing in the list of user IDs. We now can create a mapping of the user IDs to names in $users.

We loop through each of the compliments, and create an array of info-item objects. Each object must contain a label and link, and can optionally include a subtitle, image, and description. That array of objects is enclosed in another array of fields; our Compliments application might add another field called Compliments Sent and include a set of info-item objects for that.

Finally, we call profile_setInfo(), passing in a title for our info section, the type of info section, our array of data, and the user ID for which to create the info section. We are using an Object info section, so we pass 5 for the type.

Adding Info Section Buttons

Just like the Add to Profile buttons, we need to update our canvas pages to display the Facebook-provided Add to Info button. For the FBML canvas page, add the following code under the addbutton <div> in index.php:

```
<div id='infobutton'>
  <fb:if-section-not-added section='info'>
    <fb:add-section-button section='info' />
  </fb:if-section-not-added>
</div>
```

For the IFrame, add the following line for the new infobutton placeholder <div> after the addbutton placeholder <div> in index_iframe.php:

```
<div id='infobutton'></div>
```

Add this line after the showAddSectionButton() call for the Profile button in index_iframe.php:

```
FB.Connect.showAddSectionButton('info',document.getElementById('infobutton'));
```

Finally, add the following line to `main.css` to position the button in the banner:

```
#infobutton { position:absolute; top:48px; right:33px; }
```

You should now be able to go to your canvas page and click the Add to Info button. It should take you to your Info tab, where you see a new info section for Compliments.

Allowing Users to Update Info Sections

Applications can also allow users to edit info sections from the Info tab by calling `profile.setInfoOptions()` with an array of possible values for one of the fields. If you put a callback handler in the Information Update Callback URL in the Developer Settings, your application can be notified when a user updates this information. Listing 8.13 shows sample code for implementing this functionality, and Figure 8.8 shows what a user editing the options sees.

Figure 8.8 Editing an info section

Listing 8.13 Example of Allowing Users to Edit an Info Section

```
// Create an info section for My Favorite Compliment Type
$favoriteComplimentTypes = array(
  array('field' => 'My Favorite Compliment Type',
    'items' => array(
      array( 'label'=> 'A Great Cook',
        'description'=> 'I love to cook and it shows',
        'link'=> 'http//apps.facebook.com/compliments/'
      )
    )
  )
);

$facebook->api_client->profile_setInfo( 'Compliments', 5,
  $favoriteComplimentTypes, $appUserID );

// Submit the editable options for Compliment Type
$complimentTypes = array(
  array(
    'label'=> 'A Great Cook',
```

Listing 8.13 **Continued**

```
    'description'=> 'I love to cook and it shows',
    'link'=> 'http//apps.facebook.com/compliments/'),
  array(
    'label'=> 'Full of Life',
    'description'=> 'I have a zest for living',
    'link'=> 'http//apps.facebook.com/compliments/'),
  array(
    'label'=> 'Magic',
    'description'=> 'I make things happen for people',
    'link'=> 'http//apps.facebook.com/compliments/'),
);

// The first parameter must match the name of one of the 'fields' passed in
// the setInfo call above
$facebook->api_client->profile_setInfoOptions('My Favorite Compliment Type',
  $complimentTypes);
```

Working with Facebook's Caching

After the content of a profile box or info section is set, Facebook caches it until the time the application updates it. Facebook not only caches the FBML for profiles, but also the images. But, there are times when you might want to manage the cache yourself, either to refresh your images or to cache common sections of FBML.

Refreshing the Image Cache

Facebook's image caching is great news for your servers, because each image is only loaded from your servers once. However, if you ever update an image, Facebook continues to supply the cached version. It is also possible that Facebook might fail to successfully load the image, because of an error on your server, and the cache might be empty. Images stay in Facebook's cache as long as they are being used. After a period of disuse, Facebook might drop them from the cache and reload them from your server the next time a user accesses them. This means that it is possible for an image that appears now to disappear later, if an error occurs.

You can manually update the cached version of an image by passing the absolute URL to the image on your server to `fbml_refreshImgSrc()`, like this:

```
$facebook->api_client->fbml_refreshImgSrc("http://server.com/img.jpg");
```

Facebook refetches the image from your server and adjusts the `src` attribute for `<img>` tags, referencing it to something like this:

```
http://platform.ak.facebook.com/www.new/app_full_proxy.php?app=195482325614&v=
➥1&size=p&cksum=b30fbadecf8274988ca7e5f2d5bbcade&src=http%3A%2F%2Fserver.com
%3A85%2Fimg.jpg
```

Managing the FBML Cache

FBML for profile boxes are cached "forever." For applications with completely static content, this might be fine. Updating a user's profile boxes when he accesses the application might make sense most of the time; it allows the profile boxes to reflect the most current information. However, there are times when you want to update many of your users' profile boxes at once. This might be because of a general style change or there might be a content change that applies to a large set of users.

It is simple to set up a server-side cron job to iterate through all the application's users and call `profile.setFBML()` for them. However, as the number of users increases, this can take longer and longer to accomplish, and eventually be unmanageable. Thankfully, a better solution uses Facebook itself to update all the profile boxes for you.

The `<fb:ref>` FBML tag can mark blocks of FBML that can be updated across many profiles with a single call. There are two ways to use this tag: by URL and by Handle. They both can achieve the same result, but one might fit better with your application design than the other. Specifying a URL tells Facebook to call that URL to get the new content when the cache is being refreshed, while specifying a Handle lets your application directly pass the new FBML content. You can also nest `<fb:ref>` tags, but only the content of the Handle or URL specified is updated.

Listing 8.14 shows how an application might use `<fb:ref>` with a Handle. You create a block of FBML and pass it to `fbml.setRefHandle()` with a unique Handle identifier. Then, use `<fb:ref handle='youridentifier'/>` in your profile FBML content wherever you want that block of FBML to appear and pass it to `profile.setFBML()`. From then on, your application can just call `fbml.setRefHandle()` with new FBML to update all profiles that contain that Handle to use the new content. Only the section in the Handle is updated.

Listing 8.14 **Using `<fb:ref>` with a Handle**

```
//Store the FBML in a handle
$commonFBML = "<div>Today's temperature is 60 degrees F</div>";
$facebook->api_client->fbml_setRefHandle("temp", $commonFBML);

$profileFBML = "
  <div>
    <h1>Today's weather</h1>
    <fb:ref handle='temp'/>
  </div>";
$facebook->api_client->profile_setFBML(NULL, $appUserID, $profileFBML,
  NULL, NULL, NULL);
```

Listing 8.15 shows how to accomplish the same thing using a URL. In this case, you don't set cache the FBML ahead of time, but instead, you supply a callback URL from which the FBML can be retrieved. To update it, call `fbml.refreshRefUrl()` passing the

URL. The callback should just return the FBML, and is only called one time, not once per profile updated.

Listing 8.15 **Using <fb:ref> with a URL**

```
$profileFBML = "
  <div>
    <h1>Today's weather</h1>
    <fb:ref url='http://server.com/getweather.php'/>
  </div>";
$facebook->api_client->profile_setFBML(NULL, $appUserID, $profileFBML,
  NULL, NULL, NULL);

$facebook->api_client->fbml_refreshRefUrl("http://server.com/getweather.php");
```

In Compliments, we might want to update the list of available categories to all of our users at once. This is a great use for `<fb:ref>`. Listing 8.16 shows how to modify the code for `$formBlock` in the `renderPage()` function in `profile.inc` to use `<fb:ref>` for the categories list.

Listing 8.16 **`profile.inc`: Example of Using <fb:ref> for the Compliment Categories**

```
$formBlock = "
  <div class='sendCompliment'>
    <span class='sendTitle'>Send me a compliment</span>
    <form method='POST' id='complimentForm' action='".FB_APP_URL."/'>
      <div class='categories'>
        <fb:ref handle='profileCategories'/>
      </div>
      <input type='hidden' name='target' value='$appUserID'/>
      <input class='textInput' name='compliment'/><br/>
      <input class='inputbutton' type='submit' name='submitCompliment'
        value='Send'>
    </form>
  </div>";
```

Listing 8.17 shows a new `updateCategoriesRef()` function that generates the FBML for the categories and stores it in a `<fb:ref>` handle.

Listing 8.17 **`updateCategoriesRef()` Function for `profile.inc`**

```
/** Update the facebook cache for the categories FBML */
function updateCategoriesRef(){
  global $g_categories;
  $facebook =  new Facebook(FB_API_KEY, FB_APP_SECRET);
```

Listing 8.17 **Continued**

```
  $categories = "";
  foreach( $g_categories as $name => $info ){
    $categories .="
      <div class='category'>
        <img class='categoryImg' title='{$info['title']}'
          src='".LOCAL_APP_URL."/img/".$info['smallimg']."'/><br>
        <div class='categoryTitle'>{$info['title']}</div>
        <input type='radio' name='category' value='$name' />
      </div>";
  }
  $categories .= "<div style='clear:both;'></div>";

  // Store in a ref handle so we can easily update the categories for everyone
  $facebook->api_client->fbml_setRefHandle("profileCategories", $categories);
}
```

We just need to call `updateCategoriesRef()` whenever we update the `$g_categories` list in `globals.inc` to update all of our users' profiles.

Summary

This chapter talked about the profile boxes, application tabs, and info sections, as well as how to manage the Facebook cache. Here are some key points:

- Facebook has three different types of profile boxes, each with their own dimensions. Applications need to support each type of box with content that fits appropriately and serves a useful purpose. This content is preset via an API call and cached by Facebook forever.
- Profile boxes and info sections are not added automatically but must be done as a manual step by users by clicking an FBML button. IFrame canvas pages must use XFBML to display the Add to Profile and Add to Info buttons.
- Application tabs provide applications with a canvas-size surface on the user's profile. The content is pulled from a callback rather than preset via an API call. Application tabs can only use FBML.
- Info sections let applications add additional information to users' Info tabs on their profile. Text and images can be displayed. Applications can also allow users to edit this information right from the Info tab.
- Facebook caches images in FBML. Applications can update this cache for an image using `fbml_refreshImgSrc()`.
- Applications can cache and update specific blocks of FBML using `<fb:ref>`. Either a handle or an URL can be used as a unique identifier. Updating a cached block updates it across all profiles that use that `<fb:ref>` identifier.

9

Feed Stories, Feed Forms, and Templates

How an application communicates with its users and their friends is undoubtedly one of the most important contributors to its ultimate success or failure. Since the Platform's launch, Facebook has significantly changed how applications can use the available channels to correspond with their users. Mastering these channels in a way that makes an application more noticeable without becoming a nuisance to the Facebook population is paramount.

This chapter presents the groundwork of the communication options Facebook provides for applications to interact with their users. It covers the creation and publishing of Feed stories, different ways of getting stories published to the stream, and the management of story template bundles using both Facebook tools and the application programming interface (API). To increase its level of engagement, the sample application is updated to use the new features presented.

Using Feed Forms and Templates

Facebook Feed forms are one the most important and frequently used methods of publishing content to Facebook. They come in two different types, which the following sections cover. To use them, however, you need to clearly understand the creation and management of Feed templates and how they are used in the story-creation process. Feed forms and templates are one of the more complex topics that this book covers, but they are critical to understanding how to get great application content from an application into the stream.

Introducing Feed Forms

Let's start by looking at how to create our first control that can submit Feed stories to the stream. Listing 9.1 is exactly like the code from Chapter 8, "Updating the Profile," except that the `form` tag has some new attributes, and we added a label to the Submit button. Facebook requires the Submit button on Feed forms to have a label or Facebook fails to correctly parse the page as FBML. This is all a developer needs to do to convert a normal HTML form into an FBML Feed form.

Listing 9.1 **index.php Converting an HTML Form to a Facebook Feed Form**

```
<form method='POST' fbtype='multiFeedStory' id='complimentform'
  action='".LOCAL_APP_URL."feed_form_callback.php' >
  <h1>Select one of your friends and enter your compliment.</h1>

  // rest of form elided for clarity...

  <input class='inputbutton' type='submit' name='submitCompliment'
    label='Send Compliment' value='Send Compliment'/>
</form>
```

The first change mandated by Facebook is that Feed forms have an action attribute set to an absolute URL. It's been set to the full URL of a new file, `feed_form_callback.php`. The most important change is the addition of the `fbtype` attribute to the `form` tag. This indicator tells Facebook to treat this form as a Feed form and publish its data to the stream. Later in this section, you write the code for the `feed_form_callback.php` script.

Currently, Facebook provides two flavors of Feed forms: feedStory and multiFeedStory. Both allow the publishing of content to the stream. Although there are only minor syntactic differences between them, their behaviors are completely different.

The feedStory form is created by setting the form's `fbtype` attribute to feedStory. It publishes content to the current user's Wall and their friends' News Feeds.

The multiFeedStory Feed form is created by setting `fbtype` to multiFeedStory. Unlike the feedStory form, it publishes to both the Wall of the current user and one of his friends. The multiFeedStory form also requires that an FBML `<fb:friend-selector>` tag be placed on the form to allow the user to choose to which of their friends' Walls they want to publish content. The multiFeedStory form only publishes to a single friend's Wall—targeting multiple friends is not supported.

For Compliments, it makes sense to use the multiFeedStory form because the application is designed to send compliments to the user's friends. When a user submits the form, a story containing the compliment is published to the Wall of the friend he typed in the `<fb:friend-selector>` control.

An `<fb:friend-selector>` tag already exists in your form's code, but you need to remove its `idname` attribute and the hidden input control that it populates (it follows the closing `</table>` tag):

```
<input type='hidden' name='target'>
```

Facebook requires that all Feed forms use the default value for the `idname` attribute of the `<fb:friend-selector>`. If you don't remove the `idname` attribute, you receive an erroneous error dialog, like the one shown in Figure 9.1, when you submit, saying that you must select some friends, even though you have done so. This is currently a bug with the Facebook Platform, and it might be fixed by the time you read this.

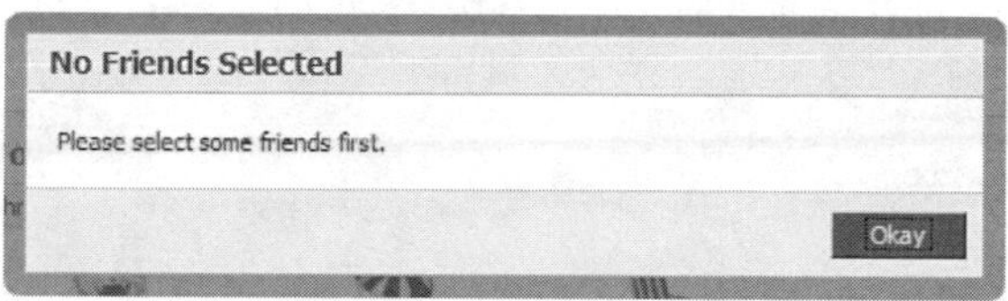

Figure 9.1 Erroneous error shown when the `idname` attribute is present in a multiFeedStory forms and friends have been selected

Now, you will remove the code that handles the form post from `index.php` and move it to a new script, `feed_form_callback.php`. Save it in the same location as `index.php`. Separating our form-processing logic from its presentation makes the code easier to understand and maintain. Add the code from Listing 9.2 to `feed_form_callback.php`.

Listing 9.2 **`feed_form_callback.php`: Handling Form POSTs**

```
<?php
   require_once 'inc/globals.inc';
   require_once 'inc/utils.inc';
   require_once 'inc/profile.inc';
   require_once 'inc/db.inc';
   dumpRequestVars(basename(__FILE__), true);
   // Handle the form submit
  if (isset($_POST['friend_selector_id']) && isset($_POST['method']) &&
      isset($_POST['compliment']) && isset($_POST['category'])) {
    $target        = $_POST['friend_selector_id'];
    $feedFormType = $_POST['method'];
    $compliment    = $_POST['compliment'];
    $category      = $_POST['category'];
    $facebook = new Facebook(FB_API_KEY, FB_APP_SECRET);
    $db = new DB();
    $db->addCompliment($facebook->user, $target, $category, $compliment );
    updateProfileBox( $facebook->user );
    updateInfoSection( $facebook->user );
    // Output the results
    $pageOutput = "
      <fb:success>
```

Listing 9.2 **Continued**

```
        <fb:message>Your Compliment to <fb:name uid='$target'/> was
sent.</fb:message>
          <fb:profile-pic uid='$target'/>
          <img class='catImg'
            src='".LOCAL_APP_URL."/img/".$g_categories[$category]['bigimg']."'/>
          <fb:name uid='$target' linked='false'/> is <b>
            {$g_categories[$category]['title']}</b> because \"$compliment\"
        </fb:success>";
  } else {
    // Output the error
      $pageOutput = "
        <fb:error>
          <fb:message>Sending the Compliment failed!</fb:message>
          Please check that the form is filled out correctly
        </fb:error>";
  }
echo($pageOutput);
?>
```

Now, it's time to test your new Feed form implementation. Navigate to your application's Canvas Page URL (*http://apps.facebook.com/<appname>/*) and fill out all the form's fields. Click the Send Compliment button. You should receive a cryptic error message similar to the one shown in Figure 9.2, which says something about an invalid JSON response.

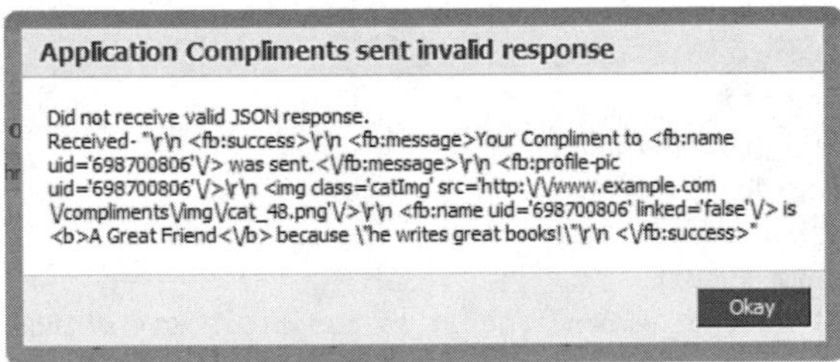

Figure 9.2 You receive an invalid JSON response error when attempting to submit your form.

Feed Templates

The reason why Facebook raises the error shown in Figure 9.2 is because it requires more information about what content it should actually publish to the target friend's Wall. It just has a set of data posted by what it thinks is a multiFeedStory form, and that data is missing something. It turns out that Facebook requires three more things in order to publish a Feed story. It needs a "template" to tell it how to render the data in the story, custom data provided by the application to fill in that template, and some code to tell it where to take the submitting user after the story is published.

All feed stories are constructed from groups of templates that a developer registers for an application. Templates are strings constructed from a set of tokens, text, and potentially some FBML. Templates groups are called *bundles*. Each bundle contains the following: a required template for a one line Feed story, an optional template for a short Feed story, and optionally, one or more templates for action links that will be appended to each story type. Here's an example of a one line story template:

```
{*actor*} sent {*target*} a compliment.
```

> **Note**
> Chapter 1, "Facebook Applications: The Basics," covered the basics of one line and short Feed stories. Later in this section, you are introduced to action links.

As the name implies, one line stories should get their point across in one line. They can contain only text and links. Short stories have both a title and a body, which allows them to provide a more information than one line stories. They can contain images, Flash, mp3, or video content. Short stories make up the core of the Facebook stream, and it's critical that you understand how to enable your applications to produce and publish them.

Tokens

Tokens are placeholders in templates that Facebook replaces with content before it publishes a story to the stream. All tokens must start and end with curly braces and asterisks. Facebook provides two standard tokens—`{*actor*}` and `{*target*}`—which it replaces with the user who published the story and the user to whom the story is targeted, respectively. Facebook actually replaces these tokens with a user's name hyperlinked to his Facebook profile. Facebook also reserves four tokens that it uses to render graphical and multimedia content in short Feed stories: `{*image*}`, `{*flash*}`, `{*mp3*}`, and `{*video*}`.

Developers can also provide their own custom tokens. For example, the Compliments application could provide a `{*compliment*}` token, which can be replaced with the content of the compliment a user publishes to a friend's Wall. If an application registers custom tokens in a template bundle, it also needs to provide the custom data that Facebook will use to replace them when a story is submitted.

For the Compliments application, we first use the Feed Template Console to register a template bundle that consists of a one line story, a short story, and an action link. Then, we modify the code to publish a short story to a friend's Wall with an image and an action link. Next, we demonstrate how to use the Facebook API to automatically publish a one line Feed story. Finally, we cover how to manage template bundles using the API.

Using the Feed Template Console

To create your first template, you use the Feed Template Console, which Chapter 4, "Platform Developer Tools," introduced. However, we suggest that, before you start using the Feed Template Console, you modify one of its features to make the template-creation process clear. The Feed Template Console is wonderful because it uses the templates and data you enter to show previews of how a Feed story based on them will appear when it's published to the stream.

As part of this process, Facebook replaces a template's `{*target*}` tokens with a list of names of five of your randomly chosen friends. There are three problems with this. First, the only way to target a single story to multiple users is through the Facebook API (which you are introduced to in the section, "Using the Facebook API"), not Feed forms. Therefore, the tool's behavior might lead you to believe that stories published to the stream might always target multiple users. This is definitely not true. Second, support for targeting multiple friends in a single story will very likely be removed in the near future. Finally, if the current user has less than five friends, Facebook simply ignores the `{*target*}` token, removing its content from all previews of the story with no explanation. This can easily be confusing.

We need to change the behavior of the Feed Template Console so that it replaces the `{*target*}` token with the name of a single friend, not a list of five. This requires skipping to the final page of the Feed Template Console's registration process to replace this list of friends chosen by Facebook with a single one. Open the Feed Template Console (*http://developer.facebook.com/tools.php?feed*). Choose the Compliments application from the drop-list, as shown in Figure 9.3.

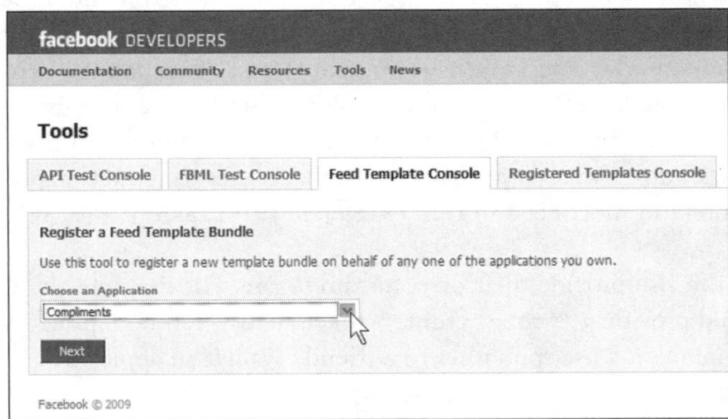

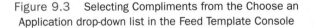

Figure 9.3 Selecting Compliments from the Choose an Application drop-down list in the Feed Template Console

To get to the final page of the Console to fix the `{*target*}` issue, click the Next button four times or until the Review and Register page appears. You're interested in the first text field, titled Sample Target IDs, as shown in Figure 9.4.

Delete all but one of the values in this list. Then, click the Back button three times or until the page titled Create a One Line Story template appears, which is discussed in the next section. Note that these steps do not need to be performed every time you register a new template, assuming you understand the behavior. But, for purposes of illustration, it would be confusing to someone new to the template-creation process to understand it.

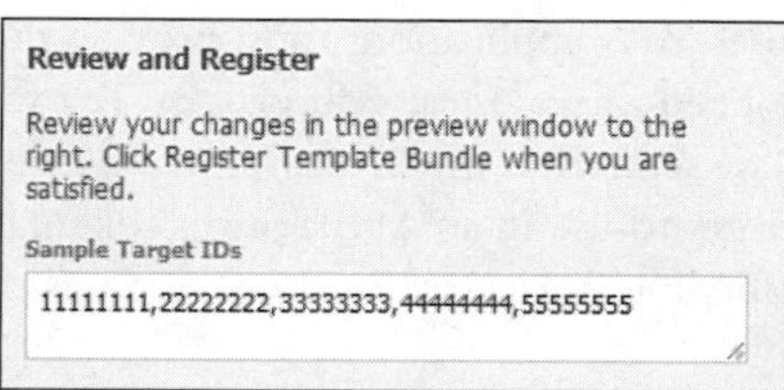

Review and Register
Review your changes in the preview window to the right. Click Register Template Bundle when you are satisfied.
Sample Target IDs
11111111,22222222,33333333,44444444,55555555

Figure 9.4 Facebook chooses five random friends' user IDs for the Feed Template Console.

One Line Story Templates

The Create a One Line Story template page allows developers to create one line story templates. As shown in Figure 9.5, the highlighted text field in the top left is prefilled with a sample one line story template containing

```
{*actor*} likes one line templates.
```

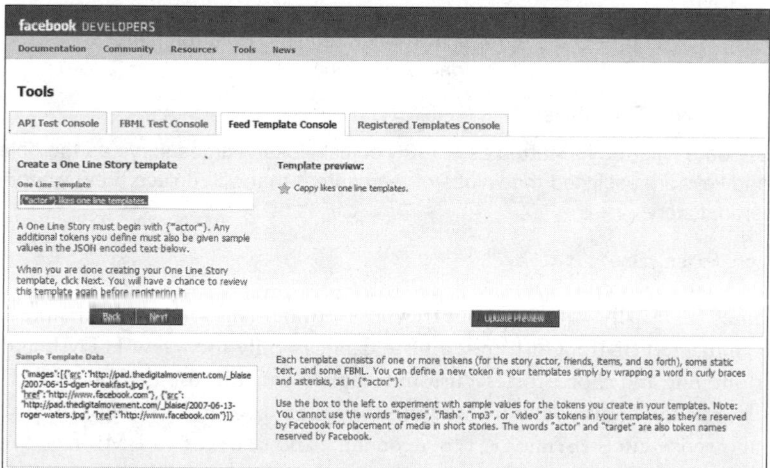

Figure 9.5 The Feed Template Console allows you to create one line Feed templates.

Directly to the right of this is the story preview area, which shows a preview of how a story will appear after it publishes to the stream. Replace the text in the One Line Template text field with

```
{*actor*} used {*app*} to tell {*target*} they are {*ctitle*} because {*ctext*}.
```

If you click the Update Preview button—which only appears after you edit the text in the One Line Template field—you receive an error dialog like the one shown in Figure 9.6. This error is generated because you need to actually provide the template in the Feed Console with the data it will use to replace your custom tokens. The data you provide in this tool is just for testing purposes. Your applications must provide the real data when Facebook requests it during the Feed form submission process. Test template data is entered in the Sample Template Data section in the lower-left hand side of the page. Facebook provides you with two images to use in an {*images*} token; however, these are not supported for inclusion in one line stories, so Facebook ignores them.

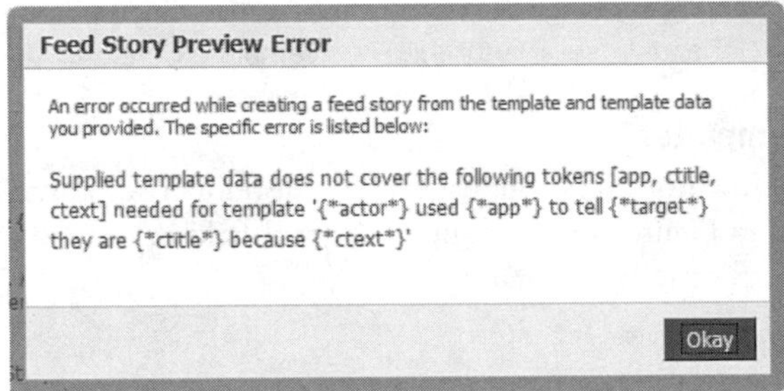

Figure 9.6 Error shown when required Feed template data is missing

JSON and Feed Templates

Template data must be formatted as a JSON object. Token names serve as the object's keys, and keys are assigned the values of the content that will replace them when rendered into the final story:

```
{"custom_token_name": value}
```

The values are usually static text, but they also can contain some HTML and Facebook Markup Language (FBML). Custom template data can only use a few HTML and FBML tags. Both one line and short stories' custom template data can use the <a> HTML tag, and short stories can additionally include the <small>, <br>, and <i> tags. Both story types are allowed to use <fb:name>, <fb:pronoun>, and <fb:ref> FBML tags. We've covered all these except the last one; however, Facebook is apparently deprecating its support for targeting multiple users with a single Feed story, and the <fb:if-multiple-actors> tag is used only in this context. For both custom tokens, you provide sample data that renders links back to the application's canvas page. It's good practice to place at least a few links in your stories to the page that allows users to authorize your application! In the Sample Template Data field, replace anything already there with the following JSON, or something similar, substituting your own valid values:

```
{
"app":"<a href='http://apps.facebook.com/<appname>/' >
   Compliments</a>",
"ctitle": "A Great Cook",
"ctext":"their tripe is the best!"
}
```

Creating and Editing Template Data

You might find it easier to generate template data in an external text editor and copy it into this field, because hand-coding JSON objects in this small text area can be difficult, especially when dealing with differences between single and double quotes. In fact, it's a best practice to keep a text file with both your templates and sample template data handy so you can easily copy and paste them into the Feed Template Console for testing without having to retype them. This also makes testing different messaging much easier.

Several free JSON editors are available online that make the process easier. Check out this book's companion website (*www.essentialfacebook.com*) for suggestions.

Click the Preview button, and a one line story should be rendered in the preview area on the right. Facebook automatically handles filling in the `{*actor*}` token with a link to your profile and the `{*target*}` token with the name of the friend whose ID you entered. Your story should look similar to what's shown in Figure 9.7.

Figure 9.7 The Feed Template Console displays a preview of one line Feed stories.

Short Story Templates

Facebook does not require an application to register a short story template; however, because one line stories are only sent to the Recent Activity section of users' Walls, as shown in Figure 9.8, their visibility in the social graph is somewhat limited. To reach as many users as possible, applications must be sure to get their Feed stories into the News Feed on the Home pages of the application user's friends, and the only way an application can do this is through publishing short stories.

To create a short story template, click Next in the Feed Template Console. The Create a Short Story template page appears. Notice that images show up in the preview area and that the story includes a profile picture of the sending user. Also, the story body is larger and contains multiple lines of text.

For the title, use the following template:

```
{*actor*} sent {*target*} a compliment with {*app*}!
```

For the template body, use this:

```
<br/>{*actor*} thinks {*target*} is {*ctitle*} because {*ctext*}
```

Now, add an image to your story. It's important to understand that you cannot add the `{*images*}` token to your sample data or template, because it is reserved by Facebook and handled specially. The `{*images*}` token is different from `{*actor*}` and `{*token*}` in that it is never used by template creators, only internally by Facebook. You just need to provide an *images* entry in your template data and, when your application submits the template data to Facebook, and it will automatically handle rendering of the images using the `{*images*}` token. Image data must be encoded in the template data as a JSON object with a key named `images` and a value that's an array of JSON objects, each of which contains a `src` and an `href` property. The `src` property must contain the absolute path to the image. The `href` property is the link where the viewer of the story should be taken if she clicks the image. Adding some sample template data with the images filled in makes it easier to understand:

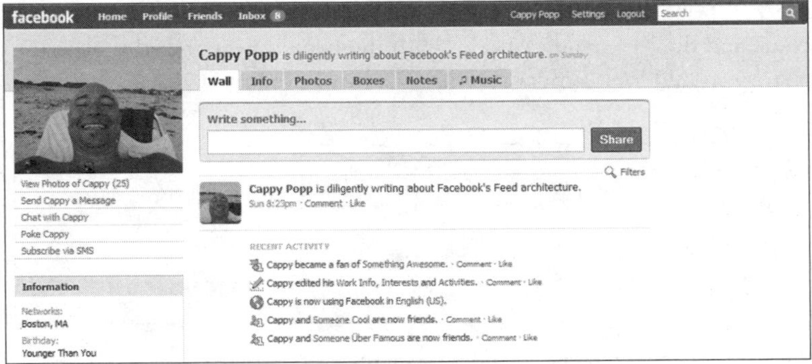

Figure 9.8 Here is the recent activity section on the author's Wall. All one line feed stories end up here.

```
{
"app":
"<a href='http://example.com/<appname>/'>Compliments</a>",
"ctitle": "A Great Cook",
"ctext":"their tripe is the best!",
"images":
}
```

Click Update Preview to verify the new template and data. You should see something similar to what's shown in Figure 9.9.

If you want to add multiple images to your template data, simply add more entries to the `images` array, which ensures that each object has a valid `src` and `href` property. For example:

```
"images":
```

Facebook allows a limited number of images to be included in an individual short story template, depending on their size. Facebook scales images to fit, but you need to create images that follow Facebook guidelines and aim to make them between 100 and 130 pixels wide and (at most) 100 pixels high. This ensures that they are clearly visible in the story and cuts down on the processing time the Facebook servers must use to scale them, if needed. Be aware that, the more images custom template data contains, the longer it takes Facebook to process and display the Feed form dialog to the user. Be mindful of the fact that it can be several long seconds before image-heavy Feed stories completely render, and your application's users might abandon it if the wait time is too long! Also, it's critical to note that Facebook forbids the use of any images hosted on Facebook, including users' profile pictures, in your short stories. Storing profile pictures is against the Facebook Terms of Service, so copying to and serving them from your own web server is not a legal option to circumvent this restriction.

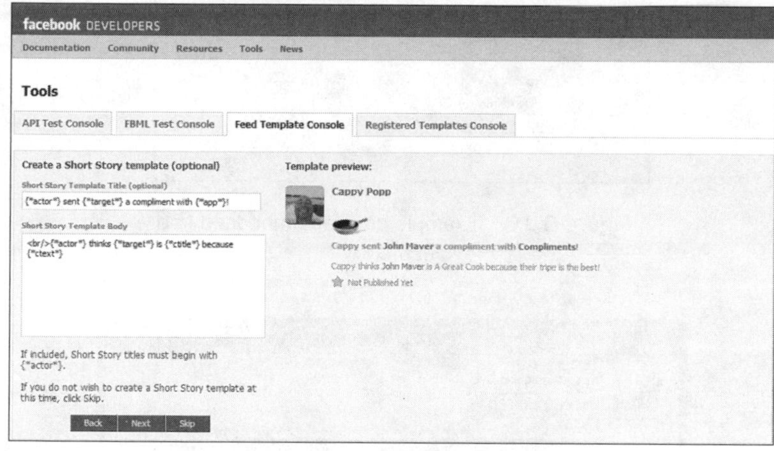

Figure 9.9 The Feed Template Console allows you to create and preview Feed short stories

Facebook also allows mp3 audio, Flash content, or videos to be included in short stories. As was the case with the `{*images*}` token, the `{*mp3*}`, `{*flash*}`, and `{*video*}` tokens are also not directly used. If an entry exists in the template data for more than one of the media types, Facebook will only use the data for one of them, in the following order of preference: Image data will always be used if present, followed by Flash, then mp3, and finally, video.

As an exercise, place a video in your Feed story template data to see how it works. To add video content, two pieces of information are required: the URL of the video and the absolute path to a preview image, which Facebook displays as a placeholder until the video Play button is clicked. The reason for the preview image is that Facebook does not allow videos (or Flash content) to play automatically when rendered in the stream or on users' profiles. Users must click the video content to actually play it. Note that the preview image does not have to be the same size as the video. Facebook expands the video to fit as best it can to fill the story body so the content can be viewed. To add a video, remove the `images` object from the sample template data and replace it with the following:

```
"video":{
"video_src":"http://www.youtube.com/watch?v=Izhh-JDigX4",
```

```
"preview_img":"http://s3.ytimg.com/vi/Izhh-JDigX4/default.jpg"
}
```

Click the Update Preview button. Rendered in a Feed form, it looks similar to what is shown in Figure 9.10 and Figure 9.11. Feel free to experiment with the other media types as you see fit.

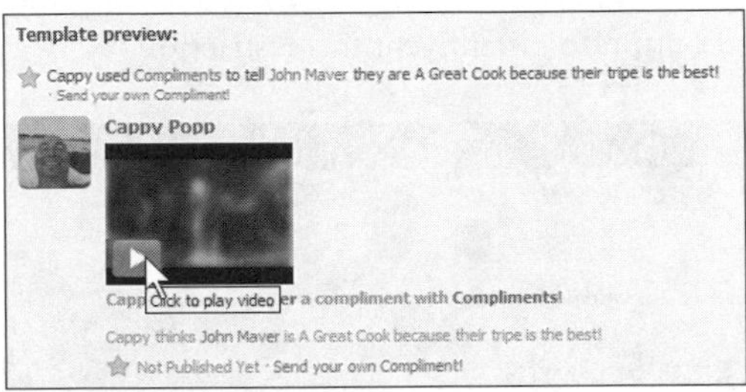

Figure 9.10 Example of video embedded in a Feed story

Figure 9.11 Clicking a video to play it within a story expands it to a viewable size.

Action Links

Next, you add an action link to your template. Action links are rendered as links at the end of the Feed story content, and they direct viewers to take some action as a direct result of reading the story. Click Next on the Feed Template Console page to see the Create an Action Link page. For the Action Link Text, enter something that starts with an action verb and entices viewers to use the Compliments application (for example, Submit Your Own Compliment!) For the URL, enter the application's URL on Facebook. Click the Update Preview button, and you see both the one line and short stories rendered with the new action links, as shown in Figure 9.12. You can only enter a single action link using the Feed Template Console. However, by using the API, you can enter more than one.

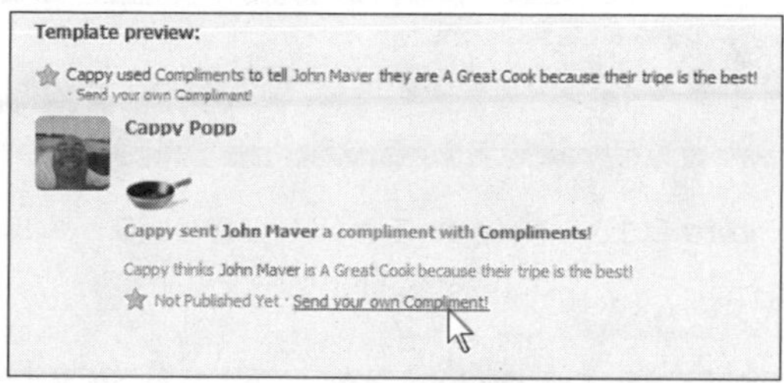

Figure 9.12 The Feed Template Console shows a preview of the placement of action links in your one line and short stories.

Registering Templates

Clicking Next on the Feed Template Console brings up the Review and Register page for your template. Notice the Sample General Body text area below the Sample Target IDs text box (discussed earlier). A short story template's general body text allows you to add more content to a Feed story. The content added here follows the rest of the text in the story, but before the action link; it is subject to the same content restrictions as the rest of the short story. You can enter a good deal of content here, but make sure that what you provide in your stories' content is relevant and interesting or viewers will not act on them—or worse, they might specifically hide or block them.

Click the Register Template Bundle button to register your template with Facebook. A popup like the one shown in Figure 9.13 appears. It's important to copy the Feed Template Bundle ID somewhere for safe keeping. Facebook needs this ID to replace the tokens in the template bundle with the custom data an application provides. If you misplace or forget it, you can always retrieve it by going to the Registered Templates Console. You should go there now to view your newly registered template bundle. Choose the application from the drop-down list; it should look similar to what's shown in Figure 9.14.

You can follow this process as many times as you like to create different stories. Facebook allows each application to register up to 100 templates, so you have plenty of room to create engaging content. Well-constructed Feed stories should describe a single event that happened between the target user and some specific action he performed in the context of the application that published the story. If possible, Feed stories should provide other media, such as images, audio, or video that reinforces the action explained in the story. When building them, avoid relative measures of time when describing actions (such as the following adverbs: just, recently, or frequently), because they have no meaning in the time context of the stream: You have no control over when target users will read or see them. Short stories must not duplicate information in their titles and bodies. One line stories should get their point across in a single line of text, if possible.

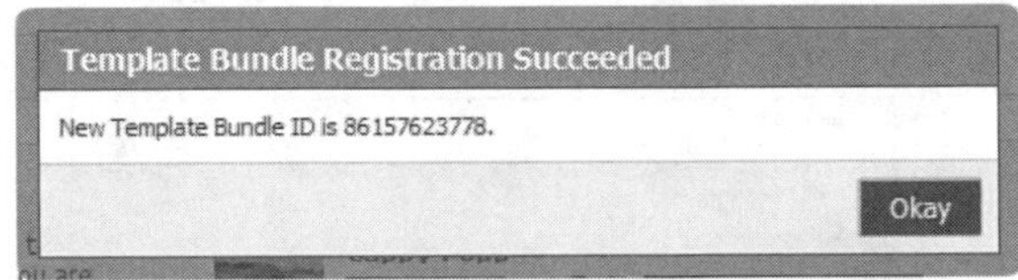

Figure 9.13 Note the Template Bundle ID. You'll need it shortly.

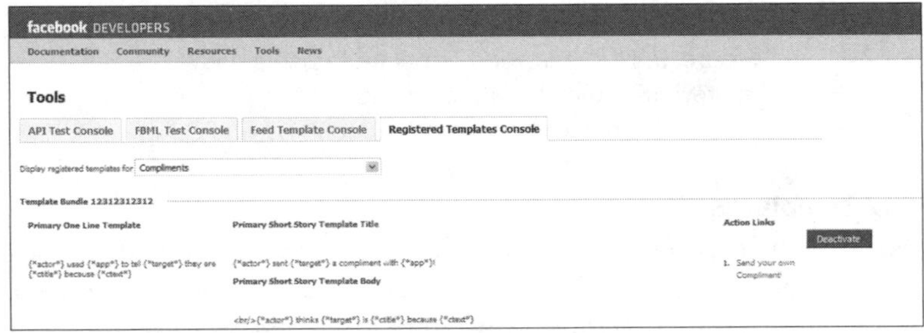

Figure 9.14 Use the Registered Templates Console to view your new template and get its ID, if needed.

Using Feed Forms to Publish to the Stream

Now that you saved your template and have its ID saved, you need to update the code in `feed_form_callback.php` to use it to publish a short story. Give it a meaningful name that describes what the template bundle is used for in your application. Open `globals.inc` and add to it the following line of code, replacing the following number with the ID you saved:

```
define('TEMPLATE_BUNDLE_MULTIFEEDSTORY', 12312312312);
```

Save `globals.inc`. Listing 9.3 shows the updated code for submitting the Feed story.

Listing 9.3 **`feed_form_callback.php`: Handling Submission of a MultiFeedStory Feed Form**

```
<?php
require_once 'inc/globals.inc';
require_once 'inc/utils.inc';
require_once 'inc/db.inc';
```

Listing 9.3 **Continued**

```
require_once 'inc/profile.inc';

dumpRequestVars(true, basename(__FILE__));

if (isset($_POST['friend_selector_id']) && isset($_POST['method']) &&
    isset($_POST['compliment']) && isset($_POST['category'])) {
  $target       = $_POST['friend_selector_id'];
  $feedFormType = $_POST['method'];
  $compliment   = $_POST['compliment'];
  $category     = $_POST['category'];

  $facebook = new Facebook(FB_API_KEY, FB_APP_SECRET);
  $db       = new DB();
  $sender   = $facebook->user;
  $db->addCompliment($sender, $target, $category, $compliment);
  updateProfileBox($sender);
  updateInfoSection( $facebook->user );
  // start filling in our template
  $categoryInfo  = $g_categories[$category];
  $imageSrc      = LOCAL_APP_URL.'/img/'.$ categoryInfo  ['bigimg'];
  $imageLink     = LOCAL_APP_URL;
  $images        = array('src'=> $imageSrc, 'href'=> $imageLink);
  $feed = array('template_id'   => TEMPLATE_BUNDLE_MULTIFEEDSTORY,
                'template_data' =>
                  array('app'   => '<a href="'.FB_APP_URL.'">Compliments</a>',
                                   'ctitle' => $ categoryInfo  ['title'],
                                   [illegible],
                                   'images' => array($images)));
  $queryString = "ffh=1&tgt=$target&cat=$category&cpl=".urlencode($compliment);
  $data = array('method'   => $feedFormType,
                'content' => array('feed' => $feed,
                                   'next' => FB_APP_URL."?$queryString"));
} else {
  $data = array('errorCode'    => FACEBOOK_API_VALIDATION_ERROR,
                'errorTitle'   => 'Sending the compliment failed!',
                'errorMessage'=> 'Please fill the form out correctly.');
}
// send the data to Facebook
echo json_encode($data);
?>
```

Using multiFeedStory to Publish to the Wall

The process of publishing a Feed story from a Feed form is comprised of multiple steps. First, the user submits the form from your application. Facebook intercepts the submission after recognizing the form data is coming from a multiFeedStory form. It then passes the form data to the URL provided in the form's action attribute. The code at this endpoint then must print a JSON-encoded object containing the template bundle ID and all custom data needed to render the Feed story. Facebook waits for the output and uses it to build the actual Feed story.

Because Facebook accepts only valid JSON as the output from this endpoint, it is important that your code not print anything else (like debug messages), or you receive an error like the one that was shown back in Figure 9.2. This also means that you cannot turn on Facebook's debug messages on this page, either!

With those steps in mind, refer to Listing 9.3. The real work begins after the call to `updateInfoSection()`. Creation of the custom data begins with the following code:

```
$feed = array('template_id'   => TEMPLATE_BUNDLE_MULTIFEEDSTORY,
              'template_data' =>
                  array('app'    => '<a href="'z.FB_APP_URL.'">Compliments</a>',
                        'ctitle' => $categoryInfo['title'],
                        'ctext'  => $compliment,
                        'images' => array($images)));
```

Notice that the code creates an associative array that contains two keys:

- **`template_id`.** Set to the template bundle ID
- **`template_data`.** Contains an array of the custom template data that is supplied to Facebook

The names of these two keys cannot be changed. Furthermore, the names of the keys in the `template_data` array must match the names of the custom tokens you placed in your template bundle. Here's the template for one line stories:

```
{*actor*} used {*app*} to tell {*target*} they are {*ctitle*} because {*ctext*}
```

You can see that `{*actor*}` and `{*target*}` are not keys in the `template_data` array, as expected. Remember that Facebook automatically replaces `{*actor*}` with the user publishing the story and `{*target*}` with the user chosen in the `<fb:friend-selector>` control on the form. But, the keys `app`, `ctitle`, and `ctext` are all present, as is the `images` token name, even though you did not directly use it while creating the template bundle.

The code then builds a query string:

```
$queryString = "ffh=1&tgt=$target&cat=$category&cpl=".urlencode($compliment);
```

This string has two purposes. Remember, at the beginning of this chapter, when we mentioned that Facebook required three things to publish a feed story? The first was a registered template bundle; second, the data to fill it; and finally, a URL to redirect to after publishing completes. This string will carry some information to that redirect for further processing.

Finally, the code constructs the final template bundle package:

```
$data = array('method'  => $feedFormType,// multiFeedStory
```

```
                'content' => array('feed' => $feed,
                                   'next' => FB_APP_URL."?$queryString"));
```

This associative array contains two keys. The first, `method`, tells Facebook which type of Feed story the data should be used to create. The second, `content`, contains an associative array with two members. The `feed` key contains the entire template data payload. The `next` key is set to the redirection URL. You could use `next_fbjs` in place of the `next` key and provide, as its value, arbitrary FBJS to execute when publishing completes.

To complete the process, the array is JSON-encoded and printed:

```
// send the data to Facebook
echo json_encode($data);
```

The JSON itself that your application sends back should look similar to what's shown in Listing 9.4. The values vary, but the keys—other than the ones representing your own custom tokens—should not. Listing 9.4 shows a complete JSON object that Facebook can use to generate a multiFeedStory.

Listing 9.4 **Sample JSON Sent to Facebook to Render a multiFeedStory**

```
{
   "method":"multiFeedStory",
   "content":{
      "feed":{
         "template_id":123456789,
         "template_data":{
            "app":"<a
href=\"http:\/\/apps.facebook.com\/<appname>\">Compliments<\/a>",
            "ctitle":"A Great Cook",
            "ctext":"his tripe is the best!",
            "images":[
               {
                  "src":"http:\/\/example.com\/<appname>\/img\/pan_48.png",
                  "href":"http:\/\/apps.facebook.com\/<appname>/"
               }
            ]
         }
      },
"next":"http:\/\/apps.facebook.com\/<appname>?ffh=1&tgt=698700806&cat=cook&cpl=
his+tripe+is+the+best%21"
   }
}
```

Now, when you submit the form, you see something like the dialog shown in Figure 9.15. You can add a comment to the text field and choose to Publish the story, at which point Facebook publishes it on the target friend's Wall. Notice that the action links are not rendered in this preview. Facebook automatically adds these, and some other links, to the story when it's published. Figure 9.16 shows the final story published to the target friend's Wall. As Figure 9.17 shows, Facebook also publishes a one line story to the Recent Activity section of your Wall.

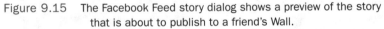

Figure 9.15 The Facebook Feed story dialog shows a preview of the story that is about to publish to a friend's Wall.

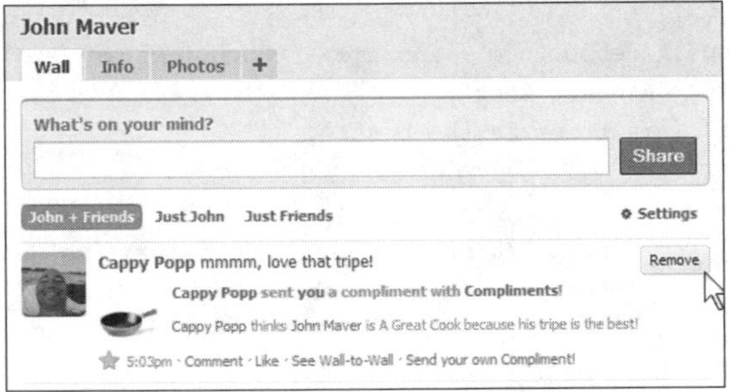

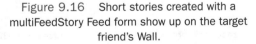

Figure 9.16 Short stories created with a multiFeedStory Feed form show up on the target friend's Wall.

Using feedStory to Publish to the News Feed

In the last few pages, you have successfully created a multiFeedStory Feed form and had it publish a short story to a friend's Wall and a one line story to your Wall. But, something is obvious. When published, it doesn't show up in the News Feed on your friends' Home pages, and this limits its exposure to a smaller audience. How can you get a Feed story published to the stream and have it show up in the News Feed?

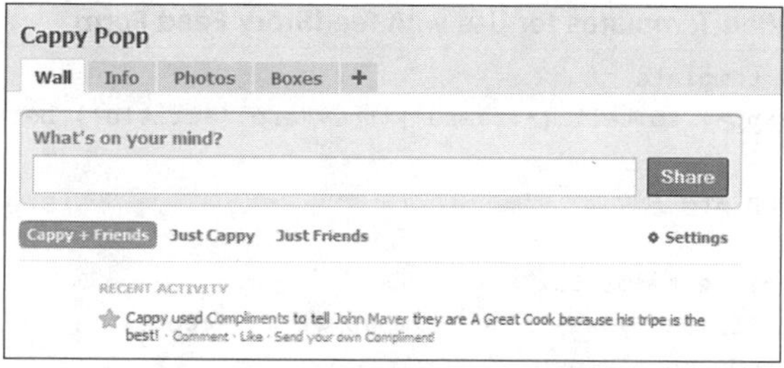

Figure 9.17 A one line story is also published to the user who submits the story.

Enter the feedStory form. As you recall, it allows an application to publish stories to the Wall of the publisher and their friends' News Feeds. Let's get started on providing this functionality to your application.

First, you need to create a new template and register it with Facebook because stories created with feedStory forms do not use the `{*target*}` token. To compensate, you need to provide something similar to take its place, or it will be replaced with an empty string in your stories. Let's test this to understand the behavior. Edit your `index.php` file and replace the `multiFeedStory` value of the form's `fbtype` attribute with the value `feedStory`. Save the file and visit the canvas page in the browser. When the form is submitted, you should see a feed story submission dialog like that in Figure 9.18. Notice that Facebook leaves the target's name (where it replaced the `{*target*}` token in the template) blank in the final story.

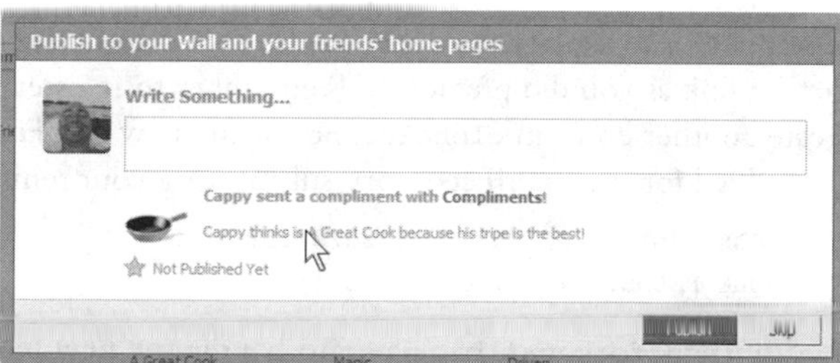

Figure 9.18 Notice how Facebook leaves the space blank where the `{*target*}` token existed for feedStory form stories (where the cursor is pointing).

To rectify this behavior, add a new template. You use the same templates from your previous effort; however, remove the `{*target*}` tokens and replace them with a couple of custom tokens, which you will replace with an `<fb:name>` FBML tag in the template data, as shown in Listing 9.5.

Listing 9.5 **Modified Templates for Use with feedStory Feed Form**

```
/* One line story template */
{*actor*} used {*app*} to tell {*friend*} they are {*ctitle*} because {*ctext*}

/* Short story template */

  // Short story title template
  {*actor*} sent {*friend_you*} a compliment with {*app*}!
  // Short story body template
 <br/>{*actor*} thinks {*friend*} is {*ctitle*} because {*ctext*}

/* Sample Template Data */
{
  "app":"<a href='http://example.com/<appname>'>Compliments</a>",
  "friend_you": "<fb:name uid='xxxxxxxx' useyou='true' />",
  "friend": "<fb:name uid='xxxxxxxx' />",
  "ctitle": "A Great Cook",
  "ctext":"their tripe is the best!",
  "images":
}
```

Remember that feed stories of either type can use the `<fb:name>` FBML tag. You use two versions of it in Listing 9.5. First, you use the `useyou` attribute on the `{*friend_you*}` token. The default behavior of this FBML tag renders the pronoun "you" instead of "User Name" if the person viewing the page is the currently logged-in user. For the `{*friend*}` token, you use the `<fb:name>` tag with its `useyou` attribute set to `false`, which renders the full name of the user, no matter who views the page. Refer to Listing 9.5, and remember to replace the Facebook user IDs and URLs with your own.

Use the same action link as you did previously. Remember to register your template and save its ID. Create another entry in `globals.inc` for the new feedForm template bundle after the one added for the multiFeedStory, substituting your template bundle's ID:

```
define('TEMPLATE_BUNDLE_MULTIFEEDSTORY', 74225284158);
define('TEMPLATE_BUNDLE_FEEDSTORY', 74225289158);
```

You need to modify `feed_form_callback.php` to handle the new feedForm data. Replace the code that builds the custom template data with the code shown in Listing 9.6.

Listing 9.6 **`feed_form_callback.php`: Modified to Handle Both feedStory and multiFeedStory Feed Forms**

```
// start filling in our template
  $categoryInfo  = $g_categories[$category];
  $imageSrc      = LOCAL_APP_URL.'/img/'.$categoryInfo['bigimg'];
  $imageLink     = LOCAL_APP_URL;
  $images        = array('src'=> $imageSrc, 'href'=> $imageLink);
```

Listing 9.6 **Continued**

```
  if( 'multiFeedStory' === $feedFormType ) {
  $feed = array('template_id'    => TEMPLATE_BUNDLE_MULTIFEEDSTORY,
                'template_data' =>
                  array('app'    => '<a href="'.FB_APP_URL.'">Compliments</a>',
                                    'ctitle' => $categoryInfo['title'],
                                    'ctext'  => $compliment,
                                    'images' => array($images)));
  } else {
  $feed = array('template_id'    => TEMPLATE_BUNDLE_FEEDSTORY,
                'template_data' =>
                  array('app'    =>
                              '<a href="'.FB_APP_URL.'">Compliments</a>',
                              'friend_you' => "<fb:name uid='$target'
➥useyou='true' />",
                              'friend' => "<fb:name uid='$target' />",
                              'ctitle' => $categoryInfo['title'],
                              'ctext'  => $compliment,
                              'images' => array($images)));
  }
```

Save the code and fill and submit the form. If you do not receive any errors, you see a short story published to your Wall, like that in Figure 9.19, and a short story published to your developer (or test user account) friend's Home page News Feed, as shown in Figure 9.20. Note that the cursor in each figure points to the data that replaced the `{*friend_you*}` token. When John views his News Feed, he sees "you" instead of his name in the title of the short story. When Cappy views his Wall, he sees John's full name.

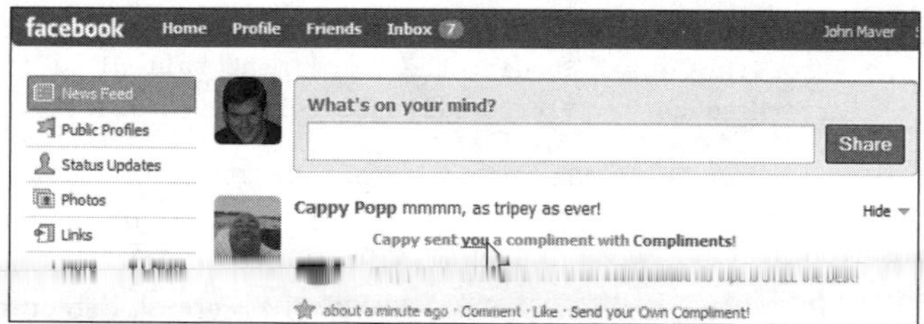

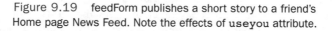

Figure 9.19 feedForm publishes a short story to a friend's Home page News Feed. Note the effects of `useyou` attribute.

To make it easier to test both types of Feed forms, it makes sense to change the code so that you can test either style at will. We'll add a request variable to the URL for the application that allows you to select which type of Feed form to use. Add the following code to `renderPage()` in `index.php`, replacing the original form tag:

```
$feedFormType = isset($_GET['feedform']) ? $_GET['feedform'] : 'multiFeedStory';
  // Show the compliment form
```

Figure 9.20 feedForm publishes a short story to the publisher's Wall. Note that the useyou attribute has no effect in this case.

```
$pageOutput .= "
  <div class='panel'>
    <form method='POST' fbtype='$feedFormType' id='complimentform'
      action='".LOCAL_APP_URL."/feed_form_callback.php' >
```

Now, if you append `?feedform=feedStory` to the application URL typed in the address bar, the form submits via a feedStory form or uses the multiFeedStory form by default.

Handling Feed Form Publication Errors

Finally, you need to understand how to tell if a story was published and what happens in case there's an error. We discuss the error condition first. Look at the ending else clause from `feed_form_callback.php` once more (refer to Listing 9.3):

```
$data = array('errorCode'    => FACEBOOK_API_VALIDATION_ERROR,
              'errorTitle'   => 'Sending the Compliment failed!',
              'errorMessage'=> 'Please fill the form out correctly.');
```

Remember that, as a user, you never see any output onscreen from the `feed_form_callback.php` script. So, what do you do if you encounter an error condition and want to alert the user? Facebook allows you to pass a JSON-encoded object that contains an error code, message title, and message body. If Facebook detects this object in your script's output, it uses it to populate and show an error dialog, like the one shown in Figure 9.21. Realize that you can have several error codes and messages depending on the logic in your script. Notice that the code only does extremely rudimentary validation of the submitted form data to make the code easy to understand; therefore, only one example is provided. A production application would undoubtedly have several to cover different error conditions. But, beware: Facebook currently supports only the value 1 for the `errorCode` value, although this is not clear from any of the Facebook documentation. If you want to use a different error code, be sure to include it in the `errorTitle` or `errorMessage` values in the array, or you get an unhelpful error saying, "Missing or invalid 'feed' parameter," not your custom error message. Luckily, the `FacebookRestClient` class provides the `FACEBOOK_API_VALIDATION_ERROR` constant. Use it all the time for the `errorCode` value, and you won't have the problem.

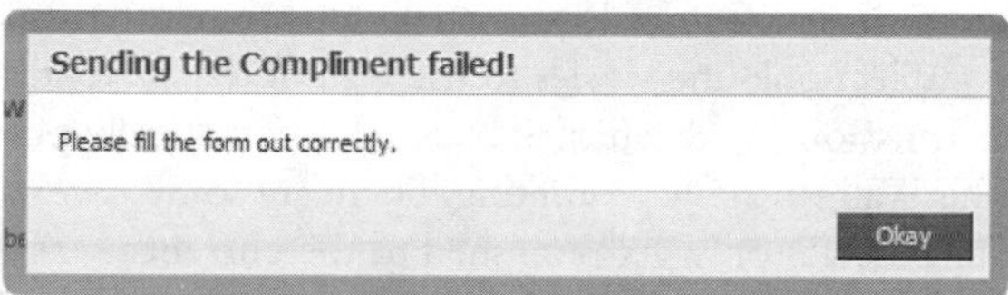

Figure 9.21 Facebook uses the error data sent to it by your code to populate this dialog.

Handling errors in this manner might seem one-sided. Production code would undoubtedly have some client-side validation, probably written in JavaScript, to check the form's data before allowing the submission. So, why use this method to display an error to the user? Because Facebook intercepts the form submission before your code ever gets the chance. This means that client-side code cannot handle the form's `onsubmit` event to execute client-side JavaScript validation. It also means that you cannot dynamically change the form's `fbtype` attribute to different Feed form values, which is why we used the request string variable. The only place to do Feed form data validation is on the server, after Facebook sends the posted data back to the URL given in the original form's action attribute.

One final, and important, note about the Feed submission process bears mention. Your code is not notified if the user cancels the story submission (either by clicking the Skip button or hitting the ESC key when the submission dialog is onscreen.) Unfortunately, there is also no way for your code to determine whether a user published a story. Facebook made a conscious decision to disallow this to cut down on applications incenting or forcing users to publish content and limit the possibility of application spamming or abuse. The only thing you can know is that the dialog is no longer visible when the action that you set in the value of your `next` or `next_fbjs` key occurs. Either you are redirected to the URL you set for the value of the `next` key or the arbitrary FBJS you set for the `next_fbjs` key executes.

Using the Facebook API

In previous sections, you created Feed templates and both types of Feed forms and used them to publish both one line and short stories to the stream on both users' Walls and News Feeds. But, there was a small catch with Feed forms. Application users had to manually allow stories to be published to the stream on their behalf. If they decided to skip the publishing step, your application did not publish any Feed stories whatsoever, which severely limits its potential for growth in the social graph.

Using the API to Publish to the Stream

One way to mitigate this restriction, at least partially, is through the Facebook API. It allows applications to publish one line stories to the Wall of the currently logged-in user without requiring permission (by default). Stories are automatically posted to the Recent Activity section on his Wall, without prompting. There are some caveats to understand, however. First, one line stories only get published to the current user's Wall, so the user's friends never see them in their News Feed. They only see them when they visit the current user's profile. Next, an application can send only a specific number of one line stories through this API per user, per day. We cover this allocation scheme in Chapter 10, "Publisher, Notifications, and Requests." Finally, only one line stories can be published by default—never short stories.

Using the API to Automatically Publish One Line Feed Stories

Applications can use the API method called feed.publishUserAction() to publish to the stream (It's called `feed_publishUserAction()` in the PHP Library.) Table 9.2 shows its prototype.

Table 9.2 **`feed_publishUserAction()`** Parameters

Parameters (In Order)		
Name	**Type**	**Description**
`template_bundle_id`	int	The template bundle ID. **Required.**
`template_data`	object	JSON-encoded object containing template data. **Required.**
`target_ids`	string	Comma-separated list of Facebook user IDs to replace the `{*target*}` token if present in the template.
`body_general`	string	Contains extra markup for the body of a short story (only). Can be directly generated by an application.
`story_size`	int	Size of the story to publish: can be either 1 for oneline stories (the default) or 2 for short stories. Use the constants from the Facebook PHP Client Library: `FacebookRestClient::STORY_SIZE_ONE_LINE` or `FacebookRestClient::STORY_SIZE_SHORT`.

Table 9.2 **Continued**

`user_message`	string	Content created by the user that's submitted with short stories as a comment. Facebook's Terms of Service require that this code be user generated.

You are probably already familiar with many of the parameters this API call takes, except for the `target_ids` and `user_message` parameters. The `target_ids` parameter is important because it makes the `feed.publishUserAction()` API call unique. It provides the only means in the Facebook Platform for applications to publish stories to multiple targets at once. The `user_message` parameter is only used when the API publishes short stories to the stream.

To automatically publish one line stories, you need to update your code to call `feed_publishUserAction()`. You could use one of your existing template bundle IDs for the one required by the API, because both included a one line story. However, because both Feed form types already publish something to the actor's Wall, it would be redundant to publish the same one line story twice when a multiFeedStory form was published. Let's create a new template that provides the number of compliments sent to a given target user.

To get this number, you have to add another method to the `DB` class. We also append a suffix to the number to make it an adjective for use in the story (1 becomes "1st," 3 becomes "3rd," and so on.) Add the code in Listing 9.7 into the `DB` class in `db.inc`.

Listing 9.7 **`db.inc`: Adding the `getComplimentCountForUser()` Function**

```
function getComplimentCountForUser($appUserID) {
    $appUserID = $this->real_escape_string($appUserID);
    $query = "SELECT COUNT(*) FROM compliments WHERE targetID = $ appUserID ";
    $result = $this->_execQuery($query);
    $row = $result->fetch_array(MYSQLI_NUM);
    return isset($row[0])? $row[0] : 0;
  }
```

This method returns the number of compliments for a given target (represented by a Facebook user ID). Now, add the code in Listing 9.8 into `utils.inc` to handle formatting this number as an adjective.

Listing 9.8 **`utils.inc`: `getAdjectiveSuffixForNumber()` Function**

```
function getAdjectiveSuffixForNumber($number) {
  if( $number == 0 ) {
    return '';
  }
  $suffixes = array('st', 'nd', 'rd');
  $mod = $number % 100;
  $ext = 'th';
```

Listing 9.8 **Continued**

```
  if( $mod > 13 || $mod < 11 ) {
    $mod %= 10;
    if($mod != 0 && $mod < 4) {
      $ext = $suffixes[$mod - 1];
    }
  }
  return $ext;
}
```

Finally, add the code to call the `feed_publishUserAction()` PHP Library method. Add the code from Listing 9.9 to the `feed_form_callback.php` file right after the code that sets up the Feed form template data. You also need a new Feed template bundle registered for your new one line stories. This is referred to as **`TEMPLATE_BUNDLE_ONELINE_1`** in Listing 9.9. Don't rush to the Feed Template Console to register it, however. We will register it in a different way than we have in previous templates. It's shown here for reference so the following code makes sense:

```
'{*actor*} just sent {*target*} {*pronoun*} {*count*} {*app*}!'
```

Listing 9.9 **`feed_form_callback.php`: Calling the `feed_publishUserAction()` PHP Library Method**

```
// top of file elided for clarity...
$queryString = "ffh=1&tgt=$target&cat=$category&cpl=".urlencode($compliment);
  $data = array('method'  => $feedFormType,
                'content' => array('feed' => $feed,
                                   'next' => FB_APP_URL."?$queryString"));
// new code follows this point...
  $complimentCount = $db->getComplimentCountForUser($target);
  $onelinedata = array( 'pronoun' => "<fb:pronoun uid='$target'
possessive='true'/>",
                        'count'   => "$complimentCount" .
                          getAdjectiveSuffixForNumber($complimentCount),
                        'app'     => "<a href='".FB_APP_URL."'>Compliment</a>  ");
  $body_general = '';
  $user_message = '';
  try {
    $facebook->api_client->feed_publishUserAction(TEMPLATE_BUNDLE_ONELINE_1,
                                                  $onelinedata,
                                                  array($target),
                                                  $body_general,

FacebookRestClient::STORY_SIZE_ONE_LINE,
                                                  $user_message);
  } catch(FacebookRestClientException $ex) {
    $data = array('errorCode'   => FACEBOOK_API_VALIDATION_ERROR,
```

Listing 9.9 **Continued**

```
                'errorTitle'   => 'One line feed story failed!',
                'errorMessage'=> 'Code '. $ex->getCode(). ': '.$ex->getMessage());
}
```

Listing 9.9 calls `feed_publishUserAction()` with a template bundle ID, the array of template data, an array of Facebook user IDs, an empty string for both the `body_general` and `user_message` parameters (which are ignored for one line stories anyway), and a constant to indicate the size of the stories to publish by default. `{*actor*}` is replaced automatically as before. `{*target*}`, however, is not automatically replaced; you need to provide the value for it in the `target_ids` parameter. Notice that the code also handles any Facebook exceptions that might be raised and uses them to fill in the data structure we'll echo back to Facebook to display an error dialog. Because we can't use the exception's code as the `errorCode`, we instead encode it in the `errorMessage` value.

A common question is, "How can an application user keep my application from sending messages on their behalf?" The answer lies in the application's user settings, shown in Figure 9.22. From the Compliments canvas page, hover the mouse cursor over the Settings link in the top Facebook menu bar. Click Compliments Settings, and a dialog titled Edit Compliments Settings appears onscreen. Click the Additional Permissions tab in this dialog, and you see a checkbox—checked by default—with the label Publish Recent Activity (One Line Stories) to My Wall.

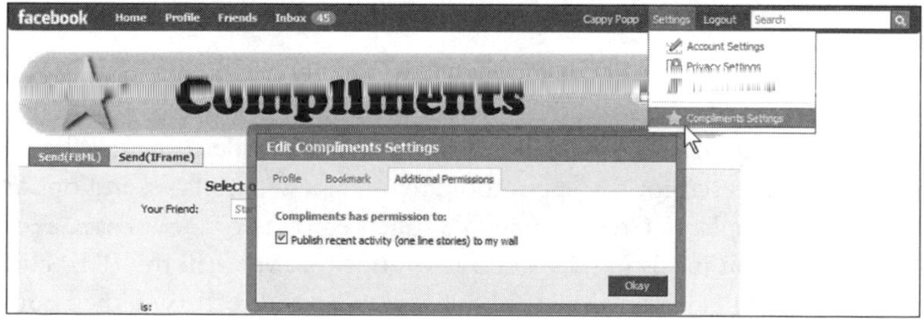

Figure 9.22 Unchecking this checkbox keeps `feed_publishUserAction()` from automatically publishing any stories to your Wall.

Try it out. Uncheck the box and try sending a friend a compliment. You get an error similar to the one shown in Figure 9.23. Facebook actually throws a `FacebookRestClientException` with a code of 200 (permissions error). But, as you recall from your code in `feed_form_callback.php` in Listing 9.9, you handle the exception and package it into the JSON-encoded data structure that Facebook uses to show the error dialog.

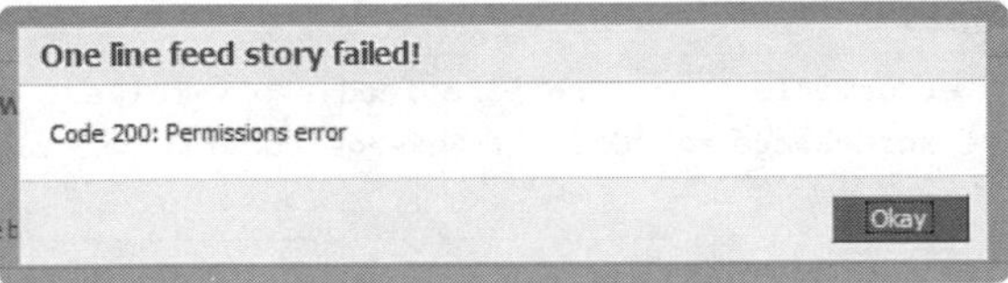
One line feed story failed!
Code 200: Permissions error
Okay

Figure 9.23 Facebook returns a permission error when attempting to automatically publish a one line story to the profile of a user who has explicitly disabled this feature in the settings for the application.

Using the API to Manage Template Bundles

Another feature offered by the Facebook API is the capability to register template bundles without using the Feed Template Console. This can be a great timesaver if you are experienced in creation and registration of templates and find the Console tedious. Also, the API provides one other feature that the Console does not: the capability to register multiple action links for a single template bundle.

Let's introduce some API methods that let you manage your template bundles via code. The Facebook API currently provides four methods for doing so:

- `feed.registerTemplateBundle()`
- `feed.getRegisteredTemplateBundles()`
- `feed.getRegisteredTemplateBundleByID()`
- `feed.deactivateTemplateBundleByID()`

Instead of delving into each of these in detail, let's write some code that uses them to manage your templates. We also add the new template we introduced, but did not register, for the `feed_publishUserAction()` call in Listing 9.9. The code shows all the templates that are currently registered for the application, register new templates, and optionally, unregister all existing templates. Create a new file called `register_feed_templates.php` and add the code shown in Listing 9.10 into it. Notice that you call the PHP client library versions of the APIs in the previous list. Create a new directory named `config` and save the script there as `register_feed_templates.php`. It is a good idea to secure the `config` directory because you do not want someone to arbitrarily execute this script.

Listing 9.10 **`register_feed_templates.php`: Managing Feed Templates with the Facebook PHP Library**

```
<?php

require_once './../inc/globals.inc';
require_once './../inc/utils.inc';

$facebook = new Facebook(FB_API_KEY, FB_APP_SECRET);
$fbapi    = $facebook->api_client;
```

Listing 9.10 **Continued**

```
$pageOutput = "
<!DOCTYPE html PUBLIC '-//W3C//DTD XHTML 1.0 Strict//EN'
    'http://www.w3.org/TR/xhtml1/DTD/xhtml1-strict.dtd'>
  <html xmlns='http://www.w3.org/1999/xhtml'
xmlns:fb='http://www.facebook.com/2008/fbml'>
  <head>
   <title>Compliments: Register Facebook Feed Templates</title>
   <style>
    h2 {padding:7px;background:#ddffbb;border:1px solid #558833;width:40%;}
    .define {padding:15px;background:#ffeebb;border:1px solid #ba0000;width:30%;
      font:14px monospace;}
    .error {padding:7px;background:red; border:1px solid black; width:40%;}
    .template{margin:1px;background:#efefff; width:40%; border:1px solid #aaaaaa;}
   </style>
  </head>
  <body>
  ";
try {
  $registeredTemplates = $fbapi->feed_getRegisteredTemplateBundles();
  if( displayRegisteredTemplates($registeredTemplates, $pageOutput) ) {
    unregisterExistingTemplates($registeredTemplates, $pageOutput);
  }
  $templateData = registerNewTemplates($pageOutput);

  if($templateData) {
    $pageOutput .= "<div>
        [illegible]
        <h3>Copy the following line(s) to globals.inc:</h3>";
    foreach($templateData as $template) {
      $pageOutput .= "
        <div class='define'>
          define('TEMPLATE_BUNDLE_{$template['name']}', {$template['bundleID']});
        </div>";
    }
    $pageOutput .= "
        <p>Be sure to remove any template definitions that were removed!</p>
        </div>";
  }
} catch (FacebookRestClientException $fbex) {
  echo '<div class="error">'
    .'Facebook error while registering templates: <br /><tt>'
    .$fbex->getMessage().'</tt></div>';
} catch( Exception $e) {
  echo '<div class="error">'
    .'Exception: <br /><tt>'
    .$fbex->getMessage().'</tt></div>';
```

Listing 9.10 **Continued**

```
}
$pageOutput .= "
    </body>
  </html>";

echo($pageOutput);
/**
* Prints formatted contents of all currently-registered Feed Templates for
* current application
*
* @param array $registeredTemplates feed templates
* @param string $output (ref) page markup
*/
function displayRegisteredTemplates($registeredTemplates, &$output) {

  if(isset($registeredTemplates[0])) {
    $output .= "<h2>Currently Registered Feed Templates</h2><br/>";
    foreach($registeredTemplates as $registeredTemplate) {
      $output .= "<div class='template'>
                    <pre>".var_export($registeredTemplate, TRUE). "</pre>
                  </div>";
    }
    return true;
  } else {
    $output .= "<h2>No Feed Templates Registered.</h2>";
  }
  return false;
}
/**
* Unregisters all existing Facebook Feed Template Bundles for the application
*
* @param array $registeredTemplates feed templates
* @param string $output (ref) markup for page
*/
function unregisterExistingTemplates($registeredTemplates, &$output) {
  global $fbapi;
  if(isset($_GET['u']) && '1' === $_GET['u']) {
   $output .= "<h2>Unregistering Existing Templates</h2>";
    for($i = 0, $len = count($registeredTemplates); $i < $len; ++$i) {
      $bundleID = $registeredTemplates[$i]['template_bundle_id'];
      $result   = $fbapi->feed_deactivateTemplateBundleByID($bundleID);
      $output  .= "<h3>Unregistering Template Bundle ID: $bundleID. Result: ".
        ($result == 1 ? "SUCCESS" : "FAIL")."</h3>";
    }
  }
}
```

Listing 9.10 **Continued**

```
/**
* registers a new Facebook Feed Template Bundle
*
* @param string $output (ref) markup for page
*/
function registerNewTemplates(&$output) {
  global $fbapi;
  $bundles = buildTemplateBundles();
  $templateData = array();
  foreach($bundles as $template) {
    $result = $fbapi->feed_registerTemplateBundle( $template['oneline'],
                                                   $template['short'],
                                                   null, // deprecated
                                                   $template['actionlinks'] );
    // if length of return is <= 4 it's an error code
    // see http://wiki.developers.facebook.com/index.php/Error_codes
    if(strlen(strval($result)) > 4) {
        $templateData[] = array('name'     => $template['name'],
                                'bundleID' => $result ) ;
    } else {
      $output .= "<div class='error'>
                    Error registering template bundle {$template['name']}.
Code: $result
                 </div";
    }
  }
  return $templateData;
}
function buildTemplateBundles() {
  $bundles = array(
    array(
      // used in multiFeedStory form submission
      'name'    => 'MULTIFEEDSTORY_1', // name we'll append to the constant
➥ definition
      'oneline' => array(
        '{*actor*} used {*app*} to tell {*target*} they are {*ctitle*} because
          {*ctext*}'
      ),
      'short'=> array (
        array(
          'template_title' => '{*actor*} sent {*target*} a compliment with
➥{*app*}!',
          'template_body' => '<br/>{*actor*} thinks {*target*} is {*ctitle*} because
            {*ctext*}'
        )
      ),
```

Listing 9.10 **Continued**

```
      'actionlinks' => array(
        array("text" => "Send your own Compliment!",
              "href" => FB_APP_URL
        )
      )
    ),
    // used in feedStory form submission
    array(
      'name'    => 'FEEDSTORY_1', // name we'll append to the constant definition
      'oneline' => array(
        '{*actor*} used {*app*} to tell {*target*} they are {*ctitle*} because
         {*ctext*}'
      ),
      'short'=> array(
        array(
          'template_title' => '{*actor*} sent {*friend_you*} a compliment with
           {*app*}!',
          'template_body' => '<br/>{*actor*} thinks {*friend*} is {*ctitle*} because
           {*ctext*}'
        )
      ),
      'actionlinks' => array(
        array("text" => "Send your own Compliment!",
              "href" => FB_APP_URL
        )
      )
    ),
    // used in feed.publishUserAction one line submission
    array(
      'name'    => 'ONELINE_1', // name we'll append to the constant definition
      'oneline' => array(
        '{*actor*} just sent {*target*} {*pronoun*} {*count*} {*app*}!'
      ),
      'short'=> null,
      'actionlinks' => array(
        array("text" => "Send your own Compliment!",
              "href" => FB_APP_URL)
      )
    ),
  );
  return $bundles;
}
```

To see it in action, enter the URL of the file in your browser's address bar. Use the full path to it on your web server, not on Facebook. For example, use *http://example.com/<appname>/config/register_feed_templates.php*, not *http://apps.facebook.com/....*

You see something similar to what's shown in Figure 9.24 and Figure 9.25. In Figure 9.24, one template is shown but several can be present, depending on the application. Note the `'?u=1'` query string that's been appended to the URL.

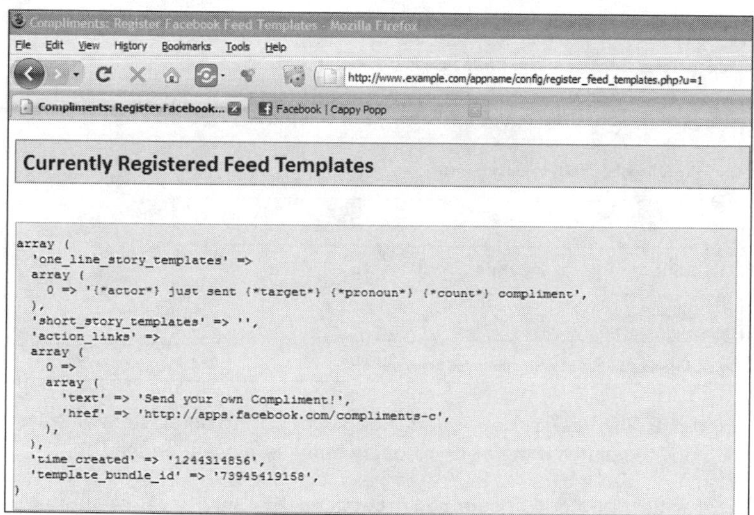

Figure 9.24 `register_feed_templates.php` displays all templates currently registered for this application.

The code then registers all new templates and renders some handy statements that you can copy to your `globals.inc` for use in your code, using the names provided in each template data structure to uniquely identify them. Notice that the code uses exception handling around its main code path and that it handles the specific `FacebookClientRestException`, which is thrown by most of the methods in the Facebook PHP Client Library.

The code first calls the `feed_getRegisteredTemplateBundles()` PHP Library method, which returns a numerically indexed array containing all the template bundles currently registered by the application. For each registered template, it uses PHP's `var_export()` function to display the preformatted template objects to the screen. If the optional u=1 is added to the query string, it unregisters each template by using the `feed_deactivateTemplateBundleByID() method`. Deactivating a template is the same thing as deleting it; after this method is called for a specific template bundle ID, you cannot retrieve it. Finally, it registers all the templates you provide in the `buildTemplateBundles()` function using the `feed_registerTemplateBundle()` method. To verify the script's action, run it once and then open the Registered Feed Templates tool for Compliments. This tool should show the newly registered templates, along with any already present, depending on whether you passed the query string variable to unregister all templates first.

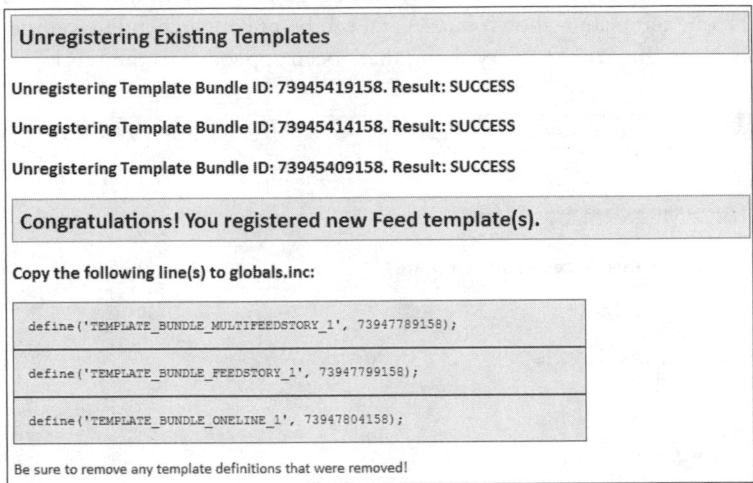
Unregistering Existing Templates

Unregistering Template Bundle ID: 73945419158. Result: SUCCESS

Unregistering Template Bundle ID: 73945414158. Result: SUCCESS

Unregistering Template Bundle ID: 73945409158. Result: SUCCESS

Congratulations! You registered new Feed template(s).

Copy the following line(s) to globals.inc:

```
define('TEMPLATE_BUNDLE_MULTIFEEDSTORY_1', 73947789158);
define('TEMPLATE_BUNDLE_FEEDSTORY_1', 73947799158);
define('TEMPLATE_BUNDLE_ONELINE_1', 73947804158);
```

Be sure to remove any template definitions that were removed!

Figure 9.25 `register_feed_templates.php` unregisters all existing templates if the `'?u=1'` query string is present on the URL.

Note the third parameter to `feed_registerTemplateBundle()`. Facebook used to have three story sizes: one line, short, and full. Full stories could include much more data and were allowed to use more HTML and FBML tags; however, they were deprecated, but the placeholder for them still exists in the API for backwards-compatibility. Always pass `null` for it. Also, check out the return value handling for the call. Its return value is either an error code or the template bundle ID of the newly registered template. Template bundle IDs are always longer than four digits, so the code checks the length of the returned ID: If it is less than four characters, we assume it is an error code—all Facebook APIs return and handle it appropriately.

Let's look at the one line template data structure in detail and how it's used in the call to `feed_registerTemplateBundle()` in Listing 9.11. We use the new template that we are registering for the one line stories we want to publish through the API.

Listing 9.11 **`register_feed_templates.php`: One Line Story Template Bundle in Detail**

```
// used in feed.publishUserAction one line submission
array(
  'name'    => 'ONELINE_1', // name we'll append to the constant definition
  'oneline' => array(
    '{*actor*} just sent {*target*} {*pronoun*} {*count*} {*app*}!'
  ),
  'short'=> null,
  'actionlinks' => array(
```

Listing 9.11 **Continued**

```
        array("text" => "Send your own Compliment!",
              "href" => FB_APP_URL)
        )
    ),
);
```

As you recall from Table 9.2, the `feed.publishUserAction()` API method takes two required parameters: the template bundle ID and the JSON-encoded template data for the stories it will publish. In the data in Listing 9.11, we provided one line template data, but not short. This is fine because the only required part of a template bundle is the one line story template. You do not have to JSON-encode this data when using `feed.publishUserAction()`; the Facebook PHP Library first checks to see if the template data is an array and automatically JSON-encodes it on your behalf if needed. Finally, look at the `actionlinks` array. If you want to provide multiple action links for this story (or any others registered in this file), you simply add another entry to the array. For illustrative purposes, you can add two action links to your story: one that contains the `feedform=feedStory` query string, which allows you to publish via a feedStory Feed form, and the other, which publishes by using the default multiFeedStory. To do this, change the `actionlinks` array like so:

```
'actionlinks' => array(
        array("text" => "Compliment via feedStory!",
              "href" => FB_APP_URL.'?feedform=feedStory'),
        array("text" => "Compliment via feedFormStory!"
"href"= FB_APP_URL)
),
```

Previously, it was said that one of the great benefits of `feed.publishUserAction()` is that it allowed the sending of stories without any user prompting or interaction. Let's observe that behavior. Save and run the `register_feed_templates.php` again and add the new template bundle ID constant definition(s) to your `globals.inc`. Now, send a compliment to someone. Do not publish the story to the stream. Click Skip or the X at the top right of the feed story publish dialog to close it. Now, browse to your Facebook profile. Notice that, although you did not publish the short story, the one line story automatically published by `feed.publishUserAction()` is still present in your Recent Activity section (see Figure 9.26).

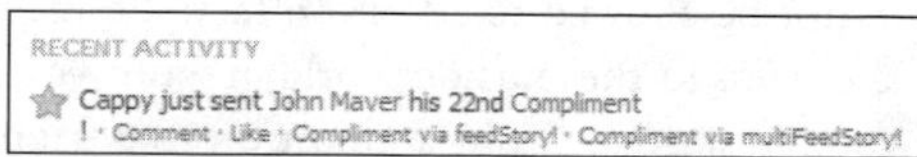

Figure 9.26 Even after canceling the normal feed story submission, Facebook still automatically sends the one line story published by `feed_publishUserAction()`.

Do you see the trailing exclamation point in the one line story in Figure 9.26? HTML rules cause this behavior: Connected words wrap together, and Facebook places the action links in a <span> element right after the one line story's text with no space between them. The easiest way to combat this is to ensure that your one line stories end with a space. Open `register_feed_templates.php` and change the template in your one line story bundle to end with a space, like so:

```
array(
      'name'    => 'ONELINE_1',
      'oneline' => array(
        '{*actor*} just sent {*target*} {*pronoun*} {*count*} {*app*}! ' // note
space
      ),
```

Facebook puts the full text of the story on one line, as shown in Figure 9.27.

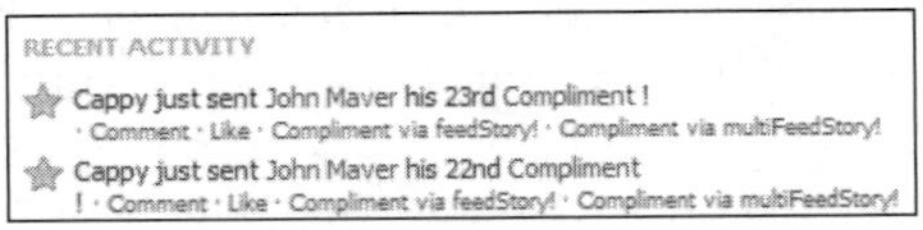

Figure 9.27 The first one line feed story is correctly terminated without wrapping, unlike the second story, where the exclamation point wraps.

Sandbox Mode and Testing Feed Stories

One concern you might have is that, if you are publishing all these stories to the stream, all of your friends—and potential competitors—are able to view them. The Feed Template Console allows you to test your stories before they publish; however, sometimes, you need to test the story in the wild. What's the best way to handle this?

This is where your application's Developer Settings come in handy. Chapter 1 covered them in detail, but there is one setting that is specifically important in this context: Sandbox mode. If you open your application's Developer Settings page and click the Advanced tab, you see the Sandbox Mode choice at the top, as shown in Figure 9.28. This should be set to Enable. There are three important reasons for this.

First, only the actual developers of your application are permitted to install and use it. Even if a friend of yours on Facebook has the absolute URL to your application's authentication page, she will not be allowed to add it. In fact, she receives an HTTP 404 File Not Found error if she tries. To the outside world, it's as if your application does not exist. Remember this if you are showing your application to a friend (or client!).

Second, your application can publish Feed stories at will while in Sandbox mode, and only other application developers ever see them! You can verify this simply. Publish a multiFeedStory short story to a friend who's a developer on the application. Verify that he can see it on his Wall, and you can see it on his Wall when you view his profile, and that

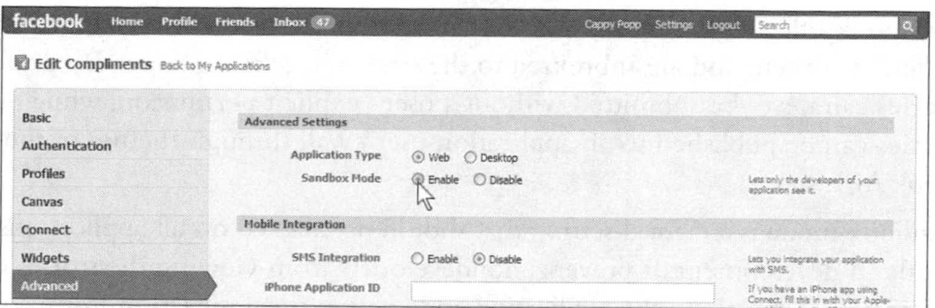

Figure 9.28 Sandbox mode is critical for testing application Feed stories while keeping them from being viewed by nondevelopers or being subject to Facebook allocation limits.

both of you can see the one line story on your Walls. Now, have a friend who's not a developer visit both of your profiles. He should see neither story.

Finally, Sandbox mode prevents your application from being subject to Facebook's strict messaging-allocation limits. We cover this in a Chapter 10 but for now, realize that applications that are not in Sandbox mode are subject to strict quotas for the different types of messages they can send per user per day and, in some cases, per user per week, to minimize spam and potential abuse.

If, by chance, you are testing an application that is not in Sandbox mode, you can still remove the stories you don't want all users to see. Notice the mouse pointer way back in Figure 9.16. The owner of this profile can click the Remove button on all stories on his Wall and they will be removed from the stream. This also removes them from their friends' Home pages.

Summary

This chapter covered many of the core features and techniques for creating, managing, and publishing Feed stories to the Facebook stream. The sample application added numerous new features, enabling it to send multiple types of messages to its users. Here are some key points:

- Feed forms are specialized HTML forms that allow an application to submit Feed stories to the stream. There are two types: feedStory and multiFeedStory, each of which targets their messages to different endpoints on users' Walls and Home page News Feeds.
- Feed forms do not allow any client-side validation opportunities; however, they do provide an error-handling capability that allows you to emulate the behavior on a callback to your server.
- Templates and template bundles are critical components in the creation of Feed stories. They can be composed, previewed, and manually registered through the Feed Template Console or managed directly using the Facebook API.

- Facebook offers two different story types: one line and short. They are composed of different content and are submitted to the stream in different ways. By default, short stories can never be submitted without a user's explicit permission, while one line stories can be published to an application user's Wall through the use of the Facebook API.
- Sandbox mode is a critical setting that should be enabled on all applications currently in development. It prevents nondevelopers from viewing the stories published to the stream by the application and excuses the application from messaging-allocation limits imposed by Facebook.

10

Publisher, Notifications, and Requests

Chapter 9, "Feed Stories, Feed Forms, and Templates," introduced you to the basics of interacting with and producing content for the Facebook stream via Feed forms and the Facebook application programming interface (API). Facebook offers several other alternative communication channels for applications and their users that can greatly expand an application's reach within the Facebook social graph, and ultimately, its potential for success.

This chapter first covers another novel way for application users to publish content to the stream via a special construct known as the Publisher. It's unique in that it is more closely associated with an application user's profile and Home page than it is with an application. This chapter also introduces you to several notification types, which are gener-[illegible] by applications without user interaction, however, they also include one of the most powerful application communication mechanisms available. Finally, we delve into requests, which are one of the more controversial and misunderstood methods of application messaging. Requests are interesting, because they encompass one of the most direct means for applications to spread: invitations. You use all of your new knowledge to update your sample application to use these features, which greatly enhances its capabilities.

Getting to the Heart of Feed: The Publisher

The Publisher is undoubtedly one of the most often used communication channels in Facebook. You see it every time you visit a Facebook profile or your own Home page: It's the control that's placed right above the Feed that lets you update your Facebook status message. Figure 10.1 shows it in its default compact state on the author's profile.

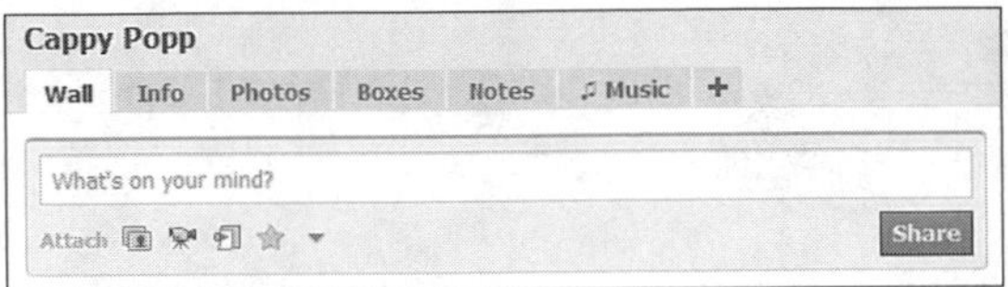

Figure 10.1 The Publisher is one of the most used pieces of functionality on Facebook, and it is found both on users' Home pages and profiles.

Introduction to the Publisher

The purpose and power of the Publisher is to allow users to insert new application-specific content directly and immediately to the stream without having to leave their profiles or Home pages. Applications can register their own custom Publishers, and content created by them is always submitted to the stream in short story Feed format, so it can contain rich media, such as images, audio, or video. Clicking inside the Publisher box's text area expands it to show all the applications that have provided Publisher integration for the current profile; clicking the small arrow to the right of these brings up the full list, as shown in Figure 10.2.

The list of available Publishers is organized automatically by Facebook. Publisher links for default Facebook applications always appear first in the list, followed by any application-specific ones ordered by how recently they were used. This arrangement is specific to the profile owner, not the viewing user, so if you visit a friend's profile, you see his Publishers arranged in an order that reflects the applications or Publishers that friend has used.

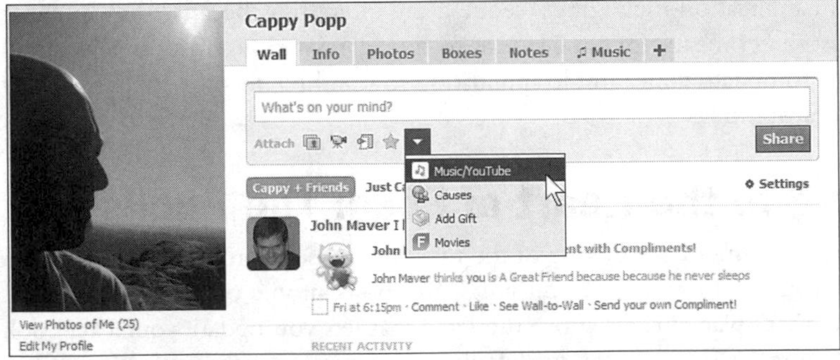

Figure 10.2 Clicking in the text input area of the Publisher shows the list of applications that integrate with it on the current page.

One of the most engaging and powerful features of the Publisher, for both application users and developers, is that it allows applications to present their own custom interactive interfaces for creating Feed content that are not subject to the same constraints that Facebook imposes on other application interaction points, such as profile boxes or application tabs. Unlike either of these, the Publisher allows applications to automatically play Flash videos and hook the `onload()` event in Facebook JavaScript (FBJS).

Take a moment to explore the different possibilities already in place on your own profile or Home page. Some are quite interactive. For example, look at the default Facebook Music/YouTube Publisher provided by iLike, shown in Figure 10.3. It offers the ability to preview and publish songs and video, and more.

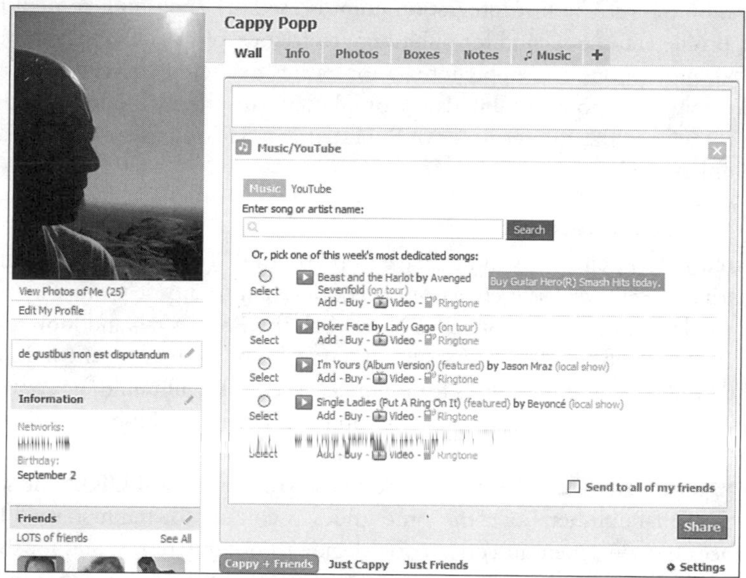

Figure 10.3 The Facebook Music/YouTube Publisher offers many interactive options for creating content.

Another reason why the Publisher is so important is that it offers a flexible and liberal means of interacting with users where they normally live on Facebook: on their friends' profiles and on their own Home page. In comparison, Feed forms are specialized HTML forms that exist on application-specific canvas pages or application tabs. Facebook handles Feed forms specially and a side-effect of this special handling makes client-side form validation impossible. A Publisher interface has no such restrictions. Publishers can use FBJS directly to dynamically enable a form's Submit button, depending on the state of the form's data or variables. When users employ the Publisher, they don't have to visit application-specific pages to publish application content; moreover, they can be presented an entirely different interface from the one you would see if you used the Publisher on your own profile or Home page.

Finally, the Publisher can directly insert content into the Home page News feed and the Wall simultaneously and instantaneously. When a user submits a Feed story from a Publisher to his own profile or Home page, a short Feed story is created in both locations and on the Home page News feed of all of their friends. Stories submitted by a user to a friend's profile are shown on the friend's profile and the Home page News feeds of that friend and all of their friends.

Integrating with the Publisher

Applications that provide Publisher interfaces have the opportunity to provide two separate integration points. The first integration point is used for publishing content to a user's own profile and the second for publishing to friends' profiles. Because Publishers are not required, applications can supply integration points for neither, one, or both. However, for illustrative purposes we'll update Compliments to provide both. From this point forward we'll refer to the former flavor of Publisher as a Self-Publisher and the latter, an Other-Publisher.

Publisher Developer Settings

To get started with Publishers, you first have to revisit the Compliments application's Developer Settings page (*www.facebook.com/developers/apps.php*). Choose Compliments from the list on the left and then Edit Settings. Now, click the Profiles tab and look for the section titled Profile Publisher. The options listed here specify the text for the links used to activate the Publishers and the URLs from which Facebook will pull their content.

The first pair of options is for the Other-Publisher. For the Publish Text value, enter Compliment. For the Publish Callback URL, enter something like *http://example.com/<appname>/publisher_callback.php*, but be sure to use your own local URL. The second pair is for the Self-Publisher. Enter the same values as you did for the first; we'll handle the differences between them in code. If you decide to use different values for the link labels, be aware that Facebook limits them to 20 characters. Your settings should look similar to what's shown in Figure 10.4.

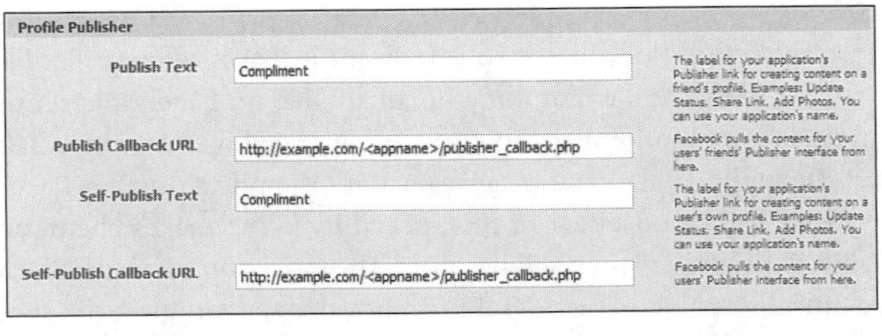

Figure 10.4 The Facebook Developer application allows you to set custom Publisher values.

Our goal is to produce a Publisher interface like the one shown in Figure 10.5. It will look identical for both the Self- and Other-Publishers; the only difference being the text that's shown when they're displayed. The Self-Publisher refers to you when it's shown on the currently logged-in user's profile or Home page, while the Other-Publisher uses the friend's first name when it's launched from their friend's profile. Figure 10.6 and Figure 10.7 show the different Feed stories that each flavor of Publisher ultimately produces when we're done.

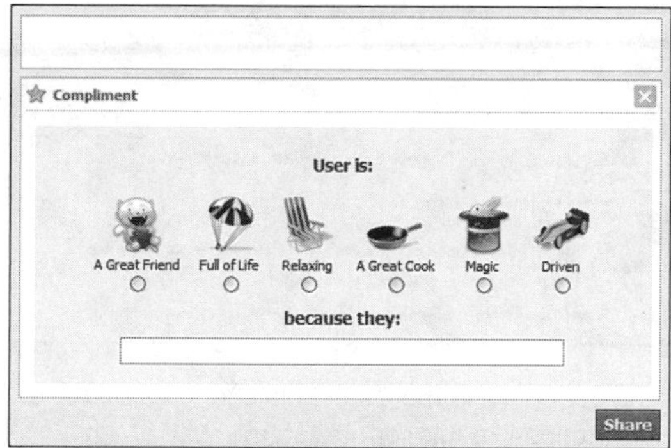

Figure 10.5 The Self-Publisher user interface looks similar to this.

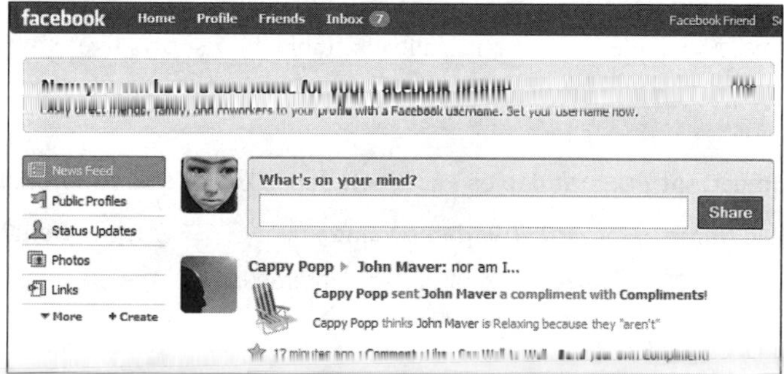

Figure 10.6 The Self-Publisher creates Feed stories like this for the user's Wall and Home page Feeds.

Creating the Publishers

Now that you have set the necessary options in the Compliments Developer Settings, you can actually implement the Publishers. First, we need to go over how Facebook communicates with the application when using a Publisher. Facebook actually requests information from the Publisher Callback URLs on two separate occasions. First, when a user clicks a Publisher link in a profile or Home page, Facebook calls it to request the FBML to display the Publisher. If a user then submits a story from that Publisher, Facebook calls it a second time to request the content for the Feed story it will publish, which is a process that was discussed in Chapter 9. Your callback's code can determine which type of request Facebook makes by checking the value of the `method` `POST` variable, which Facebook will send with each call.

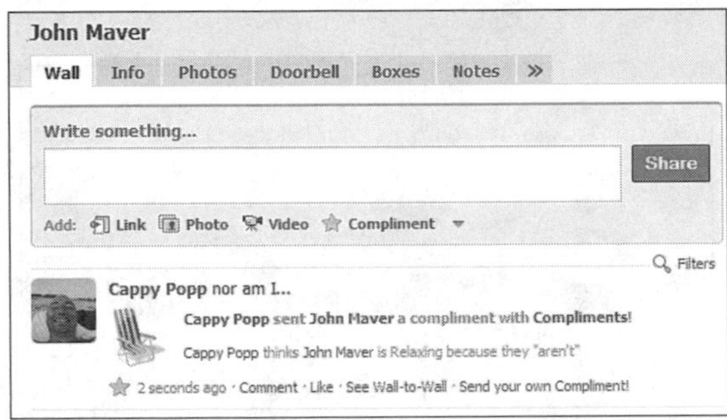

Figure 10.7 The Other-Publisher creates Feed stories like this for the target's Wall and his friends' Home page Feeds.

We'll be able to differentiate between the two flavors of Publishers rather than providing two separate implementations. We can do this because Facebook also sends this information in the `POST` variables sent to this callback. Table 10.1 shows five `POST` variables sent by Facebook that you'll come across when creating Publishers.

Table 10.1 **Important `POST` Variables Facebook Sends to the Publisher Callback URLs**

POST Variable Name	POST Variable Value	Always Sent?
`fb_sig_user`	Facebook ID of user interacting with the Publisher.	Yes.
`fb_sig_profile_user`	Facebook ID of user from whose profile the Publisher was requested.	Yes.
`fb_sig_session_key`	If sent, means the user identified by `fb_sig_user` has authorized the application that provided the Publisher.	No.

Table 10.1 **Continued**

`method`	Set to `publisher_getInterface` on first request, `publisher_getFeedStory` for Feed story content.	Yes.
`app_params`	Contains an array of the Publisher's form variable data, keyed by form element name.	No; only sent when `method` has the value `publisher_getFeedStory`.

Armed with the data in Table 10.1, we can determine that if the values of `fb_sig_user` and `fb_sig_profile_user` are equal, then the user interacting with the Publisher is also the owner of the profile (or Home page) from which it was launched; therefore, we need to display the Self-Publisher to allow this user to publish a Feed story to his own Wall and Home page News feed. If these values are different, we need to display the Other-Publisher, which allows publishing to the Wall of the user identified by `fb_sig_profile_user` and his friends' Home pages. If we want the Publisher to offer enhanced functionality to users that have authorized the application that provides it, we can check for the existence of fb`_sig_session_key` in the `POST` variables—it is only sent when this is true.

Create a new file called `publisher_callback.php` in your application root directory. We separate the code for this file over the next few listings to make it very clear. First, the core behaviors of both displaying a custom Publisher and publishing a story to Facebook are shown in Listing 10.1. Add this to `publisher_callback.php`.

Listing 10.1 **`publisher_callback.php`: Handling Publisher Callbacks From Facebook**

```
<?php

require_once 'inc/globals.inc';
require_once 'inc/utils.inc';
require_once 'inc/db.inc';
require_once 'inc/profile.inc';
require_once 'inc/notifications.inc';

// Comment out before deploying
//dumpRequestVars(true, basename(__FILE__));

$fb = new Facebook(FB_API_KEY, FB_APP_SECRET);

$publisher = $fb->user || $fb->fb_params['page_id']; // who's publishing
$target    = $fb->fb_params['profile_user']; // who they're publishing to
```

Listing 10.1 **Continued**

```
$isSelfPub = $publisher === $target; // 'true' if publisher on own profile/home

$publisherAction = $_POST['method'];

$fbResponse = '';

if( isset( $publisherAction ) &&
    isset( $publisher ) &&
    isset( $target ) ) {

  // Facebook is requesting the user interface of the Publisher
  if( 'publisher_getInterface' === $publisherAction ) {

    $markup = getPublisherUI($isSelfPub ? $publisher : $target);

    $fbResponse = array( 'content'=> array( 'fbml' => $markup,
                                            'publishEnabled' => true ),
                         'method' => $publisherAction );

  } else if ( 'publisher_getFeedStory' === $publisherAction ) {

    // Facebook is requesting the data for the Feed story

    $formValues = $_POST['app_params'];

    if( isset( $formValues ) ) {

      global $g_categories;

      if(!isset($fb->fb_params['page_id'])) {
      // save the compliment in the DB
      $db = new DB();
      $db->addCompliment( $publisher, $isSelfPub ? $publisher : $target,
                          $formValues['category'], $formValues['compliment'] );
      }

      // start filling in our template
      $categoryInfo = $g_categories[$formValues['category']];

      $imageSrc     = LOCAL_APP_URL.'/img/'.$categoryInfo['bigimg'];
      $imageLink    = LOCAL_APP_URL;
      $images       = array('src'=> $imageSrc, 'href'=> $imageLink);

      $feed = array( 'template_id' =>
                     $isSelfPub ? TEMPLATE_BUNDLE_SELF_PUBLISH_1 :
                                  TEMPLATE_BUNDLE_OTHER_PUBLISH_1,
```

Listing 10.1 **Continued**

```
                    'template_data'   =>
                      array( 'app'    => '<a href="'.FB_APP_URL.
                                         '">Compliments</a>',
                             'ctitle' => $categoryInfo['title'],
                             'ctext'  => $formValues['compliment'],
                             'images' => array( $images ) ) );

    } else {

      $fbResponse = getPublisherError('Incorrect method
        requested: Expected either publisher_getFeedStory or
        publisher_getInterface');
    }

    $fbResponse = array( 'method'  => $publisherAction,
                         'content' => array( 'feed' => $feed ) );
  } else {

     $fbResponse = getPublisherError('Missing form values from Publisher');
  }
} else {

  $fbResponse = getPublisherError('Either method, user, or target are not
    specified');
}

[illegible]
echo json_encode($fbResponse);
?>
```

Listing 10.1 uses a few utility functions. It calls the `getPublisherError()` function to create arrays that Facebook uses to notify your users of specific error conditions. This is exactly the same process you used when handling errors with Feed forms. Again, you must provide Facebook with a JSON-encoded associative array containing three keys: `errorCode` (which must always be set to 1, handily defined by the constant `FACEBOOK_API_VALIDATION_ERROR`), `errorTitle`, and `errorMessage`. The values for `errorTitle` and `errorMessage` populate an error dialog's title and body content, respectively. Listing 10.2 shows the code for the `getPublisherError()` function. Add this to the end of `publisher_callback.php`.

Listing 10.2 **`publisher_callback.php`: `getPublisherError()` Function**

```
/** Creates an error array to return to Facebook if the Publisher experiences an
error */
function getPublisherError($msg) {
  return array( 'errorCode'   => FACEBOOK_API_VALIDATION_ERROR,
```

Listing 10.2 **Continued**

```
                'errorTitle'   => 'Facebook Publisher Error',
                'errorMessage'=> $msg );
}
```

Listing 10.1 uses the `getPublisherUI()` function to provide the markup for the Publisher's user interface. Facebook requests it after sending the `publisher_getInterface` `POST` variable. `getPublisherUI()`, in turn, uses the `getCSS()` function to provide the styles for the Publisher. Listing 10.3 shows the code for both of these functions. Add these functions to the end of `publisher_callback.php`.

Listing 10.3 **`publisher_callback.php`: Publisher User Interface Functions**

```
/** Returns the CSS for the Publisher interface */
function getCSS() {
  $css = "
  <style>
    h1 { font-size: 14px; font-weight:bold; text-align:center; margin-top:6px;
         margin-bottom:6px; }
    .panel { text-align:center; background-color:#F7F7F7; padding:10px 0;}
    #complimentTable { margin: 5px auto; }
    #complimentTable .textInput { width: 85%; }
    #complimentTable td { text-align:center; }
    .category { float:left; height:75px; text-align:center; margin:8px; }
    .category img { width:48px; height:48px; }
    .category .categoryTitle { height:20px; font-weight:bold; }
  </style>";

return $css;
}

/** Gets the Publisher's FBML markup */
function getPublisherUI( $uid ) {
  global $g_categories;

  $out = getCSS();

  $out .= "
    <div class='panel'>
      <form>
        <table id='complimentTable'>
          <tr>
            <td>
              <fb:if-is-friends-with-viewer uid='$uid' includeself='false'>
                <h1>
                  <fb:name uid='$uid' firstnameonly='true' linked='false'/> is:
                </h1>
```

Listing 10.3 **Continued**

```
            <fb:else>
              <h1>
                <fb:name uid='$uid' capitalize='true' linked='false'/> are:
              </h1>
            </fb:else>
          </fb:if-is-friends-with-viewer>
        </td>
      </tr>
      <tr>
        <td>";
  foreach( $g_categories as $name => $info ){
    $out .= "
            <div class='category'>
                <img class='catImg'
                  src='".LOCAL_APP_URL."/img/{$info['bigimg']}'/><br>
                <span class='categoryTitle'>{$info['title']}</span><br/>
                <input type='radio' name='category' value='$name'/>
            </div>";
  }
  $out .= "
            <div style='clear:both;'></div>
          </td>
        </tr>
        <tr>
          <td>
            <fb:if-is-friends-with-viewer uid='$uid' includeself='false'>
              <h1>because they:</h1>
              <fb:else>
                <h1>because you:</h1>
              </fb:else>
            </fb:if-is-friends-with-viewer>
          </td>
        </tr>
        <tr>
          <td>
            <input class='textInput' name='compliment' />
          </td>
        </tr>
      </table>
    </form>
  </div>";

  return $out;
}
```

The most important parts of the code in Listing 10.1 are the sections that deal with responding to the receipt of the `method` variable in the `POST` variables received from Facebook. When the value of `method` is `publisher_getInterface`, your code must provide Facebook with a specific JSON response that provides it with the raw FBML that comprises the Publisher's user interface, as follows:

```
if( 'publisher_getInterface' === $publisherAction ) {
  $markup = getPublisherUI($isSelfPub ? $publisher : $target);
  // The reponse to publisher_getInterface
  $fbResponse = array( 'content'=> array( 'fbml' => $markup,
                                          'publishEnabled' => true ),
                      'method' => $publisherAction );
}
```

The associative array stored in the `$fbResponse` variable will ultimately be JSON-encoded before printing it back to Facebook, just like we did with the Feed form data in Chapter 9. The first entry in the array must be named `content` and be set to an associative array itself containing two entries named `fbml` and `publishEnabled`. The first entry, `fbml`, must be set to the raw FBML that renders the Publisher interface. The final entry in the array must be named `method` and be set to the value for the `method` `POST` variable, which, in this case, is `publisher_getInterface`.

The `publishEnabled` value deserves a closer look. When it is set to `true`, the Share button is always enabled, and the user can submit the Publisher content immediately. When it is set to `false`, the Share button is disabled until the application uses the `Facebook.setPublishStatus()` FBJS function to enable it. This manual enabling allows the application to perform client-side validation. Our code sets it to `true` for simplicity; obviously, this would be unwise in production code that accepts user input, and we rectify that in Chapter 11, "FBJS, Mock AJAX, and Flash."

When Facebook sets the value of the `method` `POST` variable to `publisher_getFeedStory`, it expects your code to return to it another specifically formatted JSON response containing the template data needed to produce the appropriate Feed story from the Publisher. For Compliments, this callback happens after the user submits the Publisher form. Listing 10.1 responds to this by storing the compliment in the database and then building the template data. The following excerpt focuses on how the template data is created and returned:

```
else if ( 'publisher_getFeedStory' === $publisherAction ) {
    $formValues = $_POST['app_params'];
      // elided for clarity
      $feed = array( 'template_id' => $isSelfPub ? TEMPLATE_BUNDLE_SELF_PUBLISH_1 :
                                                   TEMPLATE_BUNDLE_OTHER_PUBLISH_1,
                    'template_data'   =>
                      array( 'app'    =>'<ahref="'.FB_APP_URL.'">Compliments</a>',
                             'ctitle' => $categoryInfo['title'],
                             'ctext'  => $formValues['compliment'],
```

```
                                'images' => array( $images ) ) );
    $fbResponse = array( 'method'  => $publisherAction,
                         'content' => array( 'feed' => $feed ) );
}
```

Again, Facebook expects a JSON-encoded array in a specific format. In this case, the associative array requires two keys: `method` and `content`. The `method` key is again set to the value of the `method POST` variable. The `content` key must be assigned an associative array containing one key, `feed`, which contains all the template data required for Facebook to publish the Feed story. (It's saved in the variable `$feed` first to make the code clear.) Notice that the code refers to two new template bundle IDs: `TEMPLATE_BUNDLE_SELF_PUBLISH_1` for the template used for stories from the Self-Publisher and `TEMPLATE_BUNDLE_OTHER_PUBLISH_1` used for those from the Other-Publisher. You need to add the code for these new template bundles to the end of the `buildTemplateBundles()` function in the `register_feed_templates.php` script created in Chapter 9. The code for the new function is shown in Listing 10.4.

Listing 10.4 **`register_feed_templates.php`: Publisher Templates to Be Registered by `buildTemplateBundles()`**

```
// used in Publisher for publishing to own Wall and friends' Home Pages
array(
  'name'    => 'SELF_PUBLISH_1', //name appendedto the constant definition
  'oneline' => array('{*actor*}'), //unused, but need to have something here
  'short'   => array(
    array(
      'template_title' => '{*actor*} gave themselves a pat on the back with
                           {*app*}!',
      'template_body' => '<br/>{*actor*} thinks they are {*ctitle*} because
                          they "{*ctext*}"'
    )
  ),
  'actionlinks' => array(
    array("text" => "Send your own Compliment!",
          "href" => FB_APP_URL.'?asrc=selfpub')
  )
),

// used in Publisher for publishing to a friend's Wall, Home Page, and their
// friends' Home Pages
array(
  'name'    => 'OTHER_PUBLISH_1', //name appended to the constant definition
  'oneline' => array(
    '{*actor*} used {*app*} to tell {*target*} they are {*ctitle*} because
     they {*ctext*}'
  ),
```

Listing 10.4 **Continued**

```
'short'    => array(
  array(
    'template_title' => '{*actor*} sent {*target*} a compliment with
                         {*app*}!',
    'template_body' => '<br/>{*actor*} thinks {*target*} is {*ctitle*}
     because they "{*ctext*}"'
  )
),
'actionlinks' => array(
  array("text" => "Send your own Compliment!",
       "href" => FB_APP_URL.'?asrc=otherpub')
)
),
```

After you add these new template bundle definitions, you need to rerun the `register_template_bundles.php` script and replace all the template bundle ID constant definitions in `globals.inc`. You should now have five template bundle constant IDs defined in `globals.inc` similar to those in the code that follows, with your own IDs, of course:

```
define('TEMPLATE_BUNDLE_MULTIFEEDSTORY_1', 78457479158);
define('TEMPLATE_BUNDLE_FEEDSTORY_1', 78457499158);
define('TEMPLATE_BUNDLE_ONELINE_1', 78457504158);
define('TEMPLATE_BUNDLE_SELF_PUBLISH_1', 78457509158);
define('TEMPLATE_BUNDLE_OTHER_PUBLISH_1', 78457514158);
```

Handling Publisher Errors

When dealing with the Publisher, you are bound to encounter errors. If Facebook encounters an error that is not covered by one of the error conditions your code handles, it provides a most unhelpful response in the form of the dialog shown in Figure 10.8.

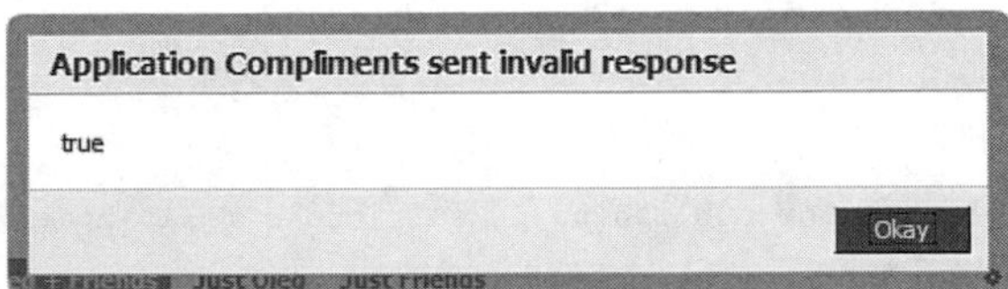

Figure 10.8 Facebook shows this when it encounters an unhandled error when dealing with The Publisher.

If you receive such an error, there are two easy ways to determine their cause. First, you can open your web server's error log and check for the error that corresponds to it; however, this can be inconvenient. An easier way is to use Firebug, the Firefox add-on discussed in Chapter 4, "Platform Developer Tools." To use it to determine what is causing your Publisher errors, perform the following steps. We've also included a screenshot to make following them easier, shown in Figure 10.9:

1. With the error dialog onscreen, open Firebug.
2. Enable the Net tab in Firebug (if it is not already) and select it.
3. Click the XHR button in the Firebug toolbar to filter out all but `XMLHttpRequest` (AJAX) traffic.
4. Locate and expand the last call to the following URL: *www.facebook.com/ajax/composer/attachment.php*.
5. Click the Response tab.

A bunch of JSON should display: The cause of the error should be the value of the `errorMessage` property. If it's a syntax error, this property shows you the line number of the offending code and the call stack leading up to it.

Notifications

Notifications are another important means of communication provided by Facebook to applications. Notifications are lightweight messages that applications can send on their users' behalf to other Facebook users. An important feature of notifications is that applications can send them without direct user interaction in some cases; however, because of past abuses by applications, Facebook strictly enforces limits on how many an application can send in a given time period.

Notifications are intended to alert users to an event, change, or activity in an application that affect them and are sent directly to the notifications area of the target user's Facebook chrome. Notice that we did not specifically say Home page or profile: The Notifications area is always visible next to the chat control on the bottom of the Facebook chrome while a user is logged into Facebook, as shown in Figure 10.10. The number of new notifications is displayed in a small red balloon above the notification icon.

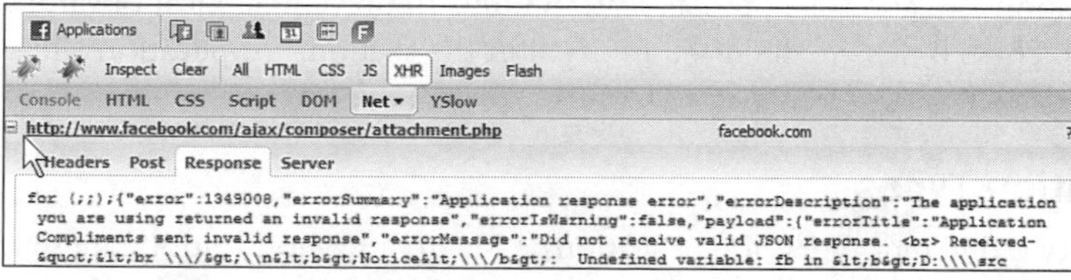

Figure 10.9 Use the Firebug extension in Firefox to discover the real cause of your unhandled Publisher errors without having to monitor your web server's error log.

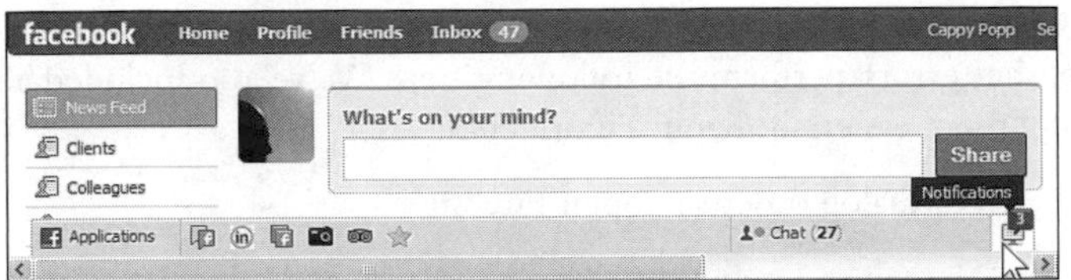

Figure 10.10 The Notifications area is always displayed in the Facebook user interface next to the chat control when a user is logged into Facebook.

To view his recently received notifications, a user can click the Notifications icon to expand a list. The full list of notifications is found on the Facebook Notifications page, which can be reached by clicking the Inbox link at the top of the Facebook user interface. The Notifications tab holds all notifications from the past several days, as shown in Figure 10.11.

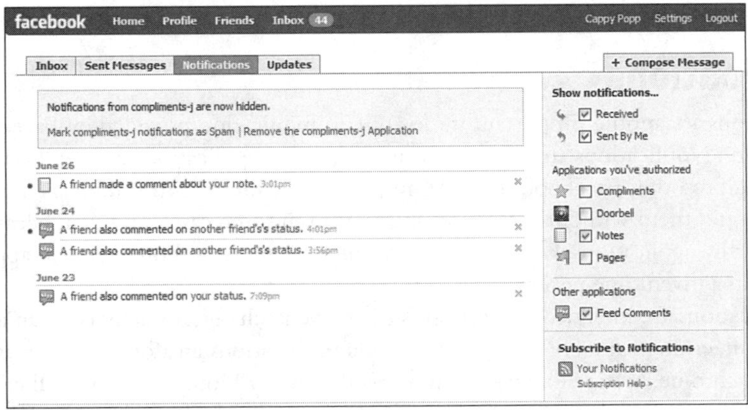

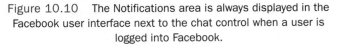

Figure 10.11 The Notifications page shows all notifications sent or received by a user over the last few days.

Notifications are also subject to allocation limits to prevent applications from spamming users. These limits are discussed in detail in the section, "Application Messaging and Allocations."

Notification Types

There are two different types of notifications. User-to-user notifications are sent on behalf of an application user to one of his friends (who might not be an application user) or to another application user (who might not be one of his friends.) Application-to-user notifications are sent by an application only to authorized application users.

User-to-User Notifications

User-to-user notifications have the potential to engage online application users in a novel way. If an application sends a user-to-user notification to another Facebook user who's currently online and logged into Facebook, that user is shown a notification popup that appears above her Notifications area (see Figure 10.12). The user who sends the notification also receives a similar popup, which allows her to cancel the sending of the notification if possible, as shown in Figure 10.13.

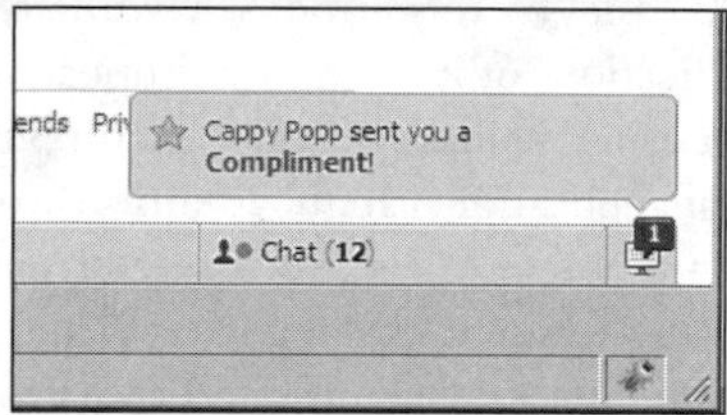

Figure 10.12 The target of a user-to-user notification receives a popup in her Notifications area if she is currently logged into Facebook.

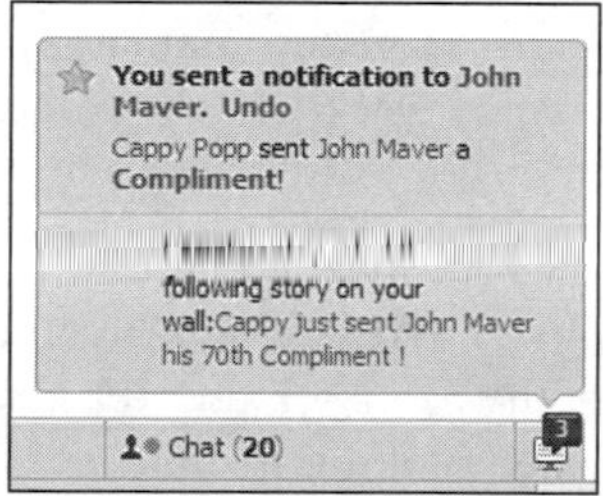

Figure 10.13 Senders of a user-to-user notifications are notified before the send initiates and are given the opportunity to undo the send action, if desired.

These popups remain visible for a few seconds before they fade out; however, the notification still shows up in the receiver's Notifications list and her Notifications tab in the Inbox. The thing to note about this behavior is that it allows applications to send a form of real-time messages to other application users or friends of the current application user. This is an excellent way to increase an application's user engagement and is great for time-sensitive or turn-based applications, such as online games where they can immediately alert users when it's their turn.

Application-to-User Notifications

Application-to-user notifications allow applications to send messages to their authorized users about actions that have occurred in the application that affect them, such as actions by multiple friends. Applications can send them to their users without needing a session to do so. Because of this, Facebook allows fewer of these to be sent to users than user-to-user notifications.

Sending Notifications with the Facebook API

Now that you understand the basics of notifications, it's time to update the Compliments application code to send notifications of its own. You'll update the application to send notifications to alert users when someone has sent them a compliment. This example is purely for illustration; in a real application, careful attention would be paid to notification messaging because of its important role in Facebook's determination of an application's messaging allocations, something which is covered later. When designing your own applications to use notifications, one thing to keep in mind is that the Facebook Platform Guidelines have specific limits on how and when they should be sent. Chapter 5, "Facebook Terms of Service and Application Programs," discussed these, but here is a summary:

- User-to-user notifications must be sent within one hour of the first action that triggered them.
- Application-to-user notifications should be from the application and not the user. They must also be about either more than one user or more than one action. They must be sent a maximum of one week after the earliest trigger and must contain the date of that trigger.

Notifications are sent using the Facebook `notification.send()` API method (`notifications_send()` in PHP). The API call returns an error code if there was a problem or a comma-separated list of the Facebook user IDs that were notified if there was not. Table 10.2 presents the parameters of this method.

Table 10.2 **`notifications_send()` Parameters**

Parameter	Type	Description
`to_ids`	array	Contains an array of Facebook user IDs of the notification's recipients. Recipients must have authorized the application or be friends of the currently logged in application user. Setting this to an empty string sends the notification to the logged-in user without his name as the first word. **Required.**
`notification`	string	Contains the notification's content. It can be up to 2,000 characters of FBML and contain text and links only. **Required.**

Table 10.2 **Continued**

`type`	string	Holds the type of the notification. Can be set to either `app_to_user or user_to_user (the default).`

The body of a notification message can only contain text or links. Because of this, it only supports a limited number of HTML and FBML tags. (Consult the online documentation for this list; it is too exhaustive to present here.) Unlike Feed stories, notifications do not require templates, template data, or template bundles. The FBML string that's passed in the notification parameter of the `notifications_send()` method contains the complete raw FBML that is used to display it.

Listing 10.5 demonstrates the code necessary to send both user-to-user and app-to-user notifications. Add this code to a new file called `notifications.inc` in your application's `inc` directory.

Listing 10.5 **`notifications.inc`: `sendUserNotification()` Function**

```
<?php
/** Sends a Facebook notification to a user; tries user-to-user first then
app-to-user */
function sendUserNotification(Facebook $facebook, $target) {

  // no <fb:name/> needed at start, provided by Facebook
  // automatically unless '' is passed as first param to API call
  $notification = "sent <fb:name uid='$target' /> a ".
                  "<b><a href='".FB_APP_URL."'>Compliment</a></b>";

  $return = null;

  try {
    $return = $facebook->api_client->notifications_send( array($target),
                                                         $notification,
                                                         'user_to_user');
    if( ! isset($return[0])) {
      // probably reached allocation limit for day, try an app-to-user
      // notification instead

      // app-to-user notifications don't include the sender's name (since they
      // are generated by the app) so we'll add it
      $notification = "<fb:name uid='{$facebook->user}'/> ".$notification;

      $return = $facebook->api_client->notifications_send( array($target),
                                                           $notification,
                                                           'app_to_user');
    }
  } catch( FacebookRestClientException $ex) {
```

Listing 10.5 **Continued**

```
    wr($ex->__toString());
  }

  return isset($return);
}
?>
```

Notice that the code first attempts to send a user-to-user notification to the user's friend. If this fails, an application-to-user notification is sent instead. Sending a user-to-user notification might fail, depending on how many user-to-user notifications the application has left in its allocation to send to that friend for the current day. Developers should use application-to-user notifications judiciously. Also, note that the FBML for the user-to-user notification does not contain an `<fb:name>` tag for the sender; this is provided automatically for user-to-user notification messages unless the `to_ids` parameter is set to an empty string.

Next, modify the code in the `feed_form_callback.php` script from Chapter 9 to call the `sendUserNotification()` function. You'll call this function when the user posts a Feed story using a multiFeedStory form, because the Feed stories they generate are targeted at a user's friends. First, add `notifications.inc` to the list of included files at the top of `feed_form_callback.php`, as shown in the following code:

```
require_once 'inc/notifications.inc';
```

Now, update the block of code in `feed_form_callback.php` that handles the multiFeedStory form to call the `sendUserNotification()` function and display an error if it fails, as shown in the following code. New code is shown in bold:

```
if( 'multiFeedStory' === $feedFormType ) {
  $feed = array('template_id'   => TEMPLATE_BUNDLE_MULTIFEEDSTORY_1,
                'template_data' =>
                    array('app'    => '<a href="'.FB_APP_URL.'">Compliments</a>',
                          'ctitle' => $comp['title'],
                          'ctext'  => $compliment,
                          'images' => array($images)));
  if(! sendUserNotification($facebook, $target)) {
    echo json_encode(
      array( 'errorCode'    => FACEBOOK_API_VALIDATION_ERROR,
             'errorTitle'   => 'Notifications Failed!',
             'errorMessage'=> 'Error sending Facebook notifications.') );
    die();
  }
}
```

Application Email

Applications can send emails to their users, but special permissions, called *extended permissions*, must be granted by a user to an application to allow it to send them. Emails are sent to the email address that the user provided when he set up his Facebook account, not to the Facebook email Inbox as you might expect. Facebook does not reveal the actual email address of the application user. Instead, it provides what's known as a proxied email address, which hides the actual email address from the application.

Extended Permissions

To understand the steps needed to allow an application to send email, we need to briefly discuss the concept of extended permissions. Extended permissions are required by Facebook to grant applications access to certain APIs that allow them to do a range of things. To give an application the right to use these features, users must have a much higher degree of trust in that application.

Facebook provides several ways for applications to request extended permissions from a user, as shown in the following list:

- By using the `<fb:prompt-permission>` FBML tag
- By using a special attribute, `promptpermission`, within an element in an HTML form
- By calling the FBJS `Facebook.showPermissionDialog()` function from FBML canvas pages
- By calling the `FB.Connect.showPermissionDialog()` function in the Facebook JavaScript Client Library for IFrame-based canvas pages or sites that implement Facebook Connect
- By directing users to a specific URL: *www.facebook.com/authorize.php?api_key=<FB_API_KEY>&v=1.0&ext_perm=<extendedpermissionname>*

The different extended permissions that can be granted to an application are found in the following list. To check which extended permissions have been granted, developers can either call the Facebook `user.hasAppPermission()` API method or check for the value(s) of the `fb_sig_ext_perms` HTTP REQUEST variable sent by Facebook to an application:

- **`email`.** Allows an application to send email to an application user. This permission can only be granted through the `<fb:prompt-permission>` tag or the `promptpermission` attribute.
- **`offline_access`.** Gives an application the right to access a user's data that requires a session when the user is offline. Effectively, this grants an application the right to use an infinite session key for the user. This permission can only be granted through

the `<fb:prompt-permission>` tag or the `promptpermission` attribute. The application must store the session key granted to the user to log them in as needed by calling the `Facebook::set_user()` PHP Library method.

- **`create_event`.** Lets an application create or modify Facebook events for users.
- **`rsvp_event`.** Allows an application to RSVP to an event on behalf of a user.
- **`sms`.** Grants an application the capability to use text messages to communicate with users.
- **`publish_stream`.** Encapsulates a lot of others; it's part of Facebook's new Open Stream API that's in beta at the time of this writing. It allows an application to set a user's status, upload photos or videos without manual approval, manage Facebook Notes, or post links to the user's profile.
- **`read_stream`.** Also part of the Open Stream API, it allows an application to read or display content from a user's stream.
- **`auto_publish_recent_activity`.** Does not appear that you can set this using the Facebook extended permissions system; however, you will notice it in the HTTP variables that Facebook sends to an application. Appears to grant applications the right to automatically publish one line Feed stories via the `feed.publishUserAction()` API method.

Sending Application Email

Now that you've been introduced to the concept of extended permissions, we'll update Compliments to send email to its users. Because we are primarily dealing with FBML in this example, we'll use the `<fb:prompt-permission>` tag to present the user with a link she can click to grant the email extended permission to the application. We'll modify `index.php` to include the tag and `main.css` to include a new style for it. Add the bold lines below after the form code in `index.php` at the end of the `renderPage()` function:

```
  <input class='inputbutton' type='submit' name='submitCompliment'
    label='Send Compliment' value='Send Compliment'/>
</form>
<fb:prompt-permission perms='email'>
  <div class='perm'>
    Click here to receive updates via email!
  </div>
</fb:prompt-permission>
```

Add the next line to your `main.css` file to add the new style for the `perm` class used in the previous code:

```
.perm { margin-top: 5px; font-weight: bold;}
```

When a user clicks the link to receive email updates, the Request for Special Permissions dialog appears, as shown in Figure 10.14. Clicking the Allow Emails button removes the link from the page the next time it is viewed.

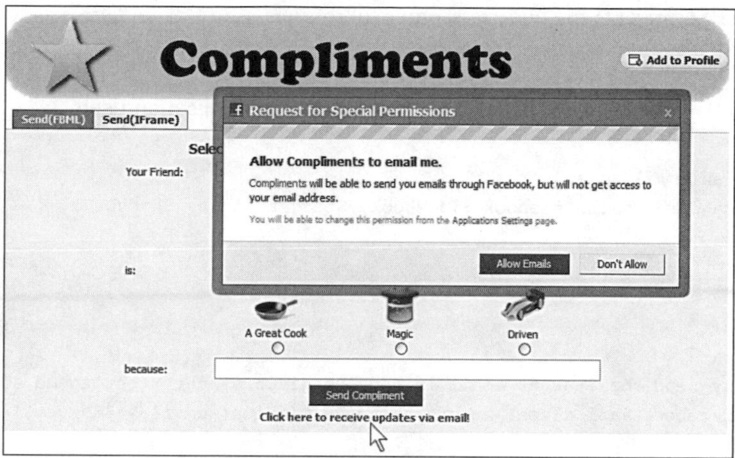

Figure 10.14 Clicking the extended permission link shows the user the Request for Special Permissions dialog.

You can always revoke the special permission by modifying the application settings, as shown in Figure 10.15 and Figure 10.16.

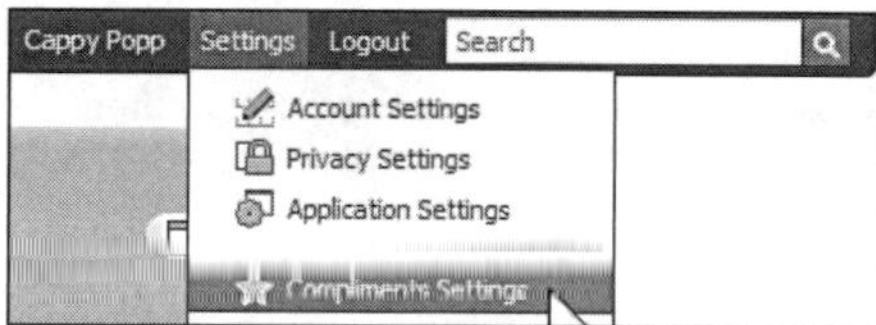

Figure 10.15 Users can access the Compliments application settings from the Facebook main navigation bar's Settings menu.

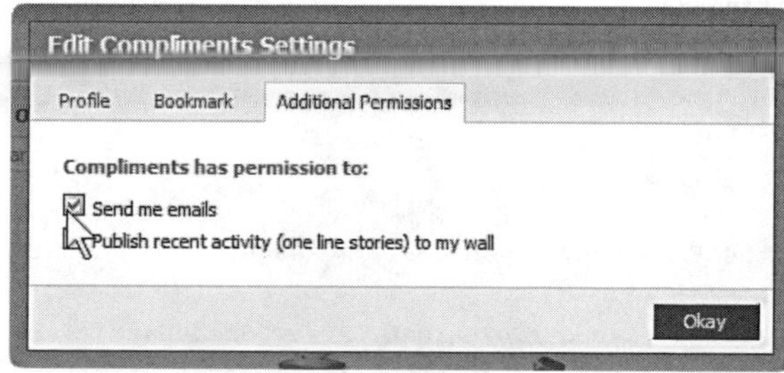

Figure 10.16 To remove the extended permission allowing the application to send emails, users can uncheck the Send Me Emails box.

Listing 10.6 presents the code to send email to users. Add this code to a new script called `email.inc` in your `inc` directory.

Listing 10.6 **`email.inc`: Sending Facebook Email to Application Users**

```
<?php
/** Sends an email to a user */
function sendUserEmail(Facebook $facebook, $target, Array $bodyData) {

  $return = '';

  try {

    // only send the $target email if they've given us the right to do so
    if( $facebook->api_client->users_hasAppPermission('email', $target)) {

      $sender = $facebook->user;

      $textBody = getTextEmailBody( $facebook, $bodyData);
      $fbmlBody = getFbmlEmailBody( $sender, $target, $bodyData);

      $subject =
        "<fb:name uid='$sender' useyou='false' /> sent you a Compliment!";

      // send the email; this API call will return a comma-separated list of
      // the users to whom the email was successfully sent or an empty string
      // otherwise
      $return =
        $facebook->api_client->notifications_sendEmail( $target,
                                                         $subject,
                                                         $textBody,
                                                         $fbmlBody );
    }
  } catch( FacebookRestClientException $ex) {
    wr($ex->__toString());
  }

  return isset($return[0]);
}

/** used to build the FBML body of an email message; used when recipient's email
client accepts HTML email */
function getFbmlEmailBody($sender, $target, Array $bodyData) {
  $appUrl = "{$bodyData['images'][0]['href']}/?appref=email";

  return "
        <meta content='text/html; charset=UTF-8' http-equiv='content-type'>
```

Listing 10.6 **Continued**

```
        <style type='text/css'>
          table { text-align: center; font-size: 16px;
                  font-family: Arial,Helvetica,sans-serif; }
          img { border: none; width: 96px; height: 96px; }
          td.compliment { color: #33cc00; font-weight: bold; }
          td p { font-size: 12px; }
        </style>
        <table>
          <tbody>
            <tr>
              <td><fb:name uid='$target' firstnameonly='true' useyou='false' />,
              </td>
            </tr>
            <tr>
              <td>
                <fb:name uid='$sender' useyou='false' firstnameonly='true' />
                thinks you are</td>
            </tr>
            <tr>
              <td>
                <a href='$appUrl'>
                  <img alt='You\'re {$bodyData['ctitle']}!'
                       title='You\'re {$bodyData['ctitle']}!'
                       src='{$bodyData['images'][0]['src']}'>
                </a>
              </td>
            </tr>
            <tr>
              <td class='compliment'>{$bodyData['ctitle']}</td>
            </tr>
            <tr>
              <td>Because you '{$bodyData['ctext']}'</td>
            </tr>
            <tr>
              <td>
                <br />
                <p>
                <a href='$appUrl'>Click here</a>
                  to send a Compliment back to
                  <fb:name uid='$sender' useyou='false' firstnameonly='true' />!
                </p>
              </td>
            </tr>
          </tbody>
        </table>";
```

Listing 10.6 **Continued**

```
}

/** gets the plain text body for an email; used if email client only accepts
text email */
function getTextEmailBody(Facebook $facebook, Array $bodyData) {
  $compliment = "";

  $userInfo = $facebook->api_client->users_getInfo($facebook->user,
                                                   'first_name');

  if(isset($userInfo[0]) && isset($userInfo[0]['first_name'])) {
    $userInfo['first_name'] = $userInfo[0]['first_name'];
  } else {
    $userInfo['first_name'] = 'A friend';
  }

  return
    "{$userInfo['first_name']} sent you a Compliment ".
    "using the Compliments application on Facebook!".PHP_EOL.PHP_EOL.
    "They think you are '{$bodyData['ctitle']}' because ".
    "you '{$bodyData['ctext']}'".PHP_EOL.PHP_EOL.
    "--".PHP_EOL.
    "Check it out at ".FB_APP_URL."!".PHP_EOL;
}
?>
```

Notice that we call two Facebook API methods to handle the task of sending email. First, we use the `users_hasAppPermission()` method to check that the target has granted the `email extended` permission. If they have, we call `notifications_sendEmail()` to actually send the email to the user. `notifications_sendEmail()` takes two parameters for the content of the body of the email it creates. The first, `$textBody` (in Listing 10.6), sets the plain text body in case the user's email only accepts text email. The second, `$fbmlBody`, provides FBML for HTML-enabled clients.

As you can see, we use a variety of markup in the FBML email body because Facebook permits a lot of tags to be used in email. Facebook always uses the FBML body if it's present and falls back on the plain-text version if it's not, but you must provide a value for one of these two or the method will fail. Also, notice that we call the `users_getInfo()` API method in the `getTextEmailBody()` function because the plain-text body parameter passed to `notifications_sendEmail()` will not be parsed as FBML; therefore, we cannot use the `<fb:name>` tag and have Facebook render the sender's name as we previously did.

To actually send the email, we'll add a checkbox to the form in `index.php`, which is checked by default. We use this value in `feed_form_callback.php` to determine whether to call `sendUserEmail()`. Add the bold code in Listing 10.7 to `renderPage()` in `index.php`.

Listing 10.7 **index.php: renderPage() Function Updated with a Checkbox to Enable Email**

```
<tr>
  <td class='label'>because:</td>
  <td class='content'>
    <input class='textInput' name='compliment' />
  </td>
</tr>
<tr>
  <td class='content' colspan='2'>
    <input type='checkbox' name='email' checked='checked' />
    Check this box to send your friend an email as well.
  </td>
</tr>
</table>
```

Now, modify the `feed_form_callback.php` script to call the `sendUserEmail()` function. Listing 10.8 shows the updated code to allow this.

Listing 10.8 **feed_form_callback.php: Calling sendUserEmail()**

```
<?php
require_once 'inc/globals.inc';
require_once 'inc/utils.inc';
require_once 'inc/db.inc';
require_once 'inc/profile.inc';
require_once 'inc/notifications.inc';
require_once 'inc/email.inc';

// some code elided for clarity...

  if( 'multiFeedStory' === $feedFormType ) {
    $feed = array('template_id'   => TEMPLATE_BUNDLE_MULTIFEEDSTORY_1,
                  'template_data' =>
                    array('app'   => '<a href="'.FB_APP_URL.'">Compliments</a>',
                          'ctitle' => $comp['title'],
                          'ctext'  => $compliment,
                          'images' => array($images)));
    if(! sendUserNotification($facebook, $target)) {
      echo json_encode(
        array( 'errorCode'    => FACEBOOK_API_VALIDATION_ERROR,
               'errorTitle'   => 'Notifications Failed!',
               'errorMessage'=> 'Error sending Facebook notifications.') );
```

Listing 10.8 **Continued**

```
        die();
    }
    if( 'on' !== $_POST['email'] ||
        ! sendUserEmail( $facebook,
                         $target,
                         $feed['template_data'] ) ) {
        wr(basename(__FILE__)." no email sent to $target.");
    }
} else { // rest of file...
```

Now, when you send a compliment to a friend that's enabled email, she should see a message, like the one shown in Figure 10.17, if she accepts HTML email. If she does not accept HTML, she'll see a plain-text email, as shown in Figure 10.18.

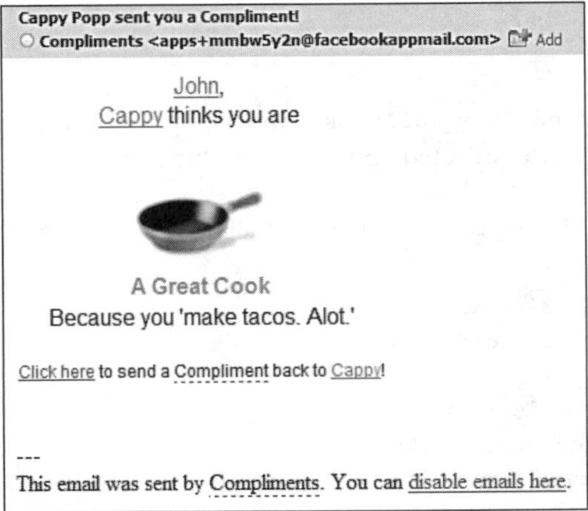

Figure 10.17 Sample HTML email sent by the Compliments application

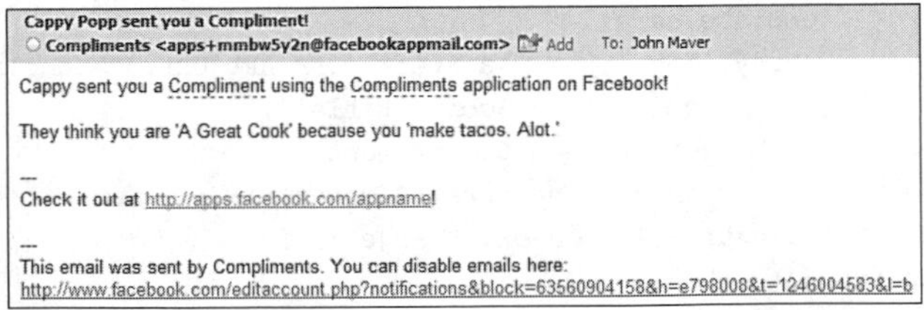

Figure 10.18 Plain-text email sent by the Compliments application

You would think that clicking one of the links at the end of emails in Figure 10.17 and Figure 10.18 to disable the sending of emails would direct the user to a similar application settings page, like that shown previously in Figure 10.15; however, these links point to the main user settings page for her Facebook account. There are no direct links to application settings for a specific application.

Requests

The next communication channel to discuss is requests. In a general sense, requests can be seen as notifications that provide a call to action. Their sole purpose is to ask a user to do something with an application, unlike Feed stories, notifications, or email. All these can provide secondary links to or suggestions for using an application, but their main focus is provide information rather than demanding a user act in an explicit way. By far, the most popular and prevalent form of requests are application invitations. Invitations obviously are designed to get an application more users. Facebook also uses them to send friend, event, and group invitations.

Overview of Requests and Invitations

No other application communication type in Facebook has been more maligned than invitations, and for good reason. In the early days of the Facebook Platform, invitations were the easiest and best way for applications to quickly gain users. However, many applications abused them terribly by requiring new users to invite all of their friends before being able to actually use them. This, of course, resulted in some applications gaining millions of users in a matter of days, but at the expense of users' patience and goodwill.

To address this problem, Facebook first put a limit on the number of friends that could be invited with a single invitation. Developers quickly countered by coding multiple successions of invitation pages into applications to achieve the same result, or by requiring users to invite friends before being able to access some critical piece of functionality in their applications. Quiz-type applications were notorious for requiring invitations to be sent before users could get their results, for example.

Facebook responded by requiring that all invitation screens shown to a user had some way for them to skip or opt out of the invitation process; moreover, it required all developers to use a standardized Facebook invitation control that all users would come to immediately recognize. This control provided a link for users to report forced invitation schemes used by applications and allowed Facebook to restrict the grossest offenders. Still, invitations clogged the News feeds of every user. Finally, Facebook launched a complete user-interface redesign that pushed invitations to a much less noticeable part of users' Home pages and removed them from their profiles entirely. Users now must manually view them from their Home page Requests section if they so desire, as shown in Figure 10.19. Notice that all of them are rolled up an Other Requests link on the user's Home page, depending on how many outstanding unviewed requests a user has. Friend, event, and group requests are always shown.

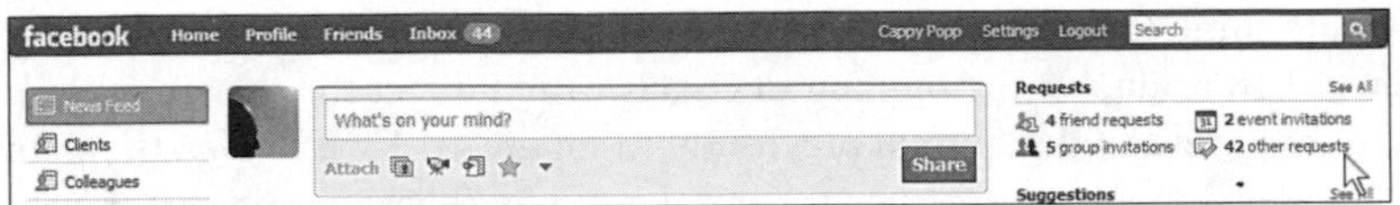

Figure 10.19 Invitations and requests have been de-emphasized in the latest revision of the Facebook user interface.

Figure 10.20 shows the effect having few outstanding requests has on a user being able to see your invitation directly.

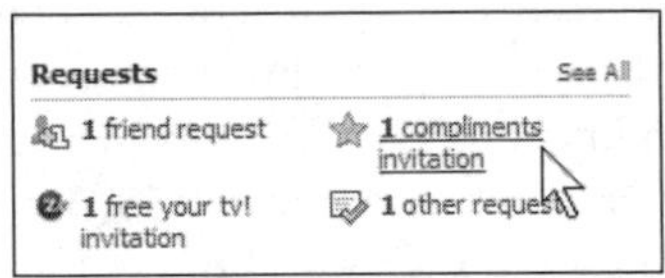

Figure 10.20 If a user only has a few pending requests, the direct link to the invitation is shown in the Requests area.

So, with all the controversy surrounding them, why should developers use requests and invitations? Because they are still a direct way for an application to gain new users, although their efficacy in doing so is undoubtedly diminished from what it once was, especially with the rise of the Facebook Feed. Nevertheless, they offer developers an important channel for viral growth, and they provide the easiest way for them to target multiple users at once. multiFeedStory Feed forms are the only other communication mechanism that allows applications to target a user's friends who have not authorized an application. However, multiFeedStory forms can only target up to three users at once. Application users can potentially send many more invitations to their friends than this, depending on the number of requests the application is allowed to send per user per day. Currently, this starts at 20; however, Facebook increases this number as an application gains users and if these users respond well to it. We discuss that process when we present allocations in the section, "Application Messaging and Allocations."

Sending Requests and Invitations

In FBML-based canvas pages, applications must present users with a standardized Facebook invitation control, shown in Figure 10.21, that's comprised of a number of specialized FBML tags. We'll add another tab to the user interface in the Compliments application to show the invite control on its own page. Listing 10.9 shows the code needed to do this.

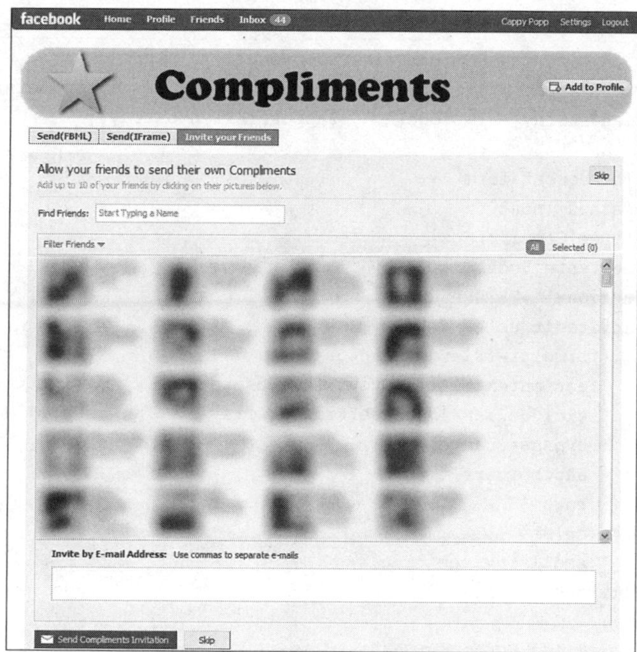

Figure 10.21 This is the invitation page with which most Facebook users are familiar.

Listing 10.9 **`invite.php`: Showing the Standard Facebook Invitation FBML Control**

```
<?php
  require_once 'inc/globals.inc';
  require_once 'inc/utils.inc';

  $facebook = new Facebook(FB_API_KEY, FB_APP_SECRET);

  $pageOutput  = getHeaderContent();
  $pageOutput .= getInviteContent();

  echo($pageOutput);

  /** Gets the markup to show the default Facebook invite control */
  function getInviteContent() {
    global $facebook;

    $content = "
    <fb:name uid=\"{$facebook->user}\" useyou=\"false\" /> loves sending
      <a href=\"".FB_APP_URL."\"> compliments </a> to their friends and
      would like you to be able to do the same!
    <fb:req-choice url=\"".FB_APP_URL."\"
      label=\"Send your Own!\" />";
```

Listing 10.9 **Continued**

```
  $content              = htmlentities($content);
  $appuserFriendsArray = $facebook->api_client->friends_getAppUsers();
  $appuserFriendsArray = implode(',', $appuserFriendsArray);

  return( "<fb:request-form
            method='post'
            type='Compliments'
            content='$content'
            action='".FB_APP_URL."'
            invite='true'>
              <fb:multi-friend-selector
                actiontext='Allow your friends to send their own Compliments'
                exclude_ids='$appuserFriendsArray'
                bypass='cancel'
                showborder='true'
                rows='5'
                cols='5'
                email_invite='true' />
          </fb:request-form>" );
}

/** renders the page header and navigation */
function getHeaderContent() {
  $header = "
    <link rel='stylesheet' type='text/css'
      href='".LOCAL_APP_URL.getFileVer("/css/main.css")."' />
    <!—[if IE]>
    <link rel='stylesheet' type='text/css'
      href='".LOCAL_APP_URL.getFileVer("/css/ie.css")."' />
    <![endif]—>
    <fb:title>Send a Compliment</fb:title>
    <div class='banner'
       style='background: url(".LOCAL_APP_URL."/img/banner.png) no-repeat;' >
      <div id='buttons' class='clearfix' >
        <div id='addbutton'>
          <fb:if-section-not-added section='profile'>
              <fb:add-section-button section='profile' />
          </fb:if-section-not-added>
        </div>
        <div id='infobutton'>
          <fb:if-section-not-added section='info'>
              <fb:add-section-button section='info' />
          </fb:if-section-not-added>
        </div>
      </div>
    </div>
```

Listing 10.9 **Continued**

```
        <fb:tabs>
          <fb:tab-item href='".FB_APP_URL."/' title='Send(FBML)' selected='true'/>
          <fb:tab-item href='".FB_APP_URL."/index_iframe.php?fb_force_mode=iframe'
            title='Send(IFrame)' />
          <fb:tab-item href='".FB_APP_URL."/invite.php'
            title='Invite your Friends' />
        </fb:tabs>";

      return $header;
   }
?>
```

Add the code in Listing 10.9 into a new file called `invite.php` in your application's root directory. You'll also need to update `index.php` to show the new tab. Update its `getHeaderContent()` function, as shown in the following code (new code shown in bold):

```
  /** renders the page header and navigation */
  function getHeaderContent() {
 // code hidden for clarity...

    $header .= "
    <fb:tabs>
      <fb:tab-item href='".FB_APP_URL."/' title='Send(FBML)' selected='true'/>
      <fb:tab-item href='".FB_APP_URL."/index_iframe.php?fb_force_mode=iframe'
        title='Send(IFrame)' />
      <fb:tab-item href='".FB_APP_URL."/invite.php'
        title='Invite your Friends' />
    </fb:tabs>";

    return $header; }
```

The new tab, and the resulting invite control the code in Listing 10.9 renders, was shown in Figure 10.21. As Figure 10.22 illustrates, clicking the invite link shows a preview of the resulting invite to the sender and allows him to add his own message or cancel its delivery. We cover the details of the FBML tags and their attributes used in Listing 10.9 in the following sections.

Invites use a set of specialized FBML tags to render an invite control. The first, `<fb:request-form>`, renders as a specialized HTML form whose sole purpose is to send requests/invites to users. Table 10.3 presents the attributes used in this tag and how they control its behavior and appearance.

The most important and frustrating part of using `<fb:request-form>` is getting the value for the `content` attribute right. Pay careful attention that all quotes are escaped correctly when using it. If you receive FBML rendering errors when rendering an `<fb:request-form>`, this attribute's value is the first place to look. View the page's source in your browser and pay attention to all the quotes, opening, and closing tags in the `content` FBML. You can also use the Facebook FBML Test Console to verify your code.

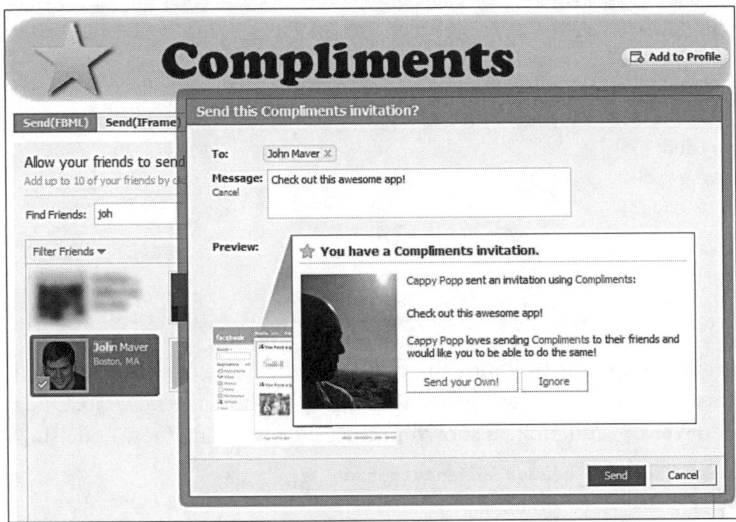

Figure 10.22 When a user clicks the link to send an invitation or request, he is shown a dialog that shows a preview of what the receiver will see on her Requests page and allows him to add his own message to the invitation.

Although it can be used to send requests to a single user, `<fb:request-form>` is used most often to target multiple users. To give it this capability, you must include one of the FBML tags that display different user selection options to the user. `<fb:friend-selector>` is the first one we'll discuss. You're already familiar with it because you used it to provide the `typeahead` control on the main form that allows you choose a friend to which you'll send a compliment. Next on the list is the `<fb:multi-friend-input>` tag. It allows you to select multiple friends and stores each one in the control as their name is typed and selected (see Figure 10.23). To actually be able to send the invitation when using either of these multiple-selection tags, you must include the `<fb:request-form-submit>` tag, which renders a Submit button on the form. The Submit button is special in that it prompts the user with a dialog to confirm the sending of the request as a way to further protect recipients from unwanted invitations.

Finally, we introduce the `<fb:multi-friend-selector>` tag. It does not require the `<fb:request-form-submit>` tag to be present on `<fb:request-form>`. It not only provides the `typeahead` functionality of the previous two tags, but it also allows a user to choose from his friends graphically, as Figure 10.24 shows. There are actually a few flavors of this tag, each of which offers similar behavior but in different-sized packages. Discussing all the potential combinations here would be overwhelming. The one we used in `invite.php` is designed to be used when an application has a full canvas page or large space to show a selection form that can show the profile pictures and names of friends. This tag renders the grid of users you see displayed in Figure 10.21 and Figure 10.22. It also offers another great feature: Users can invite their friends who aren't yet on Facebook by typing their email address in the bottom of the control. This tag provides several attributes that control its behavior, styling, and content that merit further attention. Table 10.4 provides the details.

Table 10.3 **<fb:request-form> Attributes**

Attribute	Description
`type`	Set to the type of invite/request to create and is usually set to the name of the application originating the request. **Required.**
`content`	Contains the markup of the actual request/invite. It should be FBML that only contains links and the `<fb:req-choice>` FBML tag. This is by far the most confusing attribute and piece of functionality in the request/invite creation process. You must encode the value using the PHP `htmlentities()` function or this content does not render correctly.
`invite`	Controls whether an invite or request is sent. It's set to `false` (the default) to generate a request form, `true` to generate an invite form.
`action`	Sets a custom redirect URL where users are sent after sending or skipping the request. It defaults to an application's Canvas Page URL. You cannot and must not use this to entice or force a user to invite others if she skips doing so the first time.
`method`	Specifies whether to use `GET` or `POST` for the submit, as you would for an HTML form.

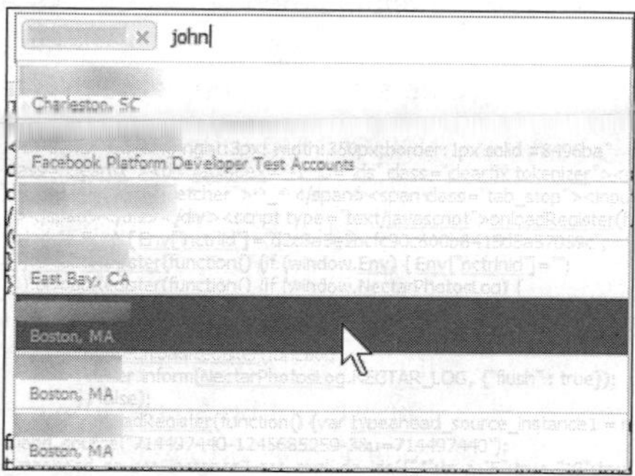

Figure 10.23 The `<fb:multi-friend-input>` FBML tag allows users to type the names of and select multiple users from their list of friends.

The `showborder` attribute has a strange side effect that can affect the style of the rendered control: If you don't set it to `true`, the control still takes up the space for the border, as shown in Figure 10.25.

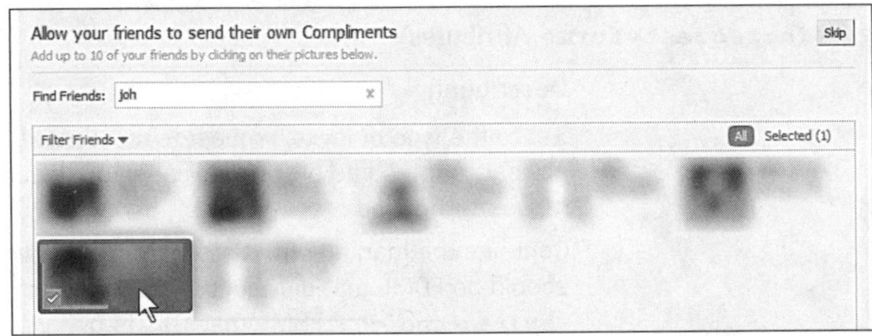

Figure 10.24 **`<fb:multi-friend-selector>`** allows both **`typeahead`** and graphical selection of users.

Table 10.4 **`<fb:multi-friend-selector>` Attributes**

Attribute	Description
`actiontext`	Used as the title of the rendered control. **Required**.
`showborder`	If set to true, this shows a border around the outside of the rendered control.
`cols`	Set this to the number of columns of Facebook user profile pictures to show in the control. This value determines the width of the control and can be set to 2, 3, or 5. Defaults to 5.
`rows`	Controls the number of rows of friends that display in the control. The default is 5, and it must be set to a value between 3 and 10.
`max`	Controls the total number of friends that can be selected in the control at once. Must be a value between 1 and 35, but is capped by the number of requests the user has remaining for the day.
`exclude_ids`	Set to a comma-separated list of Facebook user IDs, it contains all the friends of the current user that will not be shown in the selection area of the control. This attribute is extremely critical because it allows you to exclude friends of the current user, who've also authorized the application, from receiving invitations.

Table 10.4 **Continued**

Attribute	Description
`Bypass`	Used for the label of the Skip button. Set this attribute's value to `skip`, `step`, or `cancel`, which render `Skip`, `Skip This Step`, or `Cancel` for the button's label (respectively).
`email_invite`	Set this to `true` if you want to display the box at the bottom of the control to allow the user to invite friends via email who have not yet joined Facebook. Defaults to `true`.

With Border:

Without Border:

Figure 10.25 Facebook still uses the space occupied by the border when it renders `<fb:multi-friend-selector>` with `showborder` set to `false`.

Requests Versus Invitations

Because we use the terms request and invitation interchangeably, you might be confused as to the difference between the two. It's quite simple and controlled by the `invite` attribute of the `<fb:request-form>` tag we showed in Table 10.5. If the value of this attribute is `true`, Facebook renders the word invite or invitation in the markup produced for the tag. If it's `false`, it uses request instead. If you go back to Figure 10.22 and replace every instance of the word invitation with request, you'd see the difference that both the sender and receiver would see between the two.

Application Messaging and Allocations

Now that we've covered all the major ways an application can communicate with its users and implemented them all in the Compliments application, it's time for a dose of reality. Facebook strictly limits how many messages of a given type an application can send to its users. In Sandbox mode, an application is freed from many of these limits, but after it's released to the general Facebook population, it is carefully monitored and enforced.

In the early days of the Facebook Platform, few constraints were placed on application messaging, and the daily limits for each type of message were generous, especially in the numbers of invitations and notifications they could send. Applications abused these limits and, soon, users were inundated with copious amounts of application communication that many saw as spam. Facebook responded by imposing the allocation system that's in place today.

Viewing Application Allocation Limits

To view the allocation limits for Compliments, open the Developer Settings for the application. Select Compliments (if it is not already selected) and choose Statistics from the list of links along the right side of the screen, as shown in Figure 10.26. This brings up the Insights tool for Compliments. Click the Allocations tab, as Figure 10.27 shows.

Facebook limits an application's capability to send two different types of messaging: user-to-user notifications and requests/invitations. Application-to-user notifications are limited to seven per week per user, and all applications on Facebook have this limit.

Figure 10.26 To view the allocation limits for an application, click the Statistics link to display the Application Insights tool.

Because user-to-user notifications have dynamic limits, when we use the term notifications in this section, we mean user-to-user notifications. As you probably noticed in Figure 10.27, emails are also listed as being subject to an allocation limit, but these limits do not apply to new applications, only those that were launched before extended permissions were introduced. Applications can send as many emails as they want to their users after they are granted the `email` extended permission. However, Facebook still tracks user response to email by monitoring the number of times users click the disable link sent in every application-originated one.

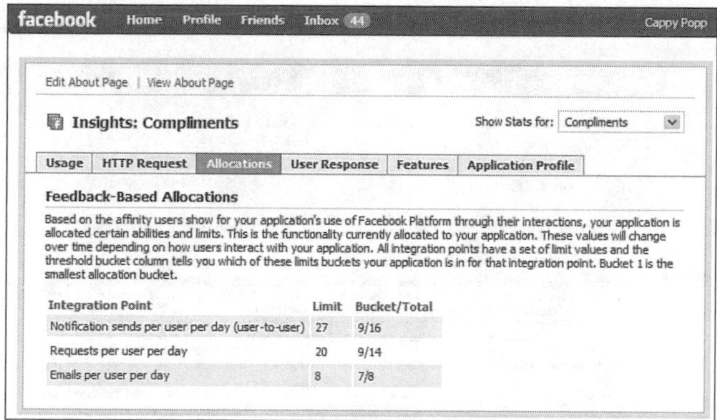

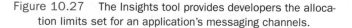

Figure 10.27 The Insights tool provides developers the allocation limits set for an application's messaging channels.

Applications are placed in groups that Facebook calls buckets that determine the maximum number of notifications and requests they can send per user per day. The upper limits of each bucket do not change linearly. Facebook does not publish these limits, but as you can see in Figure 10.27, new applications are placed a little above the middle of the scale.

How Facebook Determines Allocations

Facebook does not publicly provide the algorithms it uses to determine application allocations, but it certainly provides Platform guidelines to follow and gives developers access to some of the user-response metrics Facebook uses in the process. Facebook closely monitors how users respond to application messaging, especially notifications and requests. To see what they track for a given application and why, click the User Response tab of the Insights tool.

Not Enough Data?

Most likely, the Metric Ratio column for your application only contains the words "Not Enough Data." Because Compliments is in developer Sandbox mode, it has no users other than its developers. If the application were released to the public, these columns would contain user-response metrics. We'll address this by showing user-response data from one of our established applications, `Doorbell` (*http://apps.facebook.com/mydoorbell/*), which at the time of this writing, has more than 825,000 users.

As Figure 10.28 shows, Facebook tracks several different metrics related to application messaging and users' responses to them. Notice that all metric-ratio calculations use actions taken over the last seven days (notifications viewed, times request form shown, and so on). These metrics are one of the variables that Facebook uses to determine an application's allocations, but each of them does not carry the same weight. Facebook calculates allocations daily; it uses both data from the last seven days and some historical data to do so. The following sections detail the different user-response metrics that Facebook uses and how they're calculated.

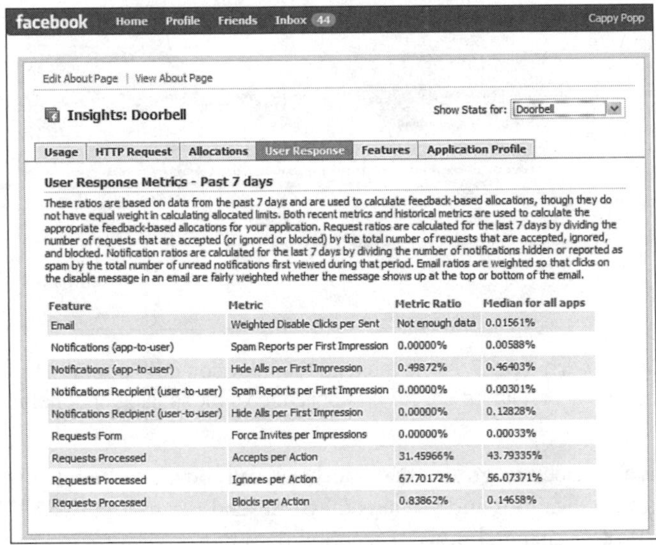

Feature	Metric	Metric Ratio	Median for all apps
Email	Weighted Disable Clicks per Sent	Not enough data	0.01561%
Notifications (app-to-user)	Spam Reports per First Impression	0.00000%	0.00588%
Notifications (app-to-user)	Hide Alls per First Impression	0.49872%	0.46403%
Notifications Recipient (user-to-user)	Spam Reports per First Impression	0.00000%	0.00301%
Notifications Recipient (user-to-user)	Hide Alls per First Impression	0.00000%	0.12828%
Requests Form	Force Invites per Impressions	0.00000%	0.00033%
Requests Processed	Accepts per Action	31.45966%	43.79335%
Requests Processed	Ignores per Action	67.70172%	56.07371%
Requests Processed	Blocks per Action	0.83862%	0.14658%

Figure 10.28 The Insights tool displays user-response metrics for the `Doorbell` application.

Notification Allocations

Facebook uses two different notification metrics when calculating allocations for an application. These apply to both user-to-user and application-to-user notifications. It is unclear which type of notification, if either, has more weight in final allocation numbers.

The first ratio, Spam Reports per First Impression, is calculated by dividing the number of notifications users flagged as spam by the number of *unread* notifications viewed for the first time over the last seven days. The denominator in this equation deserves more explanation. It means that when a user goes to his Notifications tab and flags all notifications from a *specific* application as spam, Facebook takes into account how many of the total number of notifications on the page are being viewed by that user for the first time in the last week. Figure 10.29 shows how users can tell Facebook that specific notifications are spam.

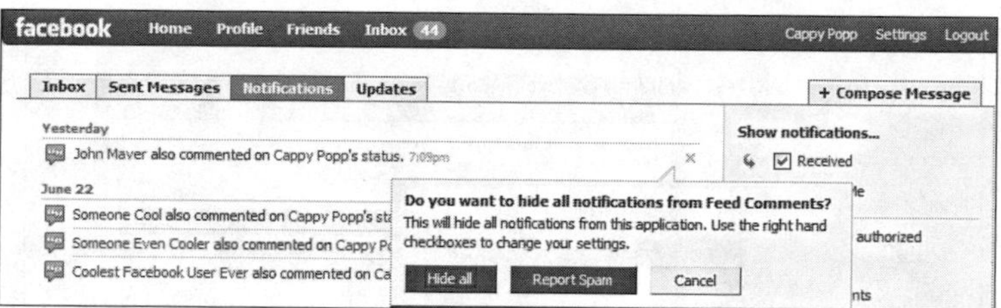

Figure 10.29 Users can hide all notifications from a specific application or report them as spam from the Notifications tab of their Inbox.

The second, Hide Alls per First Impression, is calculated by dividing the number of notifications users hid *categorically* divided by the number of unread notifications viewed for the first time over the last seven days. Figure 10.29 also shows one way users can Hide All notifications from a given application. Users can also control hiding all notifications from specific applications by using the checkboxes in the Applications You've Authorized section along the right column of the Notifications tab. Removing the checkmark from an application's checkbox has the same effect as clicking the Hide All button in Figure 10.29.

Request Allocations

Facebook calculates four metric ratios for requests. Some of these definitely have greater influence than others in the allocation determination. As previously mentioned, requests are identical to invitations and only differ by name. We use requests to refer to both types in the following paragraphs.

The ratio for the first request metric, Force Invites per Impressions, is influential. Users are shown the Report Forced Invites link on a request form if they view it more than once in a short period of time. Figure 10.30 shows an invite form after the user clicks the link. Clicking the link brings up the Forced Invite Reported dialog. Notice that a user can immediately remove any application that attempts to force them to invite others. Also, notice that the median for all applications is effectively 0%—Facebook does not take these lightly. To calculate the ratio, Facebook uses the number of times users have clicked the Report Forced Invite link in the form divided by the number of request forms shown to all users of the application.

The next three metric ratios are similar and only differ by the actions users take in response to requests. Users can accept, ignore, or block requests after they receive them, as Figure 10.31 illustrates. Facebook determines three ratios for request-related user actions: *Accepts per Action*, *Ignores per Action*, and *Blocks*. Each is calculated by dividing the number of requests accepted, ignored, or blocked (depending on the metric) by the sum of all requests accepted, ignored, or blocked.

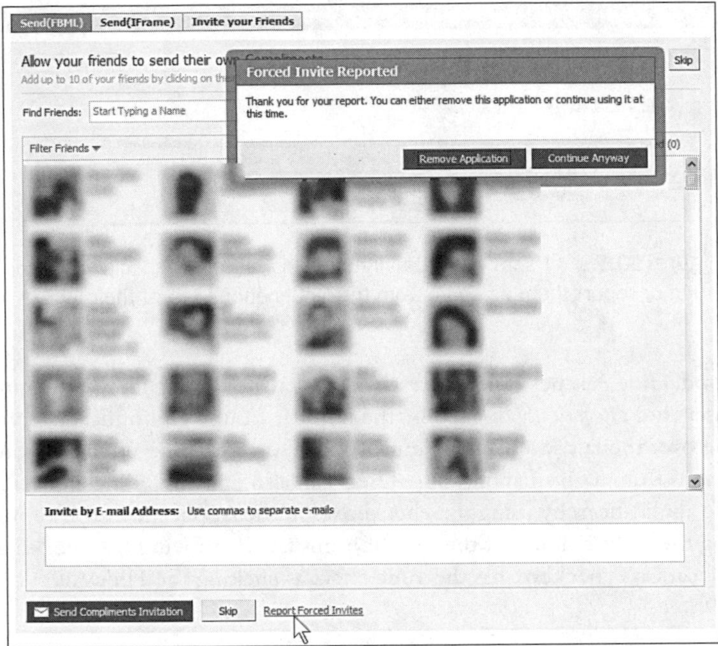

Figure 10.30 The Forced Invited Reported dialog shown after clicking the Report Forced Invites link on a request form.

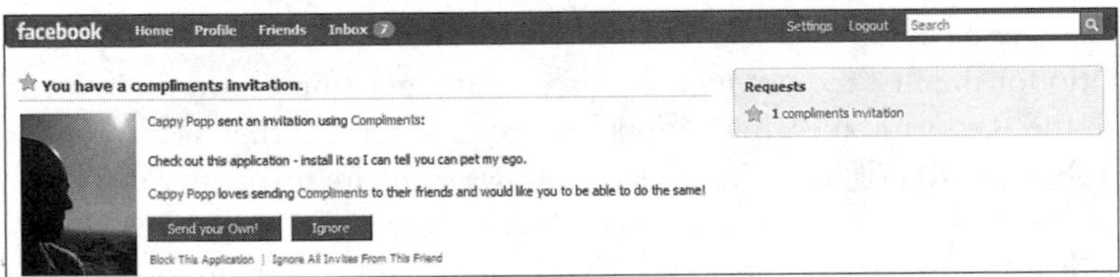

Figure 10.31 Recipients of invitations have the option to accept them, ignore them, or block them.

Email Allocations

When Facebook sends mail from an application to a user, it places a link to allow the user to disable any future emails from that application. If the link is placed at the top of the email, there is a greater chance of it being clicked by users (because it's the first thing they read) than if it's placed at the bottom. Facebook takes the placement of this link into account when calculating the Weighted Disable Clicks per Sent ratio. The ratio itself represents the number of times the links were clicked divided by the number of emails sent. Figure 10.32 shows this link in an example email message.

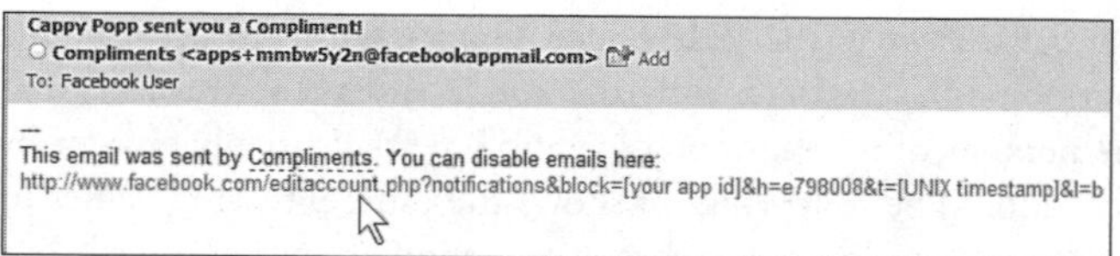

Figure 10.32 Facebook provides a link to disable the sending of emails from an application. It's up to Facebook where it's placed, but ideally, it should be at the end of the message to minimize its click-through rate.

As previously stated, email allocations and the metric ratios associated with them are no longer relevant to applications launched since Facebook introduced the `email` extended permission. The metric still is available in the Insights tool, so it deserves mention. Before the `email` permission was introduced, applications could send a small number of emails to their users every day. Currently, these applications are grandfathered and still allowed to send email without user permission. This metric only applies to them.

Tracking Allocations

The values shown for Doorbell in Figure 10.28 merit further study. First, the application currently only uses application-to-user notifications, and these are much less likely than the Facebook average to be flagged as spam, but a bit more likely to be hidden the first time they're viewed. This might impact its notification allocations, but probably not by much. Currently, the application is in bucket 13 (out of a possible 18) and is granted 60 notifications per user per day. The only requests this application sends are invitations, and they are 12 percent more likely to be ignored and a whopping 71 percent more likely to be blocked than the average application invitations, which undoubtedly directly affects its request allocations. Currently, the application is in request bucket 7 and is only allowed 6 per user per day (14 less than Compliments), which, as a new application, starts in bucket 9 and is granted 20 requests per day.

Tracking Allocations with the Facebook API

Because messaging is so important to an application's success, it's important for developers to pay close attention to the allocations their applications have been granted. We've shown one way to get them by checking the values shown on the Allocations tab from the Insights tool. This helps, but developers must manually check it for every application they own.

It would be much more convenient if there were some way for an application to check its messaging allocations itself and adjust its messaging behavior in response. Facebook provides some of this functionality via the `admin_getAllocations()` API method (`admin_getAllocations()` in the PHP client library), which returns the limit for a given message integration point. Unfortunately, the `admin.getAllocations()` method does not provide the number of messages of a specific type that have been sent by a specific user or the application. The following list shows the different string values for the `integration_point_name` parameter that this method accepts and what the method returns in response:

- **`notifications_per_day`**. Returns the number of user-to-user notifications the application can send per user per day
- **`announcement_notifications_per_day`.** Returns the number of application-to-users the application can send per week
- **`requests_per_day`**. Returns the number of requests the application can send per user per day

Best Practices

Although Facebook does not disclose either how much weight each user-response metric ratio has on its allocation calculations, nor does it provide any information on what happens if an application consistently attempts to exceed them, it is a good practice for developers to try to keep their applications from exceeding the limits they've been allocated, because this undoubtedly has some effect. The easiest way to do this is to track the number of messages of a given type sent by each application and user per day, and prevent applications from sending messages if they exceed their daily allocations. Facebook currently resets the values at 12 AM Pacific time. Developers could have a script for their applications that run daily via a `cron` job sometime after this to both store the daily limits (for efficiency) and reset all the counts. This is beyond the scope of this chapter, but keep it in mind when you're designing a robust application.

Application user ratings can also affect allocations. These ratings were introduced in May 2009, as part of the launch of a completely redesigned Application Directory. Developers have reported that applications with high user ratings are being granted higher allocations than applications with low user ratings, even if the application has poor user-response metrics. Facebook has not publicly confirmed this, but it makes sense. Getting an application verified through the Facebook Verified Apps program also has directly affects allocations: They get a two-bucket bump for both user-to-user notifications and requests after they're verified. Additionally, they are given special priority in the Application Directory, which increases their visibility to new users.

Facebook Sharing

There is yet one more way to publish content to Facebook. It's called Sharing, and Facebook provides multiple ways to access it. Sharing is interesting because it offers users a means to publish content to Facebook in two completely different ways. Sharing functionality can be added to applications via the `<fb:share-button>` FBML tag.

Publishing Content Via Sharing

The Share button rendered from `<fb:share-button>` is undoubtedly familiar to most Facebook users. Figure 10.33 shows the default appearance of this familiar button, both in its normal and hovered state. Notice the tooltip in the figure: It mentions that users can either send something to their friends or post it on their profile.

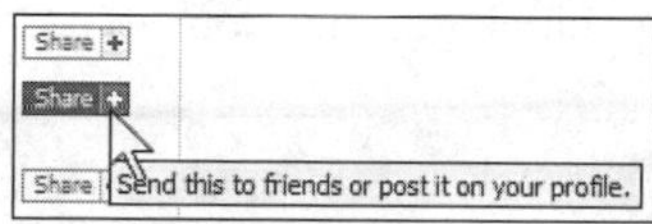

Figure 10.33 Facebook Share buttons in an application

The result of sending something to a profile combines the behavior of publishing content with Feed forms or Publishers: A Feed story is published to the user's profile, Home page, and their friends' Home pages, effectively targeting every stream-integration point. The only noticeable difference in the Feed stories produced by the Sharing system is that Facebook adds a Share action link to them that provides the same behavior as the button. In fact, Facebook adds the Share action link to many of the Feed stories it automatically publishes, such as photo notifications, imported Facebook Notes notifications, and others. Notice the Share action links in the Facebook Note Feed story in Figure 10.34.

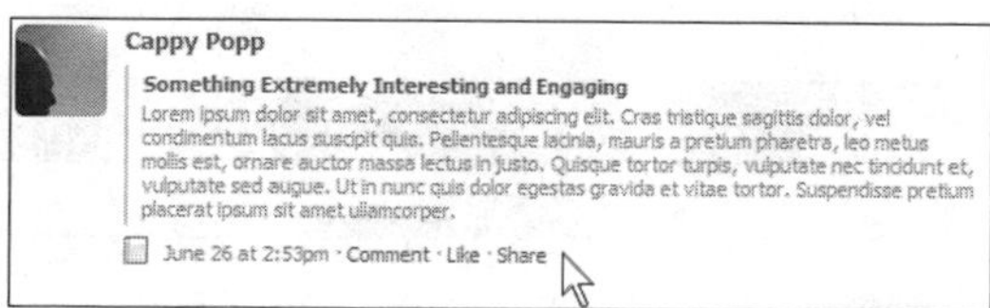

Figure 10.34 Facebook provides a Share action link at the end of many of its Feed stories.

The other publishing option offered by Sharing is unique. It allows users to send content to a maximum of 20 friends' Facebook Inboxes as Facebook messages. This is the only method for applications to send content to a user's Facebook Inbox. Unfortunately, there's no way to do this programmatically.

Sharing Preview

The interface users are presented with when attempting to share content is also unique. Figure 10.35 and Figure 10.36 show the dialog users are shown when a Share button or Share link is clicked. In Figure 10.35, the Send a Message tab is selected. Notice that, in the To: field, the user is given the option to type the name of a specific friend, a Facebook friend list, or an external email address to which he can send content. Users can also provide their own custom subject and message. Figure 10.36, on the other hand, displays an interface similar to that used for publishing stories from a Feed form.

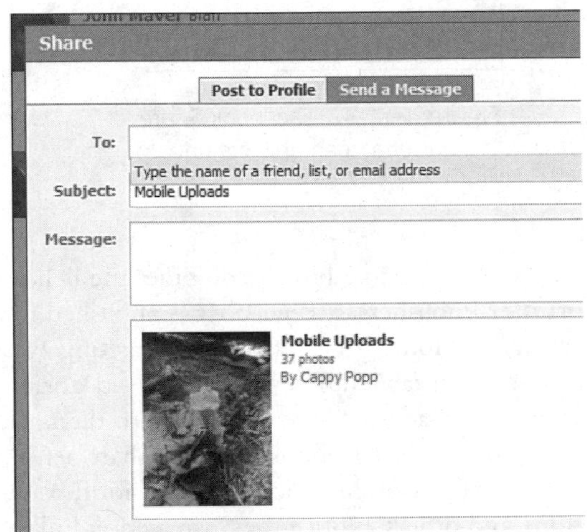

Figure 10.35 Facebook Share preview dialog Send a Message tab

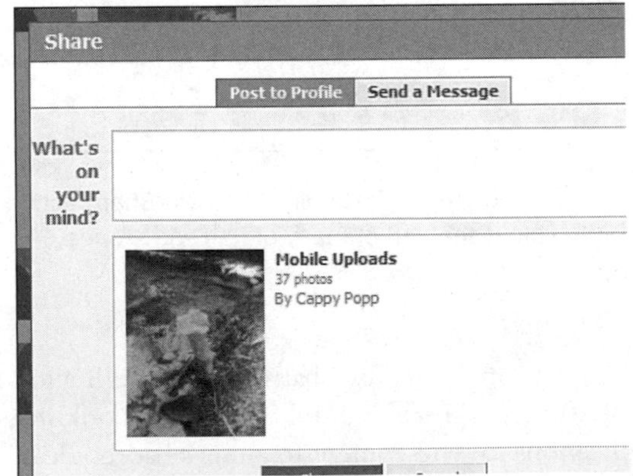

Figure 10.36 Facebook Share preview dialog Post to Profile tab

The dialog also displays a content preview that can be customized by the application for each media type that can be shared; links, photos, and multimedia all have different previews.

The following code shows how to render a button to share a link using the `<fb:share-button>` FBML tag. Figure 10.37 shows the preview dialog rendered from it when a user clicks it. Notice that there's no image shown in the preview; the *apps.facebook.com* subdomain is used as the title, and the URL is shown below it:

```
<fb:share-button class="url" href="http://apps.facebook.com/example" />
```

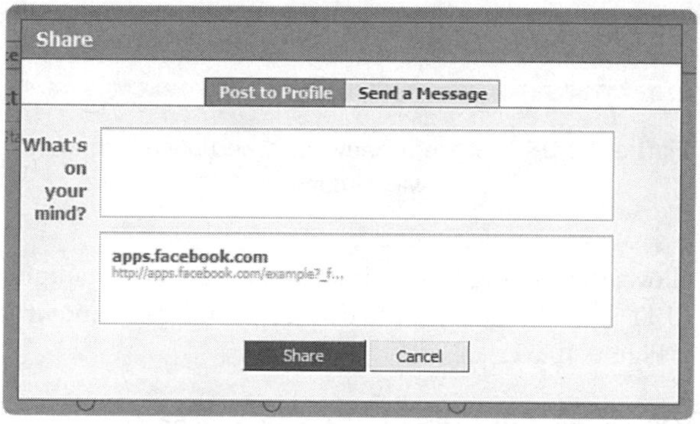

Figure 10.37 Share preview for a basic hyperlink

To make content more likely to be shared by others, it's best to make the preview of that content as engaging as possible. Listing 10.10 shows how to implement a Facebook Share button for a web page with a preview image. Figure 10.38 shows the preview generated by clicking a Share button using this code. Notice how the values from the `content` attributes from the `<meta name='title'>` and `<meta name='description'>` elements are used in the preview. The image preview is generated from the URL passed in the `<link rel='image_src'>` element.

Listing 10.10 `<fb:share-button>` FBML for a Web Page Preview

```
<fb:share-button class="meta">
  <meta name="title" content="meta title content" />
  <meta name="description" content="meta description content" />
  <link rel="target_url" href="http://www.example.com/" />
  <link rel="image_src" href="http://www.example.com/images/img.jpg" />
</fb:share-button>
```

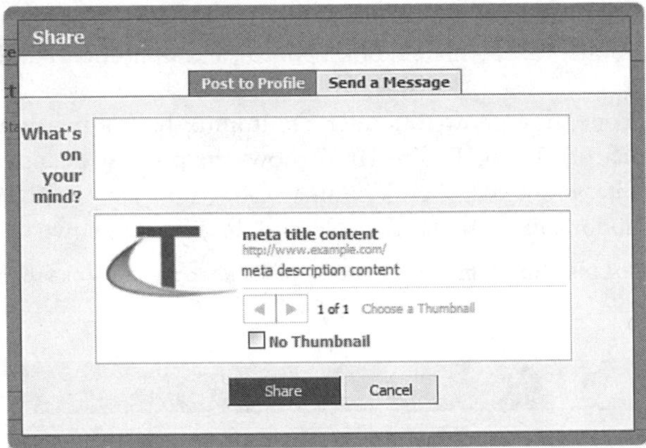

Figure 10.38 Share preview for a web page with a preview image

Facebook also allows the sharing of multimedia content. For example, the FBML shown in Listing 10.11 is used to share a podcast. The rendered content looks similar to what was shown in Figure 10.37.

Listing 10.11 **<fb:share-button> FBML for Sharing an Audio File**

```
<fb:share-button class="meta" >
  <meta name="medium" content="audio" />
  <meta name="title" content="The Greatest Podcast Ever" />
  <meta name="description" content="A weekly podcast about the greatest things
ever" />
  <meta name="audio_type" content="application/mp3" />
  <meta name="audio_title" content="Episode 20: Why Facebook is Great" />
  <meta name="audio_artist" content="John Doe" />
  <link rel="image_src" href="http://example.com/images/podcast.gif" />
  <link rel="audio_src" href="http://example.com/podcasts/podcast.mp3" />
  <link rel="target_url" href="http://example.com/podcasts/podcast.mp3" />
</fb:share-button>
```

As Listings 10.10 and 10.11 illustrate, `<fb:share-button>` can contain `<meta>` and `<link>` elements and a `class` attribute that controls its behavior. The `class` attribute should be set to `url` if the button will be used to share a link and `meta` if it will be used to share other media, such as images, audio, or video. None of these elements can contain any HTML in their content attribute values—Facebook strips it out.

When using `<fb:share-button class='meta'>`, always at least provide `title` and `description` `<meta>` elements to ensure the preview is correctly rendered. As Figure 10.38 demonstrates, `title` is the title of the preview (and of the resulting Feed story or Facebook message). `description` is the body of the preview, story, or message. If you want to provide a preview image, a `<link rel='image_src'>` element must be present with its `href` attribute set to the image's full URL. Finally, although Facebook does not require it, it's a good practice to provide a `<link rel='target_url'>` element. In many cases, a preview won't render without it.

Summary

This chapter covered some of the most important messaging channels for Facebook applications, including the Publisher, notifications, application email, and requests/invitations. It also discussed using extended permissions to allow users to grant applications access to more advanced functionality. Finally, it presented how Facebook monitors application messaging and user response to set messaging limits. Here are some key points:

- The Publisher is one of the most powerful communication channels available to application developers. There are two types available, and they allow users to publish application content directly to the stream and are not subject to allocation limits.
- Facebook provides two different types of notifications: User-to-user notifications require an active session to be sent, while application-to-user notifications do not.
- Applications can send email to their users, but users must grant an application permission to do so.
- Users can grant applications extended permissions that give them access to an array of powerful features of the Facebook API that they do not normally have. Facebook provides several ways for applications to prompt users to request them.
- Requests and invitations are not as important as they once were, but they are still the most direct way for applications to gain new users. Several controls are available to customize both the sender's and receiver's user experience when dealing with them.
- Facebook restricts the numbers of user-to-user notifications, application-to-user notifications, and invitations applications can send for a given time period. These allocation limits are directly related to how users respond to application messaging and behavior.
- Facebook Sharing allows the publishing of links, photos, and multimedia content to the stream and the Facebook Inbox.

11

FBJS, Mock AJAX, and Flash

So far, we spent a great deal of time on server-side PHP that comprises Facebook applications. However, nearly every web application today uses at least some JavaScript for client-side logic and validation. For Facebook applications, the more logic and processing that can be offloaded to the user's machine, the better. Why? First, client-side processing is free. JavaScript executes within the user's browser on his local machine. Although hosting is undoubtedly cheaper than ever, it can still quickly get expensive if an application suddenly explodes in popularity or you host several popular applications on a single server. Secondly, it decreases application response time when code can execute locally without the user's browser having to send an HTTP request to a remote server and wait for a result. Finally, it allows more dynamic user interfaces to be created through the user of DOM manipulation and technologies, such as AJAX and Flash.

Allowing External JavaScript in Facebook

Most websites or domains that allow third parties to embed JavaScript within them usually segregate that JavaScript by requiring that it be hosted in IFrames. This keeps them somewhat insulated from code over which they have little control, because the IFrame's contents are *usually* served from a different domain on a remote server. The browser's same-origin policy protects scripts from the remote domain from interacting with those running in the host page's `window` execution context. There are downsides to this approach, however. First, search engines do not index IFrames like they do normal web pages. They simply link to the content in the IFrame, not to the page that hosts it. It also takes time to load the external IFrame code; users do not want to wait for an external page to populate an IFrame if they are on a page to interact or get information.

Taking these points in context with Facebook, more issues arise. For example, FBML was designed so that application developers can access Facebook design primitives and have their code translated into normal HTML and JavaScript that could be served from a Facebook domain. Remember that applications and their canvas pages are addressed with URLs, such as the following: http://apps.*facebook.com/appname*. During the translation process, Facebook parses an application's FBML—served from a remote server—to normal HTML and JavaScript. It then wraps this code in an HTML `<div>`, surrounds it by the Facebook chrome, and serves it up like any other page on its domain. If Facebook allowed full access to JavaScript in this environment, developers could easily manipulate not only their own document structure, but the entire Facebook user interface and many of the client-side subsystems it provides, such as Chat, the Applications menu, or the Notifications area.

Profile boxes also present risks. As discussed in Chapter 8, "Updating the Profile," their contents are cached and run from Facebook servers. If Facebook allowed arbitrary JavaScript to run on profile boxes, the code would have access to all the global JavaScript objects available on the Facebook domain. The security risk to Facebook would be overwhelming, not only from a DOM manipulation or exploit standpoint, but from a privacy one: All the personal information of hundreds of millions of Facebook users would be at risk.

Even with these issues, Facebook had to provide some way to allow developers to use JavaScript in their Facebook Markup Language (FBML) applications. JavaScript is the most widely used scripting language for client-side web application development. Developers would never have adopted the FBML model of application design without it. To solve this problem, Facebook decided to use a technique, called sandboxing, to allow a modified, safer version of JavaScript to run within FBML.

Sandboxing

Sandboxing has its roots in the object capability movement of software design and security. (You can read more about it on the web at *http://en.wikipedia.org/wiki/Objectcapability_model.*) Simply put, this is a software security model that believes objects should have no innate abilities of their own unless they are passed them as a reference or sent them in a message.

The core JavaScript language and all browsers' implementations of it violate this principle in several ways. For example, in the JavaScript core language, global objects (such as `Object`, `Array`, and `String`) are always accessible to any JavaScript code and can be changed simply by modifying their `prototype` properties. Browsers add DOM interfaces to allow HTML/XML manipulation of the documents they load that are accessible to JavaScript; JavaScript functions provided by the browsers, such as `document.write()`, can allow arbitrary code or malware to be dynamically injected into web pages. The core JavaScript `eval()` function can execute arbitrary code that has access to the global environment.

All three of these are simple examples of unintended side effects (or *ambient effects*, in object-capability terms) that can lead to disaster. Not to mention the ubiquity of cross-site scripting (XSS) and cross-site request forgery (XSRF) exploits both enabled by JavaScript, which have resulted in untold millions of privacy breaches and lost revenue across the web. To allow JavaScript in some form on FBML pages, Facebook clearly had to ensure that only a sanitized subset of the full JavaScript language and DOM interfaces were made available to third-party client-side code.

How Facebook Restricts JavaScript

To create the sandbox, Facebook removed many of the offending functions and access to the global objects that might be misused. When an FBML application canvas page loads, or profile content is set via the `profile.setFBML()` Facebook API method, Facebook scans it for JavaScript. If it finds any, it automatically places it in a special namespace created by prepending every JavaScript function, object, array, variable, and event reference it finds with an identifier that contains the current application's ID. This action ensures that there are no clashes with variables defined in the global namespace and effectively removes the ability for this JavaScript to obtain any reference to global objects or functions. Facebook also hides the powerful JavaScript `eval()` function and any global functions that might be used as attack vectors.

Finally, Facebook significantly modifies the DOM object model. Access to the global `Window` object, which is the root object and default execution context in all client-side JavaScript programming, is forbidden. Also gone is the darling of most client-side web programmers, the DOM-provided `alert()` function. DOM properties themselves are also restricted and only a subset is exposed; however, instead of properties, they are replaced with `get` and `set` functions. Event handlers are also significantly modified. Many common event handlers familiar to JavaScript programmers, such as the `onload() functions`, are not available, and events themselves are also modified. These are just some of the changes that Facebook made to JavaScript to create its safer, sanitized Facebook JavaScript (FBJS).

One of the first questions new Facebook developers have about FBJS is the availability of third-party JavaScript library support. With the explosion of AJAX-enabled sites, many libraries—Dojo, Mochikit, YUI, Prototype, Scriptaculous, and jQuery, to name a few—have been developed that provide loads of extra functionality, objects, and [illegible] JavaScript developers. The short answer is that none of these libraries are available in FBJS. If you need them for your code, you must use an IFrame-based canvas page to do so.

Sandbox Creation and Initialization

To get a better understanding of the sandbox, we present a simple example using the FBML Test Console. To use it, log in to Facebook and visit the Developer Tools page at *http://developer.facebook.com/tools.php*. Click the FBML Test Console tab. Type this code into the FBML text field within the console:

```
<a href="#" id="hello">Hello World!</a>
<script>
  document.getElementById('hello');
</script>
```

Now, select Canvas from the Position drop-down menu. Next, click the Preview button and examine the HTML Source window's contents. As you can see, Facebook creates a lot of JavaScript in the background for the simple `document.getElementId()` call made from a canvas page. Listing 11.1 shows this content in detail (with irrelevant features removed or commented out), and we bolded the code from the previous small program to make it easier to see in context.

Listing 11.1 **JavaScript Generated for a Simple "Hello World" FBJS Script**

```
<a href="#" id="app2353941073_hello" onclick="(new Image()).src =
  &#039;/ajax/ct.php?app_id=2353941073&action_type=3&
  post_form_id=e7270c8ceb77f9ce89258268a463a860&position=3&&#039; +
  Math.random();return true;" fbcontext="0dab11581b51">
    Hello World!
</a>

<script type="text/javascript">

    var app_2353941073 = new fbjs_sandbox("2353941073").setBridgeHash("");

    app_2353941073.validation_vars = {
        <!— 'fb_sig'-style variables —>
    };

    app_2353941073.context = "0dab11581b51";
    app_2353941073.contextd = [JSON code not relevant to discussion];

    app_2353941073.data = {
        "user": 714497440,
        "installed": true
    };

    app_2353941073.bootstrap();

</script>
<script type="text/javascript">
    a2353941073_document.getElementById('hello');
</script>
<!— lots of JavaScript omitted —>
</script>
```

The most important thing happening in Listing 11.1 is the creation of the sandbox itself. Facebook creates the sandbox instance with the code line shown here:

```
var app_2353941073 = new fbjs_sandbox("2353941073").setBridgeHash("");
```

Notice that the new sandbox is assigned to a variable called `app_[app id]`, and the application ID is passed as a parameter to the `fbjs_sandbox()` constructor. As mentioned, Facebook uses this ID to rename all the functions and variables in your FBJS to ensure that they do not conflict with any other code in the global namespace. Listing 11.2 shows the implementation of `fbjs_sandbox()`.

Listing 11.2 **Creation of the `fbjs_sandbox` Object**

```
function fbjs_sandbox(appid) {
    if (fbjs_sandbox.instances['a' + appid]) {
        return fbjs_sandbox.instances['a' + appid];
    }
    this.appid = appid;
    this.pending_bootstraps = [];
    this.bootstrapped = false;
    fbjs_sandbox.instances['a' + appid] = this;
}
fbjs_sandbox.instances = {};
```

After the sandbox instance is created, Facebook calls the `app_[app_id].bootstrap()` function it provides to fill the sandbox. This core function constructs the FBJS sandbox and sets up the types and functions that are allowed in FBJS. Listing 11.3 shows this function in detail. We went a step further and bolded the actual FBJS objects and functions you are allowed to use so that you can easily see the way Facebook creates them.

Listing 11.3 **`fbjs_sandbox.bootstrap()` Function Filling in the FBJS Sandbox**

```
fbjs_sandbox.prototype.bootstrap = function() {
  if (!this.bootstrapped) {
    var appid = this.appid;
    var code = [
        'a', appid, '_Math = new fbjs_math();',
        'a', appid, '_Date = fbjs_date();',
        'a', appid, '_String = new fbjs_string();',
        'a', appid, '_RegExp = new fbjs_regexp();',
        'a', appid, '_Ajax = fbjs_ajax(', appid, ');',
        'a', appid, '_Dialog = fbjs_dialog(', appid, ');',
        'a', appid, '_Facebook = new fbjs_facebook(', appid, ');',
        'a', appid, '_Animation = new fbjs_animation();',
        'a', appid, '_LiveMessage = new fbjs_livemessage(', appid, ');',
        'a', appid, '_document = new fbjs_main(', appid, ');9,
        'a', appid, '_undefined = undefined;',
        'a', appid, '_console = new fbjs_console();',
        'a', appid, '_setTimeout = fbjs_sandbox.set_timeout;',
        'a', appid, '_setInterval = fbjs_sandbox.set_interval;',
        'a', appid, '_escape = escapeURI;',
        'a', appid, '_unescape = unescape;'
      ];
    for (var i in {
      clearTimeout: 1,
      clearInterval: 1,
      parseFloat: 1,
      parseInt: 1,
```

Listing 11.3 **Continued**

```
      isNaN: 1,
      isFinite: 1
    }) {
      code = code.concat(['a', appid, '_', i, '=', i, ';']);
    }
    eval(code.join(''));
  }
// come code omitted for clarity
  this.bootstrapped = true;
}
```

The code simply builds an array of the object types and global functions that make up FBJS, and then passes it to JavaScript's `Array.join()` function to make a string out of them. This string is executable JavaScript code, so it's passed as an argument to an `eval()` call to execute the joined string as code, which initializes the sandbox.

As you can see, the FBJS sandbox is built from several internal Facebook objects that expose a specific set of functions and properties to the client, many of which are covered in this chapter. In Listing 11.3, the bold names are the actual object names you use in FBJS to access each type's functions or properties. For example, if you look at Listing 11.1, you can notice the original call to `document.getElementById()` was replaced with `a[app id]_document.getElementById()`. In our code, however, we just used `document`, not `a[app id]_document`. Notice that, in Listing 11.3, the `a[app_id]_document` object is created from a line in the code array in the `bootstrap()` function. It's an instance of a type known as `fbjs_main`, but this is hidden from the user. They just use the `document` object as they normally would in regular JavaScript. The `fbjs_main` object exposes specific functions from its underlying DOM `document` object for FBJS use.

Basic FBJS

We covered a lot about the how and why of FBJS, so now it's time to learn what *is* available in FBJS. This section overviews some of the major FBJS objects and the functions or properties they offer. As with any other part of Facebook, FBJS is evolving. This section is not an exhaustive FBJS reference; it's more of a guide to some of FBJ's more interesting and important features.

> **FBJS2**
>
> In January 2009, Facebook announced a beta of the next major version of FBJS, dubbed FBJS2. It was designed to allow more access to traditional JavaScript language features, DOM functionality, and semantics. However, with the rise of Facebook Connect and the functionality recently exposed to IFrame-based canvas pages via XHTML and the Facebook JavaScript Library, Facebook has temporarily ceased work on it. It has provided a download of the actual sources for anyone interested. FBJS2 can be downloaded from *http://developers.facebook.com/fbopen/fbjs2-0.1.tar.gz*. It is not covered further in this book.

Browser Detection

Developers regularly use some method of browser detection to work around bugs in browsers' implementations, conditionally use specific features, or customize user experiences. Although JavaScript browser detection has faded in popularity in recent years as browser feature or capability testing has gained in popularity, it is still a valuable tool. Unfortunately, the browser object most often used in client-side JavaScript for detection, the `Navigator`, is not part of FBJS.

Facebook provides a way to do this, although not a very intuitive one. It involves the use of the `<fb:user-agent>` FBML tag. This tag accepts two attributes, `includes` and `excludes`, that are to be set to the value of the user agent (browser name) that the developer wants to target or exclude inside the FBML tag. Both attributes can be provided; however, `includes` are always processed first. The following example shows how the tag is used in FBML:

```
<fb:user-agent includes='firefox, ie' excludes='ie 6'>
  <!— do something exclusive of Internet Explorer 6 —>
</fb:user-agent>
```

Developers can use these tags on their canvas pages to set variables in script that can later be checked in FBJS. Taking the previous code, we can set a variable that tells us that the browser we are working with is IE 6, as shown here:

```
<script type='text/javascript'>var isIE6 = true;</script>
<fb:user-agent includes='firefox, ie' excludes='ie 6'>
  <script type='text/javascript'>isIE6 = false;</script>
</fb:user-agent>
```

You can then use the `isIE6` variable later in your FBJS code to conditionally execute code based on its value. This is just one way to detect the browser that Facebook provides. Of course, it's also possible to do this on the server side by checking and parsing the value of the PHP `$_SERVER['HTTP_USER_AGENT']` variable. Many excellent examples of doing this are available on the web.

FBJS and the DOM

One of the most important uses of client-side JavaScript is manipulating a document loaded into a browser window using the DOM functions provided by the browser in which the JavaScript is executing. Facebook realized that it had to provide some DOM manipulation functionality or developers would never adopt FBJS. Facebook implements many of the familiar DOM functions and some of the properties found in the W3C DOM Level 1 and 2 specifications; however, properties are converted into functions. Facebook did this by wrapping numerous DOM properties with `get` and (sometimes) `set` functions. For example, in FBJS, instead of using `obj.lastChild` in your code, you'd use `obj.getLastChild()`.

The following sections summarize DOM support in FBJS. We only focus on those functions or properties that have unique behaviors or syntax, have no equivalent in the

DOM, or are of special interest. The remaining DOM properties and functions are easy to figure out, and Facebook provides an exhaustive list on its site (*http://wiki.developers.facebook.com/index.php/FBJS*). Another quick way to get an idea of what functions are available is through the use of the FBML Test Console, the Firefox browser, and the Firebug Firefox add-on. To use these to get the list of available functions, go to the Facebook FBML Test Console. Enter this line of code into the FBML edit field:

```
<h1 onclick='console.log(this);'>hi</h1>
```

After you do this, click the Preview button and click the "Hi" text in the Facebook FBML Test Console Preview window. Make sure that you enabled the Firebug console so that you can see the output of the `console.log()` call in the previous code. You should see something similar to what's shown in Figure 11.1.

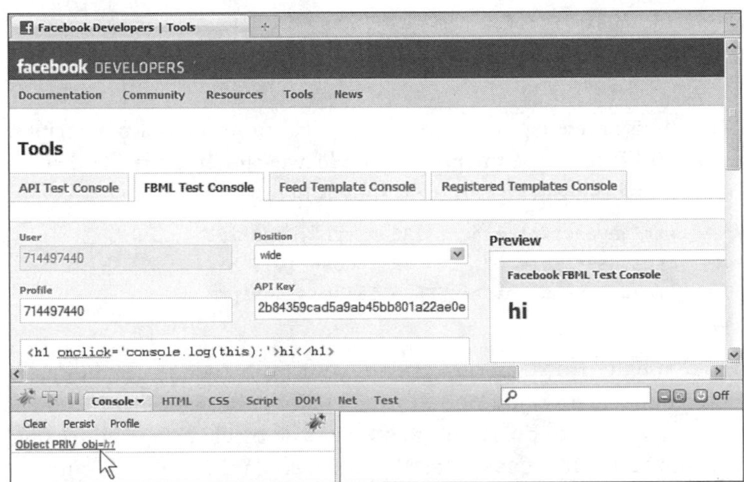

Figure 11.1 Getting the reference to an FBJS DOM element

Notice that the object reference displayed in the Firebug console window is actually a link. Click it, and you are taken to the DOM tab, which shows you the list of all the functions Facebook has added to the element. Be sure to check the Show User-defined Properties and Show User-defined Functions options in the DOM menu. Figure 11.2 illustrates the process and output. The `PRIV_obj` property displayed at the top of the DOM list is the Facebook-wrapped instance of the actual `<h1>` DOM node.

Facebook supports all the usual DOM functions that JavaScript developers are familiar with, such as `appendChild()`, `insertBefore()`, `cloneNode()`, and others. It exposes a few properties as `get` functions for which it provides no partner `set` function, because the DOM properties are read-only. Table 11.1 provides these functions, the DOM properties they wrap, and a description of their behavior.

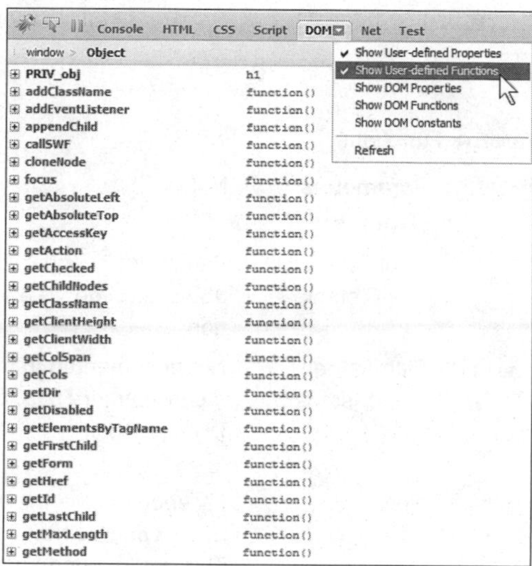

Figure 11.2 Displaying FBJS functions and properties added by Facebook to a DOM element

Table 11.1 **Overview of Select FBJS DOM Functions**

FBJS Function	DOM Property	Description
`getParentNode()`	`parentNode`	Gets a reference to the calling element's parent node. Returns null if used to go beyond the root element of your FBML code.
`getNextSibling()` `getPreviousSibling()`	`nextSibling` `previousSibling`	Gets a reference to the next or previous element at the same level in the document as the current element.
`getFirstChild()` `getLastChild()`	`firstChild` `lastChild`	Returns a reference to the first or last child of the current element.
`getChildNodes()`	`childNodes`	Returns a read-only collection of the child nodes of the current element. The list returned does *not* contain text nodes, unlike its DOM counterpart.

FBJS DOM Document Object

The `document` object wraps functionality provided by the native DOM `document` object present in all browsers as part of the W3D DOM Level 1 specification. The FBJS version offers significantly less functionality. Table 11.2 shows the details on some of the most important functions it offers.

Table 11.2 **FBJS `document` Functions**

`document` Function	Parameters (Type)	Notes
`getElementById()`	ID of DOM element (string)	Semantically equivalent to the familiar `document.getElementById()` function.
`getElementsByTagName()`	Element tag name (string)	Not documented in the Facebook documentation for FBJS, but it works like its DOM partner.
`getRootElement()`	None	Facebook hides the global `document` and `window` objects from FBJS code. This workaround lets you get access to the root node of your application content.
`createElement()`	FBML/HTML element tag name (string)	Can create normal HTML elements; however, for FBML, it is currently restricted only to the creation of `<fb:swf>` elements.
`setLocation()`	URL (string)	Replaces the normal DOM location property and can redirect the browser to a new URL.

DOM Node Content Manipulation

Facebook provides three functions that allow developers to set the content of a DOM node. When FBJS first launched, not all these functions were available, so updating the content of an existing element with HTML was somewhat difficult. The functions Facebook provides have some quirks that we cover in the following section.

`setTextValue()`

The `setTextValue()` function sets the text content of the node on which it's called. When using it, you must be aware of a couple of things. First, this only sets *text* values for the node. If you add HTML markup as part of the value you want it to set, it is included as text, not markup.

Here's a quick demonstration. Type the code shown in Listing 11.4 into the FBML Test Console FBML edit field.

Listing 11.4 **Using the FBJS `setTextValue()` Function**

```
<h1 onclick='setNodeText(this);'>Click Me</h1>
<script>
```

Listing 11.4 **Continued**

```
function setNodeText(elt) {
  elt.setTextValue('<h2>New Text</h2>');
}
</script>
```

Now, click the "Click Me" text in the FBML Preview window. You can see that the text changes from "Click Me" to "<h2>New Text</h2>." Notice that the `<h2>` tag is interpreted as text and not used to render the text in an `<h2>` element. This function only sets or replaces the text within an element; furthermore, it removes all child elements of the node on which it's called, as Listing 11.5 demonstrates. Clicking the text "Click Me" causes `setTextValue()` to replace the entire contents of the `<h1>` element, including the embedded `<span>`, with the text "<h2>Thanks!</h2>." The Facebook documentation states that no FBML or HTML tags are accepted by `setTextValue()`. Listing 11.5 shows that's not entirely true; they are accepted, but they're simply inserted as literal text.

Listing 11.5 **`setTextValue()` Removes All Child Nodes**

```
<h1 onclick='setNodeText(this);'>Click <span>me</span> please</h1>
<script>
function setNodeText(elt) {
  elt.setTextValue('<h2>Thanks!</h2>');
}
</script>
```

`setInnerFBML()`

`setInnerFBML()` sets static FBML content for an element. There's one important requirement for using it: The value you pass to it must contain a reference to a block of FBML, not a string of literal FBML. This can be somewhat confusing for those unfamiliar with its behavior. To set FBML content dynamically for an element, you need to use AJAX, which is covered later in this chapter.

An example clarifies its use. Replace the call to `setTextValue()` in Listing 11.5 with `setInnerFBML()` and execute it. Notice that the "Click me please" text does not change as expected, but the FBML Test Console does not show any errors; however, Firebug displays an error:

```
fbjs_private.get(fbml_ref) is null
fbjs_dom.prototype.setInnerFBML = function(fbml_ref) {
  var html=fbjs_private.get(fbml_ref).htmlstring;
  http://static.ak.fbcdn.net/rsrc.php/.../somefile.js
  Line 85
```

Observe in the text of this error that the `setInnerFBML()` function expects an argument named `fbml_ref`. This FBML reference variable is an object created through the use of a special FBML tag, `<fb:js-string>`. The purpose of this tag is to render a block of

FBML as an object instead of directly rendering it to the page. Facebook requires a construct like this, because it needs to parse the string of FBML into its HTML and JavaScript equivalents before the content is displayed in the element. Because `setInnerFBML()` only runs on the client, the string of FBML does not get evaluated by the FBML parser running on Facebook's servers. For example, if it were possible to pass a string to this function, calling `setInnerFBML()` with an argument such as `<fb:name uid='714497440'/>` would result in that string being rendered as the content of the element, not "Cappy Popp" as you might expect.

To use `setInnerFBML()`, you need to create an `<fb:js-string>` ahead of time and use it to call `setInnerFBML()`. Listing 11.6 shows how to accomplish this.

Listing 11.6 **Using `<fb:js-string>` and `setInnerFBML()` Together**

```
<h1 onclick='setNodeText(this);'>Click <span>me</span> please</h1>
<fb:js-string var='fbml_content'>
  <h2>Thanks!</h2>
</fb:js-string>
<script>
function setNodeText(elt) {
  elt.setInnerFBML(fbml_content);
}
</script>
```

Running Listing 11.6 in the FBML Test Console and clicking the "Click me please" text now displays "Thanks!," as expected. Observe the bold code in Listing 11.6. It illustrates how `<fb:js-string>` takes an attribute, `var`, that is set to the name of the JavaScript variable that is used as the reference to the block of FBML. This variable is passed to `setInnerFBML()`. We revisit `<fb:js-string>` when we discuss AJAX later in this chapter. For now, be aware of `<fb:js-string>`'s role in the creation of static FBML content for DOM elements.

`setInnerXHTML()`

When FBJS first launched, there was no way for developers to set pure HTML content for elements. For security reasons, the familiar DOM function `setInnerHTML()` is not part of FBJS. This posed a real problem for developers because there was no easy way to quickly add markup to an element or document. To set any kind of markup for an element, you had to either know that markup ahead of time and use `<fb:js-string>` with `setInnerFBML()`, use AJAX to have it returned dynamically, or manually add new nodes to the document using `document.createElement()`, `appendChild()`, and other DOM manipulation functions.

The `setInnerXHTML()` function rectifies this. This function takes a string of valid XHTML and inserts it as the content of the DOM node on which it's called. Be aware that the parameter passed to `setInnerXHTML()` *must* be valid XHTML. This means that it must contain markup that starts and ends with valid tags, uses all lowercase tag names, be correctly nested, and have every tag within it properly closed. Plain text not wrapped in enclosing tags is not supported. For example, this won't work: setInnerXHTML('hi'), while this does: setInnerXHTML('<span>hi</span>').

This function is notoriously fussy about the markup it accepts. For example, you must also escape characters like "&," which cannot appear in literal form in most XHTML. This is something to be aware of when you use setInnerXHTML() to add <a> tags to an element dynamically using URLs with query strings. Listing 11.7 shows the issues faced when using setInnerXHTML() for this. Type this code into the FBML Test Console and click the Create Link button rendered in the FBML Preview window.

Listing 11.7 **Using setInnerXHTML() to Build Hyperlinks**

```
<input type='button' onclick='buildLink(this);' value='Create Link' /><br /><br />
<script>
function buildLink(elt) {
  var parent = elt.getParentNode();
  var linkDiv = document.createElement('div');
  parent.appendChild(linkDiv);
  linkDiv.setInnerXHTML("<a
href='http://example.com/blah?f=1&r=2'>hyperlink</a>");
}
</script>
```

Notice that, after the button is clicked, no list is added to the Preview window. If you have Firebug running, turn on Show XML Errors in its Console tab's drop-down menu. Now, when you click the button in the Preview window, you see an error like the one shown in Figure 11.3.

The reason for the error is the embedded ampersand character in the query string of the URL in the href attribute of the <a> tag. To rectify it, we need to replace it with a numeric character reference or the string "&." Try it; you should see that links are added below the Create Link button every time it's clicked.

Form Validation

One important activity in client-side JavaScript is HTML form validation. All production code that accepts user input (using a form or otherwise) always validates user input ideally both on the client and server side to minimize security risks. FBJS provides many of the DOM properties and functions that can be used for doing client-side validation.

This section revisits the Compliments application and adds client-side form validation to it by using FBJS. We no longer use Feed forms in this chapter; instead, later in this chapter, we introduce a way to submit Feed stories from the client side in FBJS. This is more efficient because we don't need multiple round trips to Facebook's servers to submit a Feed story. To begin the process of adding client-side validation to our <form>, open the index.php file and replace the renderPage() function with the code shown in Listing 11.8. We bolded the places where code changes have occurred.

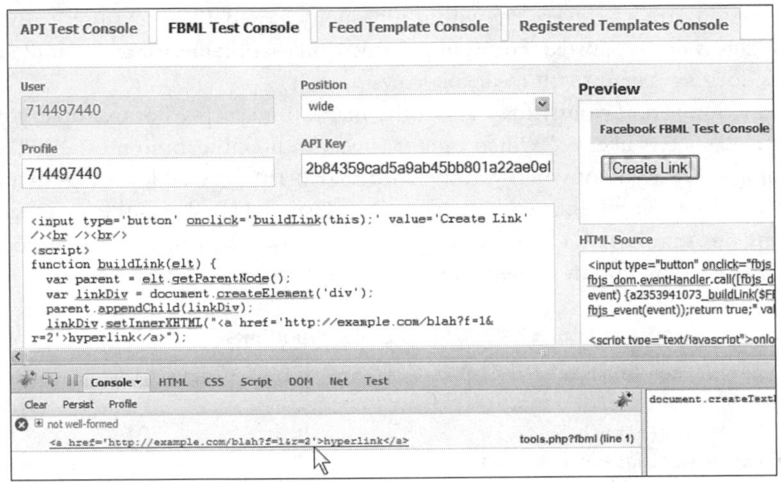

Figure 11.3 Error shown by Firebug when running the code from Listing 11.7

Listing 11.8 **`renderPage()` Function Updated for Client-Side Validation**

```
function renderPage() {
  global $g_categories;
  $pageOutput = getHeaderContent();
  $pageOutput .= "
    <script type='text/javascript'>
      function submitForm(formObj) {
        return false;
      }
     </script>
    <div id='panel' class='panel'>
      <form method='POST' id='complimentform' onsubmit='return submitForm(this);'>
        <h1>Select one of your friends and enter your compliment.</h1>
        <table id='complimentTable'>
          <tr>
            <td class='label'>Your Friend:</td>
            <td class='content' id='friend_selector'>
              <fb:friend-selector id='fsel' name='uid' idname='target' />
            </td>
          </tr>
          <tr>
            <td class='label'>is:</td>
            <td class='content' id='categories'>";
  foreach( $g_categories as $name => $info ){
    $pageOutput .= "
              <div class='category clearfix'>
```

Listing 11.8 **Continued**

```
                <img class='categoryImg'
                  src='".LOCAL_APP_URL."/img/{$info['bigimg']}'/><br>
                <span class='categoryTitle'>{$info['title']}</span><br/>
                <input type='radio' name='category' value='$name' />
            </div>";
}
$pageOutput .= "
            </td>
          </tr>
          <tr>
            <td class='label'>because:</td>
            <td class='content'>
              <input class='textInput' id='compliment' name='compliment' />
            </td>
          </tr>
          <tr>
            <td class='content' colspan='2'>
              <input type='checkbox' name='email' checked='checked' />
              Check this box to send your friend an email as well.
            </td>
          </tr>
        </table>
        <input class='inputbutton' type='submit'
          name='submitCompliment'
          label='Send Compliment' value='Send Compliment'/>
      </form>
      <fb:prompt-permission perms='email'>
        <div class='perm'>
          Click here to receive updates via email!
        </div>
      </fb:prompt-permission>
    </div>
  </div>
  ";
  echo $pageOutput;
}
```

Because we'll soon be using an FBJS equivalent to a Feed form, there is no need for the `fbType` attribute on the `<form>` element to specify a Feed form type. Also, in this chapter, we eventually POST the contents of the `<form>` using AJAX, so we also removed the `action` attribute. Finally, we added a simple `<script>` block to the top of the page, which contains a `submitForm()` function that is called when the user clicks the Submit button for the `<form>`. We added a FBJS `onsubmit()` event handler to the `<form>` element to which we pass the instance of the form. Currently, `submitForm()` just returns `false`, which means that the form will not be submitted.

Now, let's add some more FBJS to the `submitForm()` function to get all the values of the fields from the form. FBJS provides a `serialize()` function to do the work of parsing the form's data into name-value pairs. Update the `submitForm()` function to contain the code shown in Listing 11.9.

Listing 11.9 **Using the FBJS `serialize()` Function to Obtain Form Values**

```
<script type='text/javascript'>
  function submitForm(formObj) {
    var formData   = formObj.serialize();
    var name       = formData.uid;
    var compliment = formData.compliment;
    var category   = formData.category;
    // Validate the form
    if ( (name == \"Start typing a friend's name\") ||
         (name == \"\") ||
         ( category == null ) ||
         ( compliment == \"\" ) ) {
      // form not valid, return false to prevent submit
      var formIsValid = false;
    } else {
      // form is valid
      formIsValid = true;
    }
  return formIsValid;
  }
</script>
```

Here, the FBJS `serialize()` function gets an object that contains the form's `<input>` values keyed by their name. We use it to verify that each of the form's fields is set to an appropriate value and return `false` if one is not—thereby stopping the form submission in the process. Notice the use of the `formIsValid` variable: It's declared in the `if` statement but used outside this scope. This is OK because, in FBJS, like JavaScript, variables do not have block-level scope. This means that all variables declared in a function are accessible *throughout* that function, unlike block-scoped languages, such as C++ or Java.

Realize that FBJS provides other functions to handle getting or setting the values of `<form>` elements; you are by no means constrained to using `serialize()`. For example, you can use the DOM node access functions, such as `getChildNodes()`, to accomplish a similar task, recursively building a list of `<input>` values to check. FBJS provides numerous functions to use, such as the `getValue()` or `setValue()` functions to retrieve or set the contents of an `<input>` tag, `getChecked()` and `setChecked()` functions to handle checkbox control state, `getType()` and `setType()` functions to manage detection of `<input>` elements, and more.

FBJS Dialogs

One of the first hurdles that new Facebook developers encounter is the lack of dialogs to interact with users or use for simple debugging. The `alert()`, `prompt()`, and `confirm()` functions are not part of FBJS. FBJS provides its own versions of these via the FBJS `Dialog` class.

The `Dialog` class constructs two different types of dialogs: popup and contextual. Popup dialogs are displayed in the center of the page from which they are created and provide either one button (such as the `alert()` dialog in JavaScript) or two (such as the `confirm()` one). This means that the user cannot interact with the rest of the page while the dialog is displayed on screen, which is similar to the behaviors of the JavaScript dialog functions. Contextual dialogs are tied to a specific element on the page and are rendered with an arrow pointing to this element. These are perfect for alerting users to a specific location or error condition on your page.

First, let's look at how to create and use both types of dialogs in the FBML Test Console. Then, we'll update Compliments to use contextual dialogs to indicate the sources of specific form-validation failures. Open the FBML Test Console again and enter the code shown in Listing 11.10 into it. After doing so, click the Preview button and try clicking both links in the Preview window. When you click the first link, you see a popup dialog similar to the one shown in Figure 11.4. Clicking the second link displays a contextual one, which is shown in Figure 11.5.

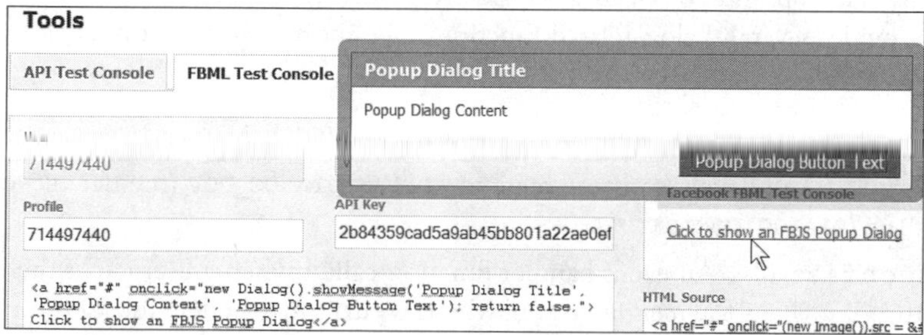

Figure 11.4 FBJS provides the popup dialog to replace the `alert()` and `confirm()` JavaScript functions.

Figure 11.5 The contextual dialog can point to specific elements on a page.

Listing 11.10 **Displaying Both Types of FBJS Dialogs**

```
<a href="#"
  onclick="var d = new Dialog();
           d.showMessage('Popup Dialog Title',
                         'Popup Dialog Content',
                         'Popup Dialog Button Text');
           return false;">
  Click to show an FBJS Popup Dialog
</a>
<a href="#"
  onclick="var d = new Dialog(Dialog.DIALOG_CONTEXTUAL);
          d.showMessage('Contextual Dialog Title',
                        'Contextual Dialog Content',
                        'Contextual Dialog Button Text');
          d.setContext(this.getPreviousSibling());
          return false;">
  Click to show an FBJS Contextual Dialog
</a>
```

Notice that, when you click one link and then the other without closing the dialog currently on screen, Facebook automatically hides the current dialog to show the next one. You cannot have more than one of these dialogs displayed on screen at a time. These can actually stack up, and you need to separately dismiss each one.

FBJS provides several dialog-related functions. The most important ones are summarized here:

- **`Dialog(type)`.** The constructor function for all dialogs. It takes a single parameter, which can have a constant value of `Dialog.DIALOG_POP` (the default) or `Dialog.DIALOG_CONTEXTUAL`.
- **`onconfirm()`.** An event handler function called when a user clicks the dialog button known as the *confirm* button, which is currently the left-most button shown. If it returns true, the dialog will be hidden.
- **`oncancel()`.** Called when a user clicks the *cancel* button (the right-most). If it returns true, the dialog will be hidden.
- **`setStyle()`.** Sets the CSS styles for a dialog's content.
- **`showMessage(title, content, button)`.** The function used in the previous example. It takes three parameters: the first, `title`, is a string used for the title text of the dialog; the second, `content`, is used for the dialog's body content; and the final, `button`, is a string used for the text of the *confirm* button, which defaults to Okay.
- **`showChoice(title, content, buttonConfirm, buttonCancel)`.** Renders an FBJS `confirm()`-style dialog with two buttons. The `title` and `content` parameters behave exactly like those for the `showMessage()`

function. `buttonConfirm` is a string used for the text of the *confirm* button (it defaults to Okay), and `buttonCancel` is a string used for the text of the *cancel* button (it defaults to Cancel).

- **`setContext()`.** Used for contextual dialogs to set the element to which they are bound, or more simply, the element at which the dialog's arrow points.
- **`hide()`.** Hides the dialog on which it's called.

Let's update the Compliments application to use contextual dialogs to point at the individual elements in the form that have failed validation. Modify the `submitForm()` function in `index.php` to match Listing 11.11.

Listing 11.11 **Updating `submitForm()` to Use FBJS Contextual Dialogs**

```
<script type='text/javascript'>
function submitForm(formObj) {
  // Create the validation dialog
  var dialog = new Dialog(Dialog.DIALOG_CONTEXTUAL);
  dialog.setStyle('color', 'red');

  var formData   = formObj.serialize();
  var name       = formData.uid;
  var compliment = formData.compliment;
  var category   = formData.category;
  var title      = 'Validation Error';

  // Validate the form
  var formIsValid = false;
  if ( (name == \"Start typing a friend's name\") || (name == \"\") ) {
    dialog.setContext(document.getElementById('friend_selector'));
    dialog.showMessage( title,
                        'Please choose someone to compliment');
  } else if ( category == null ) {
    dialog.setContext(document.getElementById('categories'));
    dialog.showMessage( title,
                        'Please enter a compliment category');
  } else if ( compliment == \"\" ) {
    dialog.setContext(document.getElementById('compliment'));
    dialog.showMessage( title,
                        'Please enter a compliment');
 } else {
   formIsValid = true;
 }
 return formIsValid;
 }
</script>
```

Try submitting the form without filling in any of its fields. Figure 11.6 illustrates what you should see. Notice that the arrow of the contextual dialog points to the `<input>` element for which validation has failed. As you fill each field, notice how the next element that fails validation is presented with its own contextual dialog.

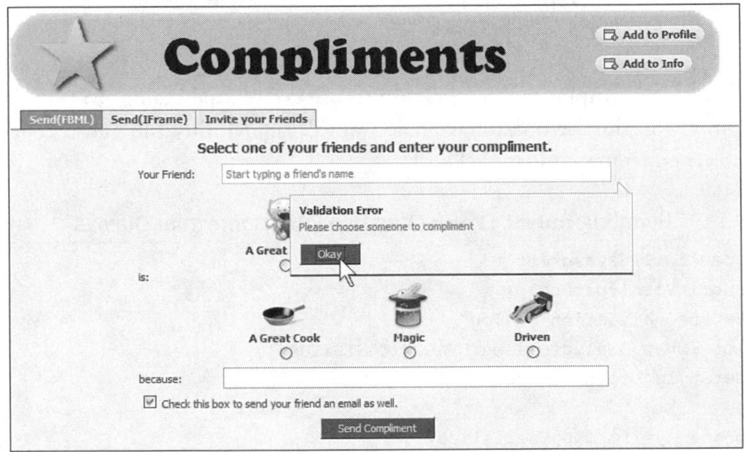

Figure 11.6 Using contextual dialogs to highlight form-validation failures

Dialogs are not restricted to simple strings as their content. Complex examples can be created from FBML; however, any FBML used in a dialog must be pre-rendered by Facebook's servers before you can use it on the client side. To accomplish this, use the `<fb:js-string>` tag, like we did when discussing the `setInnerFBML()` function, to allow Facebook to pre-render its contents and store it in a reference variable that you can pass as the content parameter to the `Dialog.showMessage()` or `Dialog.showChoice()` function.

Facebook also provides FBML equivalents of the dynamic FBJS dialogs for cases where FBJS is not possible or the developer is unfamiliar with JavaScript or FBJS syntax. The `<fb:dialog>`, `<fb:dialog-response>`, `<fb:dialog-title>`, `<fb:dialog-content>`, and `<fb:dialog-button>` tags can all create dialogs in FBML, although these are used less frequently than the FBJS versions because they lack much of the flexibility that the FBJS versions provide. They also depend on a unique Facebook technology called Mock AJAX, which is covered next.

Mock AJAX

These days, it's nearly impossible to discuss web programming of any kind without mentioning AJAX. Sites like Facebook would not even be possible without it. Imagine having to refresh the entire page every time you clicked a link within the Facebook chrome to leave a comment, flagged something you "Like," or clicked an application tab in your profile. For all its detractors, AJAX has undoubtedly revolutionized the user experience on the web. It seems ludicrous to not have access to AJAX when building a web application for any platform, not just Facebook.

> **AJAX**
>
> Asynchronous JavaScript and XML (AJAX) is comprised of a set of client-side web-development techniques that creates dynamic and interactive web content. With it, web applications can asynchronously fetch data without modifying the operation of or causing a refresh of an existing page. Much of AJAX's functionality is implemented using the browser's `XMLHttpRequest` object; however, although its name suggests it, AJAX does not actually require either JavaScript or XML.

However, when Facebook first launched the developer platform, there was no FBJS, JavaScript, or AJAX support for FBML applications. If your application needed to use AJAX, it was required to use IFrame-based canvas pages and your own implementation of AJAX primitives—most likely, via a third-party JavaScript library. But, using IFrame-based pages had a cost: You could not use the FBML controls that made it easy for developers to make applications that had the look and feel of Facebook itself. Facebook understood the pain developers faced and provided an AJAX-like functionality for FBML called *Mock AJAX*.

Today, although there is full AJAX support included as part of FBJS, Mock AJAX is still available for use on profiles, application tabs, or canvas pages, and it is required for some FBML tags, such as `<fb:dialog>`. Mock AJAX uses a set of special FBML attributes that Facebook parses from the FBML and replaces it with AJAX-like behaviors (for example, modifying only portions of element content on a page without reloading it or dynamically controlling element visibility based on user action).

We'll update Compliments to use Mock AJAX to submit the form. In the process, we cover many of the Mock AJAX attributes you can use. Note that we do not update the application to display a Feed form or actually submit a compliment to Facebook via Mock AJAX. We just update it to specifically demonstrate how Mock AJAX works.

First, create and save a new script in your application's root directory named `mock_ajax_handler.php`. The code for this file is found in Listing 11.12.

Listing 11.12 `mock_ajax_handler.php`: Mock AJAX Form Handler

```
<?php
  require_once dirname(__FILE__).'/inc/globals.inc';
  require_once dirname(__FILE__).'/inc/utils.inc';
  require_once dirname(__FILE__).'/inc/db.inc';
  require_once dirname(__FILE__).'/inc/profile.inc';
  dumpRequestVars();

  $result     = "
    <fb:dialog id='errorDialog'>
      <fb:dialog-title>Compliment Validation Error</fb:dialog-title>
      <fb:dialog-content>%s</fb:dialog-content>
      <fb:dialog-button type='button' value='OK' close_dialog='true'/>
    </fb:dialog>
```

Listing 11.12 **Continued**

```
    <a href='#' clicktoshowdialog='errorDialog' clicktohide='formResult'
      style='font-weight:bold;font-size:larger;color:yellow;background:red;'>
      Click here for form validation errors!
    </a>";

  if( !isset($_POST['uid']) || !isset($_POST['target'])) {
    $result = sprintf($result, 'You must select a friend' );
  } else if( !isset($_POST['compliment'])){
    $result = sprintf($result, 'You must enter a compliment');
  } else if( !isset($_POST['category'])) {
    $result = sprintf($result, 'You must select a compliment type');
  } else {

    $target     = $_POST['target'];
    $compliment = trim($_POST['compliment']);
    $category   = $_POST['category'];

    $facebook = new Facebook(FB_API_KEY, FB_APP_SECRET);
    $db       = new DB();

    $sender   = $facebook->user;
    $db->addCompliment($sender, $target, $category, $compliment);

    updateProfileBox($sender);

    // start filling in our template
    $comp         = $g_categories[$category];

    $imageSrc     = LOCAL_APP_URL.'/img/'.$comp['bigimg'];
    $imageLink    = LOCAL_APP_URL;

    $result = "
      <h1>Your Compliment to <fb:name uid='$target'></fb:name> was sent.</h1>
      <p>
        <fb:profile-pic size='square' uid='$target'>
        </fb:profile-pic>
        <img class='categoryImg' src='$imageSrc' ></img>
        <fb:name uid='$target'></fb:name>
        is <b>'{$comp['title']}' </b>
        because $compliment
      </p>";
  }

  echo $result;
?>
```

In Listing 11.12, the first thing to notice is the use of the `<fb:dialog>`, `<fb:dialogtitle>`, `<fb:dialog-content>`, and `<fb:dialog-button>` tags to create a Facebook popup dialog using FBML instead of FBJS. If you look at the HTML and JavaScript rendered from this FBML, you can see that it creates a dialog in a similar fashion to the way we did with FBJS. The one thing that's different here is that, unlike the FBJS dialogs, the FBML dialog cannot be shown automatically because FBML is rendered on Facebook's servers, not on the client. This is the reason for the `<a>` tag and its `clicktoshowdialog` Mock AJAX attribute. Applying this attribute to any clickable DOM element allows you to show the dialog when the element is clicked. Also note that the `<a>` element sets another Mock AJAX attribute, `clicktohide`, to the ID of a `<div>` into which we place the results of the form submission.

Now, we need to modify the form code in `index.php` to use Mock AJAX instead of a normal POST to submit the form. We just add another button to the form in `index.php` to handle submission via Mock AJAX, and we add a hidden `<div>` element to accept the results of the Mock AJAX call—the very same one whose ID was set in the `clicktohide` attribute of the `<a>` element in Listing 11.12. First, add a new `<div>` element to the page right after the closing `</script>` tag and before the `<div id='panel'>` element. Refer to Listing 11.4 for the full `<form>` code; we just show the new code in context in bold:

```
</script>
    <div id='formResult' class='success' style='display:none;'></div>
    <div id='panel' class='panel'>
      <form method='POST' id='complimentform' onsubmit='return submitForm(this);'>
```

Next, add another `<input>` button next to the existing one from the form. Again, new code is shown in bold:

```
  <input class='inputbutton' type='submit'
          name='submitCompliment'
          label='Send Compliment' value='Send Compliment'/>
  <input class='inputbutton' type='submit'
          name='submitComplimentMockAJAX'
          clickrewriteurl='".LOCAL_APP_URL."/mock_ajax_handler.php'
          clickrewriteform='complimentform'
          clickrewriteid='formResult'
          clicktoshow='formResult'
          label='Send Compliment Mock AJAX' value='Send Compliment via Mock AJAX'/>
</form>
```

Finally, add the success style to `main.css`:

```
.success {padding: 3px; text-align: center;}
```

Reload the application canvas page and click the Send Compliment via Mock AJAX button. You can see something similar to what's shown in Figure 11.7. Notice that a bold link is displayed at the top of the form, which indicates that some validation errors have occurred. Note that the current form validation code in the `submitForm()` function did not get executed: No contextual dialogs are shown when there's an error. We cover why this is so a bit later.

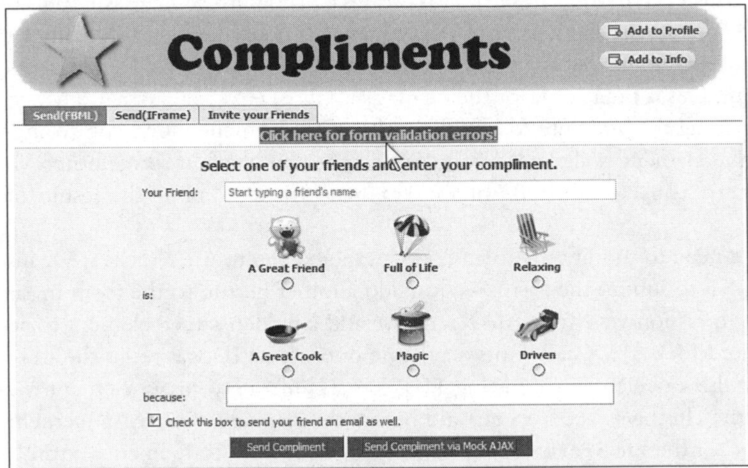

Figure 11.7 Result of submitting an incomplete form via Mock AJAX

Clicking the link displays an <fb:dialog> box like the one displayed in Figure 11.8. Notice how the original <div> with the error message and link disappears when the <fb:dialog> is displayed, and it stays hidden when the OK button on the dialog is clicked.

Figure 11.8 An `<fb:dialog>` showing our form validation errors

If you successfully fill out the form and submit it, you see something like what's shown in Figure 11.9.

Several things are happening in this example. The first thing to notice are the attributes:

- **`clickrewriteurl.`** When the user clicks the <input> button, the contents of the form identified by `clickrewriteform` are automatically POSTed to Facebook's servers and passed to this URL. This URL must be a full URL and point to a non-Facebook domain. This URL must return valid FBML, which is parsed by Facebook and sent to the element identified by `clickrewriteid`.

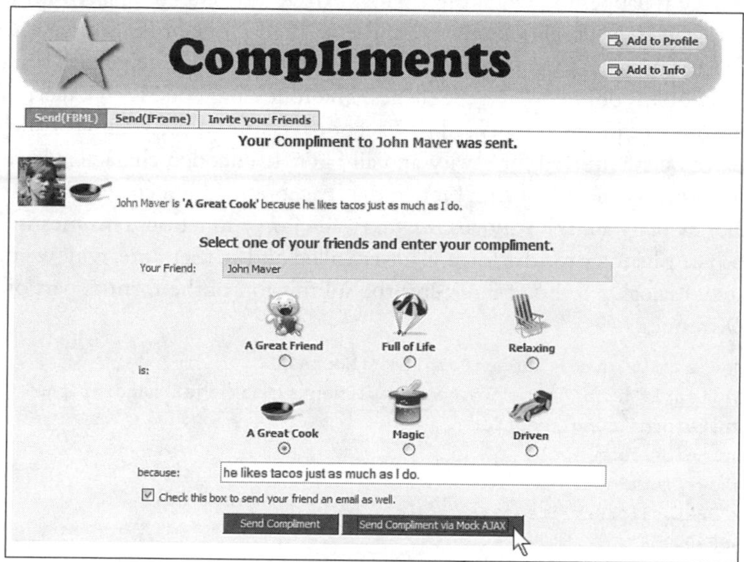

Figure 11.9 Result of successfully submitting the form via Mock AJAX

- **`clickrewriteform.`** Set to the ID of the `<form>` whose contents are POSTed to Facebook when the element that contains this attribute is clicked.
- **`clickrewriteid.`** Set to the ID of the DOM element used as the target for the FBML rendered by Facebook from that returned from the `clickrewriteurl`.
- **`clicktoshow.`** The ID of the DOM element set in this attribute is displayed when the element that contains it is clicked. In this case, when the `<input>` button is clicked, the `<div id='formResult'>` element is shown. This `<div>` originally had an inline CSS style of `display:none`.

The `mock_ajax_handler.php` file uses a couple more Mock AJAX attributes worthy of mention. This file uses a somewhat contrived example: In production code, you would rarely require a user to click to receive error messages; however, in this case, it was illustrative to demonstrate not only the `<fb:dialog>` tags in action, but also the Mock AJAX attributes that make them possible. The attributes used in this file are

- **`clicktohide.`** Placed on the `<fb:dialog-button>` element and is set to the ID of the element to hide when the `<fb:dialog-button>` is clicked. In this case, it's the `<div id='formResult'>` element in `index.php` that's hidden when the OK button on the dialog is clicked.

- **clicktoshowdialog.** Dialogs rendered via <fb:dialog> cannot be displayed without a user clicking some DOM element to allow it. We set this attribute on an arbitrary link to allow us to display form-validation errors.

What exactly is happening when these Mock AJAX attributes are placed on DOM elements? What code does Facebook render for them? If you look at the source for the canvas page after the Mock AJAX attributes are added to the <input> element, you can easily see what Facebook is doing behind the scenes. The following code is an excerpt from the <input> button after it's been rendered by Facebook. Some of the attributes, such as class and value, have been removed for clarity, and all HTML-encoded characters have been converted to human-readable forms. Notice that Facebook adds a custom `onclick()` event handler, which calls the `FBML.clickRewriteAjax()` function. This means that our own `onsubmit()` handler for the form is never called and is, therefore, why we never see the contextual dialogs. Facebook intercepts the submission of the form as part of the Mock AJAX request:

```
<input type="submit" name="submitComplimentMockAJAX"
  clickrewriteurl="http://example.com/compliments/mock_ajax_handler.php"
  clickrewriteform="complimentform"
  clickrewriteid="formResult"
  clicktoshow="formResult"
  onclick="FBML.clickRewriteAjax(
      '63560904158',
      1,
      'app63560904158_formResult',
      'http://example.com/compliments/mock_ajax_handler.php',
      $('app63560904158_complimentform'),
      '');
    FBML.clickToShow('app63560904158_formResult');
    return false;" />
```

Here is the pseudo-code for the `FBML.clickRewriteAjax()` function. As you can see, it does an AJAX call on your behalf, passing the serialized form data to a URL on Facebook's domain and setting the result data as the `innerHTML` of the DOM element specified by your `clickrewriteid` attribute:

```
function clickRewriteAjax(appID, userLoggedIn, targetElementID, handlerURL,
formObj,...) {
  var postData = formObj.serialize();
  var ajax = new Ajax-Like-Object();
  ajax.setURI('http://www.facebook.com/fbml/mock_ajax_proxy.php');
  ajax.setMethod('POST');
  postData.url = handlerURL;
  // set a bunch more postData properties...
  ajax.setData(formData);
  ajax.setHandler( function(result) {
      if(result.ok) {
        document.getElementById(targetElementID).innerHTML = result.html;
```

```
        } else {
          // handle error
        }
        return true;
    }
}
  ajax.send();
}
```

Advanced FBJS

As you can see, Mock AJAX offers a lot of functionality using a simple syntax. If you don't need the full control of all aspects of an AJAX call or object, Mock AJAX offers a simple alternative to accomplish a similar set of behaviors. It also offers some unique features to manage element visibility.

However, if you need the power of AJAX on your FBML pages, FBJS AJAX is the tool of choice. FBJS also offers the means to accomplish dynamically displaying elements through the use of specific FBJS CSS functions. For even more striking and interactive effects, it also provides a full-featured animation package. This section covers the advanced features of FBJS and AJAX.

Developers rejoiced when Facebook released AJAX for FBJS. At the time, the only alternative was to use Mock AJAX, which performed asynchronous requests like AJAX, but offered no notification callback functions or error handlers. Readers are probably already familiar with the basics of AJAX, including its benefits and shortcomings, so this book doesn't cover the details of the technology. You can find a complete reference for AJAX in Ajax for Web Application Developers by Kris Hadlock (part of the Addison-Wesley Developer's Library).

One of the nice things about FBJS AJAX is that, like many JavaScript libraries, it abstracts all the low-level details of making an AJAX call. It provides an FBJS class, aptly named `Ajax`, that handles all the low-level tasks normally associated with AJAX, such as dealing with creation of the correct `XMLHttpRequest` object for the current browser, monitoring state with `onreadystatechange` handlers, and managing data formats for the HTTP response.

FBJS AJAX provides a powerful object that's customized for use in Facebook applications that differ from normal AJAX implementations. First, calls are always asynchronous, and there is no way to use it for synchronous data transfer. Next, Facebook automatically proxies all calls made via FBJS AJAX through its servers. It does this to provide Facebook-centric POST variables to identify the current Facebook user (in the form of `fb_sig` variables that were introduced in Chapter 6, "The Basics of Creating Applications") and parse any FBML content it finds. Finally, it automatically processes AJAX responses into different Facebook-friendly formats. It can return server response data unaltered, as JSON, or even as parsed FBML. Facebook also provides a way to skip the Facebook proxy entirely if you don't need the FBML parser or don't require the normal Facebook POST variables in your AJAX handler.

The `Ajax` class provides the following three methods:

- **`Ajax()`.** Constructor for the `Ajax` class; it takes no arguments.
- **`abort()`.** Stops an AJAX call if needed, perhaps because of a timeout or another error.
- **`post( targetURL, queryObject )`.** Actually performs the asynchronous call via HTTP POST. The `targetURL` parameter must be set to a full URL on the same domain as the originating application because of the JavaScript same-origin restrictions discussed at the beginning of this chapter. `queryObject` is a simple JavaScript/FBJS object that contains the query data to be passed to the target URL.

The `Ajax` class also offers numerous properties:

- **`ondone( resultData )`.** Can be set to a callback function that takes one argument. This function is called when the AJAX request successfully completes. `resultData` is set to an object that contains the AJAX response from your server; its format depends on the response type set.
- **`onerror`.** Can be set to a callback function that's called when an error occurs during the AJAX call.
- **`requireLogin`.** A Boolean value that can be set to `true` to require the current user to log in to the application before making the AJAX call. If he refuses to do so, the call fails. When he is logged in, Facebook sends all of its usual `fb_sig` POST parameters to the AJAX target URL.
- **`responseType`.** Can be set to any of the values in the following list. If not set, `responseType` defaults to `Ajax.RAW`:
    - **`Ajax.FBML`.** Use this to have the data sent back from your server as an FBML object—like the ones created by `<fb:js-string>`—that can be used directly as the argument to `setInnerFBML()`. Using it requires that your call goes through the Facebook AJAX proxy to ensure any FBML in the request or response is parsed appropriately.
    - **`Ajax.RAW`.** Setting this causes Facebook to return the data from your server unaltered.
    - **`Ajax.JSON`.** Causes the response from your server to be parsed and returned as a JSON object. To encode your response data appropriately from PHP, use its `json_encode()` function before sending the response.
- **`useLocalProxy`.** (*Beta feature.*) Setting this to true allows your call to completely bypass the Facebook AJAX proxy. You cannot use it if you return FBML from your AJAX call. It requires that Adobe Flash Player 9 or higher is installed on the system, and requests can only be sent to port 80 on the target server.

Using `Ajax.FBML`

To understand how to use the `Ajax` class, we update Compliments to use it to submit the form data, just like we did with Mock AJAX earlier in this chapter. First, we need to update `index.php` to use the `Ajax` class to send the form contents to our target URL and handle receipt of the data and the updating of the page. Listing 11.13 shows the modified `submitForm()` function that you need to add AJAX support to the page and the changes to the `<form>` required to use it. (Changes in the `<form>` are bold.)

Listing 11.13 **Updating the `submitForm()` Function to Use AJAX**

```
function renderPage() {
  global $g_categories;

  $pageOutput = getHeaderContent();

  $ajaxURL = LOCAL_APP_URL."/ajax.php?submitform=1";
  // Show the compliment form
  $pageOutput .= "
  <script type='text/javascript'>
    function submitForm() {
    // Create the validation dialog
    var dialog = new Dialog(Dialog.DIALOG_CONTEXTUAL);
    dialog.setStyle('color', 'red');
    var formObj    = document.getElementById('complimentform');
    var formData   = formObj.serialize();
    var name       = formData.uid;
    var compliment = formData.compliment;
    var category   = formData.category;
    var title      = 'Validation Error';

    // Validate the form
    if ( (name == \"Start typing a friend's name\") || (name == \"\") ) {
      dialog.setContext(document.getElementById('friend_selector'));
      dialog.showMessage( title,
                        'Please choose someone to compliment');
    } else if ( category == null ) {
      dialog.setContext(document.getElementById('categories'));
      dialog.showMessage( title,
                        'Please enter a compliment category');
    } else if ( compliment == \"\" ) {
      dialog.setContext(document.getElementById('compliment'));
      dialog.showMessage( title,
                        'Please enter a compliment');
   } else {
    // Submit the form via AJAX
    var ajax = new Ajax();
```

Listing 11.13 **Continued**

```
    ajax.responseType = Ajax.FBML;

    // Handle the result of the AJAX call by
    // updating the canvas with a success message
    ajax.ondone = function(data) {
       var statusDiv = document.getElementById('formResult');
       statusDiv.setInnerFBML(data);
    };
    ajax.onerror = function() {
     new Dialog().showMessage('Ajax error');
    }
    var queryParams = formData;
    ajax.post('".$ajaxURL."', queryParams);
  }
}
</script>
<div id='formResult'></div>
<div id='panel' class='panel'>
  <form method='POST' id='complimentform'>
    <h1>Select one of your friends and enter your compliment.</h1>
      <table id='complimentTable'>
        <!-- table unchanged from previous listings;
             removed for clarity -->
      </table>
      <input class='inputbutton' type='submit'
        onclick='submitForm();return false;' name='submitCompliment'
        label='Send Compliment' value='Send Compliment'/>
  </form>
  <!-- unchanged from previous listings, removed for clarity -->
</div>
```

Notice that we defined the PHP variable `$ajaxURL` to hold the AJAX target URL at the top of the `renderPage()` function. Also, we removed the parameter from the `submitForm()` function and the `onsubmit()` event handler from the `<form>`, because we'll submit the form via AJAX instead of via normal HTTP POST or GET. To accomplish this, we added an `onclick()` event handler to the submit button that calls our `submitForm()` function. Finally, for clarity, we removed the Mock AJAX submit button.

We use `Ajax.FBML` as the response type because we want to update an FBML element on the page to show the result of the AJAX call. To do this, we need the FBML sent back from our server to be parsed into an FBML object reference that we can pass to `setInnerFBML()`. Later, we show how setting the `Ajax.responseType` property to `Ajax.JSON` can return both JSON and rendered FBML from an AJAX call.

Now, we add the script for handling the AJAX request. Copy Listing 11.14 into a new script file and save it in the application's root as `ajax_handler.php`.

Listing 11.14 **ajax_handler.php: AJAX Endpoint**

```
<?php
require_once 'inc/globals.inc';
require_once 'inc/utils.inc';
require_once 'inc/db.inc';
require_once 'inc/profile.inc';
require_once 'inc/notifications.inc';
require_once 'inc/email.inc';

dumpRequestVars(true, basename(__FILE__));

if ( $_GET['submitform'] ) {
  if ( isset($_POST['target']) && isset($_POST['compliment']) &&
       isset($_POST['category'])) {

    global $g_categories;
    $target     = $_POST['target'];
    $compliment = $_POST['compliment'];
    $category   = $_POST['category'];

    $facebook = new Facebook(FB_API_KEY, FB_APP_SECRET);
    if ( $facebook->user == NULL ) {
      // Work around bug in FB where sometimes the signature passed doesn't
      // actually match the one that the FB PHP library generates from the passed
      // parameters.
      /// http://wiki.developers.facebook.com/index.php/Verifying_The_Signature
      $facebook->set_user($_COOKIE[FB_API_KEY . '_user'],
                          $_COOKIE[FB_API_KEY . '_session_key'],
                          $_COOKIE[FB_API_KEY . '_expires'],
                          $_COOKIE[FB_API_KEY . '_ss'] );
    }
    $sender = $facebook->user;

    $db = new DB();
    $db->addCompliment($sender, $target, $category, $compliment);

    updateProfileBox($sender);

    $comp       = $g_categories[$category];

    $imageSrc   = LOCAL_APP_URL.'/img/'.$comp['bigimg'];
    $imageLink  = LOCAL_APP_URL;
    $images     = array('src'=> $imageSrc, 'href'=> $imageLink);
    // create the FBML to be parsed on the return
    $fbmlStatus = "<div class='success'>
                   <h1>Your Compliment to <fb:name uid='$target' /> was
```

Listing 11.14 **Continued**

```
                        sent.</h1>
                      <p>
                        <fb:profile-pic size='square' uid='$target' />
                        <img class='categoryImg' src='$imageSrc' ></img>
                        <fb:name uid='$target' />
                        is <b>'{$comp['title']}'</b>
                        because
                        $compliment
                      </p>
                    </div>";
    // Output the results
    $output = array("app"    => "<a href='".FB_APP_URL."'>Compliments</a>",
                    "target" => intval($target),
                    "images" => array($images),
                    "ctitle" => $comp['title'],
                    "ctext"  => $compliment);

    sendUserEmail($facebook, $target, $output);

    sendUserNotification($facebook, $target);

    echo $fbmlStatus;
  }
}
?>
```

Now, when the user submits the form, its serialized data will be sent via HTTP POST to `ajax_handler.php`. After you submit the form, you see something similar to Figure 11.10. Notice that the browser window does not reload, nor does the URL in the address bar change to indicate that any interaction with `ajax_handler.php` occurred, which is what you might expect of an AJAX call.

The code in `ajax_handler.php` is similar to that in `mock_ajax_handler.php` or the code we used in our Feed form callback files in Chapter 9, "Feed Stories, Feed Forms, and Templates." It first checks to make sure that all the expected POST variables we need are set, updates our database and profile box with new content, and sends the appropriate Facebook notifications. The most important thing to note for this example is that we are creating a block of FBML in `ajax_handler.php` and using PHP's `echo()` function to return it to the client code in `index.php`. Facebook intercepts the response from `ajax_handler.php`, notices that FBML is expected as the format for the response, and parses the FBML into an object before returning it to the `ondone()` handler in the `submitForm()` function in `index.php`.

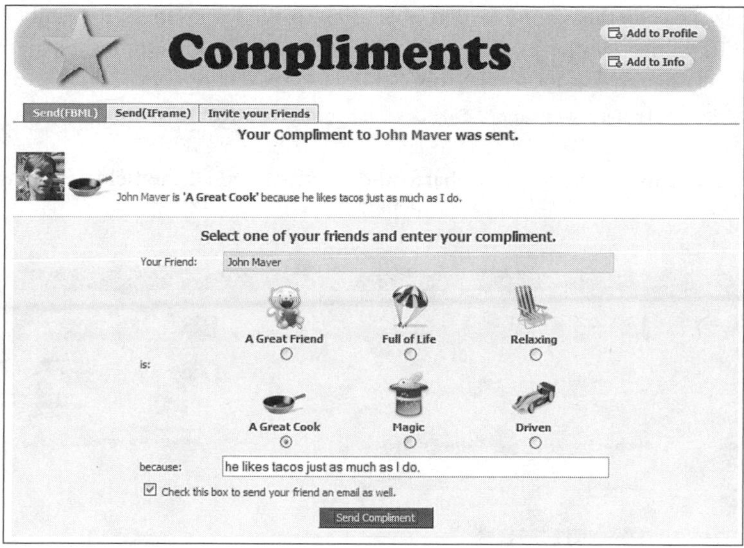

Figure 11.10 Result of a successful AJAX form submission

Using Firefox and Firebug to Monitor AJAX

One of the most powerful aids to debugging and following AJAX calls is the Firebug add-on for Firefox. It's indispensable for diagnosing AJAX errors or observing AJAX requests and responses. We explain the basics of using it to inspect the data posted to and returned from Facebook in AJAX calls and, in the process, make the FBJS AJAX lifecycle clearer.

First, by using a JavaScript breakpoint, we use Firebug to verify that our ondone() handler is being called. To accomplish this, run the application in Firefox with Firebug enabled. Set a breakpoint on the first line of the `ondone()` handler in `index.php` by doing the following:

1. Open the application canvas page in Firefox with Firebug enabled. Press the F12 key to open Firebug if the Firebug window is not visible.
2. Click the Script menu item in the Firebug menu bar.
3. Click the drop-down arrow to the right of the Script menu and ensure that JavaScript debugging is enabled. Click Enabled in the menu if it's not.
4. Refresh the page (if necessary) to load the script for the Compliments application in the Firebug Script panel.
5. Search for the `ondone()` handler using the *Firebug* search box, *not* the Firefox one. You can see two of them. Skip the first one; it's actually commented out as part of the developer view of the page. Remember that Facebook gives developers a preview of the page with the pre-parsed FBML and original non-sandboxed FBJS in one huge HTML comment at the start of the page. So, the first `ondone()` handler is

actually in code that's commented out. Click to the left of the line number of the first line of the handler in the Script window to set the breakpoint. For reference, set it on the line that looks like this:

```
var a<app id>_statusDiv = a<app id>_document.getElementById('formResult');
```

6. Submit the form, making sure that you correctly filled all the fields. Firebug stops at your breakpoint, as shown in Figure 11.11.

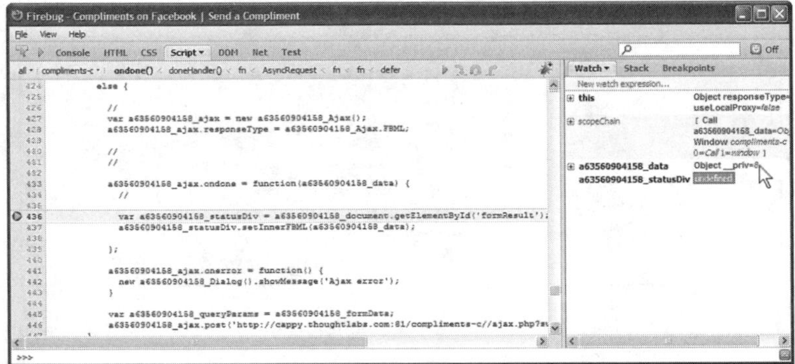

Figure 11.11 Stopping at a breakpoint while debugging FBJS using Firebug

In Figure 11.11, observe where the cursor is pointing in the Watch window in Firebug. It shows that the argument passed to the `ondone()` handler from the Facebook proxy is actually a JavaScript object. This Object instance contains the FBML reference that we pass to `setInnerFBML()` on the next line in the script.

Another important use of Firebug is to monitor the actual AJAX HTTP headers: Request and Response. The following steps describe how to do this:

1. Open the application canvas page in Firefox with Firebug enabled. Press the F12 key to open Firebug if the Firebug window is not visible.

2. Click the Net menu item in the Firebug menu bar.

3. Click the drop-down arrow to the right of the Net menu and ensure that Enabled is checked.

4. With the Net menu selected, click the XHR (short for `XMLHttpRequest`, which is the core object in AJAX) button in the toolbar below it. This filters the Net panel in Firebug to only show AJAX calls.

5. Refresh the page in the browser to update the Net panel.

6. Fill out and submit the Compliments form. An entry for the Facebook AJAX proxy URL—*http://www.facebook.com/fbml/fbjs_ajax_proxy.php*—appears in the Net panel.

7. Click the Facebook AJAX Proxy URL link in the Net panel. It expands and shows a set of tabs, the first of which, Headers, is selected by default. This shows all the HTTP Request headers sent to the Facebook server and the Response headers sent back from it to the browser. Note the Response header's content-type value. We refer to it later.
8. Click the Post tab beneath the expanded proxy URL. You see something similar to Figure 11.12.

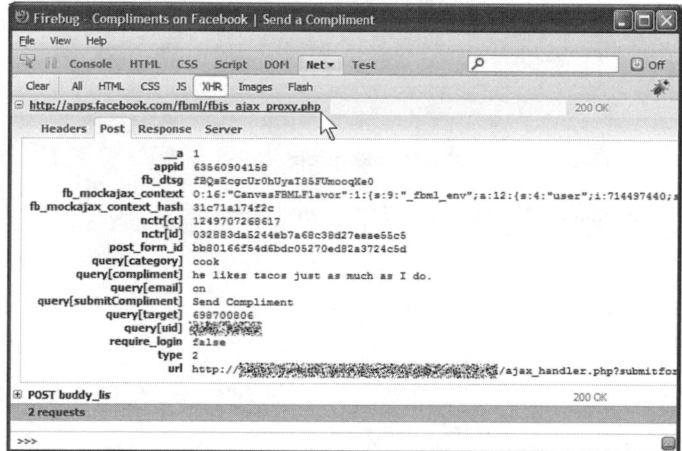

Figure 11.12 Showing the HTTP POST variables sent in an AJAX request

9. You can also view `XMLHttpRequest` calls in Firebug's Console panel by setting the appropriate options, as shown in Figure 11.13.

If you look closely at the POST variables sent to Facebook, shown in Figure 11.12, you can see that the form data is sent as part of a `query` array. Values for other Ajax class properties are also sent. First, the `require_login` variable holds the value of the `Ajax.requireLogin` property, which is currently `false` (the default). Next, the `type` variable contains the response format we expect (in this case, 2), which is actually the value of `Ajax.FBML`. Finally, `url` contains the full URL of our server's `ajax_handler.php` file.

Click the Response tab to see the raw HTTP response data returned to the browser from Facebook. Notice that it's actually JavaScript that does nothing but has a JSON object tacked on the end of it. If you look at the Response headers sent back to the browser from Facebook, you notice that `content-type` was set to `application/x-javascript; charset=utf8`. Keep this in mind as you examine the example HTTP response shown in Listing 11.15.

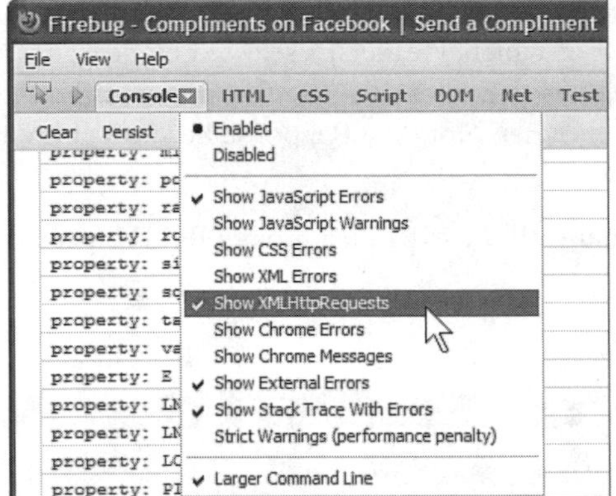

Figure 11.13 Using the Console panel to view `XMLHttpRequest` calls

Listing 11.15 **Sample AJAX Response Body from Facebook**

```
for (;;); {
  "error": 0,
  "errorSummary": "",
  "errorDescription": "",
  "errorIsWarning": false,
  "payload": {
    "data": "<!— our fully-parsed FBML —>",
    "type": 2 // Ajax.FBML
  },
  "bootload": ,
    "name": "js\/aspzj17g3yg4cc88.pkg.js",
    "type": "js",
    "src": "http:\/\/static.ak.fbcdn.net\/rsrc.php\/zCVHY\/hash\/ealyqk9w.js",
    "permanent": false,
    "sticky": false
  }. // more like this...
  {
    // etc.
  }],
  "onload": ["some JavaScript"]
}
```

We removed some of the content of the HTTP response body, formatted it to make it easier to understand, and added a few comments for clarity. If an error occurred during the execution of the call, the `error` property of the JSON object would hold an error code and both the `errorSummary` and `errorDescription` properties might contain more information about the error. The important thing to see is that our FBML response is passed in the JSON object set as the value of the `payload.data` property (shown in bold).

It's the value of `payload.data` that's passed back to the `ondone()` handler, after some post-processing on the client by Facebook's own JavaScript.

You might wonder why Facebook returns JavaScript instead of JSON if that's what the response really contains. The JavaScript in the response is actually just a shield to protect the real payload: the JSON object that follows it, of which the AJAX response data is only part. So, why does Facebook not use a JSON-specific content type, such as `application/json`? Doing so would invariably cause problems with older browsers that do not understand what to do with JSON. Users on older browsers receiving these responses likely receive a prompt asking them to save or download the content. By using the `application/x-javascript` content type, Facebook ensures that all modern browsers accept the content without prompting the user or displaying the file as plain text, because all browsers natively understand JavaScript. Also, Facebook returns and uses JSONP, also known as JSON with padding, which wraps an extra callback function around a JSON response that executes on the client when evaluated. If Facebook did not serve the content as JavaScript, these JSONP callbacks would never execute, rendering them useless. In fact, if you look at the Facebook JavaScript code, you find that, when handling asynchronous responses, Facebook simply strips the `for(;;);` string from the front of the response data and uses JavaScript's `eval()` function to convert the JSON that follows it into an instance of a JavaScript object.

We only presented one method of monitoring AJAX calls here. Other popular browsers have similar solutions for inspecting AJAX calls or debugging JavaScript. The Google Chrome and Apple Safari browsers provide a JavaScript console that show the Request and Response headers. Microsoft's new Internet Explorer 8 browser also has similar development tools built in. However, none provide the rich functionality that Firebug currently does for Firefox. These tools were presented in Chapter 4, "Platform Developer Tools," and we leave more detailed investigation as an exercise for readers.

Using `Ajax.JSON`

As promised, we now switch our AJAX code to use the `Ajax.JSON` response type. This response type allows your AJAX calls to receive not only JSON but also fully parsed and rendered FBML in a single request, which is undoubtedly a great optimization and benefit.

To begin the process, we modify our `submitForm()` function to switch the response type and store the data returned in the `ondone()` handler. The code shown in bold shows the modifications you need to make to `submitForm()`:

```
// Submit the form via AJAX
var ajax = new Ajax();
ajax.responseType = Ajax.JSON;

// Handle the result of the AJAX call
ajax.ondone = function(data) {
  var statusDiv = document.getElementById('formResult');
  statusDiv.setInnerFBML(data.fbml_markup);
};
```

In the `ondone()` handler, other than switching the response type, we just passed the value of the `data.fbml_markup` property to `setInnerFBML()`. We also need to make changes in the `ajax_handler.php` file to complete the switch to JSON, as shown in the following code. Again, we only show a portion of the file with the relevant changes in bold. The rest of the script remains unchanged:

```
// Output the results
$output = array("app"     => "<a href='".FB_APP_URL."'>Compliments</a>",
               "target" => intval($target),
                "images" => array($images),
                "ctitle" => $comp['title'],
                "ctext"  => $compliment,
                "fbml_markup" => $fbml
               );

sendUserEmail($facebook, $target, $output);
sendUserNotification($facebook, $target);

$output = json_encode($output);

echo $output;
```

Notice that we simply added a new entry to the end of the `$output` array, with a key name of `fbml_markup`, which is set to the value of the `$fbml` variable. As you probably noticed, this key shares its name with the property of the `data` parameter that's now passed to `setInnerFBML()` in the `ondone()` handler. Also, instead of sending pure FBML back from `ajax_handler.php`, we're now using the PHP `json_encode()` function to convert the `$output` array to JSON and sending *it* back to the client as a JSON object. All these changes are required to make the transition to JSON as our AJAX response type.

Let's view the effects these code changes make. Make sure that your breakpoint is still enabled in Firebug; if not, reset it to the first line of the `ondone()` handler in `index.php`. Refresh the application canvas page in the browser, fill out the form, and submit it. After the breakpoint is hit, you can see the results of the changes in the `data` argument sent to the `ondone()` handler, as shown in Figure 11.14. Observe that it now contains both pure JavaScript data for the compliment we sent and an FBML object reference that we can pass directly to `setInnerFBML()`.

Facebook allows this transmission of both JSON and FBML references by using a simple technique. When the response type is set to `Ajax.JSON`, it scans the JSON object returned from the AJAX endpoint for properties prefixed with `fbml_`, parses their values as FBML, and converts them to FBML object references, exactly like the results one gets from using the `<fb:js-string>` FBML tag. There is a catch with using `Ajax.JSON`, however. Its payload size is limited; each JSON property and value in the response is limited to a current maximum length of 5,000 characters. If you need to return more data than this limit allows, you need to use one of the other response types. If this limit is a problem—and it well might be, depending on how complex the FBML is that your handler returns—realize that you do not need to send back FBML references from your AJAX handler if you only want to create pure HTML elements using the data passed to the `ondone()` handler. Earlier, this chapter discussed the FBJS `setInnerXHTML()` function to allow you to build pure HTML dynamic DOM elements.

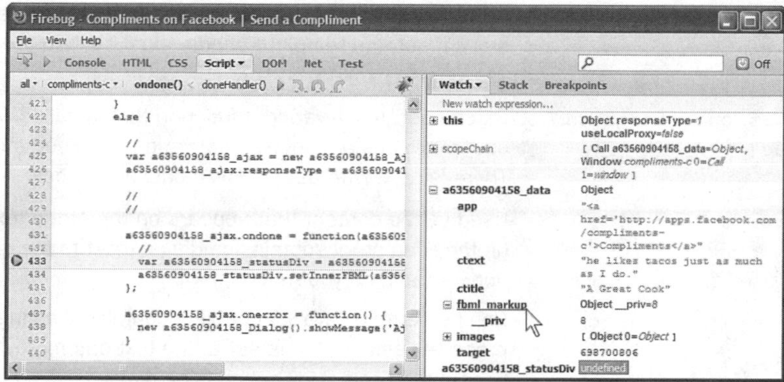

Figure 11.14 Using a response type of **`Ajax.JSON`** allows both data and rendered FBML to be returned from an AJAX handler.

Publishing Feed Stories with FBJS

The real reason why we returned both FBML and data from our AJAX handler was to introduce you to the FBJS method of submitting Feed stories, such as Feed forms or Publishers: the `Facebook.showFeedDialog()` function. It provides a Feed-publishing mechanism similar to that of the Feed forms that Chapter 9 discussed.

The real beauty of this function, however, is that, unlike all other Facebook stream-publishing mechanisms that accept direct user input that we've discussed to date, this one does not require a round trip to Facebook's servers to publish a Feed story. Remember that Feed forms required one round trip: Facebook intercepts the originating HTML `<form>` POST and calls the Feed form callback specified in that `<form>`'s `action` attribute to get the custom template data needed to populate the Feed story submission dialog. Publishers required at least two round trips: one to get the content for the Publisher's user interface and a second to get the Feed template data to populate the Feed story submission dialog.

The `Facebook.showFeedDialog()` function handles all this on the client side, which makes it more useful and responsive in most cases. This function accepts numerous parameters, which are described in Table 11.3.

Table 11.3 **Parameters of the `Facebook.showFeedDialog()` Function**

Parameter	Type	Description
`template_bundle_id`	`int`	Contains the ID of a Feed Template bundle registered using the Feed Template Console or Facebook API. **Required.**
`template_data`	`object`	Contains a JavaScript associative array that contains the custom data needed to populate the Feed Template.
`body_general`	`string`	Can contain extra markup for use in the body of a short story.

Table 11.3 **Parameters of the `Facebook.showFeedDialog()` Function**

Parameter	Type	Description
`target_id`	`int`	Set to the Facebook user ID of the actor of the Feed story. If set, the template bundle must contain the `{*target*}` token.
`continuation_callback`	`function`	Can be set to a JavaScript function that is called when a user publishes *or* cancels publication of a Feed story. There is no way to detect which caused the call.
`user_prompt`	`string`	Used as the content that appears on top of the text field on the Feed story submission dialog (next to the question, "What's on your mind?")
`user_message`	`object`	Can be set to a JavaScript object containing a single property, value, which is set to the text entered by a user in the Feed story submission dialog.

The `Facebook.showFeedDialog()` function behaves differently depending on the value of the `target_id` parameter passed to it. If this is set, the function behaves like a multiFeedStory Feed form. Short Feed stories published with it in this mode appear of the recipient's Wall and the Home page News Feeds of all the recipient's friends. A one line Feed story is also published to the sender's Wall Feed in his Recent Activity section. Unlike a multiFeedStory Feed form, however, only *one* recipient is allowed. When the `target_id` is set to null, the function behaves like a feedStory Feed form. Short stories submitted by it appear on the sender's Wall Feed and the Home page News Feeds of their friends.

Now, we use this function to submit a Feed story (targeted to the recipient of our compliment) in the AJAX `ondone()` handler. We add another FBJS function to `index.php` to handle the logic. Listing 11.16 provides the code for the new `getFeedDialog()` function. Copy it to the end of your `index.php` file.

Listing 11.16 **Implementing the `getFeedDialog()` Function**

```
/** returns HTML for the Feed Dialog **/
function getFeedDialog() {
  $output = "
    <script type='text/javascript'>
      function showFeedDialog(templateData) {
        // The short story template for reference
        //{*actor*} sent {*target*} a compliment with {*app*}!
        //<br/>{*actor*} thinks {*target*} is {*ctitle*} because {*ctext*}
        var targetID = [templateData.target];
        var templateID = ".TEMPLATE_BUNDLE_MULTIFEEDSTORY_1.";
        var bodyGeneral = '';
        var callback = feedDialogDone;
        var feedDialogPrompt = 'Publish your Compliment';
```

Listing 11.16 **Continued**

```
        // NOTE: this is for illustrative purposes only. Setting the
        // user_message to text not physically entered by a user
        // violates the Facebook Developer guidelines.
        var feedDialogUserMsg = {value:'I love sending Compliments!'};

        Facebook.showFeedDialog(templateID, templateData, bodyGeneral, targetID,
                                callback, feedDialogPrompt, feedDialogUserMsg);
      }

      function feedDialogDone(){
        document.setLocation('".FB_APP_URL."');
      }
    </script>
  ";
  return $output;
}
```

In Listing 11.16, observe the `showFeedDialog()` function. It takes a single argument that contains the data returned to our `ondone()` handler. Notice that we use the properties of the argument to build the parameters for the `Facebook.showFeedDialog()` function. Pay special attention to the comment about directly setting its `user_message` parameter in application code. You cannot (and must not) do this in production; the `user_message` *must* be generated by a physical Facebook user or the application violates the Facebook Developer Guidelines. This means that, at the least, it would fail the application verification process. We just included it in this sample to show the correct syntax for using it.

We need to update the code in index.php to actually call the `getFeedDialog()` function. Add a line of code to do so at the top of the `renderPage()` function in `index.php`, as demonstrated in the following bold code:

```
function renderPage() {
  global $g_categories;

  $pageOutput = getHeaderContent();

  $ajaxURL = LOCAL_APP_URL."/ajax_handler.php?submitform=1";
  $pageOutput .= getFeedDialog();
  // Show the compliment form
  $pageOutput .= "
    <script>
```

Next, we need to call the `showFeedDialog()` function from the `ondone()` handler. The modified code in the `submitForm()` function is shown in bold:

```
// Submit the form via AJAX
var ajax = new Ajax();
ajax.responseType = Ajax.JSON;
```

```
// Handle the result of the AJAX call by displaying a feed dialog
// and updating the canvas with a success message

ajax.ondone = function(data) {
  showFeedDialog(data);
  var statusDiv = document.getElementById('formResult');
  statusDiv.setInnerFBML(data.fbml_markup);
};
```

Now, it's clear why the `Ajax.JSON` response type is so handy. We get back formatted FBML to update our user interface and the data needed to create a Feed story. Now, when you submit the form, you are prompted with a Feed story submission dialog like the one shown in Figure 11.15. Clicking either the Publish or Skip button on the dialog causes the code in the `feedDialogDone()` function to execute, which refreshes the page and resets the controls on it to their default state.

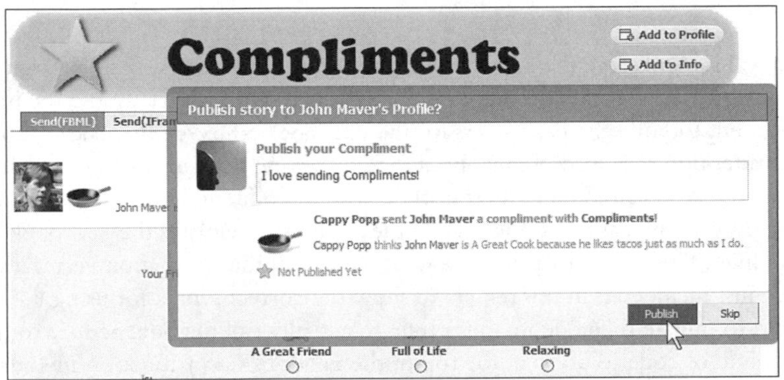

Figure 11.15 Feed story submission dialog generated by the `Facebook.showFeedDialog()` function

FBJS and CSS

One of the great things about using JavaScript and the DOM is that it provides the ability to retrieve or set CSS styles dynamically using the DOM element's style property; however, this property is not available in FBJS. FBJS replaces it with the `getStyle()` and `setStyle()` functions.

The `getStyle()` function can get the value of a specific CSS style on a DOM element. It takes a string argument of the CSS style property and returns its value. It has one major shortcoming. It only returns inline styles set on an element, not ones applied through external `<style>` tags. This, of course, is inconvenient because most HTML code these days uses external CSS applied in this manner. Also, to use CSS style attributes that contain a dash in their names—like font-size, text-align, or margin-top, for example—you must convert them to camel-cased versions before passing them to either of these FBJS functions to ensure that they behave similarly on all browsers. To convert a dashed property name to camel case, simply remove the dash, capitalize the word after it, and combine the two words. For example, text-align becomes textAlign.

If you run Listing 11.17 in the FBML Test Console in WebKit-based browsers, such as Chrome or Safari, calling the `getStyle()` function with a dashed name works, while on Firefox and Internet Explorer, it does not. On all four browsers, the camel-cased version works. None of them work when querying for non-inline CSS styles.

Listing 11.17 **Using the FBJS `getStyle()` Function**

```
<style>
.foo {color:red;}
</style>
<div class='foo'
     style='text-align:center;font-weight:bold;'
     onclick='styleTests(this);return false;'>Click Me</div>
<script>
function styleTests(obj) {

  var dashed      = "'" + obj.getStyle('text-align')+ "'";
  var camelCased  = "'" + obj.getStyle('fontWeight')+ "'";
  var extCSSValue = "'" + obj.getStyle('color') + "'";

  // Google Chrome, Safari show: 'center' - 'bold' - ''
  // Firefox and IE show: 'undefined' - 'bold' - ''
  new Dialog().showMessage('FBJS getStyle() tests',
       dashed + ' - ' + camelCased + ' - ' + extCSSValue);
}
</script>
```

The `setStyle()` function can set a single style on an element or multiple ones at a time. To set multiple styles on an element, you need to incorporate them as properties of an FBJS object literal and pass that object to the `setStyle()` function. The properties of this object are set to the names of the CSS styles to set; their values are set to strings containing the style information. We use this to set multiple styles on an element in the next section, "FBJS Animation." The following code shows the various right and wrong ways to call `setStyle()`. The most common mistakes developers make when using this function involve either not passing the second argument as a string or omitting the units ("px" for example) when setting a dimensions of an element:

```
element.setStyle('fontWeight', 'bold'); // correct on all browsers
element.setStyle({fontWeight: 'bold'}); // correct on all browsers
element.setStyle('font-weight', 'bold'); // does not work on IE or Firefox
element.setStyle('fontWeight:bold'); // fails
element.setStyle('fontSize', 20); // fails, second argument must be string
element.setStyle('fontSize', '20'); // fails, need to append 'px' to the value
```

FBJS also contains some functions for managing CSS classes on elements. The following list explains how they're used:

- **`addClassName(name)`** and **`removeClassName(name)`.** The former adds the CSS class `name` to an element (to its `className` DOM property, specifically); if it's not already present, the latter removes it.
- **`getClassName()`** and **`setClassName(name)`.** The former gets the value of the `className` property of an element, and the latter sets it to the value passed in the `name` parameter.
- **`toggleClassName(name)`.** Adds the named CSS class if not already present on the element (and removes it if it is).
- **`hasClassName(name)`.** Returns `true` if the element's `className` property contains the named CSS class; otherwise, it returns `false`.

FBJS Animation

As part of FBJS, Facebook provides a rich set of JavaScript-based animation functions that can make your user interfaces more interesting and dynamic. Facebook actually provides a version of the animation functions in a library for use in pages outside Facebook. You can download it from *http://developers.facebook.com/animation*. Internally, Facebook uses a version of this library extensively in its client-side user interface code and exposes the same library via the FBJS `Animation` class. You see it in action every time you use Facebook. For example, if you run Listing 11.17, notice how the FBJS dialogs gradually fade from view rather than instantly disappearing when their Okay buttons are clicked. This behavior is implemented behind the scenes using functions of the `Animation` class.

We briefly discuss it here and update the Compliments application to dynamically show the `<div>` that holds the FBML returned from our AJAX handler. Modify the code in the `ondone()` handler to match Listing 11.18. Now, if you submit the form, you see the `<div>` at the top of the form gradually appear by scrolling across and down to fill its full height and width over the course of one second or so. A few seconds later, the Feed story submission dialog appears.

Listing 11.18 **Using Facebook FBJS Animation**

```
ajax.ondone = function(data) {

      var statusDiv = document.getElementById('formResult');

      statusDiv.setStyle({
        display: 'none',
        border: '3px solid #bdc7d8',
        padding: '0px 3px',
        textAlign: 'center'
      });
```

Listing 11.18 **Continued**

```
      statusDiv.setInnerFBML(data.fbml_markup);

      // create an instance of the Animation class, passing a
      // reference to the DOM element to animate
      var anim = Animation(statusDiv);

      // keep the height of the statusDiv at 0px...
      anim.to('height', '0px').from('height', '0px');

      // ...while expanding the statusDiv to its full width
      anim.to('width', 'auto').from('width',  '0px');

      // now expand the statusDiv to its full height; however, add a
      // checkpoint to make sure the width expansion finishes first.
      // The blind() calls ensure that text does not wrap while the
      // statusDiv expands
      anim.show().blind().checkpoint().to('height', 'auto').blind();

      // do the whole thing in 1 second
      anim.duration(1000);

      // The number below is multiplied by duration value
      // to get resulting milliseconds to wait before firing
      // checkpoint. In this case, duration is set to 1000 so
      // the checkpoint below will call the function passed as its
      // second argument 5 seconds after the animation finishes
      var feedDialogDelayFactor = 5;

      anim.checkpoint(feedDialogDelayFactor, function() {
        // show the Feed story submission dialog as before
        showFeedDialog(data);
      });

      // start the animation sequence
      anim.go();
};
```

A lot is happening in this code. We start with the call to the FBJS `setStyle()` function. Notice that we're setting multiple styles on the `<div>` element using an object literal whose keys are set to the (potentially camel-cased) names of the CSS style properties and whose values are set to strings. After these styles are applied to the element, we set the FBML content of it by using the FBML object returned from our AJAX call.

The animation code starts on the next line. First, we create an instance of the `Animation` class by passing its constructor a reference to the DOM element we want to animate. The lines following its instantiation look complex; however, nearly all the

`Animation` functions (and most FBJS DOM functions) return references to the object on which they're called, which allows you to chain multiple function calls together in a single line of code.

The `Animation.from()` and `Animation.to()` functions *tween* CSS styles of an element. The `Animation.from()` function overrides the existing style used as the starting point for the animation. In this case, even if the `<div>` had its width set to 200px, it would start with a width of 0px in this animation. Tweening, or inbetweening, in animation is the process of smoothly inserting frames *in between* the start and end of an animation to make it look fluid. So, the following lines of code expand the width of the `<div>` from 0px to its full width—smoothly—while keeping the height of the `<div>` at 0px the entire time. If we did not do this, the `<div>` wipes in from left to right instead of expanding to its full width and then expanding vertically.

```
anim.to('height', '0px').from('height', '0px');
anim.to('width', 'auto').from('width', '0px');
```

The next code line is more involved. It's shown here for reference:

```
anim.show().blind().checkpoint().to('height', 'auto').blind();
```

First, the `Animation.show()` function explicitly sets the `<div>`'s CSS display attribute to "block" to ensure that it behaves as a block-level element. Next, the `Animation.blind()` function keeps the text—or any other content that might wrap—in an element from wrapping or constantly repositioning to fill the intermediate sizes of the element being animated. It's much easier to see than explain. If you uncomment the line in Listing 11.18 that does not use `blind()`, you see the effects of using it. Without it, the content of the `<div>` is visible no matter what, and it constantly readjusts itself to fill the space provided. Not very smooth animation. The `blind()` function adds a special container `<div>` as a child of the element we're animating. It's set to a fixed width and height that keeps the content from wrapping until the animation is complete. When the animation completes, the `<div>` is removed.

The `checkpoint()` function breaks the animation into steps to ensure that one animation completes before the next one starts. In this case, it lets the `<div>` expand to its full width before expanding it vertically. The `duration()` function takes a value (in milliseconds) that sets the length of the entire animation sequence. Here, we set it to 1 second. Next, and most importantly, we use another `checkpoint()`; however, this time, we pass it two arguments. The first argument is multiplied by the duration to get the number of milliseconds to wait after the animation completes before calling the anonymous function passed as the checkpoint's second argument. This function simply calls our `showFeedDialog()` function—5 seconds after the animation finishes. Finally, the `Animation.go()` function starts the entire animation process. It's actually called last because it's usually called at the end of a long line of chained animation functions and signifies the end of that chain.

The animation functions offer more functionality than what we've discussed here. It's actually enjoyable to experiment with it in the FBML Test Console. We encourage you to try it out on your own to see what it can do.

FBJS Events

One of the most important shifts in programming for the web occurred when developers shifted from using only static HTML to provide content to modern event-driven programming. No longer was the web static. The rise of dynamic HTML, the DOM, CSS, JavaScript, and technologies like AJAX allowed developers to make users' experience on the web more interactive and have revolutionized the way people use the web. Without these technological shifts, sites like Facebook would not be possible.

At the core of the interactive web are events and event handlers. Effectively using them is an important skill that all web developers should master. As the W3C codified the DOM and its base functionality, different means of handling events emerged from the different browsers. Currently, the W3C DOM `addEventListener()` function is the most widely accepted means of registering an event listener on a single target, and FBJS bases its events on this model. FBJS abstracts the browser differences from developers so they can use a familiar and consistent syntax to make their applications more interactive and responsive. Using events in FBJS is somewhat different than doing so with the DOM. We point out those differences as we encounter them.

To help you understand events more clearly, we provide some examples. We also try to follow the tenets of what's known as *unobtrusive JavaScript*. This is a recent paradigm in client-side web programming that holds that script on a page should not draw attention to itself or intrude on the viewers experience or the content on the page. It needs to degrade gracefully and show the viewer no error messages if it fails. Ideally, and most importantly, it's separated from the markup of the page as much as possible, preferably in external files. You can read more about it on the Web Standards Project site at *www.webstandards.org/action/dstf/manifesto/*.

FBJS Event Handling

FBJS allows developers to add or remove event handlers to DOM elements by using the `addEventListener()` and `removeEventListener()` functions. They both require two parameters, which are discussed in a moment. Currently, the Facebook documentation for FBJS states that these functions *require* a third parameter, `useCapture`, that the W3C DOM functions of the same name do; however, the Facebook documentation is incorrect. Because there is a discrepancy between the Facebook documentation and the actual implementation of these functions in FBJS, we discuss this third parameter anyway. It's important to understand what it does and how FBJS uses it. Table 11.4 describes the arguments to these functions.

Table 11.4 **Parameters of the `addEventListener()` and `removeEventListener()` Functions**

Parameter	Type	Description
`type`	`string`	Contains the name of the event for which to register/remove a handler, such as "click," "submit," and so on.
`listener`	`function`	Contains the name of the FBJS function to add/remove as the event handler. It can also be an inline anonymous function.
`useCapture`	`boolean`	Set to true if you want to handle the event before it reaches its final target; false, otherwise. This parameter is *not required* by FBJS, where it's always false.

The `useCapture` parameter might be confusing to some. It helps to understand the W3C DOM Event flow model, which is detailed at *www.w3.org/TR/DOM-Level-3-Events/events.html#Events-flow*. Simply put, events propagate from the root of the DOM to their ultimate target and then back up to the root. Multiple DOM elements can register event handlers for the same event. Elements that register handlers for an event are called *targets* for that event. Those higher in the DOM tree are known as the target's *ancestors*, and the one immediately preceding it is the target's *parent*. Events go through three phases during their lifecycle:

1. **Capture phase.** Occurs as the event travels down through the target's ancestors to its parent. If the target had passed `true` for the `useCapture` parameter of the `addEventListener()` function (a process known as *initiating capture*), it would allow it to handle the event before it reached any targets beneath it in the DOM hierarchy or tree. Similarly, if a target's parent or ancestor had done the same, it would be able to handle the event before the target.

2. **Target phase.** Happens as the event reaches its final target. Normal event listeners operate at this phase to handle the event.

3. **Bubbling phase.** Events not only travel down through the DOM to reach their target, but they also travel back *up*. The process of doing so is known as *bubbling*. Handlers registered for this phase handle the event *after* it's been handled by the target, or more colloquially, as the event bubbles back up the DOM tree. Event listeners that have initiated capture are never called during this phase.

In FBJS, the `useCapture` parameter of `addEventListener()` is always set to `false`, which means that we will only ever be able to handle the event during the target or bubbling phase (whichever comes first).

FBJS also provides a couple of utility functions for dealing with event handlers. The `purgeEventListeners()` function takes a single argument—the type of the event—and removes all the currently registered handlers for it from the element on which it's called. `listEventListeners()` takes the same argument and returns an array of all the handlers registered for the event type it's passed.

A final note: FBJS does not support the older form of event handler registration that was available before `addEventListener()` was introduced. This older model exposed events as properties of an element to which handler functions could be directly assigned, like this: `element.click = function(){}`. These properties are not available in FBJS.

> **Event Handling and Internet Explorer**
>
> We have not discussed the differences in event handling between different browsers. All modern browsers, with the notable exception of Internet Explorer, use W3C-style event handling. Internet Explorer—including version 8—uses a completely different and nonstandard event handling syntax, using the functions `attachEvent()` and `detachEvent()`. Thankfully, FBJS handles the differences internally so that you don't have to.

Implementing FBJS Event Handling

Now, let's update our application to use an FBJS event handler. First, we add a new event handler to the page for our submit button on the `<form>` instead of using the inline `onclick()` handler as our first step on the path to writing unobtrusive code. In doing so, we begin to move our FBJS code to an external file instead of including it in `index.php`. To begin, create a new directory named `js` in the root of your application. Add the code in Listing 11.19 to a new file and save it as `fbjs.js` in this new directory.

Listing 11.19 **`fbjs.js`: Adding an Unobtrusive `onclick()` Handler**

```
// keep our script out of global scope;
// not really required here since FBJS is already
// sandboxed but good practice
(function() {

  var functionsToCallOnLoad = [ addEventHandlers ];
  // since FBJS does not expose the onload event handler for the page
  // we'll fudge one by running this function 10 ms after the page loads
  var interval = setInterval( function() {
    var root = document.getRootElement();
    if(root) {
      clearInterval(interval);
      for( var i = 0, len = functionsToCallOnLoad.length; i < len; ++i ) {
        functionsToCallOnLoad[i]();
      }
    }
  }, 10);

  function $(element) {
    if ('string' == typeof element) {
      element = document.getElementById(element);
```

Listing 11.19 **Continued**

```
    }
    return element;
  }
  function addEventHandlers() {

    var submitButton = $('submitButton');

    if(submitButton) {
      submitButton.addEventListener('click', function(event){
        submitForm();
        event.stopPropagation();
        event.preventDefault();
        return false;
      }, false);
    }
  }
})();
```

The first thing to notice about Listing 11.19 is that the entire file is enclosed in an anonymous function, which is executed immediately after the script loads. The reason for this is to ensure that none of the variables or functions clash with any others defined in the global namespace by using the function's scope as a temporary namespace. This is an important practice to use when writing external JavaScript files for a page, especially if you don't control the other scripts that the page can load. In this case, it's not that important because all of your FBJS code runs in a sandbox that virtually guarantees that no name conflicts will occur; however, it is a best practice to follow nonetheless, and it helps in our approach to write unobtrusive code.

The next part of the code gets around a limitation of FBJS: the lack of access to the page's `onload()` handler. In normal DOM scripting, a developer usually defers any JavaScript that interacted with the DOM until the page on which it's used is fully loaded. At this point, the `window` object fires the `load` event. Typically, the developer registers a handler for this event and, in it, runs any script that needed to run as soon as users can interact with the document. But, in FBJS, we must provide a workaround by using the `setInterval()` function to do a time-based deferral of our script's execution. Not a perfect solution, but it's effective in most cases. Here, we use `setInterval()` to poll every 10ms to check for the existence of our canvas page's root element. When it's found, we clear the interval and execute our startup code.

We organized the functions that we need to run immediately by using an array. When our startup code executes, it walks this array, calling each function in turn. For this example, we only added the `addEventHandlers()` function to this array.

Note the utility `$()` function. It's used to put some syntactic sugar on the process of getting a reference to a DOM element using its ID. Much less work is needed to type `$()` to get a reference to a DOM element than typing `document.getElementById()` each time. Many commercial JavaScript libraries do something similar.

Finally, we can add our new event handler. In the `addEventHandlers()` function, we first get a reference to the submit button DOM instance and, with it, we call the FBJS `addEventListener()` function. In our case, the event handler it sets is always called during the target phase because we cannot initiate capture in FBJS, and there are no elements deeper in the DOM tree that have registered handlers for the event.

Notice that we then call two functions on the event instance that's passed to our handler. The first, `stopPropation()`, immediately halts the event's progress through the event phases. This means that if there were another target further along in the DOM that had registered a handler for this event—and we set `useCapture` to true when calling `addEventListener()` on the submit button—the final target element would never receive the event. This also prevents any other handlers from receiving it as the event bubbles back up. The next function, `preventDefault()`, stops the default action the event causes on the implementation of the target. For example, the normal default action for the click event in an `<input type='submit'>` button might be to submit the `<form>` in which it's found. By calling `preventDefault()`, we cancel this action because we are submitting the form ourselves using AJAX.

Now, we need to update our submit button to use the new event handler. The first thing we need to do is include the external `fbjs.js` file in our canvas page. The following code shows the line we need to add to the `getHeaderContent()` function in `index.php` to do it:

```
function getHeaderContent() {
  $header = "
    <link rel='stylesheet' type='text/css'
      href='".LOCAL_APP_URL.getFileVer("css/main.css")."' />
    <!–[if IE]>
    <link rel='stylesheet' type='text/css'
      href='".LOCAL_APP_URL.getFileVer("css/ie.css")."' />
    <![endif]–>
    <fb:title>Send a Compliment</fb:title>
    <script src='".LOCAL_APP_URL.getFileVer("js/fbjs.js")."'
type='text/javascript'></script>
    <div class='banner'
      style='background: url(".LOCAL_APP_URL."/img/banner.png) no-repeat;' >
```

Next, we modify the existing submit button to remove the `onclick()` handler it's currently using. Because we're adding the event handler in FBJS dynamically, we just need to remove the `onclick` attribute completely, as shown here:

```
<input id='submitButton'
        class='inputbutton'
        type='submit'
        name='submitCompliment'
        label='Send Compliment'
       value='Send Compliment'/>
```

That's all the changes required to use FBJS event handling in our application. Test it out and verify that submitting the form behaves exactly like it did before our changes. Clicking the submit button submits the form exactly as before. The next step of making our FBJS more unobtrusive is to completely remove the FBJS from `index.php` and place it into `fbjs.js`. We leave that as an exercise for you.

Using Flash

Abobe Flash is a popular, powerful, and mature technology for implementing interactive applications for the web (and elsewhere). According to Adobe, more than 98 percent of all PC web browsers have at least version 9 of the Flash Player installed. Flash has always been a popular choice for developers to use in creating engaging Facebook applications. In fact, many of the top applications on Facebook today use it.

Recently, a new library, fully supported by both Facebook and Adobe, was released to allow developers to use Flash or Flex and ActionScript 3 (the JavaScript-like scripting language supported by Flash) to create complete Facebook applications that can run either within Facebook or externally. This library gives Flash the ability to call the Facebook API directly, much like the PHP library does. This is a huge time-saver; prior to its release, developers had no way to easily call the Facebook API from their SWF files; moreover, they had to manage all the communication between their Flash SWF files and their Facebook applications themselves.

One of the most frequent issues that developers deal with in using Flash in traditional Facebook web applications is how to communicate between their Flash objects and the application pages on which they're placed. This section covers that in detail. For more information on the Facebook ActionScript 3 Library, visit the Adobe Developer Connection site at *www.adobe.com/devnet/facebook/*.

Hosting Flash Content in Facebook Applications

Flash content can be inserted in Facebook profiles, application tabs, or canvas pages. Remember that developers have a choice to use either IFrame- or FBML-based canvas pages. Hosting Flash content from within an IFrame-based page is similar to hosting it on a normal web page. Generally, the Flash is placed on the page using an HTML `<object>` tag or using JavaScript detection and embedding scripts. FBML canvas pages are slightly different and, for these, Facebook provides a special FBML tag, `<fb:swf>`, to host Flash content within FBML.

The `<fb:swf>` tag can be used directly or created using FBJS. The `<fb:swf>` tag accepts a large number of attributes, which are explained in Table 11.5.

Using FBJS to embed a Flash SWF on a page is done with the FBJS `document.createElement()` function; this tag is currently the *only* FBML tag that can be created using FBJS in this way. Several FBJS functions parallel many of the attributes found in the `<fb:swf>` tag; instead of presenting them in a table, we discuss them in code.

Table 11.5 **<fb:swf> Attributes**

Attribute	Type	Description
swfsrc	string	Must be set to the full path to the SWF file. Cannot be a Facebook domain. **Required.**
imgsrc	string	Set to a full URL of an image to use as a placeholder for the SWF on Facebook profiles and application tabs. Defaults to a blank "dummy" image if none is provided. Ignored on canvas pages.
height	int	Height of the SWF and the image set in imgsrc.
width	int	Width of the SWF and the image set in imgsrc.
imgstyle	string	CSS style attributes for the image set in imgsrc.
imgclass	string	CSS class for the image set in imgsrc.
flashvars	string	Can be set to a list of name=value pairs separated by & characters (basically like a query string). Must be URL encoded.
swfbgcolor	string	Set to the color of the SWF's background, in hexadecimal notation. The value set in the SWF is ignored. Defaults to 000000, or black; however, the wmode attribute influences it.
waitforclick	boolean	Set to false to allow Flash to start playing automatically on canvas pages. If set to true, it requires the user to click the SWF before it begins playing. On profiles and application tabs, it's ignored unless an AJAX call happens first. Defaults to true.
salign	string	Analogous to the salign attribute used on an HTML <embed> tag. Can be set to top (t), left (l), bottom (b), right (r), or any valid combination of these.
align	string	Set this to the alignment for the movie in the browser: left, center, or right. Defaults to left.
loop	boolean	Set to true if you want the Flash movie to loop; otherwise false. Defaults to false.
quality	string	Set to the quality you want the SWF to be rendered in: best, high, medium, or low. Defaults to high.
wmode	string	Sets the opacity for the Flash movie. Can be transparent, opaque, or window. Defaults to transparent, which results in the swfbgcolor attribute's value being ignored.

Creating a SWF That Can Communicate with FBJS

To understand how Flash can communicate with our application, we need to create the base SWF file to use. Listing 11.20 contains a complete Document class for a Flash SWF written in ActionScript 3. It's basic and simply illustrates how to use the Facebook ActionScript 3 Library to enable two-way communication between FBJS and Flash. You can simply include this code in a new Flash ActionScript 3 project, add a reference to the Flash ActionScript 3 Library, and build. We provide the .fla on this book's website. Figure 11.16 shows it running from within the Compliments application. Much of the code in Listing 11.20 is specific to Flash user-interface coding, and we won't cover that here. Several great references on the web, including the Adobe Developer Center, can give you the essentials of building Flash applications. We focus on the communication between Flash and Facebook.

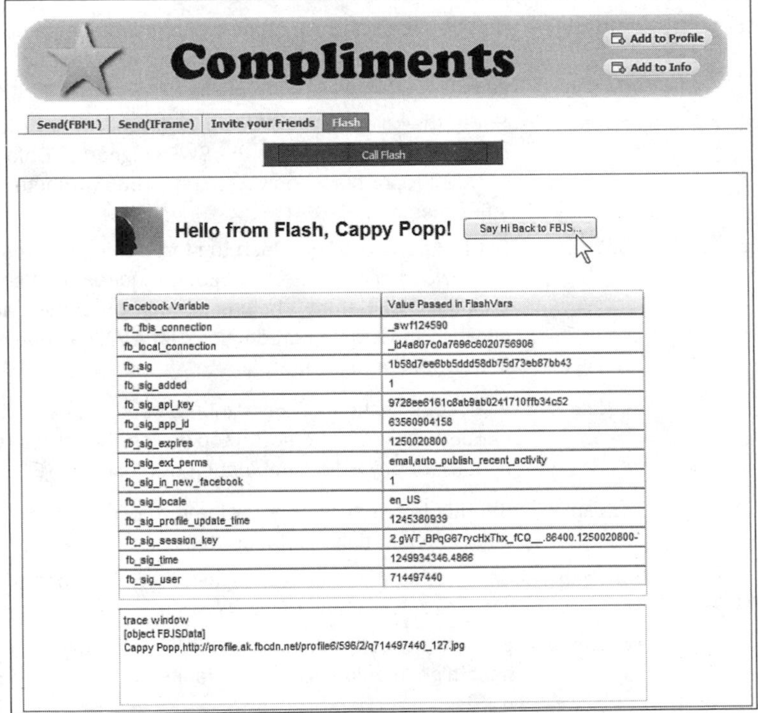

Figure 11.16 The Compliments Flash application that communicates with Facebook and FBJS

Creating the `compliments.swf` File for Facebook

For this example, we assume that you have Adobe Flash CS4 or newer installed. If you have Adobe Flex Builder, Flash Develop, or some other development environment installed, consult its help or documentation on how to include an ActionScript class file into a project. To create the SWF for this project in Adobe Flash CS4, follow the steps in the following list. If you just want to compile your own SWF from the `compliments.fla` project file included with the book's code listings, simply open the `compliments.fla` file, publish the movie, and copy the resulting `compliments.swf` to your Facebook application's root directory.

1. Open Flash and create a new `.fla` file by choosing Flash File (ActionScript 3.0).
2. Copy and save the `compliments.as` file from our code listing into a directory of your choice.
3. Save the project as `compliments.fla` in the same directory into which you copied the `compliments.as` file.
4. Open the Window menu and check the Properties entry.
5. Change the size of the Stage to be 750x550px. To do this, click the Edit button next to the Size entry in the Properties panel and change Dimensions to 750px for the width and 550px for the height.
6. Open the Publish Settings dialog by clicking the Edit button to the right of the Profile entry in the Properties panel.
7. On the Format tab, *uncheck* everything but Flash (.swf).
8. On the Flash tab, choose Flash Player 9 from the Player drop-down at the top of the dialog.
9. Make sure that ActionScript 3.0 is selected in the Script drop-down.
10. Click the Settings button to the right of the the Script drop-down.
11. In the Document Class text field at the top of the dialog, enter Compliments. Click the pencil icon to the right of the text field and verify that the `compliments.as` file opens in the Flash IDE code editor.
12. Click OK at the bottom of the dialog.
13. Click Publish at the bottom of the next dialog.
14. Verify that the compliments.swf file has been created in the same directory as the compliments.as and compliments.fla files.
15. Modify the `Compliments` class to contain your application's Facebook API key for the `API_KEY` constant's value. Save the class file.
16. Publish the `compliments.swf` file once more.
17. Copy the `compliments.swf` to the root directory of your Compliments application.

Listing 11.20 **`Compliments.as`: ActionScript 3 Class for Communicating with FBJS**

```
package {

  import fl.controls.Button;
  import fl.controls.TextArea;
  import fl.controls.DataGrid;
  import fl.controls.dataGridClasses.*;
  import fl.data.DataProvider;

  import flash.display.Loader;
```

Listing 11.20 **Continued**

```
import flash.display.LoaderInfo;
import flash.display.MovieClip;
import flash.display.Stage;
import flash.display.StageAlign;
import flash.display.StageScaleMode;
import flash.events.Event;
import flash.events.MouseEvent;
import flash.events.StatusEvent;
import flash.events.ErrorEvent;
import flash.net.URLRequest;
import flash.net.URLLoader;
import flash.text.TextField;
import flash.text.TextFormat;
import flash.text.TextFieldAutoSize;

import com.facebook.data.FBJSData;
import com.facebook.errors.FacebookError;
import com.facebook.events.FacebookEvent;
import com.facebook.Facebook;
import com.facebook.utils.FBJSBridgeUtil;
import com.facebook.session.WebSession;
import com.facebook.utils.FacebookSessionUtil;

public class Compliments extends MovieClip {

  // Constants:
  // This needs to be replaced with your API key
  private static const API_KEY:String = 'YOUR API KEY';

  // Facebook AS3 Library variables
  private var fbSessionUtil:FacebookSessionUtil;
  private var fbBridgeUtil:FBJSBridgeUtil;

  // Flash variables
  private var flashVarsParams:Object;

  // UI variables
  private var button:Button;
  private var textField:TextField;
 private var dataGrid:DataGrid;
  private var textArea:TextArea;

  // constructor
  public function Compliments() {
    init();
  }
```

Listing 11.20 **Continued**

```
  private function createDataGrid(): void {
    dataGrid = new DataGrid();
    dataGrid.setSize(550, 315);
    dataGrid.x = (stage.stageWidth - dataGrid.width) / 2;
    dataGrid.y = 120;
    dataGrid.columns = [ new DataGridColumn("FBVars"), new
      DataGridColumn("FBVals") ];
    dataGrid.columns[0].headerText = 'Facebook Variable';
    dataGrid.columns[1].headerText = 'Value Passed in FlashVars';

    var facebookData:DataProvider = new DataProvider();
    for(var i:* in flashVarsParams) {
      facebookData.addItem( { FBVars:i, FBVals:flashVarsParams[i] } );
    }
    facebookData.sortOn("FBVars");
    dataGrid.dataProvider = facebookData;

    addChild(dataGrid);
  }

  private function createTraceField():void {
    textArea = new TextArea();
    textArea.setSize(550, 100);
    textArea.x = (stage.stageWidth - textArea.width) / 2;
    textArea.y = dataGrid.height + dataGrid.y + 10;
    addChild(textArea);
    textArea.appendText('trace window\n');
  }

  private function createTextField():void {
    textField = new TextField();
    textField.autoSize = TextFieldAutoSize.LEFT;
    textField.background = true;
    textField.border = false;

    var format:TextFormat = new TextFormat();
    format.size = 20;
    format.bold = true;
    format.font = 'Arial';
    textField.defaultTextFormat = format;

    textField.visible = false;

    addChild(textField);
  }

  private function createButton(): void {
```

Listing 11.20 **Continued**

```
    button = new Button();
    button.label = 'Say Hi Back to FBJS...'
    button.width = 140;
    button.visible = false;
    button.addEventListener(MouseEvent.CLICK,
           onCallFBJSClicked, false, 0, true);
    addChild(button);
  }

  private function onCallFBJSClicked (event:MouseEvent): void {
    trace('onCallFBJSClicked');
    fbBridgeUtil.call('callFromFlash', ['Hi from Flash!']);
  }

  private function doTrace(msg:String): void {
    textArea.appendText(msg + "\n");
    trace(msg);
  }

  private function init():void {

    stage.scaleMode = StageScaleMode.NO_SCALE;
    stage.align = StageAlign.TOP_LEFT;

    // Contains the 'fb_sig' parameters passed
    // by Facebook to the SWF when it loads on a Facebook-chromed
    // page
    flashVarsParams = loaderInfo.parameters;
    // create simple UI widgets
    createDataGrid();
    createTraceField();
    createTextField();
    createButton();

    // Auto-determines session type from loaderInfo,
    // will be 'WebSession' for regular FBML/IFrame app
    // null is FB_APP_SECRET key, stored in loaderInfo
    // to protected from decompilation
    fbSessionUtil = new FacebookSessionUtil(API_KEY, null, loaderInfo);
    fbSessionUtil.addEventListener(FacebookEvent.CONNECT,
                                  onFacebookConnect, false, 0, true);

    // could make calls directly to Facebook API
    // using fbSessionUtil.facebook property!
```

Listing 11.20 **Continued**

```
      isAppAllowed(flashVarsParams.fb_sig_session_key);
    }

    private function onFacebookConnect(event:FacebookEvent):void {
      // Succesfully logged in, & have valid authentication for your session type
      if (event.success) {
        trace(event.toString());
      } else {
        trace('error connecting to Facebook ' + event);
        trace(event.error.errorCode, event.error.errorMsg,
event.error.requestArgs, event.error.reason);
      }
    }

    private function isAppAllowed(sigSessionKey:String):void {

      if (sigSessionKey != null) {
        fbSessionUtil.verifySession();
        setupFBJSBridge();
      } else {
        trace('error: App not authorized by user ' + flashVarsParams.fb_sig_user);
      }
    }

    private function setupFBJSBridge(): void {
      fbBridgeUtil = new FBJSBridgeUtil( API_KEY,
      flashVarsParams.fb_local_connection,
      flashVarsParams.fb_fbjs_connection );
      fbBridgeUtil.addEventListener(FacebookEvent.COMPLETE, fbjsCallbackHandler);
    }

    private function fbjsCallbackHandler(event:FacebookEvent):void {

      doTrace(event.data.toString());
      if (event.success) {
        var argsFromFBJS = (event.data as FBJSData).results;
        doTrace(argsFromFBJS.toString());
        loadFacebookProfilePic(argsFromFBJS[0],
        argsFromFBJS[1]);
      }
      if (event.error) {
        doTrace('error');
      }
    }

    private function loadFacebookProfilePic(name:String, picUrl:String): void {
```

Listing 11.20 **Continued**

```
      var loader:Loader = new Loader();
      var request:URLRequest = new URLRequest(picUrl);

      loader.contentLoaderInfo.addEventListener(Event.COMPLETE, completeHandler);
      loader.addEventListener(MouseEvent.CLICK, clickHandler);

      addChild(loader);

      try {
        loader.load(request);
      } catch (e:Error) {
        doTrace(e.toString());
      }

      function completeHandler(event:Event):void {

        trace("completeHandler: " + event);
        loader.contentLoaderInfo.removeEventListener(Event.COMPLETE,
          completeHandler);

        loader.x = 100;
        loader.y = 30;

        textField.text = 'Hello from Flash, ' + name + '!';
        textField.x = loader.x + loader.width + 10;
        textField.y = loader.y + (loader.height - textField.height) / 2;
        textField.visible = true;

        button.y = loader.y + (loader.height - button.height) / 2;
        button.x = textField.x + textField.width + 10;
        button.visible = true;
      }

      function clickHandler(event:MouseEvent):void {
        trace("clickHandler: " + event);
        var loader:Loader = Loader(event.target);
        loader.unload();
        textField.visible = false;
        button.visible = false;
      }
    }
  }
}
```

In Figure 11.16, the Flash SWF occupies everything within the thin border below the Call Flash button, which is part of the Facebook application. Initially, the area above the DataGrid containing the Facebook variable data sent to the SWF is empty; clicking the Call Flash button calls an ActionScript method exposed by the Flash SWF, passing the name of the currently authorized user and the path to his profile picture as parameters to this method. Flash then displays these items above the grid and presents the user with a button with the label Say Hi Back to FBJS. Clicking this button sends a message back to FBJS, which displays it in the FBJS popup dialog shown in Figure 11.17.

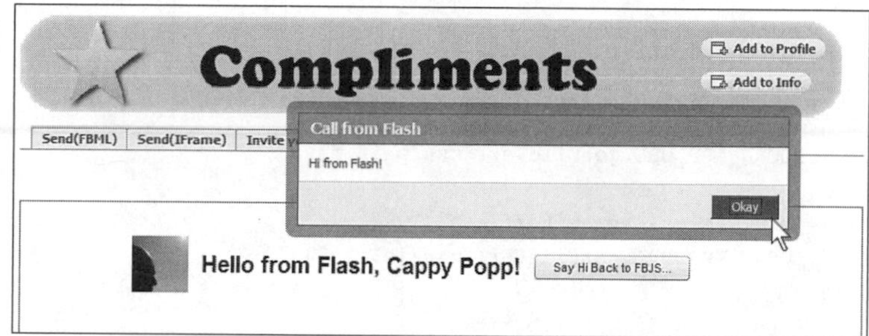

Figure 11.17 Result of clicking the Flash button to communicate back to FBJS from Flash

Hosting and Communicating with Flash from FBJS

The first thing to understand is how the communication channel between Facebook and our Flash application is structured. To gain this understanding, we need to provide the other half of the puzzle, namely the Facebook FBML and FBJS code that interacts with the Flash SWF. This is shown in Listing 11.21. Save this code in a file in the Compliments application root called `flashdemo.php`.

This adds another tab to the application named Flash that will host the Flash content; however, to have it work from all the application's pages, you need to include the following line of code as the last line of each of their `<fb:tabs>` tags:

```
<fb:tab-item href='".FB_APP_URL."/flashdemo.php' title='Flash' />
```

Notice that, in this case, we did not place the FBJS code in a separate file.

Listing 11.21 **`flashdemo.php`: Communicating with Flash Using FBJS**

```
<?php
require_once 'inc/globals.inc';
require_once 'inc/utils.inc';

$facebook = new Facebook(FB_API_KEY, FB_APP_SECRET);
$picUrl = '';
$name   = '';
// get the current user's full name and profile picture URL
$userInfo = $facebook->api_client->fql_query(
'SELECT pic_square, name FROM user WHERE uid='.$facebook->user );

if(isset($userInfo) && is_array($userInfo) && isset($userInfo[0])) {
```

Listing 11.21 **Continued**

```
  $picUrl = $userInfo[0]['pic_square'];
  $name = $userInfo[0]['name'];
}

echo(getHeaderContent());

function getHeaderContent() {
  $header = "
    <link rel='stylesheet' type='text/css'
      href='".LOCAL_APP_URL.getFileVer("css/main.css")."' />
    <!—[if IE]>
    <link rel='stylesheet' type='text/css'
      href='".LOCAL_APP_URL.getFileVer("css/ie.css")."' />
    <![endif]—>
    <fb:title>Send a Compliment</fb:title>
    <div class='banner'
      style='background: url(".LOCAL_APP_URL."/img/banner.png) no-repeat;' >
      <div id='buttons' class='clearfix' >
        <div id='addbutton'>
          <fb:if-section-not-added section='profile'>
              <fb:add-section-button section='profile' />
          </fb:if-section-not-added>
        </div>
        <div id='infobutton'>
          <fb:if-section-not-added section='info'>
              <fb:add-section-button section='info' />
          </fb:if-section-not-added>
        </div>
      </div>
    </div>
    <div id='status'> </div>
    <fb:tabs>
      <fb:tab-item href='".FB_APP_URL."/' title='Send(FBML)' />
      <fb:tab-item href='".FB_APP_URL."/index_iframe.php?fb_force_mode=iframe'
        title='Send(IFrame)' />
      <fb:tab-item href='".FB_APP_URL."/invite.php'
        title='Invite your Friends' />
      <fb:tab-item href='".FB_APP_URL."/flashdemo.php'
        title='Flash' selected='true'/>
    </fb:tabs>";

  return $header;
}

?>
<!— ***CRITICAL*** —>
```

Listing 11.21 **Continued**

```
<!— The fbjs-bridge is  REQUIRED to allow communication
     back and forth between Flash and FBJS. MUST BE placed
     above any fb:swf tag or it will fail! —>
<fb:fbjs-bridge/>

<div style='text-align:center; margin: 10px 0px;'>

  <input id='callFlash_id' onclick='callFlash(); return false;'
         type="button" class="inputsubmit"
         style='width:250px; height:25px'
         name="callFlash" value="Call Flash" />
</div>

<!— The element that will hold our SWF —>
<div style='border:1px solid #5973A9' id="swfContainer"></div>

<script type='text/javascript'>

  var swfId = 'compliments_swf_id';

  // create the <fb:swf> tag dynamically
  var swf = document.createElement('fb:swf');
  swf.setId(swfId);

  // set these to the same values you did in your .fla file
  // or Flex project
  swf.setWidth('750');
  swf.setHeight('550');

  // center the SWF on the page
  swf.setAlign('center');

  // *BUG* in Facebook currently causes this to fail...
  // swf.setSWFBGColor('5973A9');

  // don't require users to click on the SWF to activate it
  // on canvas pages (or profiles after an AJAX call)
  swf.setWaitForClick(false);

  // set to full path to SWF on our web server
  swf.setSWFSrc('<?php echo(LOCAL_APP_URL.'compliments.swf'); ?>');

  // add the SWF to the <div> we've provided
  document.getElementById('swfContainer').appendChild(swf);
  //==============================================================
```

Listing 11.21 **Continued**

```
// callFlash
//
// This calls the 'asFunction' method IN the Flash SWF, passing
// the currently-logged-on user and the path to their profile picture
//
function callFlash() {
  var s = document.getElementById(swfId);
  if(s) {
    var r = s.callSWF( "asFunction",
                       "<?php echo($name); ?>",
                       "<?php echo($picUrl); ?>" );
  } else {
    new Dialog().showMessage('FBJS Bridge Error',
                             'Unable to call Flash method');
  }
}

//==============================================================
// callFromFlash
//
// This is BY the Flash SWF
//
function callFromFlash(msg) {
  new Dialog().showMessage('Call from Flash', msg);
}
</script>
```

Now that we have both sides of the channel in place, let's discuss how it all works. We discuss the Facebook side of things first. Notice that we create the `<fb:swf>` tag dynamically using `document.createElement()`. Why do we do it this way? One important reason: If you use the `<fb:swf>` tag, it is harder to get the ID of the HTML `<embed>` element the Facebook parser renders for it. You can use DOM navigation methods to find it, assuming that it's the only `<embed>` object within your application's sandbox, but it's not guaranteed, and this ID is needed to use the FBJS DOM `callSWF()` function to call into the SWF.

Setting SWF Background Colors with FBJS

Currently, there is no way to set the SWF background color using FBJS because there's a bug in the FBJS `setSWFBGColor()` function. The bgcolor attribute of the `<fb:swf>` FBML tag works perfectly; therefore, if the background color is important for you to set in your code, you must use the FBML tag instead of creating it dynamically with FBJS.

However, the most important line in Listing 11.21 is a seemingly simple one: `<fb:fbjs-bridge/>`.

Communicating Between Flash and FBJS Using `<fb:fbjs-bridge>`

The `<fb:fbjs-bridge>` tag is the key to enabling communication between Flash and FBJS. It was originally designed to deal with a change Adobe made in Flash Player version 9. Previous versions of the player allowed developers to easily change the browser's current location using ActionScript or JavaScript, a trick many Flash developers used to allow their users to navigate through their applications. However, Adobe changed this behavior in version 9 of its player by requiring that all HTML code hosting SWFs not running on the *same domain* as the hosting HTML set the `allowscriptaccess` attribute in the `<object>` or `<embed>` tags for the SWF to a value of `always`. This allows the SWFs to access any JavaScript on their hosting page and, therefore, direct the browser at will.

This was a big problem for Facebook Flash developers for two reasons. First, as discussed, Facebook does not allow the `<object>` or `<embed>` tags in FBML canvas pages, so developers could not set this attribute themselves. Secondly, it sets this property to `never` for security reasons when the `<fb:swf>` FBML tag is parsed. Because FBML canvas pages—and therefore any SWFs within them—*always* run on a different domain than Facebook's, this effectively broke many Facebook applications that used this technique.

To fix it, Facebook and its developer community came up with a unique solution that basically used a bridge SWF to act as broker between application SWFs and the pages that hosted them. The way it works is transparent to users. When the Facebook FBML parser encounters the `<fb:fbjs-bridge>` tag, it generates an `<embed>` or `<object>` tag on the page (depending on the browser) containing the invisible bridging Flash SWF on the page. Its job is to open a communication channel between the FBJS code and SWFs on the page and provide the Flash Player navigation behavior for which it was originally designed.

From this point, we refer to it as the fbjs-bridge SWF. Note that its FBML tag *must* appear on the page before any `<fb:swf>` tag that wants to use it or none of the functionality we describe in the following sections will work for it. For safe measure, it's best to put it as close to the top of a page as possible.

If you look at the HTML generated for our SWF embedding code, you can see why the bridging SWF is needed, as shown in this pseudo-code:

```
<embed
    allowscriptaccess="never"
    id="app63560904158_compliments_swf_id"
    src="<path>/compliments.swf
    <!– some flashvars omitted and url-encoding removed –>
    flashvars="
      fb_sig_user=<user id>&
      fb_sig_session_key=<session key>&
      fb_sig_api_key=<api key>&
```

```
        fb_local_connection=_id4a809a2a486922285231199&
        fb_fbjs_connection=_swf156848"
        fbjs="_swf156848"
/>
```

The first attribute, `allowscriptaccess`, is critical. Setting this to `never` expressly forbids the SWF from accessing *any* JavaScript on the page, as mentioned. Notice that Facebook automatically passes its list of session variables to the SWF in the `flashvars` attribute. Using Flashvars is just one way to pass information to the SWF; we could have used it to pass the user's name and profile picture URL this way if we'd chosen to do so instead of calling a method in our SWF. When using it, you need to be aware of some things. Flashvars can only be 64K total size, which might seem like a lot, but it might not be if you pass all the information about an application user who has thousands of friends with it, on top of all the data Facebook might be passing. Also, it's a one-way trip. There's no way to call back into FBJS when using it. There are two important `flashvars` Facebook sends to our SWF that are important in the bridging process: `fb_local_connection` and `fb_fbjs_connection`. We return to them in a moment.

The fbjs-bridge provides two important pieces of functionality. First, because the embedding code, which hosts it, always has its `allowscriptaccess` attribute set to `always`, it's able to interact with JavaScript on the page in a way we discuss a bit later. Also, it handles *bridging* all the method calls to and from our SWF using ActionScript `LocalConnection` objects. `LocalConnection` objects allow SWFs to invoke methods on each other. There are important same-domain issues to be aware of when using them, which we do not discuss here; however, luckily, Facebook and the ActionScript 3 Library handle them transparently for us.

Communicating Between SWFs Using `LocalConnnection`

The way `LocalConnection` objects work is simple. Both SWFs that want to communication must create an instance of a `LocalConnection` object. One SWF is deemed the *receiver*, which exposes methods to the other, known as the *sender*. They interact in the following way. First, the receiver calls the `LocalConnection.connect()` method passing a string to identify the "channel" on which it will accept calls from the sender. It sets the methods it wants to expose using an object assigned to the `LocalConnection.client` property. The *sender* then uses the `LocalConnection.send()` function to call the function exposed by the receiver on this channel. `send()` takes three arguments: first, the same channel name used by the receiver, second, the method name in the receiver to call, and finally, an array of arguments to pass to it.

Both SWF and the fbjs-bridge SWF perform both roles, depending on the direction of the communication. The `fb_fbjs_connection` channel name is used when our SWF is the receiver, exposing an ActionScript function named `asMethod()`, that the fbjs-bridge SWF can call. Conversely, `fb_local_connection` is used when our SWF wants to call the FBJS bridging method exposed by the fbjs-bridge SWF, appropriately named `callFBJS()`.

Communicating Between the `<fb:fbjs-bridge>` and FBJS Using `ExternalInterface`

The `ExternalInterface` object allows the SWF (via the Flash Player) to communicate with JavaScript on the hosting page. It works similarly to `LocalConnection`, instead using a callback mechanism to allow communication from JavaScript to the fbjs-bridge SWF. The SWF uses `ExternalInterface.addCallback()` to register a callback with the Flash Player that JavaScript can call. The fbjs-bridge SWF can call a JavaScript method on the page using the `ExternalInterface.call()` method, thanks to its generous `allowscriptaccess` setting.

FBJS provides the `callSWF()` function for developers to use. It calls through `ExternalInterface` into the fbjs-bridge SWF, which forwards the call via its `LocalConnection.send()` method to our SWF. On the contrary, when the SWF wants to call our FBJS `calledFromFlash()` function, it goes through the fbjs-bridge SWF, who forwards the call.

Finally, let's look at the ActionScript code. We use the Facebook ActionScript 3 Library's `FbjsBridgeUtil` class internally to handle all the internals of using the `LocalConnection` objects for us. We just use event handlers in our Compliments class to handle the calls to and from it.

In Listing 11.20, the `setupFBJSBridge()` function is called when we've been successfully set up a session with Facebook using the ActionScript Library. Notice that we pass it the names of the channels the `LocalConnection` objects will use. Internally, the Library's `FBJSBridgeUtil` class simply handles setting up both of the `LocalConnection` objects and handles dispatching the method calls for us. One caveat: It only exposes a single method to FBJS, named `asMethod()`. If you need to expose multiple methods, there are other alternatives available, or you can use this as a basis for creating your own solution.

Listing 11.22 sums up the entire discussion thus far, showing which objects are responsible for which calls at which time.

Listing 11.22 **FBJS, `<fb:fbjs-bridge>`, and External SWF Communication**

```
// ——————————————
// In our SWF
// ——————————————

// [1] when acting as receiver for the fbjs-bridge
var swfReceiver:LocalConnection = new LocalConnection();

swfReceiver.client = {
asFunction: function(...params):void {
    // display profile pic and welcome message
    // create button for user to click to send back to FBJS
  }
};
swfReceiver.connect(fb_fbjs_connection); // name passed in flashvars
```

Listing 11.22 **Continued**

```
// [2] when acting as a sender to the fbjs-bridge
var swfSender:LocalConnection = new LocalConnection();

// ...when acting as sender to call fbjs-bridge`
function onButtonClick(event:Event): void {

  swfSender.send( fb_local_connection, // value passed in flashvars
  "callFBJS",          // hard-coded name of fbjs-bridge method
  "callFromFlash",     // argument 1 to fbjs-bridge
  "Hello from Flash!") // etc...
}

// ———————————————
// In the fbjs-bridge SWF
// ———————————————

// [3] ...when acting as receiver from our SWF
var bridgeReceiver:LocalConnection = new LocalConnection();

bridgeReceiver.client = {
callFBJS: function(fbjsMethodName:String, params:Array):void {
    // call the FBJS (JavaScript) function we've exposed
    ExternalInterface.call(fbjsMethodName, params);
  },
navigateToURL: function(targetURL:String):void {
    // we have the right to call this here
    // because we have allowscriptaccess='always' set
    navigateToURL(targetURL);
  }
};
bridgeReceiver.connect(fb_local_connection);

// [4] ...when acting as a sender to our SWF
var bridgeSender:LocalConnection = new LocalConnection();

ExternalInterface.addCallback("callFlash", _callFlashImpl);

function _callFlashImpl(methodName:String, userName:String, picURL:String): void {

  bridgeSender.send( fb_js_connection, // value known when page rendered
  methodName,       // 'asMethod'
  userName,         // argument 1 to our SWF
  picURL)           // etc...
  // NOTE: likely uses bridgeSender.apply(null, [args]) since it does not know
  // how many args it may take ahead of time, but this is clearer...
```

Listing 11.22 **Continued**

```
}

// ──────────────────
// In our FBJS
// ──────────────────

var swf = document.getElementById('swf_id');
swf.callSWF('asFunction', arg1, arg2);

function callFromFlash(msg) {
  // show msg
}

// ──────────────────
// In the FBJS DOM Sandbox
// ──────────────────

fbjs_dom_impl.callSWF(method, args) {
  fbjs_bridge_obj.callFlash(method, args);
}
```

Summary

This chapter covered how Facebook has built FBJS to be safe for it to expose on pages running on its domain while providing a rich set of features for Facebook application developers. Here are some key points:

- Facebook places all FBJS code in its own sandbox to keep it from conflicting with other JavaScript code but also to protect itself from malicious JavaScript. As part of this process, all the global JavaScript objects and many of the DOM interfaces are restricted or missing from FBJS, but Facebook provides novel ways of DOM interaction and dynamic scripting.
- FBJS provides a `Dialog` class, which gives developers an alternative to the JavaScript DOM `alert()`, `prompt()`, and `confirm()` functions not available in FBJS.
- Mock AJAX is an earlier implementation of AJAX that Facebook exposed for developers before it released its full FBJS AJAX support; however, it offers a unique set of features and provides a lot of functionality for minimal coding effort.
- The FBJS `Ajax` class provides developers with a powerful AJAX library that handles much of the low-level coding and cross-browser issues faced by directly using the `XmlHTTPRequest` object.
- FBJS provides a client-side alternative to Feed forms and Publishers via the `Facebook.showFeedDialog()` function, which can publish Feed stories without the need for round trips to the Facebook servers.

- Facebook added a powerful Animation library to FBJS, which can be downloaded and used outside of Facebook.
- The FBJS event handling model is based on W3C-style event handling and handles all the browser incompatibilities internally so you don't have to.
- Flash is a powerful technology for creating interactive content. Using it to communicate with FBJS code is not a simple task, but Facebook provides some powerful primitives to make the job easier.

Integrating Facebook into an External Website

12

Facebook JavaScript Client Library

The Facebook JavaScript Client Library lets developers access most of the functionality of the Facebook application programming interface (API) from Facebook applications with IFrame canvas pages or an external website. This chapter goes over what the Library offers and how to use it. In this chapter, the Compliments application is updated to use the Facebook JavaScript Client Library.

The Facebook JavaScript Client Library differs from Facebook JavaScript (FBJS) in several ways. Although FBJS was designed to allow developers to use a subset of JavaScript that could run on Facebook Markup Language (FBML) pages, profiles, and application tabs, the Facebook JavaScript Client Library offers access to the Facebook API and user interface (UI) controls. Additionally, FBJS works only on FBML canvas pages, whereas the Facebook JavaScript Client Library works only within IFrames and external sites.

The line between the Facebook JavaScript Client Library and Facebook Connect is more difficult to define. The release of Facebook Connect extended the Facebook JavaScript Client Library to include XFBML and single sign-on functionality to external sites. Chapter 13, "Facebook Connect," goes into more detail on Facebook Connect, focusing on integrating Facebook into an external site. This chapter focuses on using the Facebook JavaScript Client Library inside Facebook Application IFrame canvas pages; however, the same techniques can be used on external sites.

The Facebook JavaScript Client Library requires a Facebook application to work. This application supplies the API key that initializes the Library and the Connect URL to allow the Library to communicate with Facebook. If you are going to use the Library on an IFrame canvas page, you can simply set the Connect URL for your existing application. For use on an external website, the application won't need to have anything set besides the Connect URL. We set this up for the Compliments application in Chapter 8, "Updating the Profile."

The Facebook JavaScript Client Library has some additional requirements to allow it to work across domains. The authentication model is also slightly different than what the normal Facebook Platform API uses. This chapter discusses the differences in the following Cross-Domain Communication section.

Cross-Domain Communication

For security reasons, web browsers put some restrictions on JavaScript communication between different web domains. The Facebook JavaScript Client Library makes use of a trick involving IFrames to get around them, while still maintaining security. It is based on the ability of IFrames from the same domain to talk to each other, regardless of where they are located in the DOM hierarchy. Refer to Figure 12.1 as you review the following steps to see how the communication works.

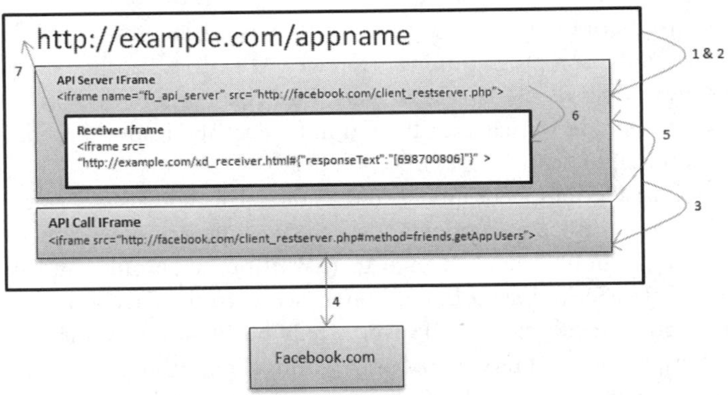

Figure 12.1 Facebook JavaScript Client Library communicates across domains using IFrames.

1. When the main external web page loads, it includes the Facebook JavaScript Client Library loader object and initializes it with the location of a special file, usually called `xd_receiver.html`, which the developer placed on his server. This file loads some JavaScript that acts as a receiver for calls from the main page. In almost all cases, this cross-domain receiver file has exactly the same code displayed in Listing 12.1.

2. During initialization, the Library creates an IFrame (API Server IFrame) with its `id` attribute set to `"fb_api_server"` and `src` attribute set to *http://facebook.com/client_restserver.php*. This API Server IFrame contains another IFrame (Receiver IFrame) with its `src` attribute set to the `xd_receiver.html` file on the external domain. The location must be a relative path from the page that uses the Library.

3. When the main page calls a Facebook JavaScript Client Library API function, the Library creates a new IFrame (API Call IFrame) with the `src` attribute set to *http://facebook.com/client_restserver.php* and adds the API call and parameters as a bookmark. This IFrame tag might look like this:

   ```
   <iframe
   src="http://facebook.com/client_restserver.php#method=friends.getAppUsers">
   ```

4. This new API Call IFrame does the actual API call to Facebook and receives the result. This is possible because this IFrame's `src` attribute is set to the Facebook domain.

5. The API Call IFrame then calls the JavaScript in the API Server IFrame, passing the results of the API call. Both of these IFrames are on the Facebook domain.

6. The API Server IFrame changes the `src` attribute of its child Receiver IFrame to include the results as a bookmark, like this:

   ```
   <iframe
   src="http://example.com/xd_receiver.html#{"responseText":"[698700806]"}/>
   ```

7. The Receiver IFrame is on the same external domain as the main page; therefore, it can communicate back to the original JavaScript that called the API and return the results.

Listing 12.1 **`xd_receiver.html` Contents**

```
<!DOCTYPE html PUBLIC "-//W3C//DTD XHTML 1.0 Strict//EN"
  "http://www.w3.org/TR/xhtml1/DTD/xhtml1-strict.dtd">
<html xmlns="http://www.w3.org/1999/xhtml" >
<head>
  <title>Cross-Domain Receiver Page</title>
</head>
<body>
  <script src="http://static.ak.facebook.com/js/api_lib/v0.4/XdCommReceiver.js?2"
   type="text/javascript"></script>
</body>
</html>
```

Using the Library

The Library is simple to use. You select the features to dynamically load, initialize it with the API key and cross-domain receiver file, and use one of the many classes that the Library provides.

FeatureLoader

The first step to using the Facebook JavaScript Client Library is to include `FeatureLoader`. This object is defined in a JavaScript file provided by Facebook that allows developers to dynamically choose which parts of the Library to load. Include the following line in your code, but make sure that it is after the `<head>` tag so that it can modify the `<body>` elements:

```
<script
  src="http://static.ak.facebook.com/js/api_lib/v0.4/FeatureLoader.js.php"
  type="text/javascript">
</script>
```

After the JavaScript from the script block is loaded, the only Facebook JavaScript Client Library functionality available is the `FB.Bootstrap` class. It contains functions to initialize the Library and choose which of its features to load. The functions of the `FB.Bootstrap` class all have aliases in the main `FB` namespace, so `FB.Bootstrap.init()` can also be called as `FB.init()`, and `FB.BootStrap.requireFeatures()` becomes `FB_RequireFeatures()`. We use the aliases in the examples.

Including Features

The Facebook JavaScript Client Library is comprised of several sublibraries called features. Table 12.1 lists the available features and their dependencies. The XFBML feature set is the easiest one to use because it loads all the others, and it is the default if no specific feature set is requested.

Table 12.1 **Facebook JavaScript Client Library Features**

Feature	Depends On	Description
`Base`	None	Boot loading
`Common`	`Base`	Common code and utility functions
`XdComm`	`Common`	Cross-domain communication
`Api`	`XdComm`	Access to the Facebook API
`CanvasUtil`	`XdComm`	Functionality for IFrame canvas pages, such as Feed forms and IFrame resizing
`Connect`	`API and CanvasUtil`	Facebook Connect session management, user management, Feed form dialogs, permission dialogs, and the profile and info section Add buttons.
`XFBML`	`Connect`	Rendering for XFBML elements

The `FB.init()` function does all the feature loading for you. `FB.init()` takes your application's API key and the relative location of the cross-domain file as parameters and loads the XFBML feature set. The features are loaded asynchronously, so make sure that they are completely loaded before you try to access them. You can do this by calling `FB.ensureInit()` after calling `FB.init()`. Listing 12.2 shows how to do this.

Listing 12.2 **Using `FB.ensureInit()` to Wait for Loading to Complete**

```
<script
  src="http://static.ak.facebook.com/js/api_lib/v0.4/FeatureLoader.js.php"
  type="text/javascript">
</script>
<script type="text/javascript">
  var apiKey = 'XXXXXXXXXXXXXX';
  var xdReceiverPath = 'xd_receiver.html';
  FB.init(apiKey, xdReceiverPath);
  FB.ensureInit( function() {
    FB.Facebook.apiClient.requireLogin( function() {
      // use the Library features
    });
  });
</script>
```

If part of your application or website doesn't need all the Connect functionality at once, you can choose to load individual features at different times using the `FB_RequireFeatures()` function. This function takes an array of features to load and a callback function that will be called after they finish loading. If a feature has already been loaded, a second request for it will just reuse it. Listing 12.3 shows an example of using this function. You still need to call `FB.init()` with your application's API key and the path to the cross-domain receiver file.

Listing 12.3 **Using `FB_RequireFeatures()` to Load Specific Features**

```
<script
  src="http://static.ak.facebook.com/js/api_lib/v0.4/FeatureLoader.js.php"
  type="text/javascript">
</script>
<script type="text/javascript">
  var apiKey = 'XXXXXXXXXXXXXX';
  var xdReceiverPath = 'xd_receiver.html';
  FB_RequireFeatures(['API', 'CanvasUtil'], function() {
    FB.init(apiKey, xdReceiverPath);
    // use the Library features
  });
</script>
```

Authentication

Because the Facebook JavaScript Client Library runs on the client, its authentication process is different from that used of the server-side Facebook PHP Library or REST API. All Facebook REST API calls made via the Library require the user to be authorized for the application, and they can only be used to perform operations as the current user. This is because, by default, the Library doesn't use the Secret key that each application is issued when it is created. Instead, it uses a temporary secret key that is generated using the session, called the session secret. Putting the Secret key on the client side would make it visible to anyone using the application, which is a significant security risk because it would allow anyone to impersonate the application.

Client-side authentication for the Library is handled by the `FB.apiClient.requireLogin()` function. This function first checks the URL of the IFrame or external website for a `session` parameter that contains the session key. If this parameter isn't present, the user is redirected to the Facebook login page. Users are prompted to authorize the application, if they haven't already, and the temporary session is generated. This session consists of a session key, session secret, and session expiration timestamp. To make sure that it is the application that called `requireLogin()`, the Callback URL from the application's developer settings is used as the base URL, with the new session parameter appended. The user is redirected to this new URL. This time, `FB.apiClient.requireLogin()` uses the `session` parameter to extract all the session information.

If your application must use any of the Facebook `admin` and `permissions` APIs or needs to create or modify any profile content for another user, you must force the Library to use your application's Secret key. Listing 12.4 shows how to do this to get your application's `app_id` from the application properties. We must use the `apiClient.callMethod()` function directly, because the `apiClient` class doesn't expose a function for the admin API calls. If `FB.Facebook.appSecret` isn't set, `callMethod()` will fail to recognize the facebook.admin.getAppProperties `function and will` return an error of "unknown method." The `appSecret` must also be set before `FB.Facebook.init()` is called, which happens inside `FB.init()`. Listing 12.4 uses `FB_RequireFeatures` to load the `FB.Facebook.apiClient` class.

Listing 12.4 **Setting the App Secret**

```
script
  src="http://static.ak.facebook.com/js/api_lib/v0.4/FeatureLoader.js.php"
  type="text/javascript">
</script>
<script type="text/javascript">
  var apiKey = 'XXXXXXXXXXXXXX';
  var xdReceiverPath = 'xd_receiver.html';

  FB_RequireFeatures(['Api'], function() {
    FB.Facebook.appSecret = 'XXXXXXXXXXXXXX';
```

Listing 12.4 **Continued**

```
    FB.init(apiKey, xdReceiverPath);
    FB.ensureInit( function() {
      FB.Facebook.apiClient.requireLogin( function() {
        var parameters = { properties :['app_id', 'callback_url'] };
        FB.Facebook.apiClient.callMethod('facebook.admin.getAppProperties',
                                  parameters, function(result, exception) {
          //Use the admin properties
        });
      });
    });
  });
</script>
```

The session information is stored in a set of cookies. If you are using the Facebook PHP library for other parts of your application, it also uses the same cookies, so the user's session state will be shared between the two libraries. The Facebook JavaScript Client Library uses the five cookies in Table 12.2 to validate the signature. Each cookie is prefixed with the API key of the application and is set on the application's domain, such as .example.com.

Table 12.2 **Session Cookies Used by the Library for Validation**

Cookie	Description
`API_KEY_user`	The currently logged in user's ID.
`API_KEY _session_key`	The current session key.
`API_KEY _expires`	The time that the current session expires.
`API_KEY _ss`	The session secret. This is used instead of an application's Secret key that generally should not be sent across client side.
`API_KEY`	This is the signature generated from the other cookie values.

The signature is verified from the first four cookies using the following steps.

1. The API_KEY prefix is removed from the cookie name.
2. A string is created by combining the cookie name and its value in the format `"name=value"`.
3. The strings from all the cookies are concatenated in alphabetical order by cookie name.
4. A hash of the string is created using the `md5()` function.
5. The value of the hash should match the value of the signature cookie. Thankfully, both the Facebook JavaScript Client and PHP libraries validate this for you.

Calling Facebook JavaScript Client Library Functions

The Library API functions can be executed immediately or in batch. In all the previous listings, we passed a function as an argument to the Library calls. This function is used as a callback taking two arguments—`result` and `exception`—holding the function results or failure exception information, respectively. The API call is executed immediately, executing the callback when it is done.

For handling many API calls, it is more efficient to do the calls in batch, sending a single request to Facebook to get all the data at once. Up to 20 API calls can be batched at a time. To batch the calls, you create an instance of a `FB.BatchSequencer` and pass it to all the API calls instead of a callback function. This adds those calls to the batch sequence, but it doesn't execute them. After the last call is added to the batch, you call the `BatchSequencer`'s `execute` function. The batched calls are executed in parallel on the server, but you can set the `BatchSequencer`'s `isParallel` property to `false` if you need to have them run in order. Listing 12.5 shows an example of batching calls. A batch sequencer is created and passed to `users_isAppUser()` and `friends.get()`. These functions return immediately, setting the `appUser` and `friends` variables to `PendingResult` objects by the API calls before the batch operation happens. When the `execute` function completes, those `PendingResult` variables are updated to contain the `result` and `exception` information for the corresponding call.

Listing 12.5 **Batching API Calls**

```
<script
  src="http://static.ak.facebook.com/js/api_lib/v0.4/FeatureLoader.js.php"
  type="text/javascript">
</script>
<script type="text/javascript">
  var apiKey = 'XXXXXXXXXXXXXX';
  var xdReceiverPath = 'xd_receiver.html';

  FB.init(apiKey, xdReceiverPath);
  FB.ensureInit( function() {
    FB.Facebook.apiClient.requireLogin( function() {
      var batch = new FB.BatchSequencer();
      var appUser = FB.Facebook.apiClient.users_isAppUser(batch);
      var friends = FB.Facebook.apiClient.friends_get(null, batch);
      batch.execute(function() {
        //appUser and friends are now updated with the results of the call
      });
    });
  });
</script>
```

Key Library Classes

The Facebook JavaScript Client Library contains many classes. This section goes over the most important classes from the Library, with examples.

FB.apiClient

The `apiClient` class contains a wrapper for the Facebook API. Most of the API functions have wrapper methods, but for those that don't, you can call the `apiClient.callMethod()` function yourself, passing in the API method name and encoding the parameters like we did for the `admin.getAppProperties()` call.

Besides providing the API wrapper functions, the apiClient class also provides utility functions to get information about the current session, including the logged in user's Facebook user ID. Listing 12.6 shows how to get those values. Notice that we use `apiClient` as an alias for the `FB.Facebook.apiClient` class for convenience. We will use this from now on.

Listing 12.6 **Getting Session Information**

```
<script
  src="http://static.ak.facebook.com/js/api_lib/v0.4/FeatureLoader.js.php"
  type="text/javascriptv">
</script>
<script type="text/javascript">
  var apiKey = 'XXXXXXXXXXXXXX';
  var xdReceiverPath = 'xd_receiver.html';

  FB.init(apiKey, xdReceiverPath);
  FB.ensureInit( function() {
    var apiClient = FB.Facebook.apiClient;
    apiClient.requireLogin( function() {
      var uid = apiClient.get_session().uid;
      var sessionKey = apiClient.get_session().session_key;
      var secret = apiClient.get_session().secret;
    });
  });
</script>
```

FB.Bootstrap

`Bootstrap` is the class that is made available by the `FeatureLoader` script and is used to control which features are loaded. We used the `FB_RequireFeatures()`, `FB.init()`, and `FB_ensureInit()` functions in previous examples.

FB.Connect

`Connect` houses session-management functions for Facebook Connect applications and some utility functions for showing dialogs. We defer discussing the Connect session-management functions until Chapter 13. The `Connect.showAddSectionButton()` function is the only way to let users add a profile box or info section for IFrames. `Connect.showFeedDialog()` allows IFrame-based canvas pages to present users with a Feed form dialog to publish stories to the stream, like the Feed forms discussed in Chapter 9, "Feed Stories, Feed Forms, and Templates."

Listing 12.7 shows how to add an Add to Profile button to a canvas page. The placeholder `<div>` for the Add button must be added to the page first, and its ID is passed to the `showAddSectionButton() function`.

Listing 12.7 **Adding an Add to Profile Button**

```
<script
  src="http://static.ak.facebook.com/js/api_lib/v0.4/FeatureLoader.js.php"
  type="text/javascript">
</script>

<div id='addbutton'></div>

<script type="text/javascript">
  var apiKey = 'XXXXXXXXXXXXXX';
  var xdReceiverPath = 'xd_receiver.html';

  FB.init(apiKey, xdReceiverPath);
  FB.ensureInit( function() {
    FB.Connect.showAddSectionButton('profile',
                                    document.getElementById('addbutton'));
  });
</script>
```

A Feed dialog can be shown using `FB.Connect.showFeedDialog()`.; however, a session is required, so make sure that `requireLogin()` is called first. Listing 12.8 shows an example of how to display a Feed dialog with `FB.Connect.showFeedDialog()` using of the templates we registered in Chapter 9. Figure 12.2 shows the resulting Feed dialog. This dialog produces a short story that can only target one user. The difference between the Facebook JavaScript Client Library dialog and `Facebook.showFeedDialog()` function is in these three parameters: `require_connect`, `story_size`, and `callback`. The `require_connect` parameter is for Facebook Connect integrations and allows the dialog to automatically prompt the user to login to Facebook. `story_size` is deprecated and should always be `null`. `callback` is a function that is automatically called after the dialog is closed. The Feed dialog launched from `showFeedDialog()` does not provide a way to notify the caller of whether the user actually published the story. We add a Feed dialog to the Compliments application in the section, "Updating Compliments' IFrame Page."

Figure 12.2 Feed dialogs displayed using `FB.Connect.showFeedDialog()` look just like the FBJS versions created by `Facebook.showFeedDialog()`.

Listing 12.8 **Showing a Feed Dialog**

```
<script
  src="http://static.ak.facebook.com/js/api_lib/v0.4/FeatureLoader.js.php"
  type="text/javascript">
</script>
<script type="text/javascript">
  var apiKey = 'XXXXXXXXXXXXXX';
  var xdReceiverPath = 'xd_receiver.html';

  FB.init(apiKey, xdReceiverPath);
  FB.ensureInit( function() {
    FB.Facebook.apiClient.requireLogin( function() {
      // The short story template
      //{*actor*} sent {*target*} a compliment with {*app*}!
      //<br/>{*actor*} thinks {*target*} is {*ctitle*} because
      //{*ctext*}
      var templateID = '230103595614';
      var templateData =
       {"app": "Compliments",
        "ctitle": "A Great Cook",
        "ctext": "His tripe is the best!",
        "images":};
      var targetID = [714497440];
```

Listing 12.8 **Continued**

```
      var bodyGeneral = '';
      var story_size = null;
      var require_connect = FB.RequireConnect.doNotRequire;
      var callback = function() {
        alert('dialog shown');
      }
      var feedDialogPrompt = 'Publish your Compliment';
      var feedDialogUserMsg = {value:'I love sending Compliments!'};

      FB.Connect.showFeedDialog(templateID, templateData, targetID,
                                bodyGeneral, story_size,
                                require_connect, callback,
                                feedDialogPrompt, feedDialogUserMsg );
    });
  });
</script>
```

`showPermissionDialog()` is another way to display permission requests instead of using the `<fb:prompt-permission>` tag. It displays a series of dialogs for each permission requested and passes a string with the ones that the user accepted to a callback. This acceptance information is only provided if you use this function; the `<fb:prompt-permission>` tag will not supply this. Figure 12.3 shows one of these dialogs, and Listing 12.9 shows the code to produce it. This code requests both the `status_update` and `email` extended permissions and results in two dialogs, one for each permission.

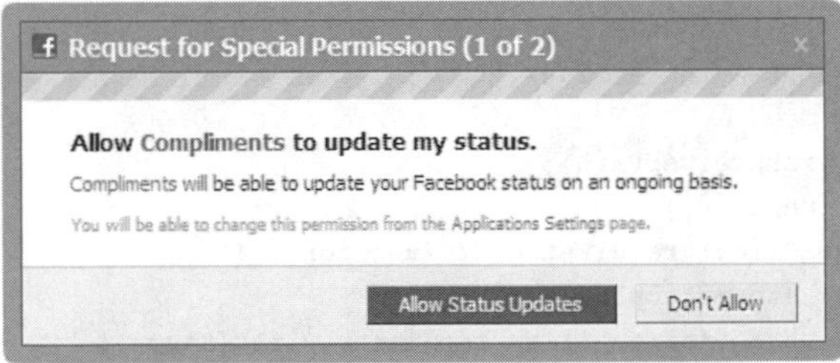

Figure 12.3 Displaying a Permissions dialog using the `FB.Connect.showPermissionsDialog()` function to get `status_update` and `email` extended permissions

Listing 12.9 **Showing a Permission Dialog**

```
<script src="http://static.ak.facebook.com/js/api_lib/v0.4/FeatureLoader.js.php"
 type="text/javascript"></script>
<script type="text/javascript">
  var apiKey = 'XXXXXXXXXXXXXX';
```

Listing 12.9 **Continued**

```
  var xdReceiverPath = 'xd_receiver.html';

  FB.init(apiKey, xdReceiverPath);
  FB.ensureInit( function() {
    FB.Connect.showPermissionDialog('status_update,email',
      function(permissions) {
        //do something with the permissions that the user allowed
      }
    );
  });
</script>
```

FB.FBDebug

The `FBDebug` class provides some useful utilities for tracing your own messages and seeing the trace messages from the Library. The type of trace messages shown are controlled by the `FBDebug.logLevel` variable. Each level shows all the traces from the lower levels. Table 12.3 shows the various levels and the types of information that they show. Listing 12.10 shows the trace output for some sample code, with each line prefixed with the trace level required to show it.

Table 12.3 **FBDebug Levels**

Level	Description
0	Tracing off
1	Error messages, session key value, API call results
2	Cross-domain communication data handler registration, XFBML errors, and CanvasClient information
3	HTTP call tracing with URLs and data
4	Cross-domain received packet dumps
5	Cross-domain channel communication, IFrame creation and removal, general cache information
6	Cache key usage

Listing 12.10 **Trace Dump and Levels for Example Code**

```
FB_RequireFeatures(['XFBML'], function(result, exception){
  FB.FBDebug.isEnabled = true;
  FB.FBDebug.logLevel = 6;
  FB.FBDebug.dump("custom trace message");

  FB.init(apiKey, xdReceiverPath);
```

Listing 12.10 **Continued**

```
    FB.ensureInit( function(result, exception) {
      FB.Facebook.apiClient.requireLogin( function(result, exception) {
        FB.Facebook.apiClient.friends_getAppUsers(function(result, exception) {
          FB.FBDebug.dump(result, 'getAppUsers results');
        });
      });
    });
  });

Produces this output:
1 - string: custom trace message
1 - Cannot use Flash on Firefox due to a possible bug in Flash
2 - Register data handler loginServer
2 - Register data handler fbLogout
1 - session key = 2.LZrDwfH8SNH8NKeDWTnSyA__.86400.1245009600-698700806
2 - Register data handler http_client
3 - XdHttpRequestClient: send request for
http://api.facebook.com/restserver.php?method=friends.getAppUsers
3 - <<<<<<< http://example.com/appname/?
➥fb_sig_in_iframe=1&fb_sig_locale=en_US&fb_sig_in_new_facebook=1&fb_sig_time=
➥1244920024.0249&fb_sig_added=1&fb_sig_profile_update_time=1241522567
➥&fb_sig_expires=1245009600&fb_sig_user=698700806&fb_sig_session_key=
➥2.LZrDwfH8SNH8NKeDWTnSyA__.86400.1245009600-698700806&fb_sig_ss=
➥MnCxv__a0B_zxM39hO7BWQ__&fb_sig_ext_perms=auto_publish_recent_activity&
➥fb_sig_api_key=52bcc10ac263e1d0d2645182e01e0c99&fb_sig_app_id=
➥195482325614&fb_sig=8d465c17579c2ee5573a5d84c980b087
3 - Server.send: handler=http_server
3 - data: 0: 0 1: POST 2: /restserver.php?method=friends.getAppUsers 3:
method=friends.getAppUsers&api_key=52bcc10ac263e1d0d2645182e01e0c99&format=
➥JSON&call_id=86&v=1.0&session_key=2.LZrDwfH8SNH8NKeDWTnSyA__.
➥86400.1245009600-698700806&ss=1&sig=b32f8e2ef809bb487106613b59dea597 4:
Content-Type: application/x-www-form-urlencoded
3 - endPoint: frameName: fb_api_server relation: 2 channelUrl:
http://api.facebook.com/static/v0.4/xd_receiver.php?r=163033 UID: 0 origin:
null
2 - Send with native postMessage: 1rd try
2 - Send with native postMessage: 2rd try
2 - Register data handler http_server
4 - received full packet: sc: http://example.com/appname/xdreceiver.html sf:
➥iframe_canvas sr: 1 h: http_server nd: 0: 0 1: POST 2: /restserver.php?
➥method=friends.getAppUsers 3: method=friends.getAppUsers&api_key=
➥52bcc10ac263e1d0d2645182e01e0c99&format=JSON&call_id=253&v=1.0&
➥session_key=2.LZrDwfH8SNH8NKeDWTnSyA__.86400.1245009600-
➥698700806&ss=1&sig=55a4b9911aff67e4bd58c2a43667b57b 4: Content-Type:
➥application/x-www-form-urlencoded df: 2 id: 0 sid: 0.741
```

Listing 12.10 **Continued**

```
4 - sender: frameName: iframe_canvas relation: 1 channelUrl:
➥http://example.com/appname/xdreceiver.html UID: 0 origin: null
3 - XdHttpRequestServer: make XHR request to
➥http://api.facebook.com/restserver.php?method=friends.getAppUsers
1 - POST http://api.facebook.com/restserver.php?method=friends.getAppUsers
4 - received full packet: sc: http://www.facebook.com/xd_receiver_v0.4.php sf:
➥loginStatus sr: 2 h: loginServer nd: 0: 0 1: loginStatus 2: InitLogin
➥3: session: uid: 698700806 session_key: 3.ZKT5K8i0AO31IOtq59yQ0g__.
➥86400.1245009600-698700806 secret: MnCxv__a0B_zxM39hO7BWQ__ expires:
➥1245009600 sig: ecf3b700aa3c807be9a2d3c004627de7 settings:
➥feedStorySettings: one_line: 1 short: 1 inFacebook: true connectState:
➥1 baseDomain: publicSessionData: null 4: false df: 2 id: 0 sid: 0.626
4 - sender: frameName: loginStatus relation: 2 channelUrl:
➥http://www.facebook.com/xd_receiver_v0.4.php UID: 0 origin: null
3 - XdRpcServer.Received: InitLogin
3 - XdHttpRequestServer: send result back http_client
3 - <<<<<<< http://api.facebook.com/static/v0.4/client_restserver.php?
➥r=163033&debug_level=3
3 - Server.send: handler=http_client
3 - data: status: 200 statusText: OK responseText: [714497440,1161559271] id: 0
3 - endPoint: frameName: iframe_canvas relation: 1 channelUrl:
➥http://example.com/appname/xdreceiver.html UID: 0 origin: null
2 - Send with native postMessage: 1rd try
4 - received full packet: sc:
➥http://api.facebook.com/static/v0.4/xd_receiver.php sf: fb_api_server
➥sr: 2 h: http_client nd: status: 200 statusText: OK responseText:
➥ [714497440,1161559271] [illegible]
4 - sender: frameName: fb_api_server relation: 2 channelUrl:
➥http://api.facebook.com/static/v0.4/xd_receiver.php UID: 0 origin: null
3 - XdHttpRequestClient: got result
1 - getAppUsers results :
1 -  0: 714497440 1: 1161559271
```

Seeing the trace output requires that there is a script debugger attached to the browser, such as Firebug for Firefox or the Script Debugger for Internet Explorer. At one point, the Library supported dumping output to a DOM object on the page with `id='_traceTextBox'`, but this no longer works.

The following are the tracing functions in this class:

- **`FBDebug.dump(object, title)`**. Writes out an object with a title you specify
- **`FBDebug.writeLine(string)`**. Writes out a string
- **`FBDebug.logLine(logLevel, string)`**. Writes out a string when the `FBDebug.logLevel` is set to a value >= to the level passed in the logLevel parameter

- **`FBDebug.assert(condition, message)`.** Pops up a dialog allowing you to break into the debugger if the `condition` fails.

FB.UI

The UI class houses a few different Facebook-style popup dialogs that you can use to display pre-rendered HTML or FBML strings. The `FB.UI.PopupDialog` class requires you to pass an existing DOM element that contains the content for the dialog. Listing 12.11 shows a simple example of using this dialog to display HTML. First, the `<div>` containing the text to display is created but not added to the document. Next, a new `PopupDialog()` is constructed, passing a dialog title, the content `<div>`, and false for the last two parameters, `showLoading` and `hideUntilLoaded`. `showLoading` displays a loading indicator in the dialog's title bar, and `hideUntilLoaded` keeps the dialog hidden until the content is finished loading. However, at the time of this writing, the dialog never believes that it has loaded, which makes these parameters unusable. We use the `setContentWidth()` function to set the dialog's inner width to 200 pixels. Finally, the dialog is shown and should look like what is shown in Figure 12.4.

Figure 12.4 A simple popup dialog displaying HTML

Listing 12.11 **Using `FB.UI.PopupDialog()`**

```
<script
  src="http://static.ak.facebook.com/js/api_lib/v0.4/FeatureLoader.js.php"
  type="text/javascript">
</script>
<script type="text/javascript">
  var apiKey = 'XXXXXXXXXXXXXX';
  var xdReceiverPath = 'xd_receiver.html';

  FB.init(apiKey, xdReceiverPath);
  FB.ensureInit( function() {
    var dlgContent=document.createElement("div");
    dlgContent.innerHTML = "Hello,viewer";
    var dialog = new FB.UI.PopupDialog("Hello", dlgContent, false, false);
    dialog.setContentWidth(200);
    dialog.show();
  });
</script>
```

The `FB.UI.FBMLPopupDialog` takes an FBML string to display inside the dialog. Listing 12.12 shows an example of displaying the viewing user's profile picture using the `<fb:profile-pic>` FBML tag. You could also use this dialog to display an `<fb:request-form>` for enabling user invites. Figure 12.5 shows what this dialog looks like.

Figure 12.5 An FBML popup dialog displaying FBML content

Listing 12.12 Using **FB.UI.FBMLPopupDialog()**

```
<script
  src="http://static.ak.facebook.com/js/api_lib/v0.4/FeatureLoader.js.php"
  type="text/javascript">
</script>
<script type="text/javascript">
  var apiKey = 'XXXXXXXXXXXXXX';
  var xdReceiverPath = 'xd_receiver.html';

  FB.init(apiKey, xdReceiverPath);
  FB.ensureInit( function() {
    var uid = FB.Facebook.apiClient.get_session().uid;
    var fbml = "Hello <br/><fb:profile-pic uid='"+uid+"'/>";
    var dialog = new FB.UI.FBMLPopupDialog("Hello", fbml);
    dialog.setContentWidth(200);
    dialog.show();
  });
</script>
```

FB.XFBML

XFBML is Facebook's method of allowing IFrame canvas pages and external sites to use FBML tags. There are a few constraints for what can be used and several methods of rendering the tags. Briefly, XFBML tags that appear on the page are automatically rendered by default into their HTML equivalents by `FB.init()`. We start by reviewing the types of tags that can be displayed and then go over how they are rendered. For these tags to be rendered, the `fb` namespace must be added to the `<HTML>` tag, like this:

```
<html xmlns=http://www.w3.org/1999/xhtml
  xmlns:fb="http://www.facebook.com/2008/fbml">
```

Client Side Tags

Only a subset of the FBML tags can be directly placed onto a page. Most of the common user information tags are included in this list. All XFBML tags require closing tags rather than the single tag using `/>` at the end. These FBML tags are directly supported:

- **`<fb:name>`.** Displays a user's name.
- **`<fb:profile-pic>`.** Displays a user's profile photo. An optional parameter, `facebook-logo`, displays a small Facebook logo overlay on pictures.
- **`<fb:pronoun>`.** Displays "he", "she", and so on, for a user.
- **`<fb:grouplink>`.** Displays a link to a group.
- **`<fb:eventlink>`.** Displays a link to an event.
- **`<fb:user-status>`.** Displays a user's current status.
- **`<fb:photo>`.** Displays a Facebook photo.
- **`<fb:prompt-permission>`.** Displays a link to prompt the user for an extended permission.
- **`<fb:share-button>`.** Displays a share button for a URL, pictures, audio, and video.
- **`<fb:comments>`.** Displays a Wall-like box that allows users to add comments to the page. Chapter 13 goes over this in more detail.

XFBML also has some of its own tags that are directly supported, including a special tag for including the rest of the FBML tags:

- **`<fb:container>`.** Conditionally displays HTML. We go through an example of this later.
- **`<fb:serverfbml>`.** A wrapper tag that handles displaying the FBML tags that aren't listed here. We go over how this works later.
- **`<fb:connect-form>`.** Displays a form to allow users to invite their friends to use Facebook Connect on an external site. We cover this in Chapter 13.
- **`<fb:login-button>`.** Displays a Facebook Connect login button. We cover this in Chapter 13.
- **`<fb:unconnected-friends-count>`.** Displays the number of a user's friends who have not linked their Facebook account to the site using Facebook Connect.

Server Tags

To display the rest of the FBML tags, you need to wrap them in an `<fb:serverfbml>` tag. The contents of these tags are rendered by Facebook and displayed in an IFrame.

Listing 12.13 shows how to put an `<fb:request-form>` tag on the page. It is important that the `<fb:serverfbml>` tag is inside a `<body>` tag or it will not be rendered. The resulting form is displayed in Figure 12.6.

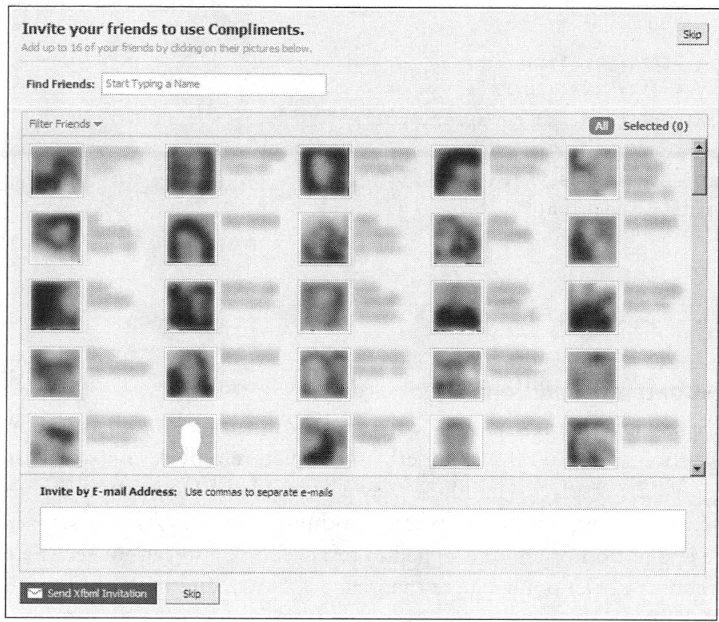

Figure 12.6 Using the `<fb:serverfbml>` tag to display a `<fb-request-form>`

Listing 12.13 **Using `<fb:serverfbml>` Tag to Display an Invite Request Form**

```
<script
  src="http://static.ak.facebook.com/js/api_lib/v0.4/FeatureLoader.js.php"
  type="text/javascript">
</script>
<body>

<fb:serverfbml>
  <script type="text/fbml">
    <fb:fbml>
      <fb:request-form method="POST" invite="true" type="Compliments"
        content="Tell your friends about Compliments.
                <fb:req-choice url='http://apps.facebook.com/appname'
                label='Try Compliments' />  ">
        <fb:multi-friend-selector showborder="false"
          actiontext="Invite your friends to use Compliments.">
```

Listing 12.13 **Continued**

```
      </fb:request-form>
    </fb:fbml>
  </script>
</fb:serverfbml>

<script type="text/javascript">
  var apiKey = 'XXXXXXXXXXXXXX';
  var xdReceiverPath = 'xd_receiver.html';

  FB.init(apiKey, xdReceiverPath);
  FB.ensureInit( function() {
  });
</script>
</body>
```

Displaying Content Conditionally

`<fb:container>` allows you to display content only if certain conditions are met. Listing 12.14 shows how to display a user's profile picture only to users who are allowed to see it. Figure 12.7 displays what those viewers would see. However, if the viewing user is not allowed to see the other user's picture, nothing shows up. Viewers who have not authorized the application or are not logged in to Facebook also cannot see the picture. (However, there is a brief point where the image is shown and then hidden. The section, "Rendering XFBML Elements," goes over how to prevent this.)

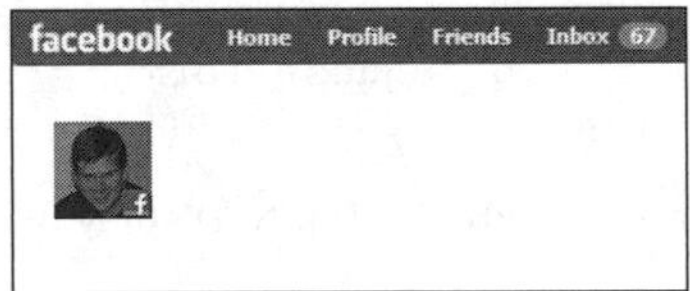

Figure 12.7 Users who authorize the application and are allowed to view the user's picture see this image.

Listing 12.14 **Conditionally Showing a Profile Picture**

```
<script src="http://static.ak.facebook.com/js/api_lib/v0.4/FeatureLoader.js.php"
 type="text/javascript"></script>
<fb:container condition="FB.XFBML.Conditions.ifCanSee('698700806', 'photosofme')">
  <fb:profile-pic uid="698700806" facebook-logo="true" linked="false">
  </fb:profile-pic>
</fb:container>
<script type="text/javascript">
  var apiKey = 'XXXXXXXXXXXXXX';
  var xdReceiverPath = 'xd_receiver.html';
```

Listing 12.14 **Continued**

```
  FB.init(apiKey, xdReceiverPath);
  FB.ensureInit( function() {
  });
</script>
```

Rendering XFBML Elements

There are three ways to show XFBML content that match the various ways you might add HTML elements to your page in general. The first is to directly place the tags on the page, as we did in Listings 12.13 and 12.14. For the subset of tags that that are listed as client-side, Facebook automatically parses the DOM as part of `FB.init()` and replaces them with the HTML equivalents. This is controlled by the `FB.XFBML.Host.autoParseDomTree` field, which defaults to `true`. You can set this to `false` before calling `FB.init()` to control when elements are rendered manually, as shown in Listing 12.15.

The second way is to add XFBML tags dynamically via JavaScript. You can call `FB.XFBML.Host.parseDomTree()` to render tags on the entire page or `FB.XFBML.Host.parseDomElement()` to render just a single element. Listing 12.15 shows how to manually render a `<fb:profile-pic>`. A container `<div>` is added to the document to hold the dynamically created elements. `FB.XFBML.Host.autoParseDomTree` is set to `false` to prevent `FB:init()` from automatically rendering the XFBML elements. This means that, before `FB.XFBML.Host.parseDomElement()`, is called, a generic profile picture is displayed, as shown in Figure 12.8. `FB.XFBML.Host.parseDomElement()` then replaces this with the user's profile picture.

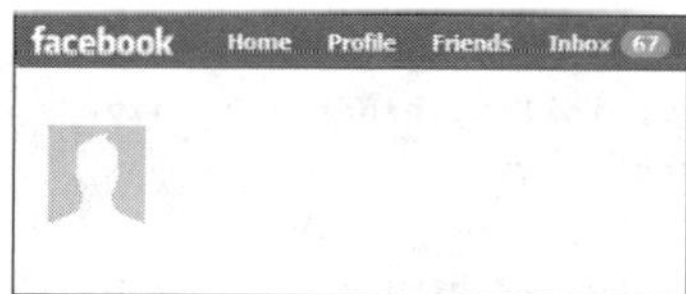

Figure 12.8 A generic profile picture displayed briefly before the final picture fully loads

Listing 12.15 **Manually Rendering XFBML Elements**

```
<script
  src="http://static.ak.facebook.com/js/api_lib/v0.4/FeatureLoader.js.php"
  type="text/javascript">
</script>
<div id='container'></div>
<script type="text/javascript">
  var apiKey = 'XXXXXXXXXXXXXX';
  var xdReceiverPath = 'xd_receiver.html';
```

Listing 12.15 **Continued**

```
  FB_RequireFeatures(['XFBML'], function() {
    FB.XFBML.Host.autoParseDomTree = false;
    FB.init(apiKey, xdReceiverPath);
    FB.ensureInit( function() {
      var api = FB.Facebook.apiClient;
      api.requireLogin( function() {
        var uid =  api.get_session().uid
        var container = document.getElementById('container');
        container.innerHTML = '<fb:profile-pic uid="'+uid+'">
                               </fb:profile-pic>';
        FB.XFBML.Host.parseDomElement(container);
      });
    });
  });
</script>
```

To prevent elements from showing up before they are fully rendered, like the generic profile picture in Listing 12.15, you can hide them initially and then use the `FB.XFBML.Host.get_areElementsReady()` object to make them visible when they are rendered. Listing 12.16 shows how to do this. The default profile picture will not be shown, and the profile picture we saw in Figure 12.7 appears.

Listing 12.16 **Hiding Elements Until They Are Rendered**

```
<script
  src="http://static.ak.facebook.com/js/api_lib/v0.4/FeatureLoader.js.php"
  type="text/javascript">
</script>
<div id='container' style='visibility:hidden;'></div>
<script type="text/javascript">
  var apiKey = 'XXXXXXXXXXXXXX';
  var xdReceiverPath = 'xd_receiver.html';

  FB_RequireFeatures(['XFBML'], function() {
    FB.XFBML.Host.autoParseDomTree = false;
    FB.init(apiKey, xdReceiverPath);
    FB.ensureInit( function() {
      var api = FB.Facebook.apiClient;
      api.requireLogin( function() {
        var uid =  api.get_session().uid
        var container = document.getElementById('container');
        container.innerHTML = '<fb:profile-pic uid="'+uid+'">
                               </fb:profile-pic>';
        FB.XFBML.Host.parseDomElement(container);
        FB.XFBML.Host.get_areElementsReady().waitUntilReady(
```

Listing 12.16 **Continued**

```
        function() {
          document.getElementById('container').style.visibility =
            "visible";
        });
      });
    });
  });
</script>
```

The third way is to create HTML elements with attributes that match their FBML equivalents and then use `FB.XFBML.Host.addElement()` to replace them with rendered FBML. Listing 12.17 creates a `div` to be turned into a `<fb:profile-pic>`, sets the `uid` attribute to the logged in user, and calls `FB.XFBML.Host.addElement()` to render it. The same profile picture from Figure 12.7 is shown.

Listing 12.17 **Dynamic Replacement for XFBML Elements**

```
<script
  src="http://static.ak.facebook.com/js/api_lib/v0.4/FeatureLoader.js.php"
  type="text/javascript">
</script>

<div id='pic'></div>

<script type="text/javascript">
  var apiKey = 'XXXXXXXXXXXXXX';
  var xdReceiverPath = 'xd_receiver.html';

  FB.init(apiKey, xdReceiverPath);
  FB.ensureInit( function() {
    var api = FB.Facebook.apiClient;
    api.requireLogin(function(exception){
      var uid = FB.Facebook.apiClient.get_session().uid;
      var pic = document.getElementById("pic");
      pic.setAttribute('uid', uid);
      FB.XFBML.Host.addElement(new FB.XFBML.ProfilePic(pic));     });
  });
</script>
```

Testing XFBML

There isn't a developer tool for testing XFBML like the FBML Test Console; however, Facebook does include one in its RunAround sample application (located at *www.somethingtoputhere.com/demo/xfbml_console/index.html*). It also lets you control the FBDebug setting, so it is easy to try out various calls and see exactly what is happening.

The page still displays the outdated trace output box with `id='_traceTextBox'`, but this will not display anything. Instead, it appears in your script debugger console.

Updating Compliments' IFrame Page

The Compliments application's FBML page was updated in Chapter 9 to display a Feed form when a user sends a compliment, and Chapter 11, "FBJS, Mock AJAX, and Flash," used FBJS to do some validation on the compliment form, displaying a dialog for errors. We will update the IFrame page with similar functionality by using `FB.Connect.showFeedDialog()` to show the Feed form and `FB.UI.FBMLPopupDialog()` to display validation errors.

The first set of changes is in `index_iframe.php`. Update the `renderForm()` function with the bold code shown in Listing 12.18.

Listing 12.18 **Updates to `renderForm()` in `index_iframe.php`**

```
/** outputs the page content **/
function renderPage() {
  global $facebook;
  global $g_categories;

  $pageOutput = getHeaderContent();

  $ajaxURL = LOCAL_APP_URL."/ajax.php?submitform=1";
  $output = getFeedDialog();
  $output .= "
    <script>
      function getRadioValue(radio){
        var value = '';
        var element = document.getElementsByName(radio);
        var bt_count = element.length;
        for (var i = 0; i <bt_count; i++) {
          if (element[i].checked == true) {
            value =  element[i].value;
            break;
          }
        }
        return value;
      }

      function submitForm() {
        // Create the validation dialog
        var dialog = null;
        var dlgContent=document.createElement('div');
        var errorText = document.createElement('div');
        errorText.classname = 'error';
```

Listing 12.18 **Continued**

```
        dlgContent.appendChild(errorText);
        var button = document.createElement('input');
        button.type = 'button';
        button.className = 'inputbutton okbutton';
        button.value = 'OK';
        button.onclick = function() { dialog.close(); return false; };
        dlgContent.appendChild(button);
        dialog = new FB.UI.PopupDialog('Hello', dlgContent, false, false);
        dialog.setContentWidth(300);

        // Validate the form
        if ( document.getElementById('target').value == '' ) {
          errorText.innerHTML = 'Please choose someone to compliment';
          dialog.show();
        }
        else if ( getRadioValue('category') == '' ) {
          errorText.innerHTML = 'Please enter a compliment category';
          dialog.show();
        }
        else if ( document.getElementById('compliment').value == '' ) {
          errorText.innerHTML = 'Please enter a compliment';
          dialog.show();
        }
        else {
          // Submit the form via AJAX

          // Handle the result of the AJAX call by displaying a feed dialog
          // and updating the canvas with a success message
          var successHandler = function(o) {
            var data = YAHOO.lang.JSON.parse(o.responseText);

            showFeedDialog(data.target, data.category,
                           data.compliment, data.img);

            var status = \" \
              <div class='success'> \
                <h1>Your Compliment to <fb:name uid='\"+data.target+\"'> \
                  </fb:name> was sent.</h1> \
                <p> \
                  <fb:profile-pic size='square' uid='\"+data.target+\"'> \
                  </fb:profile-pic> \
                  <img class='categoryImg' \
                    src='\"+data.img+\"' /> \
                  <fb:name uid='\"+data.target+\"'></fb:name> \
                  is <b>'\"+data.category+\"' </b> \
```

Listing 12.18 **Continued**

```
              because \"+data.compliment+\" \
            </p> \
          </div>\";
        var statusDiv = document.getElementById('status');
        statusDiv.innerHTML = status;
        FB.XFBML.Host.parseDomElement(statusDiv);
      };
      var callback = {
        success: successHandler
      }
      var formObject = document.getElementById('complimentform');
      YAHOO.util.Connect.setForm(formObject);
      var request = YAHOO.util.Connect.asyncRequest('POST','".$ajaxURL."',
       callback);
    }
  }
  </script>
...
```

The `submitForm()` function is similar to the same function in `index.php`, except that here we use `FB.UI.PopupDialog()` for form validation. The dialog is dynamically created but not shown, with the `errorText` variable set within each field validator. If validation fails, the dialog is shown with the error. The user can close the dialog by clicking the OK button, which calls the `FB.UI.PopupDialog()`'s `close()` function.

If validation succeeds, we use another feature of the YUI JavaScript Library: the Connect class. This class allows us to set our form data to be serialized to a URL using AJAX. After the AJAX call returns, a new function, `showFeedDialog()`, is passed the results, which are now the items needed to fill out the template data for the feed story. A Feed dialog is displayed, and after it is closed, the `status` `<div>` is updated with the compliment details. We are now using XFBML to display the target user's name and profile picture.

`getFeedDialog()` returns a script block containing the `showFeedDialog()` function. It takes the passed-in template data and fills out the parameters to `FB.Connect.showFeedDialog()`. This script block is returned to the `getComplimentForm()` function to be displayed with the form. Add the code in Listing 12.19 to `index_iframe.php`.

Listing 12.19 **`getFeedDialog()` in `index_iframe.php`**

```
/** returns HTML for the Feed Dialog **/
function getFeedDialog() {
  $output = "
    <script type='text/javascript'>
      function showFeedDialog(targetID, category, compliment, img) {
        // The short story template
```

Listing 12.19 **Continued**

```
        //{*actor*} sent {*target*} a compliment with {*app*}!
        //<br/>{*actor*} thinks {*target*} is {*ctitle*} because {*ctext*}
        var templateData = {\"app\": \"Compliments\", \"ctitle\": category,
          \"ctext\": compliment,
          \"images\":};
        var targetID = [targetID];
        var templateID = ".TEMPLATE_BUNDLE_MULTIFEEDSTORY_1.";
        var bodyGeneral = '';
        var story_size = null;
        var require_connect = FB.RequireConnect.doNotRequire;
        var callback = null;
        var feedDialogPrompt = 'Publish your Compliment';
        var feedDialogUserMsg = {value:'I love sending Compliments!'};

        FB.Connect.showFeedDialog(templateID, templateData, targetID,
                                  bodyGeneral, story_size, require_connect,
                                  callback, feedDialogPrompt,feedDialogUserMsg);
      }
    </script>
  ";
  return $output;
}
```

All these code changes produce the familiar Feed dialog in Figure 12.9 after the user submits the compliment.

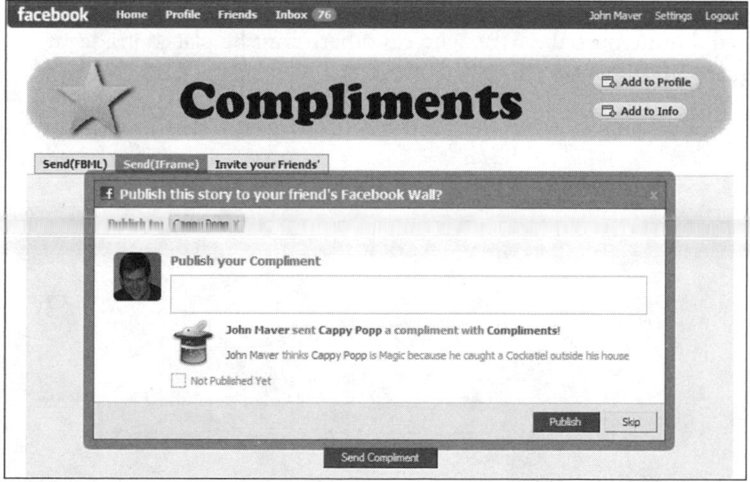

Figure 12.9 Compliments application displaying a Feed dialog using the Facebook JavaScript Client Library

Summary

This chapter talked about how the Facebook JavaScript Client Library works across domains, handles dynamic loading of features and authentication. It also discussed the key Library classes, with examples of how to call Facebook API functions, display dialogs, enable tracing, and render XFBML. Here are some key points:

- You can manually control which features of the Library get loaded or have them all loaded automatically by using different functions in the Bootstrap class. You must always call `FB.init()` with the application's key and a cross-domain receiver file.
- The `FB.apiClient` class contains wrappers for the Facebook REST API. Users must have authorized the application to call API functions. To call functions in the `admin` or `permissions` API, or to set another user's profile FBML, you must pass your application's Secret key to the Library. Do this carefully and on nonpublic pages, because this can expose your key to anyone with access to a page where this happens.
- The `FB.Connect` class is the only way for IFrame applications to create the Add to Profile and Add to Info buttons. It also provides other dialogs for permissions and feed stories. The rest of this class is used for Facebook Connect user and session management and is covered in Chapter 13.
- The `FB.FBDebug` class enables tracing for developer applications and the Library. A debugger must be attached to the browser to see the output.
- The `FB.UI` class provides Facebook-style dialogs for displaying HTML and FBML. The FBML dialog can render FBML directly without using XFBML equivalents.
- The `FB.XFBML` class allows the use of XFBML tags on the page. These tags are rendered by the Library into the FBML equivalents. A subset of these tags can be placed directly onto the page, whereas others must be placed inside an `<fb:serverfbml>` tag.

13

Facebook Connect

Facebook Connect was launched in December 2008. At the time, Facebook was a walled garden—all content stayed within the site. MySpace, Google, and other networks were lining up to use the OpenSocial platform to allow applications to be built once and run on multiple platforms. Facebook then launched Beacon to allow external sites that users visited to post Facebook status updates on the users' behalf. Unfortunately, Beacon had public-relations issues. The default setting for publishing updates was on, and users did not like having everyone know what they were doing without their permission.

Facebook Connect went in a different direction. Users explicitly use Connect to log in to external sites using their Facebook credentials. These websites then become more valuable to them because they have the ability to incorporate information from their Facebook friends. Currently, more than 15,000 websites have implemented Facebook Connect into their sites. Many of these sites have seen a massive increase in registrations, engagement, and friend referrals. This chapter goes over the major features of Facebook Connect.

Facebook Connect Features

Facebook Connect extends the Facebook JavaScript Client Library and offers external sites several key features:

- **Trusted authentication.** Users can link their Facebook credentials with the external site instead of having to create an entirely new account. The authentication process is handled by Facebook with the results returned to the site.
- **Real identity.** Users bring their Facebook information with them, without having to reenter everything on the external site.
- **Dynamic privacy.** When a user changes or removes information on Facebook, those changes are automatically reflected on the external site.
- **Friends access.** The user brings their friends with them to the site, allowing the external site to provide information about what their friends are doing. Connect

can also allow a site to suggest that the user invite friends who are also registered on the site to enable Connect for their accounts.

- **Social distribution.** The external site can publish a user's actions as status updates.
- **Commenting and the live stream.** Users can add comments and status updates that immediately appear on their Facebook profiles.

The following sections review each feature.

Trusted Authentication

Most users dream of a single username and password that can identify who they are and be used everywhere. They dislike having to set up everything over and over again on each new network. Many solutions to this problem have been proposed and tried: Microsoft Passport, OpenID, and Google Friend Connect being some of the most famous.

Facebook chose to create its own version of single sign-on that works with a user's Facebook credentials. With its large user base, Facebook can expect that it will be adopted by many sites that want to capture those users.

Facebook Connect does not have to be the only method for logging into a site. It can be an alternative to regular account creation or just an add-on that adds Connect functionality to an existing account.

When a user goes to a Connect-enabled site, she is presented with a login button that looks like the one shown in Figure 13.1.

Figure 13.1 The default `<fb:login-button>` rendered

This button uses the `<fb:login-button>` XFBML tag. When a user clicks the link, he is presented with a login dialog hosted by Facebook, shown in Figure 13.2. After logging in to Facebook, the user is then logged into the site.

Logging out of Facebook or any Facebook Connect site also logs a user out of all Facebook sites. This is by design; the user has a single identify that is either logged in or logged out.

Real Identity

Facebook users have already spent the time identifying their friends, filling out profile information, and adding a profile picture. A big benefit of Facebook Connect is that this information travels with them to each Connect site. These sites also benefit, because they get access to most of this information with the knowledge that it is usually kept current. This allows them to customize users' experience to their interests; for example, a book store might highlight books that match the user's favorite genres, or a travel site might automatically show deals that start in a user's current location.

Figure 13.2 The Facebook Connect login dialog is displayed when the user clicks the `<fb:login-button>`.

Connected sites do not get access to the user's email address—all Facebook platform applications have this same limitation. They do get access to the user's proxied email address, as outlined in Chapter 10, "Publisher, Notifications, and Requests," so sending email to users is still possible, as long as they have been properly prompted and have granted that extended permission. Connected sites usually do this immediately after a user Connects to their sites for the first time, because otherwise, there isn't an easy way to contact them in the future. Figure 13.3 shows an email extended permission dialog.

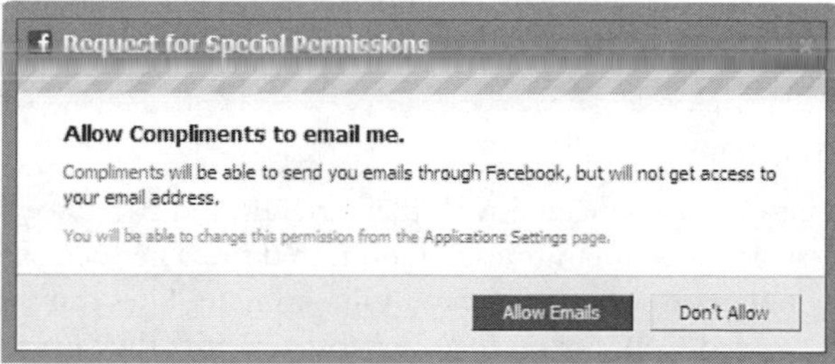

Figure 13.3 Email extended permissions must be requested and granted by a user before a Connected site can send them email.

Dynamic Privacy

Facebook Beacon failed in part because users perceived that they didn't have control over their information. Facebook Connect enables users to use the same privacy settings that they created on Facebook to only show certain sets of information to certain groups of people. Because the user's information for Connect sites comes from Facebook, any changes that the user makes to her account—managing friends, sharing more or less information, and so on—is reflected in the Connected site. Figure 13.4 shows how a user controls privacy for applications and Connected sites.

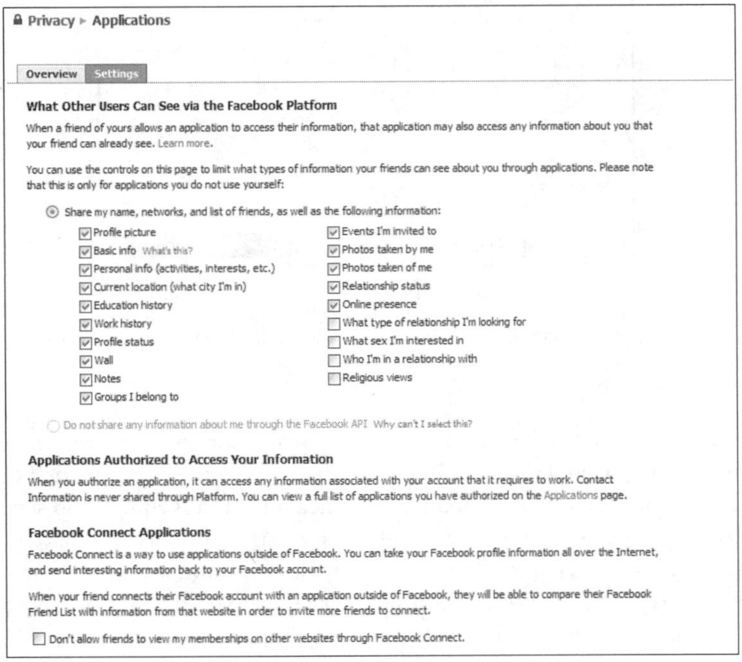

Privacy ▸ Applications

Overview | Settings

What Other Users Can See via the Facebook Platform

When a friend of yours allows an application to access their information, that application may also access any information about you that your friend can already see. Learn more.

You can use the controls on this page to limit what types of information your friends can see about you through applications. Please note that this is only for applications you do not use yourself:

(•) Share my name, networks, and list of friends, as well as the following information:

- [x] Profile picture
- [x] Basic info What's this?
- [x] Personal info (activities, interests, etc.)
- [x] Current location (what city I'm in)
- [x] Education history
- [x] Work history
- [x] Profile status
- [x] Wall
- [x] Notes
- [x] Groups I belong to
- [x] Events I'm invited to
- [x] Photos taken by me
- [x] Photos taken of me
- [x] Relationship status
- [x] Online presence
- [ ] What type of relationship I'm looking for
- [ ] What sex I'm interested in
- [ ] Who I'm in a relationship with
- [ ] Religious views

( ) Do not share any information about me through the Facebook API Why can't I select this?

Applications Authorized to Access Your Information

When you authorize an application, it can access any information associated with your account that it requires to work. Contact Information is never shared through Platform. You can view a full list of applications you have authorized on the Applications page.

Facebook Connect Applications

Facebook Connect is a way to use applications outside of Facebook. You can take your Facebook profile information all over the Internet, and send interesting information back to your Facebook account.

When your friend connects their Facebook account with an application outside of Facebook, they will be able to compare their Facebook Friend List with information from that website in order to invite more friends to connect.

- [ ] Don't allow friends to view my memberships on other websites through Facebook Connect.

Figure 13.4 Changes that a user makes in his privacy settings are reflected on Facebook and Connected sites.

Friends Access

Facebook users want to stay connected with their friends, and Facebook Connect lets them bring those friends with them to each Connected site. The social graph provides opportunities for Connected sites to add extra value to users. Sites can show which of a user's friends have enabled Connect on the site, what activities they have performed, and suggest actions for the user based on what those friends have done.

Facebook Connect also allows users to send invitations to their friends to join a site via the normal multi-Friend selector or via Friend Linking. Friend Linking allows sites to submit email addresses to Facebook to see if they are currently Facebook users. If they are, the site can use an `<fb:connect-form>` XFBML tag to allow users to invite those friends to Connect their accounts. Figure 13.5 shows this form in action.

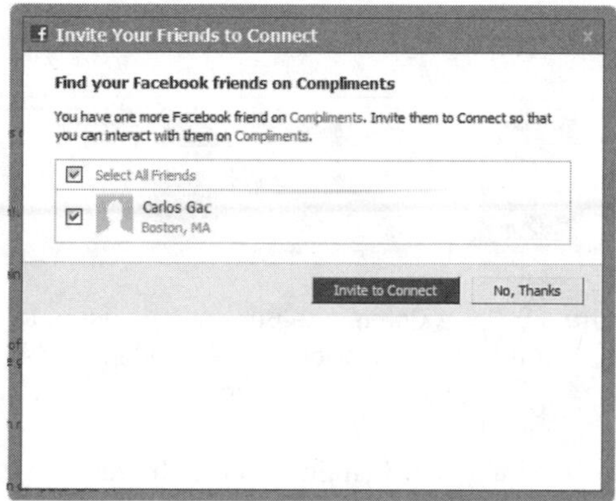

Figure 13.5 `<fb:connect-form>` allows users to invite friends to Connect who have registered on your site with a regular email address.

Social Distribution

Connected sites can publish user activity as Facebook Feed stories by using the `FB.Connect.showFeedDialog()` function. As with Facebook applications, Feed stories can be effective in getting new users to the site, as long as they contain useful or relevant content. These stories show up in Facebook on the users' Wall and in their friends' streams. For example, a music site might allow users to tell their friends about a particular song or album when they mark it as a favorite. Figure 13.6 shows a Feed dialog generated from the `FB.Connect.showFeedDialog()` function.

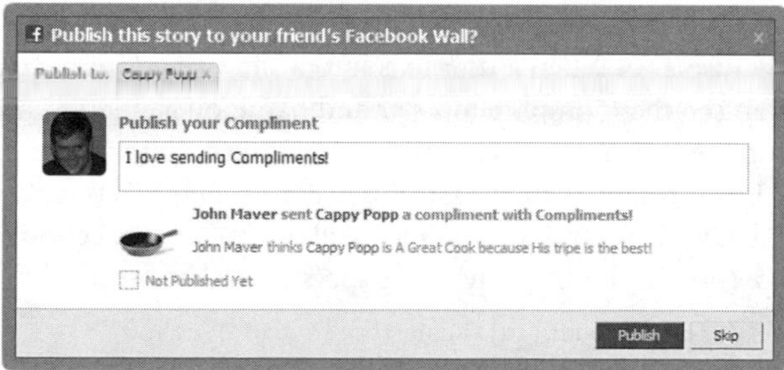

Figure 13.6 Connected sites can display Feed dialogs in response to user actions to create stories that will appear in the stream.

Commenting and the Live Stream

Connect provides a comment box that can be added to a site using the `<fb:comments>` XFBML tag. Both Facebook users and nonusers can enter comments, but Facebook users have the opportunity to have their comments posted to their profiles. Figure 13.7 shows a Comments Box.

Figure 13.7 A Comments Box enables users to enter text that will appear on the site and in stories in the Facebook stream.

Facebook used the 2009 Presidential Inauguration as the first large, public test of the Live Stream Box and have subsequently released it for use on Connect sites. Users can post their own and see other users' updates in real time. These updates are also posted back to their profile, with a link to the Live Stream Box, so that others can participate. Users can see all updates or just their friends'. This can be useful for implementing a chat as part of an online event or for general on-site communication. Figure 13.8 shows a Live Stream Box.

Setting Up Facebook Connect

We already set up most of what is needed for Facebook Connect in Chapter 12, "Facebook JavaScript Client Library," because Facebook Connect builds on this library. However, Connect adds a few more important fields that are discussed next. Figure 13.9 shows the Connect Settings section on the Connect tab in the Developer Settings in the Facebook Developer application.

We previously set the Connect URL as the location Facebook Connect and the JavaScript Library use to find the `xd_receiver.html` file. The Facebook Connect logo is used on the dialogs displayed when a user logs into a site using Connect, as was shown in Figure 13.2. You can see the Compliments star and name on the left.

When a user receives a request to Connect to an external site from a friend, the Account Preview URL is sent as the link to his account. The URL entered should be in the following format, with `id` and `hash` as optional parameters. Facebook replaces `{account_id}` and `{email_hash}` with values specific to that user:

```
http://example.com/?id={account_id}&hash={email_hash}
```

The Base Domain field tells Facebook Connect to store its cookies in the base domain, such as *example.com* instead of a subdomain, so that Connect can be used across multiple subdomains, such as *www.example.com* and *blogs.example.com*.

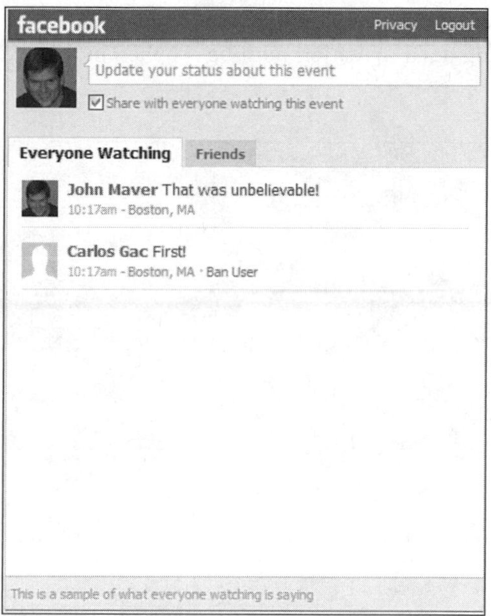

Figure 13.8 Live Stream Boxes enable real-time conversations between users on an external site.

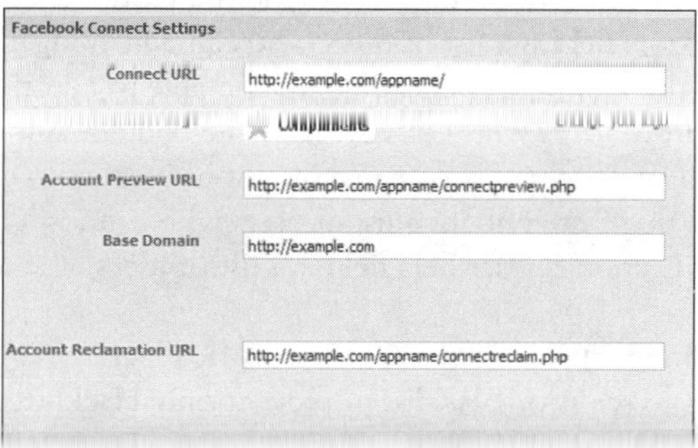

Figure 13.9 The Connect Settings on the Connect tab in the Developer Settings

Facebook uses the Account Reclamation URL field for users who have Connected to an external site and then deleted their Facebook account. This is described in more detail in the section, "Reclaiming Accounts."

The Friend Linking settings are shown in Figure 13.10. The Friend Linking Access field enables a Connected site to match an external site's user email addresses with Facebook accounts. The Native Friend Linking field should be checked if the site already enables users to search or import their friends. Both fields are only enabled after a review by Facebook, and supporting documentation must be supplied in the text boxes below them.

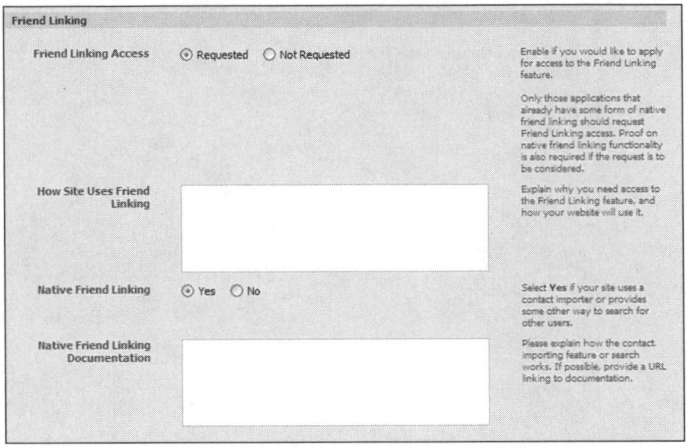

Figure 13.10 The Friend Linking settings on the Connect tab in the Developer Settings

The Widgets tab contains settings for widgets and the Comments Box (see Figure 13.11). The Administrators field is a list of users who can edit Widget settings. All users listed as developers of the Connect application are also able to edit these settings. The Moderators field is a list of users who can moderate the content and modify the whitelists and blacklists for a widget. A whitelist contains the list of users who can see or interact with a widget, while a blacklist contains a list of users who cannot. These are set on a per-widget basis. The Notification Subscribers field is a list of users who are notified when a widget's content changes.

The Permissions Mode setting for the Comments Box can be set to Whitelist to only allow whitelisted users to see it or Blacklist to prevent only blacklisted users from seeing it. The Whitelist and Blacklist fields are lists of those users who are allowed to interact with the widget and those who are not, respectively. Finally, the Allow Anonymous Comments check box allows non-Facebook users to interact with the Comments Box. Widgets, including the Comments Box and Live Stream Box, are detailed in the section, "Widgets."

Another change that sites using Facebook Connect have to make is to include *http://static.ak.connect.facebook.com/js/api_lib/v0.4/FeatureLoader.js.php* instead of the Facebook JavaScript version, *http://static.ak.facebook.com/js/api_lib/v0.4/FeatureLoader.js.php*, to get the `FeatureLoader` loaded. You can always get the latest Facebook Connect information from *http://wiki.developers.facebook.com/index.php/Category:Facebook_Connect*.

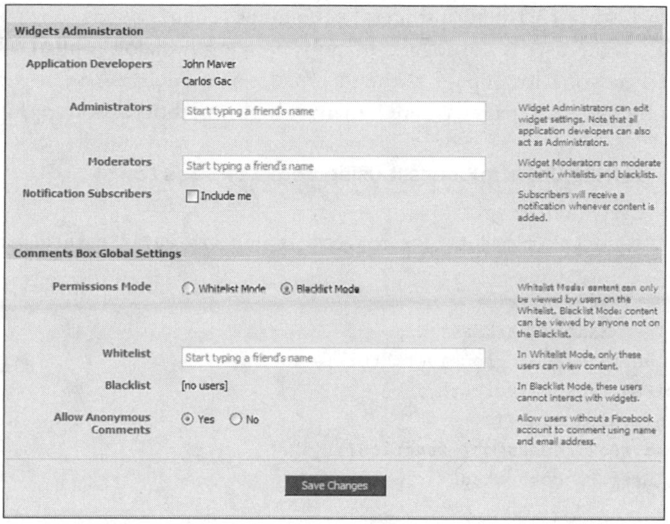

Figure 13.11 The Widgets settings on the Widgets tab in the Developer Settings

User Authentication

Authentication for Facebook Connect is the most complicated part of the implementation. This is because external sites already have user management systems in place and must integrate Facebook Connect into them. A successful integration must handle both new account creation and linking of existing accounts.

Authentication consists of two concepts: being *logged in* and being *connected*. Being logged in means that a user is logged in to Facebook. A user's logged in state is global: She is either logged in to Facebook and all Connected sites or logged out of Facebook and all Connected sites. Being connected is similar to authorizing a Facebook application; the user has linked her account with the site and authorized it to interact with Facebook. A user must be logged in to be connected.

Detecting Login Status

When the Connect library is first loaded, it uses the cross-domain communication method outlined in Chapter 12 to get the user's login status. It creates an IFrame with its `src` attribute set to *http://www.facebook.com/extern/login_status.php*. This page reads the Facebook cookies, retrieves the user's login status, and passes it back to the site's `xdreceiver.html` IFrame, which passes it back to the main IFrame. The Connect library then stores that login state in cookies for the external domain and sets its internal variables to the login state.

If a page wants to ensure that all visitors are logged in to Facebook and have authorized the site, it can call the `FB.Connect.requireSession()` function after Library initialization, as Listing 13.1 demonstrates. `FB.Connect.requireSession()` first checks the cookies, and if the user is not logged in, pops up a login dialog instead of doing a redirect to the Facebook login page as the `FB.apiClient.requireLogin()` function does. This can be useful on pages where a manual login method is not appropriate.

Listing 13.1 **Forcing Users to Connect Using `requireSession()`**

```
<script type="text/javascript"
  src="http://static.ak.connect.facebook.com/js/api_lib/v0.4/FeatureLoader.js.php">
</script>
<script type="text/javascript">
  var apiKey = 'XXXXXXXXXXXXXX';
  var xdReceiverPath = 'xd_receiver.html';
  FB.init(apiKey, xdReceiverPath);
  FB.ensureInit( function() {
    FB.Connect.requireSession( function() {
      // The user is connected
    });
  });
</script>
```

Pages can dynamically handle the user's connection state by either passing extra parameters to the `FB.init()` function or by calling the `FB.Connect.ifUserConnected()` function. Both are asynchronous and accept parameters that are either a URL to navigate to or a function to call for each connection state. Listing 13.2 shows how to use the `FB.init()` and `FB.Connect.ifUserConnected()` functions. In the real world, these functions are never used together. A developer chooses one or the other depending on what makes the most sense for the site. In the example, we pass callbacks to each function. When the user's connection state is detected, the callback for that state is called. This technique is useful for dynamically displaying information based on login state, such as the Connect button, or for sending logged-in users to a members-only page.

Listing 13.2 **Dynamically Handling the User's Connection State**

```
<script type="text/javascript"
  src="http://static.ak.connect.facebook.com/js/api_lib/v0.4/FeatureLoader.js.php">
</script>
<script type="text/javascript">
  var apiKey = 'XXXXXXXXXXXXXX';
  var xdReceiverPath = 'xd_receiver.html';
  function onLoggedIn(UID) {
   // The user with UID is connected
  }
  function onLoggedOut() {
```

Listing 13.2 **Continued**

```
  // The user is not connected
  }
  FB.init(apiKey, xdReceiverPath,{'ifUserConnected' : onLoggedIn,
                                  'ifUserNotConnected' : onLoggedOut });

  FB.ensureInit( function() {
    FB.Connect.ifUserConnected(onLoggedIn, onLoggedOut);
  });
</script>
```

You can also register a function to be called when the user is logged in using the `FB.Facebook.get_sessionWaitable().waitUntilReady(callback)` function. This is called immediately after the page loads if the user was already logged in. Otherwise, it is called after a user logs in using Facebook Connect. It can also dynamically add Connect content to a normal page. Listing 13.3 shows how to use this function to receive a callback when the user is logged in.

Listing 13.3 **Getting Notified When the User Is Logged In**

```
<script type="text/javascript"
  src="http://static.ak.connect.facebook.com/js/api_lib/v0.4/FeatureLoader.js.php">
</script>
<script type="text/javascript">
  var apiKey = 'XXXXXXXXXXXXXX';
  var xdReceiverPath = 'xd_receiver.html';
  function sessionCallback(sessionInfo) {
    // The user is connected
  }
  FB.init(apiKey, xdReceiverPath);
  FB.ensureInit( function() {
    FB.Facebook.get_sessionWaitable().waitUntilReady( sessionCallback );
  });
</script>
```

The final way for a page to handle a user's connection state is to have the page reload if the session state changes. By passing the `reloadIfSessionStateChanged` parameter to the `FB.init()` function, the page monitors the cookie session state and forces the page to reload when it changes. This state change might be triggered by any login dialog on the page, but it won't happen in response to the user logging out of Facebook or the site in another browser. Listing 13.4 shows how to set this parameter. This might be useful if there are several places on the site where users can be prompted to log in, such as a Comments Box. This parameter cannot be passed at the same time as the `ifUserConnected` and `ifUserNotConnected` parameters.

Listing 13.4 **Reloading the Page When the Session State Changes**

```
<script type="text/javascript"
  src="http://static.ak.connect.facebook.com/js/api_lib/v0.4/FeatureLoader.js.php">
</script>
<script type="text/javascript">
  var apiKey = 'XXXXXXXXXXXXXX';
  var xdReceiverPath = 'xd_receiver.html';
  FB.init(apiKey, xdReceiverPath,{'reloadIfSessionStateChanged' : true });
  FB.ensureInit( function() {
  });
</script>
```

Logging the User In

When the user isn't logged in, sites can use the `<fb:login-button>` XFBML tag to display several styles of buttons that users can click to log in, or the site can display a button it has manually created that performs the same actions via JavaScript.

If the user is already logged in, clicking the button does not show the log in dialog again. It is best to hide the button or use the `autologoutlink` parameter to change it into a logout button, as shown in Figure 13.12.

Figure 13.12 Using `<fb:login-button>` to display a logout button via the `autologoutlink` parameter

You can place this XFBML tag on your site, usually next to your normal site log in functionality. It can take the optional parameters shown in Table 13.1. Most of these parameters govern the look of the button and can be set to match the site's design. Using the `small` and `short` parameter values shows only a small Facebook "f" that can be placed next to a login link at the top of the page. The `autologoutlink` parameter can be used instead of dynamically hiding the button when the user is logged in. The `onlogin()` function can direct logged in users to a different page (see Listing 13.5).

Table 13.1 **`<fb:login-button>` Parameters**

Parameter	Type	Description
`condition`	string	JavaScript code that evaluates to a Boolean that determines whether the button is visible or hidden.

Table 13.1 **<fb:login-button> Parameters**

Parameter	Type	Description
`size`	string	Set to the size of the button image, either small, medium, or large. The default value is large.
`autologoutlink`	bool	Displays "logout" if the user is connected and logged in. Otherwise, the login button is shown all the time. The default value is false.
`background`	string	Set to the type of background antialiasing the button image will have. Pick from white, dark, or light to match the page background you have. The default value is light.
`length`	string	Sets the text of the button: Connect for short or Connect with Facebook for long. The default value is short.
`onlogin`	string	URL to navigate to or JavaScript to execute when the user is logged into Facebook. There is no equivalent function for when the user is logged out.

Listing 13.5 **Using the <fb:login-button> onlogin Parameter**

```
<script type="text/javascript"
  src="http://static.ak.connect.facebook.com/js/api_lib/v0.4/FeatureLoader.js.php">
</script>
<fb:login-button onlogin="window.location='http://example.com/loggedin.php';">
</fb:login-button>
<script type="text/javascript">
  var apiKey = 'XXXXXXXXXXXXXX';
  var xdReceiverPath = 'xd_receiver.html';
  FB.init(apiKey, xdReceiverPath);
  FB.ensureInit( function() {
  });
</script>
```

Examples of login buttons using the various sizes and lengths are located at *http://wiki.developers.facebook.com/index.php/Facebook_Connect_Login_Buttons*.

You can create your own login button and handle the click with JavaScript, but you must use a Facebook-provided image for the button. In the `onclick()` handler, call `FB.Connect.requireSession()`. Listing 13.6 shows the code for displaying a login button without using the XFBML tag. In most cases, however, `<fb:login-button>` is what you use.

Listing 13.6 **Creating a Custom Login Button**

```
<script type="text/javascript"
  src="http://static.ak.connect.facebook.com/js/api_lib/v0.4/FeatureLoader.js.php">
</script>
<a href="#" onclick="FB.Connect.requireSession(function(){
  window.location='http://example.com/loggedin.php';});" >
  <img src="http://static.ak.fbcdn.net/images/fbconnect/login-buttons/
connect_light_large_short.gif" />
</a>
<script type="text/javascript">
  var apiKey = 'XXXXXXXXXXXXXX';
  var xdReceiverPath = 'xd_receiver.html';
  FB.init(apiKey, xdReceiverPath);
  FB.ensureInit( function() {
  });
</script>
```

Logging Out the User

When a user logs out of a Facebook Connect site, he also logs out of Facebook. Depending on how you have integrated Facebook Connect into your existing user management system, you might want to give users the ability to manually log out. There are a few ways to do this.

One option is to use `<fb:login-button>` with `autologoutlink` set to true. This pairs well with passing the `reloadIfSessionStateChanged` parameter to `FB.init()`, so that, after the user clicks logout, the page reloads to display the logged-out state.

Another option is to provide your own button or link, and call either the `FB.Connect.logout()` or `FB.Connect.logoutAndRedirect()` function when a user clicks it. `FB.Connect.logout()` takes a callback function, which you can use to handle any site-specific logout logic, while `FB.Connect.logoutAndRedirect()` takes a URL that users are directed to after the session logout occurs.

Listing 13.7 shows a simple example of handling login and logout and appropriately displaying the `<fb:login-button>` or logout link. The `displayLoggedIn()` and `displayLoggedOut()` functions passed to `FB.init()` are called immediately after the session state is detected by the Connect library and shows the login or logout links. When a user clicks the login or logout buttons, the `handleLogin()` or `handleLogout()` functions are called, which can handle any site cleanup and then display the opposite button.

Listing 13.7 **Handling Login and Logout**

```
<script type="text/javascript"
  src="http://static.ak.connect.facebook.com/js/api_lib/v0.4/FeatureLoader.js.php">
</script>
<script type="text/javascript">
```

Listing 13.7 **Continued**

```
  var apiKey = 'XXXXXXXXXXXXXX';
  var xdReceiverPath = 'xd_receiver.html';
  function displayLoggedOut() {
    document.getElementById('login').style.display = 'inline';
    document.getElementById('logout').style.display = 'none';
  }

  function displayLoggedIn() {
    document.getElementById('login').style.display = 'none';
    document.getElementById('logout').style.display = 'inline';
  }

  function handleLogin() {
    displayLoggedIn();
  }

  function handleLogout() {
    displayLoggedOut();
  }

  FB.init('".FB_API_KEY."', 'xdreceiver.html',
{'ifUserConnected' : displayLoggedIn,
'ifUserNotConnected' : displayLoggedOut
}
);
  FB.ensureInit( function() {
  });
</script>
```

Disconnecting Users from Facebook

If a user decides to disconnect his Facebook account from a Connected site, he can do it on the site. To do this, the site must use the `auth.revokeAuthorization()` Facebook application programming interface (API) call. As discussed in Chapter 12, this API function is not available via the Facebook JavaScript Client Library, unless you pass your application's Secret key to `FB.init()`. The easiest, and safest, way to handle this is to redirect users to a page where this call can be executed on the server.

Users can also disconnect their account via the Application Settings page on Facebook by removing your site from the Authorized group under External Websites. When this happens, your site's Post Remove URL is pinged, which gives your site the capability to do any needed cleanup.

After a user's account is disconnected, the site cannot call any Facebook API functions on their behalf until the user chooses to reconnect his account.

Reclaiming Accounts

If a user creates an account on your website using Facebook Connect and chooses to delete his Facebook account from Facebook, Connect allows your site to provide a URL for that user to access his account using site-specific credentials.

To enable this, fill out the Account Reclamation URL field in the Developer Settings for your Connect application. When a user deletes his Facebook account, Facebook sends him an email with reclamation URLs for sites where he has enabled Facebook Connect.

Listing 13.8 shows an example of how to handle reclamation. The Account Reclamation URL receives two `GET` parameters: the Facebook user ID of the account and the user ID hashed with your Connect application's Secret key. The PHP library provides a helper function called `verify_account_reclamation()` that compares an `md5` hash of the user ID and the Application Secret to the received hash. If they match, the call action is legitimate and your site needs to help the user enable a native login.

Listing 13.8 **Handling Account Reclamation**

```
function handleReclaimation() {
  // The userid reclaiming
  $userID = $_GET['u'];

  // The verification hash
  $hash = $_GET['h'];

  // verify that this comes from the actual user
  if ( verify_account_reclamation($userID, $hash) ){
    // this is the real user, so enable them to login natively
  }
}
```

Friend Linking

Most websites already have a native method of managing user accounts, which usually requires email addresses as either the login or as part of the required information. Friend Linking lets your website send those email addresses to Facebook so that it can try to match them with Facebook users. The website can then use the `<fb:connect-form>` XFBML tag to display a form that lets connected users send requests to their unconnected friends to link up their accounts. The friends that appear in this form are the ones that Facebook matched from the email-address uploads.

The caveat with Friend Linking is that Facebook must approve a website before it can be used. As the section, "Setting Up Facebook Connect," discussed, description fields must be filled out in the Developer Settings to help convince Facebook that a site merits access. Facebook has stated that they have a turnaround of two–five days for approval.

Once approved, the Friend Linking process begins by sending the email addresses to Facebook using the `connect.registerUsers()` API function. This function takes one key parameter—accounts—which we go over here. This is an array of up to 1,000 arrays. The inner arrays each represent one user account. Each account array is composed of an `email_hash` and optional `account_id` and `account_url` properties. The `email_hash` must be generated in a particular format, which Listing 13.9 shows as the `generateEmailHash()` function.

Listing 13.9 Generating the `email_hash` for `connect.registerUsers()`

```
function generateEmailHash($email) {
  //normalize email - remove white space, convert to lower case
  $email = trim(strtolower($email));

  //Compute the CRC32 value of email and convert to unsigned int
  $CRC = crc32($email);
  $CRC = sprintf('%u', $crc);

  //Compute the MD5 hash of email
  $MD5 = md5($email);

  //Concatenate the CRC32 value with the MD5 separated by underscore
  $email_hash = "{$CRC}_{$MD5}";

  return $email_hash;
}
```

After the hash is created, you can create the accounts array. Only one of the two optional properties needs to be added to the array. `account_id` represents a unique identifier on your site for that user, and it is what Facebook uses to substitute for the `{account_id}` parameter in the Account Preview URL setting, and the `email_hash` value is substituted for the `{email_hash}` parameter. If you set the `account_url` property, that URL is used instead of the Account Preview URL. After creating the `accounts` array, pass it to the `connect.registerUsers()` API function, as Listing 13.10 shows.

Listing 13.10 Calling `connect.registerUsers()` with Native User Accounts

```
// Get array of user email addresses and identifiers from site database
$userInfo = getUserInfo();

$accounts = array();
foreach ($userInfo as $user) {
  $email_hash = generateEmailHash($user["email"]);
  $account_id = $user["id"];
  $array_push($accounts,
              array("email_hash" => $email_hash, "account_id" => $account_id));
}
$result = connect_registerUsers($accounts);
```

A site can check to see if there are unconnected users before displaying the `<fb:connect-form>` tag by calling the `connect.getUnconnectedFriendsCount()` function, which returns the number of unconnected users found by the `connect.registerUsers()` method. The `<fb:unconnected-friends-count>` XFBML tag can display this number on the page.

Listing 13.11 shows how to display `<fb:connect-form>`. Notice how it must be contained within a `<fb:server-fbml>` tag. The `action` attribute is the location the form redirects to after submitting the request or after the user clicks the Close button. You can also call the `FB.Connect.inviteConnectUsers()` library function to display the form in a popup dialog. The recipient receives the request shown in Figure 13.13.

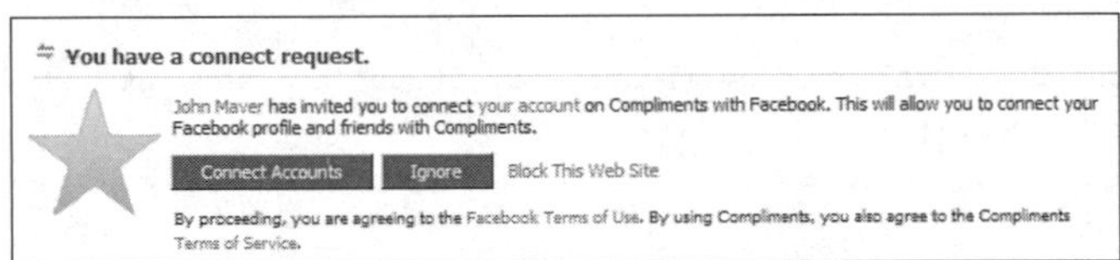

Figure 13.13 `<fb:connect-form>` sends a request to the selected unconnected users.

Listing 13.11 **Displaying `<fb:connect-form>`**

```
<script type="text/javascript"
  src="http://static.ak.connect.facebook.com/js/api_lib/v0.4/FeatureLoader.js.php">
</script>
<fb:serverfbml style="width:400px;">
  <script type="text/fbml">
    <fb:connect-form action="http://example.com/requestcomplete.php">
    </fb:connect-form>
  </script>
</fb:serverfbml>
<script type="text/javascript">
  var apiKey = 'XXXXXXXXXXXXXX';
  var xdReceiverPath = 'xd_receiver.html';
  FB.init(apiKey, xdReceiverPath);
  FB.ensureInit( function() {
  });
</script>
```

Widgets

Facebook provides several widgets for use on websites. Widgets are self-contained XFBML controls that utilize Facebook Connect. Currently, Facebook has released two widgets for Connected sites: the Comments Box and the Live Stream Box. Each widget is discussed in this section.

Comments Box

The Comments Box, as previously described in the section "Facebook Connect Features," adds a box that enables users to enter comments about the content on a page. Figure 13.14 shows a Comments Box on an external site before a user logs in. Users can either enter a comment by entering their name and email address or by logging in via Facebook Connect, either on the site itself or on the Comments Box.

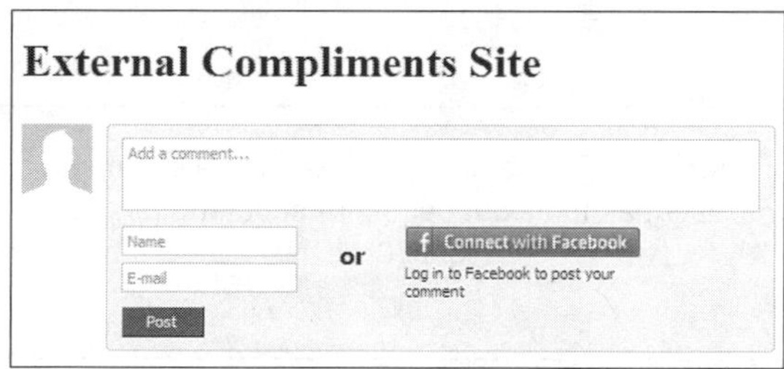

Figure 13.14 A Comments Box offers two methods of logging in to enter a comment.

When a user enters her name and email address, Facebook considers any comments she enters as coming from an anonymous source. Her name and email address are not passed to the hosting website; they are just used to display the user information next to the comment. Figure 13.15 shows the expanded entry fields that are displayed when a user begins to enter her information. A user also must pass a CAPTCHA to submit her comment; CAPTCHAs verify that a human is entering the form data rather than a computer (or *bot*) using text identification. Underneath the form in Figure 13.15 is a sample anonymous comment.

If a user chooses to use Facebook Connect to log in, the Comments Box changes to what's shown in Figure 13.16. The user has the option to also post her comments to her own Facebook profile. Comments posted from Connected users display the user's picture shown at the bottom of Figure 13.16 and, if she has the box checked, a Feed story similar to what is shown in Figure 13.17 is posted to the Wall tab of her profile and her friends' streams on their Home pages. Each story contains a link back to the Connected site on which it was created.

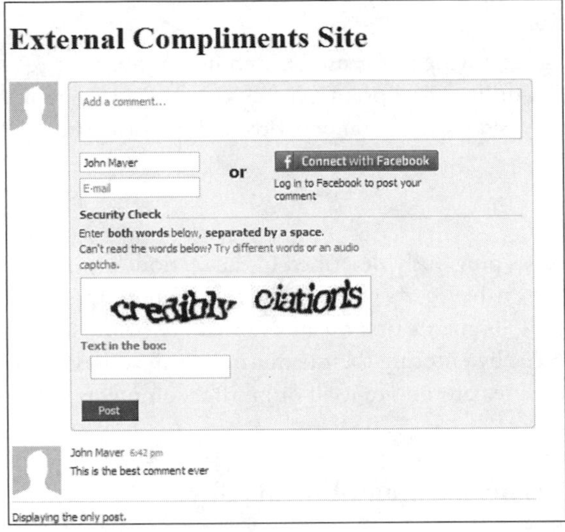

Figure 13.15 To enter an anonymous comment, a user has to fill out her information and pass a CAPTCHA.

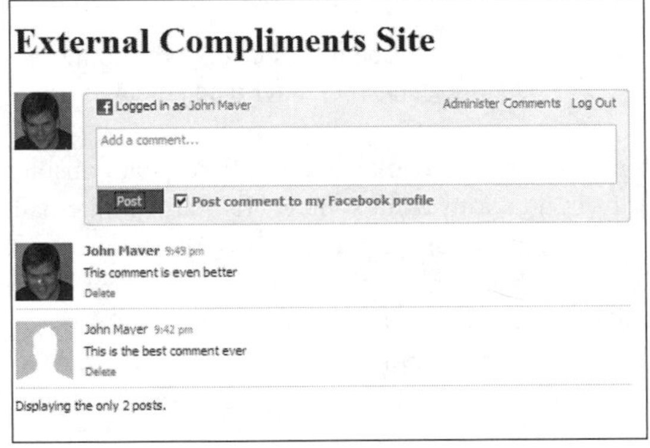

Figure 13.16 Users who are logged in with Facebook Connect see this Comments Box.

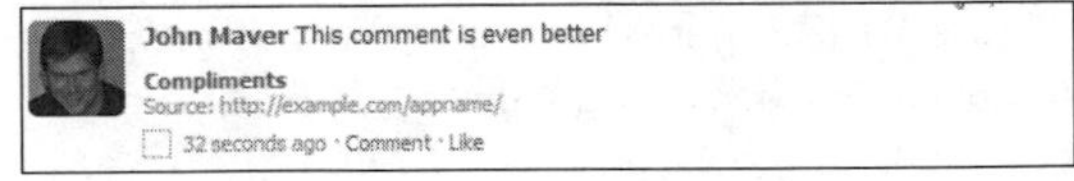

Figure 13.17 A Feed story created by adding a comment to a Comments Box

Next to the submitted comments shown in Figures 13.16, there is a Delete link. This is shown to users listed as Administrators or Moderators in the Developer Settings for the Connected site. At the top of Figure 13.16, also notice the Administer Comments link, which is only shown to Administrators. Clicking this link displays the Widget Settings form shown in Figure 13.18, which is almost identical to the Widgets tab in Developer Settings.

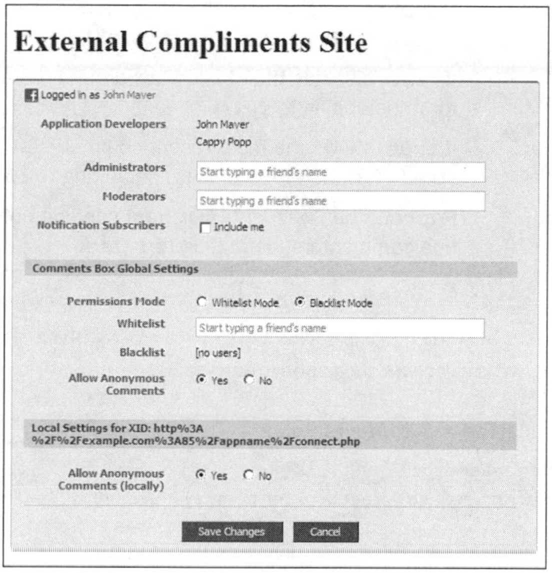

Figure 13.18 Administrators can manage the Comments Box settings by clicking the Administer Comments link on the Comments Box.

To add a Comments Box to your site, use the <fb:comments> XFBML tag. This tag can take the optional attributes listed in Table 13.2.

Table 13.2 **<fb:comments > Attributes**

Tag	Type	Description
xid	string	A unique identifier for these comments. You need to specify your own, because the default is a URL-encoded version of the page URL, which can change if the parameters change. You can use this ID later to programmatically retrieve the comments.
numposts	int	The maximum number of comments to display, defaulting to 10.
width	string	The width of the Comments Box, defaulting to 550px.

Table 13.2 **<fb:comments > Attributes**

Tag	Type	Description
`css`	string	A URL of a stylesheet to use for the Comment Box. Restrictions on these styles are displayed next.
`title`	string	The text to display above the source URL in news stories, defaulting to the web page title.
`url`	string	The URL that is used in the news stories for the source and links, defaulting to the current page URL.
`simple`	bool	If `true`, disables the shaded box around the comment entry form, defaulting to `false`.
`reverse`	bool	If `true`, shows the most recent comments at the bottom instead of at the top of the list, defaulting to `false`.
`quiet`	bool	Prevents the Comments Box from sending notifications to previous commentors, defaulting to `false`.

Listing 13.12 shows how to incorporate a Comments Box into a site. We pass set the `xid` attribute so that we can access these comments later.

Listing 13.12 **Displaying a Comments Box**

```
<script type="text/javascript"
  src="http://static.ak.connect.facebook.com/js/api_lib/v0.4/FeatureLoader.js.php">
</script>
<fb-comments xid='main_1' /></fb-comments>
<script type="text/javascript">
  var apiKey = 'XXXXXXXXXXXXXX';
  var xdReceiverPath = 'xd_receiver.html';
  FB.init(apiKey, xdReceiverPath);
  FB.ensureInit( function() {
  });
</script>}
}
```

Live Stream Box

The Live Stream Box is similar in concept to the Comments Box, but it enables real-time communication rather than long-lived comments. It is scalable, supporting millions of simultaneous users. It also allows users to switch between what everyone is saying and what their friends are saying. Figure 13.8 showed an example.

Listing 13.13 demonstrates how to display a Live Stream Box. The `<fb:live-stream>` XFBML tag can take three optional attributes: `width` of the Box, `height` of the Box, and the `xid` unique identifier of the Box.

Listing 13.13 **Displaying a Live Stream Box**

```
<script type="text/javascript"
  src="http://static.ak.connect.facebook.com/js/api_lib/v0.4/FeatureLoader.js.php">
</script>
<fb:live-stream width="400" height="500" xid="1"></fb:live-stream>
<script type="text/javascript">
  var apiKey = 'XXXXXXXXXXXXXX';
  var xdReceiverPath = 'xd_receiver.html';
  FB.init(apiKey, xdReceiverPath);
  FB.ensureInit( function() {
  });
</script>
```

The Live Stream Box doesn't have the complex administration options of the Comments Box. It just has a Ban User link, which is visible to Administrators and Moderators, next to user posts.

Summary

This chapter covered how Facebook Connect sits on top of the Facebook JavaScript Client Library, extending its features to integrate the Facebook social graph into external websites. We also reviewed the major features of Facebook Connect. Here are some key points:

- Facebook Connect enables single sign-on for external sites, allowing users to log in with their Facebook account. This resulted in large increases in registrations for Connected sites, and these registrations represent real users.
- Users take their settings and information with them to Connected sites, which gives them control over what others can see and enables changes on Facebook to propagate across all of their Facebook Connect sites.
- Integrating the Connect login mechanisms with a website's native user management system can be the most difficult part of the process. Connect provides migration functions and controls to make this easier, such as the `<fb:connect-form>`.

- There are several ways to detect and react to a user's connected state, from the `<fb:login-button>` to the `ifConnected` callback function passed to `FB.init()`. These methods enable sites to display different content to their native and Connected users.
- Facebook Connect provides functions and widgets that enable activities on a Connected site to publish stories to the stream, including links back to the originating website. This can result in more traffic from good content.

IV

Post Launch

14

Measuring Application Success

After spending all the effort to design and implement a stellar Facebook application, developers expect great success and acclamation from users. It can be disconcerting, therefore, when the application fails to attract or retain users. Without a mechanism in place to understand exactly what is causing the failure—difficult workflow, unappealing wording or imagery, or incorrect assumptions—an application is doomed to grow slowly or rely on luck to hit success. A/B testing, along with collecting the metrics to measure its effects, helps developers get their applications to spread on Facebook.

This chapter discusses A/B testing and tuning and goes over what metrics the built-in Facebook Insights and third-party libraries provide and what they mean.

Metrics: Why They Matter

A Facebook application has many channels available to communicate with users: the stream, notifications, email, profile boxes, and requests. Each channel has an associated loop that the application's developers hope will be viral. The goal is to make each channel's communication bring in new users or re-engage existing ones. You can achieve this through understanding the viral loops, implementing metrics to gather data on how users interact with the application, and using A/B testing to tune the application.

> **Note**
>
> Virality is a term that that describes the growth rate of applications and is based on a metaphor of infectious diseases, such as viruses. Virality is based on the number of people who can spread the disease (users) and how easily it can infect others (cause new installations).

Viral Loop

You can measure the virality (or k-factor) of a communication channel generally as k = *communication* * *engagement of others*. So, if an application's users each send requests to 5 friends, and 25 percent of those friends install the application, that channel has a virality of 1.25. Anything above 1 means that the application is growing virally, with the goal being to maximize this value for each channel. An application's overall k-factor is the sum of the individual channel k-factors. So, if an application has notifications at .3, invitations at .7, and news stories at .6, the overall k-factor of 1.6 means that the application is growing well.

Each channel can be measured in even more depth by tracking the entire communication process: Each invitation is opened by 50 percent of the recipients, 60 percent of those users add the application, and 80 percent of those users don't uninstall it right away. With 5 requests sent, that is a k-factor of 5 * .5 * .6 * .8 = 1.2, as shown in Figure 14.1. A good application makes sure that it uses as many of these communication channels as possible and optimizes each one's effectiveness. This does not mean spamming; in fact, measurement of the viral channels can show exactly how much contact users want or can tolerate from your application.

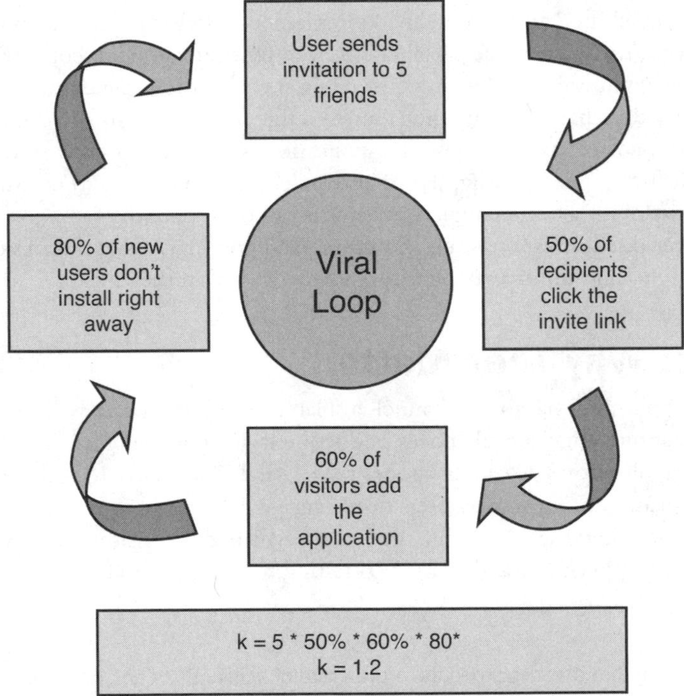

Figure 14.1 Viral loop for application invitations

It is important to measure both the overall k-factor and the percentage of each stage in the loop continuously, especially if your application is making changes to how it uses these channels. You then immediately know whether those changes had a positive effect or stalled your growth. It also helps deal with the eventual drop-off in the effectiveness of each channel, as users become inured to its effects or Facebook switches the platform to focus on newer communication methods.

Jesse Farmer, on his blog (*http://20bits.com*) describes two models for how users come to install an application:

- **Threshold model.** Users install applications because enough of their friends have. Each person has his own internal threshold: Some will try anything and others resist specifically because all of their friends are using it. The Threshold model is only valid after an application already has some type of user base.
- **Cascade model.** Also called word of mouth, this model says that a user installs an application as a result of a friend directly interacting with them, such as an invitation or notification. Friends who are more influential have a higher chance of affecting behavior. The Cascade model is what the k-factor measures for a communication channel. Applications rely on the Cascade model until they reach a sufficient number of users for the Threshold model to apply.

Collecting Metrics

Metrics are critical to understanding both the viral loop and how users respond to application features. Developers can implement their own metrics-collection system to track feature usage and conversions. Facebook also provides some general metrics in the form of its Insights tools and some FBML tags to add Quantcast or Google Analytics to canvas pages. Third-party developers, such as Kontagent, released instrumented versions of Facebook client libraries to enable more detailed tracking. The section, "Metrics Dashboards," discusses them.

Metrics enable you to make decisions based on data rather than assumptions. Combining metrics with a methodology like A/B testing, which is discussed in the next section, can lead to effective tuning of application features and communication channels. With a reasonable number of users, the time between starting to test and getting enough data to support a decision can be short.

Not all metrics need to be based on running software. Some metrics might simply be the results of in-person user-experience testing using mockups or paper testing. By validating new concepts and features early in the development cycle, you can save time and headaches later. This also allows for much quicker development cycles, which enables applications to evolve to meet users' needs.

When in doubt, test. However, metrics must be limited to things that matter and you can take action on. Too much data about the little things can cause you to lose focus on areas that you can actually improve. The metrics should also be part of measuring desired outcomes—new user installs, repeat user visits, and virtual currency purchases. This helps you decide where to apply your development resources: If increasing the number of news stories generated by 10 percent increases your user count by 20 percent, but increasing your notification response by 30 percent increases user count by only 10 percent, news-story generation is where you need to spend time.

Segmenting metrics into larger categories can help you get a quick feel for how an application is doing. You might use groupings, such as Acquisition, Engagement, Retention, and Revenue. Be careful that you also understand what they are based on, so that you don't miss important indicators. For example, aggregate metrics like Daily or Monthly Active Users measure both new users and existing users. It is possible for this number to increase only because new users come once and never return. Eventually, an application like this will die out when enough users have had their one pass at it. So, watch the summaries, but drill down into the aggregate metrics.

Some large development shops, like Slide, have 10 percent of their staff devoted to metrics, but that is obviously not feasible for individual developers or small companies. Applications can start out using Facebook Insights with no additional work needed and get some basic application usage data. Developers can also add basic tracking to the application by appending tags to the end of URLs used in communication channels, which makes it simple to find out how users are getting to the application, as shown in Figure 14.2. Facebook has recently added support for tracking the origins of user application authorizations. You can append `app_ref=<upto8chars>` to the Facebook add URL, like we do here, to see the results in Facebook Insights for that application:

```
http://www.facebook.com/add.php?api_key=YOUR_API_KEY&app_ref=<upto8chars>
```

Origins of installs

Origin	installs
app	379
directory	639
invite	50,793
profile	1,165
search	113

Figure 14.2 Simple tracking of application-installation origins using home-grown metrics

A/B Testing

A/B testing, sometimes called split-testing, means comparing the effects of two things. Most often, option A is the existing version, and option B is the new version. In a Facebook application, these two options can be entire workflows, the text of a news story, or the layout of a canvas page. An application randomly displays either option and uses metrics to determine which one had the desired effect. A/B tests can also help determine the order of steps in a workflow, such as presenting a Feed dialog before or after displaying the results of an action. The results of A/B tests can be surprising, because it replaces assumptions with real data; users might not prefer a better-looking interface or be able to use a new feature at all.

Facebook uses A/B testing itself, most publicly in the release of its new application menu. Facebook wanted to ensure that users discovered and used the Bookmarks effectively, and it went through many design iterations before finalizing on what we have today.

If you make A/B testing a normal part of the development process (which is simple to do), you and your developers are more likely to use it. The alternative is to rely on intuition or do what the whitepaper "Practical Guide to Controlled Experiments on the Web: Listen to Your Customers not to the HiPPO," by the Microsoft Experimentation Platform Team (*http://exp-platform.com/hippo.aspx*) refers to as listening to the HiPPO (Highest Paid Person's Opinion). This is a person with the power to make decisions who might not have the data to back it up. This paper describes how efforts at Amazon, Microsoft, Dupont, and NASA have seen a greater return on investment and increased innovation because of this type of testing.

Let's go through an example for the Compliments application. Currently, it is seeing only a 2 percent install rate for the notifications that it generates when a user sends a compliment. The current text users receive is "John Maver sent you a Compliment!" We think that a call to action might improve this, so we want to test "John Maver sent you a Compliment! Click here to send your own." A simple A/B test would be to change our PHP code that sends the notifications to what is shown in Listing 14.1. We create strings for both the old and new notifications and pick a number between 1 and 2. If the number is 1, we show the old notification and if it is 2, we show the new one.

Listing 14.1 **Sample Code to Randomly Send Notifications for A/B Testing**

```
$notification1 = "sent <fb:name uid='$target' /> a ".
                 "<b><a href='".FB_APP_URL."&n=1'>Compliment</a></b>";

$notification2 = "sent <fb:name uid='$target' /> a ".
                 "<b>Compliment</b>.".
                 "<a href='".FB_APP_URL."&n=2'>Click here to send your own</a>.";

if ( rand(1 , 2) == 1 ) {
  $notification = $notification1;
else {
  $notification = $notification2;
}

$return = $facebook->api_client->notifications_send( array($target),
                                                      $notification,
                                                      'user_to_user');
```

We ran this test for a day, and Table 14.1 shows the results.

Table 14.1 **Day 1 Results for Notification A/B Test**

Option	Visitors	Clicks	Conversion Rate
`Original`	51	1	2%
`New`	50	6	12%

It looks like the new notification is a winner, but we have to check that it is statistically significant. The more notifications we send out, the more likely that the results aren't just random noise. To determine its significance, we can use the following calculation (a Pearson's Chi-Square test with a confidence of 95 percent):

N = Total number of clicks = 7

D = (Option 1 click – Option 2 clicks) / 2 = 2.5

D^2 = 6.25

The results are significant if D^2 is greater than N. 6.25 is not bigger than 7, so we don't have enough test results yet. We need to let this test run longer. After another day, we get the results shown in Table 14.2.

Table 14.2 **Day 2 Results for Notification A/B Test**

#Option	Visitors	Clicks	Conversion Rate
`Original`	100	2	2%
`New`	100	12	12%

This time, the calculation is

N = 14

D = 5

D^2 = 25

25 is greater than 13, so our new notification is a good change and needs to be made permanent.

Note

Pearson's Chi-Square test is a statistical procedure for comparing the distribution of results versus expectations. More recently, the G-test has becoming increasingly used as computers are able to handle the more time-consuming calculations.

One downside to A/B testing is that if the new option isn't good, all the users that experience it are getting a bad experience. You can mitigate this by reducing the percentage of users seeing the new option below 50 percent, but you then need to wait longer for the results to be statistically significant. It also doesn't tell you why users picked one over the other; you have to conduct interviews to figure that out.

Metrics Dashboards

A dashboard is a single place to reference all the metrics you have collected and possibly perform additional analysis or display trends. If you are collecting your own custom metrics, we encourage you to build a simple dashboard. This section goes over the dashboards supplied by Facebook and the Kontagent Analytics package.

Facebook Insights and the Metrics API

We already covered using Facebook's Insights tool to monitor user response to messaging and Facebook messaging allocations in Chapter 10, "Publisher, Notifications, and Requests." However, this tool provides more data than this for application developers; moreover, much of the data that backs it is available through the Facebook application programming interface (API). This gives developers a great opportunity to develop their own custom monitoring solutions, dashboards, and A/B testing frameworks.

Looking at Metrics in Facebook Insights

Figure 14.3 shows the Insights tool containing actual data for Active Users (Engagement) from a live application, currently with several hundred thousand active monthly users. Notice that there are several tabs' worth of data available to the developer. The following sections discuss not only the metrics on each tab, but also how to get them programmatically. Additionally, we explain how the metrics named in the Insights tool map to the names used to access them using the API.

The first tab, Usage, contains several different metrics that focus on user engagement with the application and that application's interaction with the Facebook Platform. Table 14.3 describes them in detail. The first column shows the name of the metric as shown in the Insights tool, the second is the name of the metric as it's used when accessing it the Facebook API, which we cover later. Granularity explains the number of different values that are available for a given metric type.

Table 14.3 **Facebook Insights: Usage Metric**

Metric (Insights)	Metric (API)	Description	Granularity
Active Users (Engagement)	`active_users`	Total number of active users for the application	Last 1-,7-, and 30 days

Table 14.3 **Facebook Insights: Usage Metric**

Metric (Insights)	Metric (API)	Description	Granularity
Active Users (API)	`unique_api_calls`	Number of users whose use of the application resulted in a Facebook API call	Last 1-,7-, and 30 days
Canvas Page Views	`canvas_page_views`	Total number of application canvas page views	Last 1-,7-, and 30 days
Unique Canvas Page Views	`unique_canvas_page_views`	Total number of users who viewed at least one of an application's canvas pages	Last 1-,7-, and 30 days
Average HTTP Request Time on Canvas Pages (ms)	`canvas_http_request_time_avg`	The average time required to finish an individual HTTP request for the application's canvas pages	Last 1-,7-, and 30 days
Average FBML Render Time on Canvas Pages (ms)	`canvas_fbml_render_time_avg`	The average time is took Facebook to render the application's canvas pages	Last 1-,7-, and 30 days
Unique Blocks	`unique_blocks`	The number of users who blocked the application	1 day only
Unique Unblocks	`unique_unblocks`	The number of users who unblocked the application	1 day only
API Calls	`api_calls`	Total number of API calls made by the application	Last 1-,7-, and 30 days
Unique API Calls	`unique_api_calls (alias)`	Number of users whose use of the application resulted in a Facebook API call (alias)	Last 1-,7-, and 30 days

The next tab, HTTP Request, has three sections: the status codes summary, recent HTTP requests, and a graph of an HTTP status codes returned over the selected time period. Figure 14.4 shows the status code summary and recent HTTP requests. The summary shows that most requests that are returned are status code 200, which is great;

however, almost 25 percent of those return no data, which is something that the developer might want to look into. The recent requests show the full URL for the HTTP request, which can help diagnose problems.

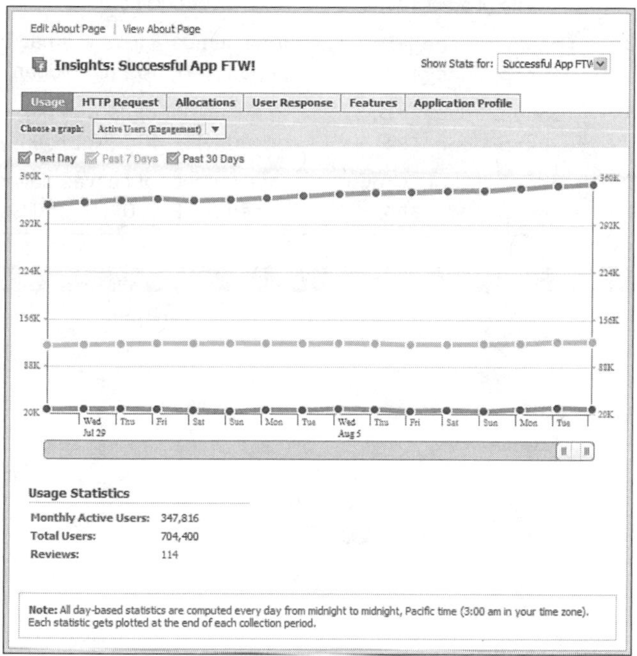

Figure 14.3 The Facebook Insights tool shows data for different time periods. Here, it shows Active Users (Engagement) for a popular Facebook application.

Figure 14.5 displays trend data for individual HTTP status codes. This can be useful to look through, because patterns in usage or errors show up that might not otherwise be found.

Table 14.4 correlates the name of the HTTP request metric in the Insights tool with the name used for it when using the API. Only some of the status codes are discussed here. Facebook provides metrics for all the major HTTP status codes supported by the protocol.

Table 14.4 **Facebook Insights: HTTP Request Metrics**

Metric (Insights)	Metric (API)	Description
HTTP Code 0	`canvas_page_views_http_code_0`	Total number of canvas pages that timed out while loading
HTTP Code 200	`canvas_page_views_http_code_200`	Total number of canvas pages that returned HTTP 200 (OK)

Table 14.4 **Facebook Insights: HTTP Request Metrics**

Metric (Insights)	Metric (API)	Description
HTTP Code 200 (ND)	`canvas_page_views _http_code_200ND`	Total number of canvas pages that returned OK and *no data*
HTTP Code 403	`canvas_page_views _http_code_403`	Total number of canvas pages that returned HTTP 403 (Forbidden)
HTTP Code 404	`canvas_page_views _http_code_404`	Total number of canvas pages that returned HTTP 404 (Not Found)
HTTP Code 500	`canvas_page_views _http_code_500`	Total number of canvas pages that returned HTTP 500 (Internal Server Error)

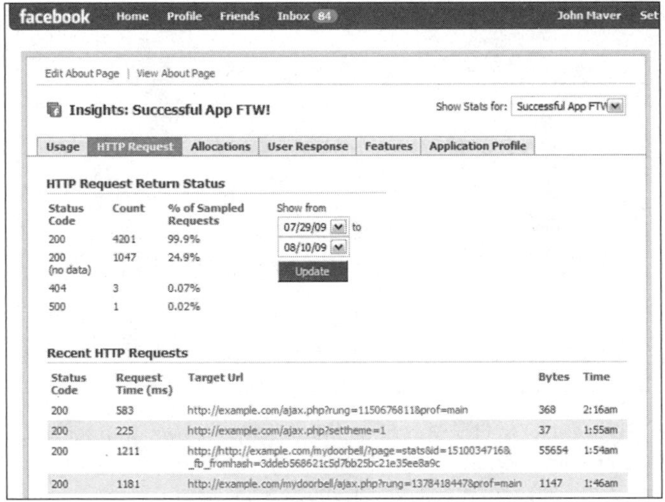

Figure 14.4 The HTTP Request tab in Insights shows the status codes that the application has been returning.

Finally, the Features tab shows metrics that are not currently available from the Facebook API and represents aggregated data for feature-based user interactions on Facebook as they relate to an application. Dozens of metrics are available, too many to list in this section; however, some of them are incredibly useful because they are given *nowhere else* in Facebook, the API, or from third-party tools. For example, Figure 14.6 shows the number of canvas page views for a popular Facebook application over a six-month period. Figure 14.7 shows some of the unique metrics available on this tab. The major categories of these metrics are summarized in the following list:

- **Canvas.** Aggregated metrics for canvas pages, including total number of links clicked on all of an application's canvas pages and errors encountered when serving or viewing them.

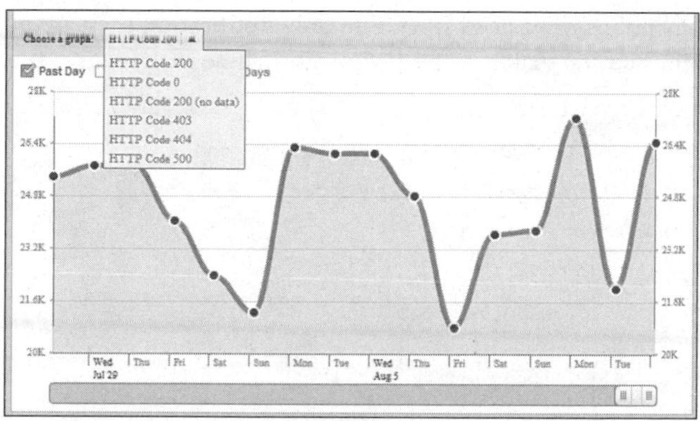

Figure 14.5 The HTTP Request tab in Insights also has a graph that shows the status codes that the application has been returning over time.

Figure 14.6 The Features tab provides interesting metrics, such as a long historical view of total canvas page views.

- **Feed.** Incredibly valuable, because this category provides developers with metrics telling how many times an application's users clicked the Publish or Cancel (Skip) buttons in Feed submission dialogs (from either Feed forms, Publishers, or other sources). As discussed in Chapter 9, "Feed Stories, Feed Forms, and Templates," and Chapter 10, there is no way for developers to programmatically know whether a user actually published a Feed story. The only notification they are given is when they've dismissed the dialog, published or not. These metrics give those numbers.

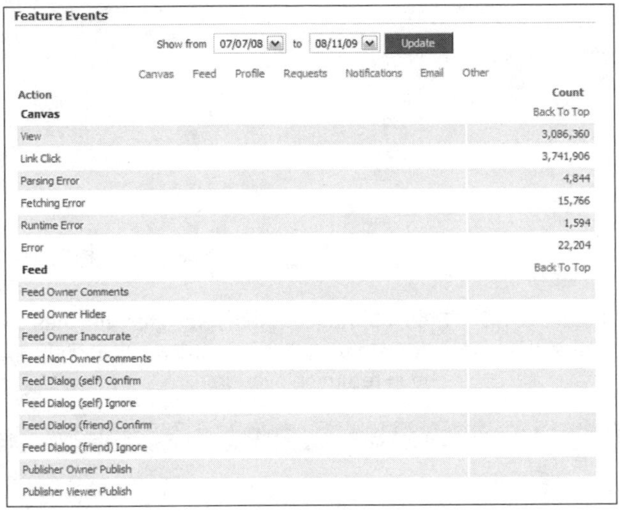

Feature Events

Show from 07/07/08 to 08/11/09 Update

Canvas Feed Profile Requests Notifications Email Other

Action	Count
Canvas	Back To Top
View	3,086,360
Link Click	3,741,906
Parsing Error	4,844
Fetching Error	15,766
Runtime Error	1,594
Error	22,204
Feed	Back To Top
Feed Owner Comments	
Feed Owner Hides	
Feed Owner Inaccurate	
Feed Non-Owner Comments	
Feed Dialog (self) Confirm	
Feed Dialog (self) Ignore	
Feed Dialog (friend) Confirm	
Feed Dialog (friend) Ignore	
Publisher Owner Publish	
Publisher Viewer Publish	

Figure 14.7 Some of the unique metrics offered on the Features tab of the Insights tool include ones found nowhere else, such as these for canvas page errors and Feed dialog interactions.

- **Profile.** Gives metrics and interaction data for Facebook profile boxes and application tabs, which, as we discussed throughout this book, are cached and served from Facebook's own servers and not the developers' servers. Facebook provides information on the number of times users add or remove profile boxes, Info sections, or application tabs for an application, and how many clicks were made on them by the actual owners of the profiles or by viewers.
- **Requests.** Gives similar data to the User Response tab discussed in Chapter 10; however, they also provide the number of times application users clicked the Skip button on the requests or invitations generated by it.
- **Notifications.** Centers around only user-to-user notifications and gives detailed information on the number of times they were clicked by their recipients and the number of them flagged as spam by recipients and incorrectly tagged as spam by senders, among others.
- **Email.** Gives the numbers of emails successfully sent during a given time period and the number of total number of users who granted or revoked the email extended permission to the application.
- **Other.** Catch-all category that provides developers with information on numbers of violation reports submitted to Facebook by users in a specific time period (for

example, drugs, violence, or privacy violations). It also provides details on the number of times the application was bookmarked.

Using the Facebook API to Get Metrics

Facebook provides a programmatic way to get more detailed application metrics by using the API. Developers can use the `admin.getMetrics()` function or FQL to query the `application` and `metrics` tables; we go over each. This metrics data can be merged with any custom application metrics into a developer dashboard.

The `admin.getMetrics()` function uses the metrics FQL table to return the information in Table 14.3 and Table 14.4. Up to 30 days of metrics can be returned at a time, using 1 day (86,400 seconds), 7 day (604,800 seconds), or 30 day (2,592,000 seconds) periods. Listing 14.2 shows how to get the number of total active users for the last 30 days and the results from the PHP client library.

Listing 14.2 **Using `admin.getMetrics()` to Get the Total Active User Count over the Last 30 Days**

```
$result = $facebook->api_client->admin_getMetrics(strtotime("-29 days"), time(),
 86400, array('active_users'));

/** Results
array
  0 =>
    array
      'end_time' => string '1247641200' (length=10)
      'active_users' => string '754,383' (length=1)
  1 =>
    array
      'end_time' => string '1247727600' (length=10)
      'active_users' => string '754,440' (length=1)
  2 =>
    array
      'end_time' => string '1247814000' (length=10)
      'active_users' => string '755,221' (length=1)
...
*/
```

Using FQL, we can access the `application` table to get the daily, weekly, and monthly active user values. Listing 14.3 shows sample code that fetches all three values.

Listing 14.3 **Using `admin.getMetrics()` to Get the Total Active User Count over the Last 30 Days**

```
$query = "SELECT daily_active_users, weekly_active_users, monthly_active_users
          FROM application
          WHERE app_id  = ".FB_APP_ID;
```

Listing 14.3 **Continued**

```
$result = $facebook->api_client->fql_query($query);

/** Results
array
  0 =>
    array
      'daily_active_users' => string '27479' (length=5)
      'weekly_active_users' => string '124004' (length=6)
      'monthly_active_users' => string '347816' (length=6)
*/
```

Kontagent

Kontagent (*www.kontagent.com*) provides several metrics and monitoring options for Facebook applications. It offers both free and premium services. The premium service offers more options; however, even its free services add incredible value, on top of Facebook metrics collected via Insights. Plus, it provides a free dashboard that provides in-depth graphs of all the metrics it collects. Its services are based on a data-collection REST API that applications call directly or through one of their free libraries. Currently, it provides free libraries for PHP, Ruby on Rails, and .NET. To use Kontagent to collect metrics for their applications, developers have three options:

- **Wrapper libraries.** Using the wrapper libraries is the easiest but least customizable option. Developers don't need to make many changes to their code, except including a few files and modifying a few calls to pass extra parameters for tracking. In the Kontagent PHP wrapper, for example, developers simply create an instance of Kontagent's `Kt_Facebook` class, which extends the PHP Library's `Facebook` class, and use it instead to make their API calls. Kontagent transparently handles data collection and calls the automatically appropriate Facebook methods.
- **Low-level wrapper.** For PHP developers who use a custom Facebook wrapper library, Kontagent provides a low-level wrapper that abstracts the direct calls to the Kontagent REST API. Developers just directly call their analytics functions and make the calls to Facebook as normal.
- **REST API.** For those developers that use either the Facebook REST-like API directly or client libraries (such as the ActionScript 3 Library discussed in Chapter 11, "FBJS, Mock AJAX, and Flash," for example) that Kontagent cannot wrap, Kontagent provides a complete REST API to directly report metrics.

Kontagent Metrics

Kontagent collects several metrics that Facebook's Insights tool does not. The following list describes several features that its APIs provide for free. More importantly, it does this *without* violating the Facebook Terms of Service, which means that developers can focus on *acting* on data rather than worrying that they are collecting, storing, or using it in violation of Facebook policy:

- **Facebook viral channel monitoring.** Kontagent tracks most major Facebook messaging channels, including invitations, requests, notifications (both user-to-user and application-to-user), and Feed stories. Developers can categorize calls to these channels by using developer-defined categories or subtypes to make A/B testing of messaging much easier, automatically.
- **Viral growth tracking.** Using its TrueVirality feature, Kontagent tracks not only viral growth (k-factor), but does so for each viral channel and tracks origination points of each install.
- **Detailed demographics.** Kontagent breaks Facebook user demographics down by age, gender, geographic location, and more. This allows easy identification of applications' most active users.
- **Engagement monitoring.** Developers can use this feature to easily find what parts of their applications are being used and filter the results demographically. The authors have actually used this feature to discover, much to their surprise, that their successful applications' largest and most active demographic was not whom they predicted, and, in fact, were not even from the *countries* they expected. This information is critical: It allows developers to tie applications to their target audiences intimately and quickly provide content that can be customized or localized to their most active segments.

Kontagent also offers a paid premium service that provides more features, including automatic monetization tracking, feature-based testing, benchmarking, advertising/traffic monitoring, and more.

Kontagent Dashboards

Not only does Kontagent provide an API, it also provides a free dashboard that developers can use to get a graphical view of their applications' performance, metrics, or demographics. Most of the dashboards provide detailed filtering options, such as the ability to view installs broken down by age, gender, time, and geographic location. Figure 14.8 shows the demographic filtering in action.

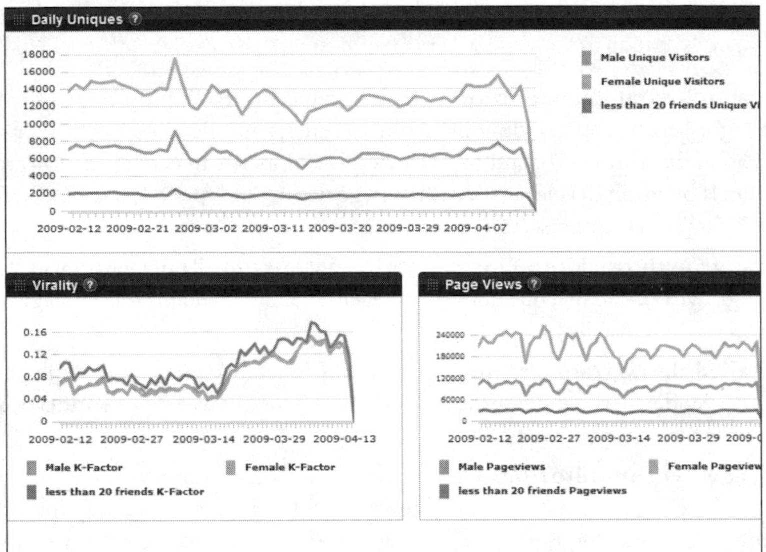

Figure 14.8 Kontagent provides free dashboards for viewing its metrics and monitoring results.

Summary

This chapter discussed the viral loop, why metrics are important, how to use A/B testing, and Facebook Insights and Kontagent's Analytics package. Here are some key points:

- The virality of a communication channel is measured by the amount of communication multiplied by the resulting engagement. The goal is to get this value to be larger than 1 for an application to grow virally.
- Metrics are better than intuition for making sure that the changes made to an application have a useful impact. Without them, the HiPPO tends to dominate.
- A/B testing is the comparison of two options by randomly displaying them to users. It is important to make sure that the data is statistically significant to rule out the effects of chance. Using metrics collected during the test, developers can determine whether a new option is a useful change to make to an application.
- Facebook Insights automatically provides developers with metrics and graphs about how many users are accessing the application, page views, and HTTP Request status codes.
- Developers can use the API to retrieve application metrics for use in their own dashboards. These can be pulled for a 30-day period in 1, 7, or 30-day increments.
- The Kontagent Analytics library provides two levels of advanced application metrics. Developers can either use the Kontagent library as a wrapper for a Facebook client library or add individual calls to the Kontagent REST API to track metrics. Kontagent provides an interactive dashboard to help with metrics analysis.

15

Spreading and Monetizing Applications

This chapter describes the ways developers can help their application spread. It discusses how to seed the application with users via advertising, co-promoting, and other methods. It also goes over some of the ways that applications can generate income.

Spreading Your Application

The days of building a Facebook application and having it rocket to millions of users overnight are gone. Too many applications are vying for attention and the Platform has tightened up many of the viral channels that were exploited by early applications. In some ways, this is a blessing. Even if you have conducted exhaustive private beta tests using Sandbox mode, real-world users are likely to do things with your application that surprise you. Having more time to react to user feedback at the start helps refine workflow issues and ferret out bugs. Figure 15.1 shows a possible growth curve for an application.

In most cases, applications must develop an initial critical mass of users that then spread the application to their friends and enable growth. This section goes over several ways for applications to do this. We assume that your application follows the best practices outlined in Chapter 2, "Making Great Applications," for identifying the target demographic, adding value, and enabling engagement.

However, before you spend a dime on promoting your application, make sure that you have exhaustively analyzed and fine-tuned your application as Chapter 14, "Measuring Application Success," detailed. If your application has difficult workflows, users aren't coming back, or the viral channels are not helping it spread, any money you throw at it is going down the drain.

After you are sure that your application is as good as it can be, you can look at promoting it on Facebook, both within the site and other applications, using ads. Two kinds of ads can help spread an application. The first are Facebook Ads, which Facebook provides. They are shown throughout the Facebook user interface along the right side of the screen. The second is using some of the many Ad Networks that supply ad inventory for other applications to display.

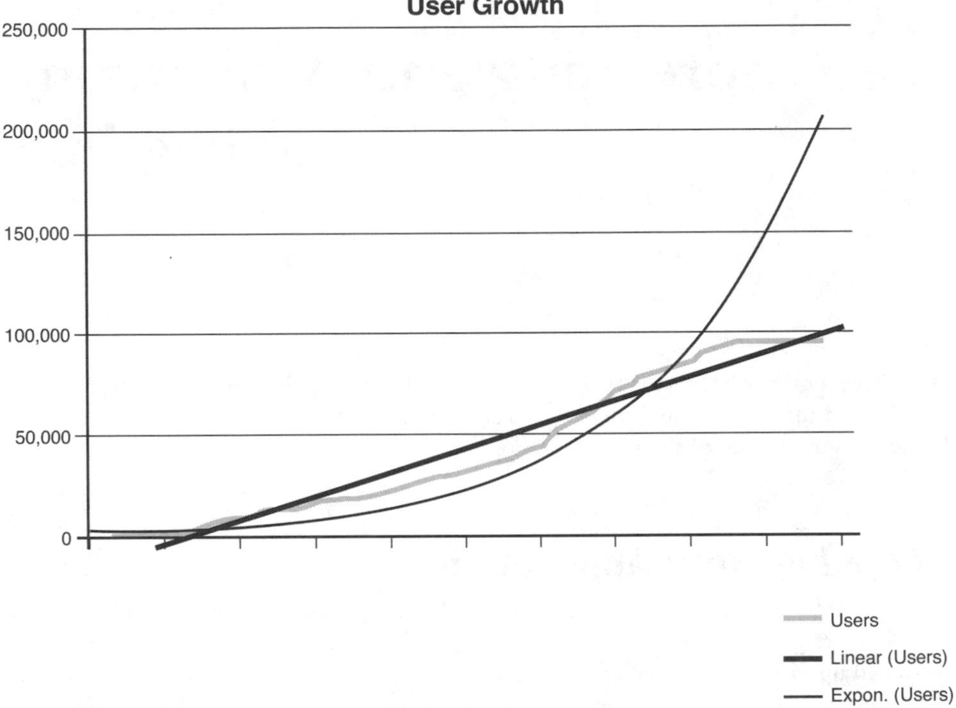

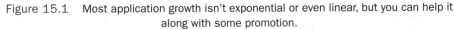

Figure 15.1 Most application growth isn't exponential or even linear, but you can help it along with some promotion.

Facebook Ads

Facebook has two ad tiers: Home page Ads and Standard Ads. Home page Ads integrate into users' Home pages, as shown in Figure 15.2. This is key real estate with a lot of views, and the pricing reflects that. Home page Ad campaigns have minimum purchases in the tens of thousands of dollars and a $5–7 CPM cost. This is probably only an option for applications with large budgets.

Standard Ads appear on all the other Facebook pages, including application canvas pages. Figure 15.3 shows what these ads look like.

Standard Ads use a self-service model that is useful not only for creating targeted ads, but also for understanding the size of Facebook demographics and for doing A/B testing of ad messaging; you can create many different ads with slightly different content or targets and measure the response. Here is a walkthrough of creating an ad for the Compliments application.

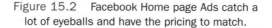

Figure 15.2 Facebook Home page Ads catch a lot of eyeballs and have the pricing to match.

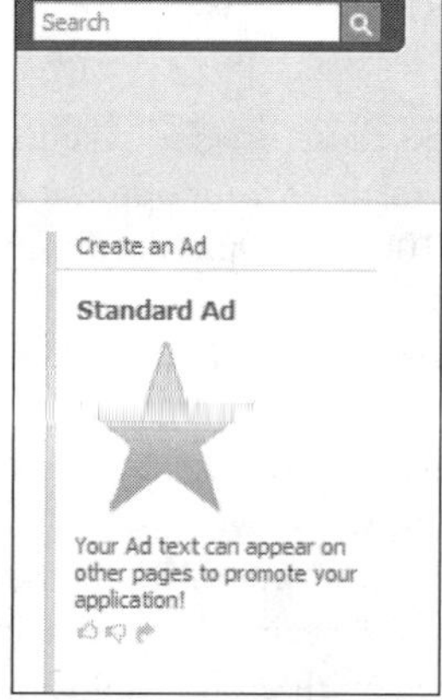

Figure 15.3 Facebook Standard Ads can appear on all the other Facebook pages.

Go to the Facebook Ads Manager (*www.facebook.com/ads/manage/*) and click the Create Ad button. You then see the Design Your Ad section (see Figure 15.4). Click the I Want to Advertise Something I Have on Facebook link and select Compliments from the Facebook Content dropdown. Fill out the rest of the Title and Body as we do in the image. Notice that each field is limited in the number of characters.

Your Title and Description need to describe the application briefly without overwhelming the viewer with details. They must also include a call to action to install the application. The text cannot contain any formatting or blank lines, so you might have to play with the text to make it look like it is spaced correctly. You also cannot use or refer to Facebook in the text. That also includes abbreviations, such as FB.

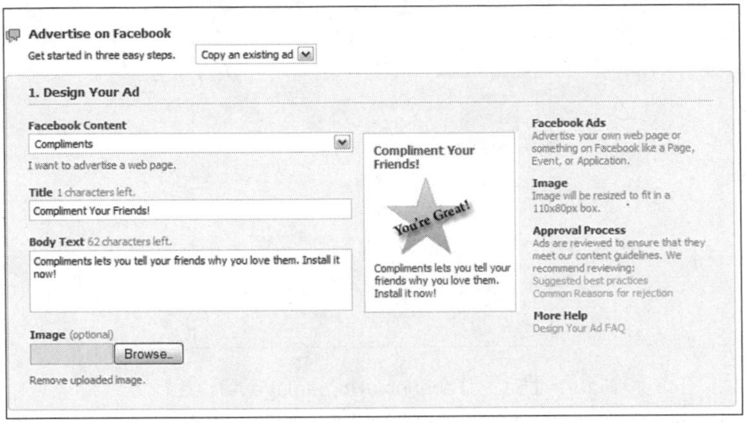

Figure 15.4 Designing a Facebook ad requires carefully crafting the message and image to stand out and drive action.

The Image should stand out and cause users to take notice. It need not be your application logo, but it must somehow relate to your application. The one strange thing about the Image is that it is limited to 110px by 80px. This is smaller than the width of the ad box and slightly shifts it to the left.

Each ad must be approved before it runs, so make sure that you review Facebook's Common Ad Mistakes (*www.facebook.com/ads/mistakes.php*) and Advertising Guidelines (*www.facebook.com/ad_guidelines.php*). If your ad is rejected, modify it to remove the offending text or image and resubmit it.

After you create the ad content, it is time to set the targeting settings shown in Figure 15.5. This process can be enlightening, because Facebook updates the Estimate of the people matching the parameters with each change. In the figure, we chose to target users who live in the United States aged 18 and older who have set "awesomeness" as one of their interests. This provides us with an estimate of 34,860 people. If we had removed all targeting except United States, the estimate would be 75,694,320 people. If we restrict this even further by specifying people who live in Boston, 18 and up, who like "awesomeness" and are male, we get just 160 people. So, targeting helps you focus your ads on specific groups. The smaller the group, the more likely your ad is to be shown.

The one key item we want to set is the Target Users Who Are Not Already Connected To field. We don't want our ads to be shown to users who have already installed our application, so enter Compliments in that box.

The pricing section is shown in Figure 15.6. You can choose to create a new named campaign or add this ad to an existing one. Because this is our first ad, we choose a new one. We call it Gain Critical Mass.

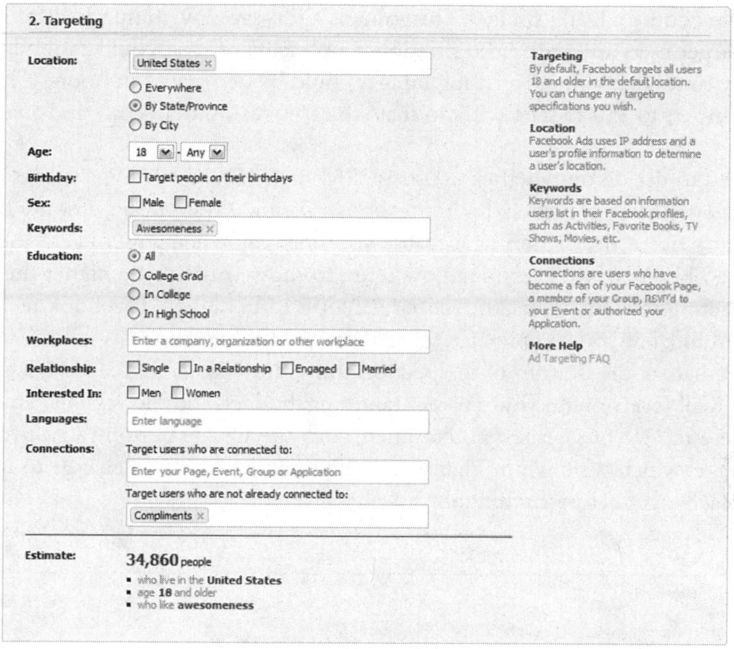

Figure 15.5 Targeting Facebook Ads makes sure that they are shown to the users you want to install your application.

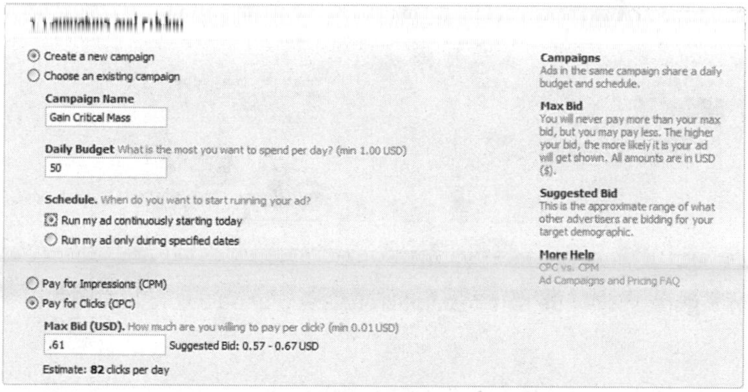

Figure 15.6 Setting the budget and bid for an ad determines how often it will be shown.

Next, we choose a Daily Budget. This value is a life-saver. With hundreds of millions of potential target users and with no restrictions in place, Facebook could easily show your ad so many times that your advertising budget could be decimated in hours, if not sooner. We leave this set to $50 to start with, so that we can tweak our ad copy and analyze the results.

You need to decide on whether to use a CPM or CPC model. CPM means cost per thousand views (Mille is French/Latin for thousand), and CPC means cost per click. CPC is safer to go with at the beginning, because you only pay when a user clicks the ad. Facebook uses a bid system to determine how often to show your ad; the higher the bid versus ads targeting the same users, the more likely it is to be shown. Facebook recommends a maximum bid, but you can pick anything above 1 cent.

The Estimate at the bottom of that section shows how many clicks or views Facebook thinks you will receive with your current targeting, budget, and bid, so you can play with each of these to get your desired results. Then, click the Create button to go to the Review Ad page, which is shown in Figure 15.7. This page gives you a change to make any last-minute changes before running the ad.

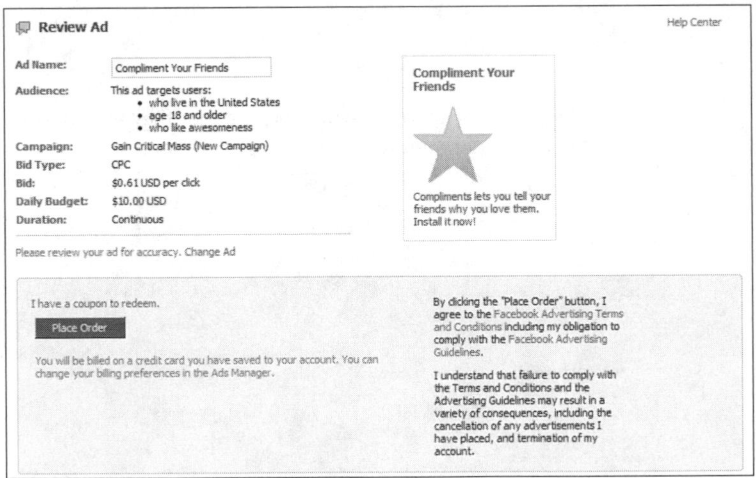

Figure 15.7 Be sure to carefully review your ad before it goes live.

After you verify the information and click the Place Order button, go back to the Ads Manager page on which we started. Your new campaign is displayed (see Figure 15.8). You can see that it is marked as Pending review—no ads are shown until Facebook approves it.

After it is approved and starts to run, your campaign receives daily status updates. In Figure 15.9, we display some data for a test ad that ran for about 2 hours. You can see that the ad was displayed over 270,000 times and resulting in 70 clicks. We might spend some time trying to improve the ad content or better target it to improve that click-through ratio from .03 percent.

Gain Critical Mass (running) edit Daily Budget $10.00 USD Since 07/31/2009

Name	Status	Max Bid ($)	Type	Imp.	Clicks	CTR (%)	Avg. CPC ($)	Avg. CPM ($)	Spent ($)
Compliment Your Friends	Pending review	0.61	CPC	Your ad is awaiting approval. [?]					
Totals				0	0	0.00	0.00	0.00	0.00

Figure 15.8 Before they start running, newly created ads must be approved by Facebook.

Daily stats for the week of: Aug 01

Date	Imp.	Clicks	CTR (%)	Avg. CPC ($)	Avg. CPM ($)	Spent ($)
08/01/2009	270,405	70	0.03	0.46	0.12	32.43
Lifetime	270,405	70	0.03	0.46	0.12	32.43

Figure 15.9 Facebook provides daily statistics on how each ad is doing for impressions and clicks.

Ad Networks

Some of the early leader application developers, such as RockYou and Slide, have been able to gather millions of daily users, and they now offer the opportunity to display ads inside their own applications. Other ad networks, such as Cubics (www.cubics.com), allow you to display your ads inside any application that publishes their ads. Ads in these networks have the potential to offer higher click-through ratios than Facebook Ads, because these users are likely to install additional applications since they already have installed at least one to see the ad.

Applications supply these networks with a set of ad images in a variety of sizes and an end-point URL. In some cases, you spend a preset amount to get a set number of CPM or CPC, such as $5,000 to get 6,500 clicks. Other services use a budget/bid system similar to Facebook. When planning your ad campaign, it is a good idea to get a feel for the prices of these other networks.

Developer Link Exchanges

Many developers are unhappy with the thought of having to advertise to spread their application, and a few options emerge for sharing links instead. Link exchanges work by developers putting their application's URL into a pool. Applications earn credits for displaying other application's links on their canvas page. Applications use credits when their application's link is displayed by other applications. No one has to pay anything and everyone benefits. fbExchange (*http://fbexchange.com*) and Cubics both offer link exchanges, and new ones seem to pop up all the time. Figure 15.10 shows what a link exchange ad from might look like.

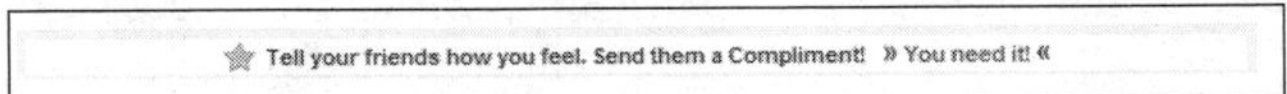

Figure 15.10 Link exchanges provide a free alternative to advertising for promoting an application.

The Facebook Developer Forums also have requests from other developers to share links. It can be worth some time searching for these posts and building relationships with other developers to help spread your application for free.

Monetizing Your Application

After you launch and grow your application, one of your goals might be to make some money from it. We go over several ways to do this in this section. However, something to keep in mind is that you want to make sure that your monetization efforts don't drive away your users with pages filled with flashing ads or virtual goods that don't relate to the application.

Displaying Ads

A huge number of companies offer application developers ads to publish inside their application canvas pages. These ads can either be from external advertisers or from other Facebook applications. Each works to acquire an inventory of advertisers, so all a developer needs to do is add a few HTML tags onto his canvas pages to display them. It is best to try to integrate ads from the beginning of the application's design process. If you develop a user base with an ad-free application, and then try to monetize the application using ads, you might experience heated resistance. Figure 15.11 shows a typical banner ad for another application.

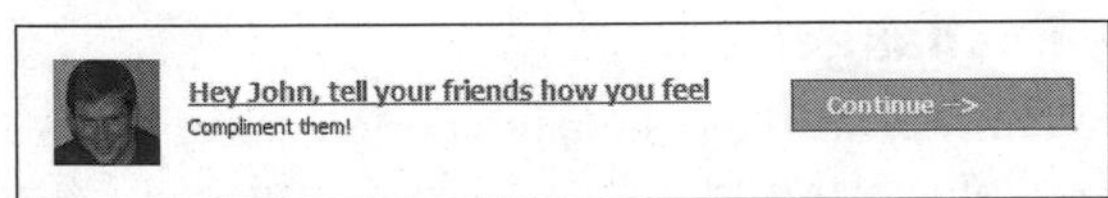

Figure 15.11 Banner ads can be as simple as this or graphically rich with flash animations.

Applications with a lot of traffic can earn a reasonably good income using ads. However, different ad networks can generate different returns, and these returns can change over time. It is best to either set up multiple ad networks in some type of rotation or change your ad network from time to time, so that you can evaluate and compare their payouts and performance. Most of the ad networks provide detailed statistics of impressions and clicks along with daily totals, so you can track how individual ad networks are doing for your application.

The rate of return is based on how relevant the ads shown are to the application users and how visible the ads are. It is best to place them so that they are always visible and to use the ad networks' customizations of ad categories to target your demographic. Some developers have reported earning as little as $.04 CPM and as high as $4.78 CPM; however, it is probably fair to base your estimates on something like $.50 CPM. Cost per Action (CPA) ads can pay more, requiring users to fill out surveys or install toolbars to generate revenue.

Here are a few Facebook-aware ad networks to get you started. All of them support multiple ad sizes, have dashboards with performance statistics, and provide code snippets that are easy to integrate with an application. Experiment with each of them to determine which type of ad resonates with your users:

- Ad Parlor (*www.adparlor.com*)
- Ad Chap (*www.adchap.com*)
- Cubics (*www.cubics.com*)
- RockYou (*http://ads.rockyou.com*)

Be aware that some of the other ad networks either won't work at all or won't work effectively on FBML canvas pages because of their use of JavaScript or the need for contextual analysis. You can also look at the Advertising/Monetization topic in the Facebook Developer Forums to find out about new networks and other developers' experiences.

Ads and User Data

In July 2009, after a series of highly publicized user complaints, Facebook clamped down on third-party ad networks. Users complained that ad networks were using their Facebook photos and other information without permission, sometimes even inappropriately. One well-known example involved a husband seeing an ad for singles containing a picture of his wife. Other examples included advertisements for applications implying that a user's friend had challenged them when, in fact, the friend was not even an application user.

In response, Facebook suspended several ad networks and informed the rest that they needed to follow the data privacy rules outlined in the Facebook Terms of Service. Applications are not allowed to pass their users' private data information to third parties, such as advertisers, without their users' permission. This should lead to better quality ads being displayed, although perhaps with a lower click-through rate.

Sponsors

If your application effectively targets a niche or has a large enough user base, you can attract corporate sponsors. A great example of this was the Vampires application. Because of its three million users, Sony Pictures got its developer, RockYou, to rebrand the application around the movie *30 Days of Night*. The rationale was that someone interested in Vampires would probably be interested in movies about vampires.

Don't be afraid to contact companies who would make good sponsors. A fast-growing application for a relevant niche might be a great financial opportunity for both parties. The Compliments application might approach a greeting card company, as compliments are a subcategory of their industry.

Affiliate Links

Applications that feature goods and services can generate income by using affiliate links. You can see the use of affiliate links in applications like LivingSocial, where books have links to buy them on Amazon.com or on iLike, where you can buy music on iTunes. Because having easy purchase links can be considered a valuable feature to users, developers should definitely explore this option.

Many affiliate programs exist beside Amazon and iTunes. In fact, the Internet is rife with them. It is just a matter of finding products and services that both match your users' interests and are relevant to your application. The Compliments application might include audio ringtones as part of the compliment and links to buy the full song on iTunes.

Subscriptions

The freemium model has taken hold on the web, offering a free version that is good enough to attract and retain users and a premium version that is enticing enough to get them to pay to upgrade. The same philosophy can work for applications. Zoosk (*http://apps.facebook.com/zooskers/*), a dating application, has a premium service for $9.99/month that enables additional communication options and enhanced placement of your dating profile. As of this writing, it's one of the top applications on Facebook with millions of monthly active users.

You can roll your own subscription billing service using a payment service, such as PayPal, as the backend—PayPal provides an API just for this purpose. A company called Zuora (*http://developer.zuora.com/facebook*) offers an end-to-end subscription management service and several Facebook applications are using it, such as Teach the People (*http://apps.facebook.com/teachthepeople/*).

If your application has value that people are willing to pay for monthly, the tools now exist to make implementation relatively simple. The Compliments application might enable users to send a limited number of compliments for free or only send pre-canned messages, while the premium model would be unlimited and offer Flash- or video-based compliments.

Andrew Chen has some excellent posts on effectively using a freemium model along with a downloadable spreadsheet (*http://andrewchenblog.com/2009/01/19/how-to-create-a-profitable-freemium-startup-spreadsheet-model-included/*). His key point is that the value you get out of your paying customers has to be more than how much it costs to acquire them plus the cost of running your application. You can calculate the lifetime value for a user with the following formula. Our example uses a 50 percent retention rate and revenue of $10 each month. With 1,000 users, our Long Term Value (LTV) is $20,000. By increasing the retention by 50 percent, you can double your LTV.

```
Ret = Retention % for the period observed
Rev = Revenue per user for the period observed
Long Term Value (LTV) = 1 / (1-Ret) * Rev
LTV = 1 / (1-.5) * 10 * 1000 = $20,000
LTV = 1 / (1-.75) * 10 * 1000 = $40,000
```

Virtual Goods, Currencies, and Economies

Many developers believe that the best way to monetize is by charging for virtual goods. A simple and successful example of using virtual goods for monetization is Facebook's Gift (*www.facebook.com/giftshop.php*) application, where users spend $1 to send a virtual gifts to friends, or by creating an entire virtual economy like Mafia Wars (*http://apps.facebook.com/inthemafia/*). Facebook currently pulls in $75 million a year from Gifts, so users are definitely willing to pay for goods they find valuable. However, some developers report that only 5–15 percent of users will ever pay for any virtual goods in an application, so this would combine well with an advertising strategy.

There are a few options for selling virtual goods. The first is to do a straight cash purchase. You can implement this via the PayPal API or other online payment vendors. Something to watch out for with applications that sell items is that, unless your application is complex to reproduce, another developer might release a "free" version to compete. The Free Gifts application became successful doing this and was able to monetize via ads and sponsorships.

The next option is to implement a point-based system, where users accrue points—or some equivalent—via actions they take in your application and then giving them the option to purchase more of them using real money. Generally, you design this system so that users can quickly gain many more points by buying them outright than they ever could by using the application normally, or the points they can purchase are very limited or hold special significance in the application. For example, the Mafia Wars application lets users spend points on additional features, such as skill upgrades or additional family members. Mafia Wars has created its own payment system for handling point transactions.

If you don't want to implement your own point-management system or you want to enable more options for users, you can integrate services from an external provider. The Spare Change service (*http://sparechangeinc.com/*) allows users to buy points that work across over 700 Facebook applications. Users can add money to their Space Change account from any application supporting it. If they choose to spend their points on your application, you earn the cash equivalent Social Gold and Gambit are some other popular point payment systems, and Facebook is currently beta testing its own payment system.

Other services, such as OfferPal (*www.offerpalmedia.com*) or SuperRewards (*www.srpoints.com*), go beyond just purchasing points. Users can also perform tasks, such as subscribing to Netflix or downloading a ringtone to earn points. Each service takes a small cut of the transactions, but that might be worth it for having them deal with refunds and other customer-service issues dealing with payments.

The biggest and potentially most rewarding method of selling virtual goods is to create an entire virtual economy. Your application provides a marketplace for either reselling existing goods or for selling user-created goods. Your application takes a cut of all transactions.

Here are some basic tips for successfully offering virtual goods:

- Offer enough free content that people don't feel that you are trying to use them. Make the paid content better enough in their eyes to justify its cost.
- Keep the available content updated for both paid and free virtual goods. This ensures that all of your users always have something new to buy.
- Introduce scarcity via limitations on quantity, time, or higher prices. Some users pay premiums for unique items, and scarcity causes users to purchase sooner.
- Make the content relevant to the application. Compliments might offer gifts to be sent along with the compliment or premium compliments that incorporate multimedia to make them much more engaging and desirable for their targets and the users who send them.
- Integrate a ladder concept, where goods get better and more expensive as users interact with the application longer. This encourages both increased usage and generates scarcity.
- Goods can also be decoration. The (Lil) Green Patch application (*http://apps.facebook.com/greentrees/*) sells decorations with the added twist that they only last for a few weeks before they must be purchased again.
- Monitor and analyze the system to make sure that the workflows are streamlined. Finding out user purchase patterns can help refine how you offer goods and the method used to buy them.

Summary

This chapter discussed using ads to promote your application and make money from it. We also discussed other methods of monetization. Here are some key points:

- Use Facebook Home page Ads to promote your application on the high visibility Facebook Home page or Facebook Standard Ads to display ads on the sidebar of pages.

- Facebook Ads Manager allows you to explore the sizes of different demographics on Facebook and target specifically who will see your application's ads. You can run multiple ads with different targeting parameters or content and compare the performance.
- You can use a link exchanges with other developers to promote your application for free.
- Displaying banner ads or integrated ads can make some money for your page, but because of low CPM rates, it requires a large number of page views to make it worthwhile.
- Sponsors and affiliates can increase revenue for applications that target specific niches or are concerned with real-world goods and services.
- Virtual goods offer the biggest income opportunity, but they take some effort and tuning to work effectively. There are many ways to integrate them: direct payment, points, offers, and entire virtual economies.

16

Improving Application Performance and Workflow

This chapter covers advanced techniques for increasing application performance, using Facebook's built-in query language for accessing data, and working with multiple developers.

Facebook only gives your application about 8 seconds to return content from the canvas pages and callbacks before it times out. For canvas pages, this results in displaying an error to the user. For AJAX callbacks, it means that the user's last action won't look like it worked. If your application loads, but is slow, users will become frustrated and stop using it. This chapter details some methods for improving your application's performance using batching and the Facebook Query Language (FQL).

When multiple developers are working on a project in multiple locations, it can be convenient to create separate applications. We go over how to create a configuration file and setup script that allow developers to easily use their own settings, while maintaining a single set of source files.

Batching API Calls

Batching application programming interface (API) calls decreases page load times by reducing the number of round trips to the Facebook server. We covered this for users of the Facebook JavaScript Client Library in Chapter 12, "Facebook JavaScript Client Library;" in this chapter we show how to use the batching API using the PHP client library. Our example will be setting the profile box FBML content for multiple users. Listing 16.1 shows how to do this both with and without batching.

Listing 16.1 extracts the first ten friends of the logged-in user and then executes the `separateCalls()` function to individually call `profile_setFBML()` for each user ID. This is the normal way to execute API functions. The `batchedCalls()` function is then called. Inside, before calling `users_getInfo()`, this function calls `begin_batch()`, which causes the PHP client library to delay executing subsequent API calls. `profile_setFBML()` is called for each user, but notice that the result is returned by reference. This is because the

API call isn't executed until after `batch_end()` is called. At that point, the references are filled in with the actual results. In local tests, batching the API calls was about 5–6 times faster than individually executing the calls.

Listing 16.1 **Batching API Calls**

```
$users = array_slice( $facebook->api_client->friends_list, 0, 10 );
separateCalls( $facebook, $users );
batchedCalls( $facebook, $users );

function separateCalls( $facebook, $users ) {
  $results = array();
  foreach ( $users as $userID ) {
    $results[] = $facebook->api_client->profile_setFBML( NULL, $userID,
      "Some FBML", NULL, NULL, NULL );
  }
}

function batchedCalls( $facebook, $users ){
  $results = array();
  $facebook->api_client->begin_batch();
  foreach ( $users as $userID ) {
  $results[] = & $facebook->api_client->profile_setFBML( NULL, $userID,
      "Some FBML", NULL, NULL, NULL );
  }
  $facebook->api_client->end_batch();
}
```

> **Note**
>
> Currently, there is a bug in the Facebook PHP client library with the `profile_setFBML()` declaration. It doesn't return its value as a reference, so the `results` array in the `batchedCalls()` function won't be set. You can fix this by changing the declaration to include an `&` in `facebookapi_php5_restlib.php`:

```
function &profile_setFBML($markup, ...
```

There are a few constraints with batching. First, you can only batch 20 API calls at a time. Second, you cannot use the results of one API call in another API call in the same batch (for example, calling the `friends_getAppUsers()` function and then using the IDs returned as parameters in a call to the `users_getInfo() function`). The solution to this problem is to use FQL, which the next section covers. You can, however, force the batched calls to be executed sequentially instead of in parallel, which is the default. Do this by setting the `batch_mode` variable like this:

```
$facebook->api_client->batch_mode =
  FacebookRestClient::BATCH_MODE_SERIAL_ONLY;
```

You can set it back like this:

```
$facebook->api_client->batch_mode =
  FacebookRestClient::BATCH_MODE_PARALLEL;
```

All the batched calls are executed on the Facebook servers, even if one of them has an error. Unfortunately, the PHP client library throws a `FacebookRestClientException` exception the first time it encounters an error as it parses the results of the batch run. This means that only those result references the library has already set at that point have values, and you won't know what happened with the rest of the batched calls.

FQL

FQL provides developers with a SQL-like interface to the data store that backs the Facebook Platform. It has several advantages over using the API functions. First, you can constrain the data returned, which can reduce query times and bandwidth. Second, you can replace multiple API calls with FQL statements that use multiple tables instead. FQL speed improvements are large enough that many of the API calls themselves just wrap FQL queries internally. We start with an overview of FQL queries, use the `fql.multiquery()` function to perform multiple queries that can reference each other, and finish with looking at how to run queries on page load using Preload FQL.

FQL Overview

FQL queries are in this format:

```
SELECT [fields] FROM [table] WHERE [conditions] [ORDER BY {[field]}]
  [LIMIT {[offset,] row count}]
```

The `FROM` clause must reference a single table, as shown in Table 16.1. You can access the full list of tables that comprise the Facebook data store at *http://wiki.developers.facebook.com/index.php/FQL_Tables*. Facebook defines a few fields for each of these tables as being *indexable*, which means that indexes have been created for them in the data store for performance reasons. The `WHERE` clause must contain at least one indexable field, but not everything in the `WHERE` clause must be indexable.

Table 16.1 **FQL Tables and Equivalent API Functions**

Table Name	Description	API Equivalent
`album`	Information about a photo album, such as the name.	`photos.getAlbums()`
`application`	Information about a specific application, such as name and usage metrics.	`admin.getAppProperties()`

Table 16.1 **FQL Tables and Equivalent API Functions**

Table Name	Description	API Equivalent
`comment`	Information about a set of user comments, such as the comment's creator and text.	`comments.get()`
`cookies`	Information about a user cookie, such as the cookie's name and value.	`data.getCookies()`
`connection`	Information about a user's connections, such as which Public Profiles they are a Fan of and who their friends are.	`pages.isFan()` and `friends.areFriends()`
`event`	Information about an event, such as the name and date.	`events.get()`
`event_member`	Information about a user's status for an event, such as whether they have RSVP'd.	`events.get()`
`friend`	Information about a whether two users are friends.	`friends.areFriends()`
`friend_request`	Information about whether a friend request has been sent from or received by the logged-in user.	No equivalent
`friendlist`	Information about the friend lists the logged-in user has created.	`friends.getLists()`
`friendlist_member`	Information about which users are a member of a friend list.	`friends.getLists()`
`group`	Information about a specific group, such as the name and description.	`groups.get()`
`group_member`	Information about the members of a group, such as the position they have.	`groups.get()` and `groups.getMembers()`
`link`	Information about a specific link, such as the title and URL.	`links.get()`

Table 16.1 **FQL Tables and Equivalent API Functions**

Table Name	Description	API Equivalent
`mailbox_folder`	Information about a user's Inbox folders, such as name and unread count. This requires the `read_mailbox` permission for access.	`message.getThreadsInFolder()`
`message`	Information about a message in an Inbox thread, such as author and body. This requires the `read_mailbox` permission for access.	`message.getThreadsInFolder()`
`metrics`	Information about an application's metrics, such as the total number of users and page views.	`admin.getMetrics()`
`note`	Information about a specific note, such as the content and title.	`notes.get()`
`notifications`	Information about the notifications for a user, such as title and application id.	`notifications.getList()`
`page`	Information about a Public Profile, such as the name and profile picture.	`pages.getInfo()`
`page_admin`	Information about a Public Profile administrator, such as the page ID and type they administer.	`pages.getInfo()` and `pages.isAdmin()`
`page_fan`	Information about a Public Profile Fan, such as the page ID and type they are a fan of.	`pages.getInfo()` and `pages.isFan()`
`permissions`	Information about the extended permissions a user has granted, such as email and offline access.	`Permissions.checkGrantedApiAccess()`
`photo`	Information about a specific photo, such as its URL and caption.	`photos.get()`

Table 16.1 **FQL Tables and Equivalent API Functions**

Table Name	Description	API Equivalent
`photo_tag`	Information about a specific photo's tags, such as the co-ordinates and text.	`photos.get()` and `photos.getTags()`
`profile`	Information about a user's profile, such as their profile picture and URL.	`user_getInfo()` and `pages.getInfo()`
`standard_friend_info`	Information about whether two users are friends. This should only be used outside of an active session, such as for cron jobs. You should use the friend table during an active session.	`friends.get()` and `friends.areFriends()`
`standard_user_info`	Information about a specific user. This should only be used outside of an active session, such as for cron jobs. You should use the user table during an active session.	`users.getInfo()` and `users.getStandardInfo()`
`status`	Information about a user's status, such as the time and message.	`status.get()`
`stream`	Information about posts in a user's stream, such as the post time and message.	`stream.get()`
`stream_filter`	Returns a filter key that is can be used to filter queries on the stream table, such as by friend list or networks.	`stream.getFilters()`
`thread`	Information about the conversation threads in a user's Inbox, such as the subject and recipients. This requires the `read_mailbox` permission for access.	`message.getThreadsInFolder()`
`user`	Information about a specific user, such as birthday and last name.	`users.getInfo()` and `users.getStandardInfo()`

Let's go over a few quick examples. Listing 16.2 shows an API call to `friends.getAppUsers()` and then its equivalent in FQL, using the `fql.query()` function. The `friends.getAppUsers()` function returns the user IDs of all the friends of the currently logged-in user who have authorized the application. The FQL query appears to be more complex, so let's walk through it.

The `user` table has the `is_app_user` field, which represents whether a user has authorized the application. The `friend` table defines relationships between two user IDs using fields `uid1` and `uid2`. FQL can only reference a single table in the `FROM` clause, so we can't use both the `friend` and `user` tables in it. We want to end up with a set of user IDs, so we use the `user` table in `FROM`. That means that the `WHERE` clause has to use a subquery to access the `friend` table. The subquery gets the IDs of the users who are friends of the logged-in user. The `WHERE` clause constrains the uids that match the subquery by those users who also have `is_app_user` set to 1.

Listing 16.2 **Simple API Call and Its FQL Equivalent**

```
$appUsers = $facebook->api_client->friends_getAppUsers();

$query = "
  SELECT uid FROM user WHERE uid IN (
     SELECT uid2 FROM friend WHERE uid1 = $loggedInUser
  )
  AND is_app_user = 1";
$appUsers = $facebook->api_client->fql_query( $query );
```

Previously, we talked about using the IDs returned from `friends_getAppUsers()` in calls to `users.getInfo()` to get all their birthdays. Listing 16.3 shows how to implement that in a single FQL query.

Listing 16.3 **Combining Multiple API Calls in One FQL Query**

```
SELECT uid, birthday
FROM user
WHERE uid IN ( SELECT uid2 FROM friend WHERE uid1 = $loggedInUser)
      AND is_app_user = 1
```

Notice that all we had to do was add the `birthday` field to the previous query. FQL also lets you access subfields, such as the country from the user's current location. Listing 16.4 shows how to do this for a particular user.

Listing 16.4 **Accessing Subfields Directly**

```
SELECT current_location.country
FROM user
WHERE uid = $userID
```

> **Note**
> Unfortunately, the FQL Tables wiki page does not display the subfields for each table. For that, you need to go to the equivalent API function wiki page at *http://wiki.developers.facebook.com/index.php/API*.

We mentioned that the `WHERE` clause must reference an indexable field. If you wanted to get all the photos for a particular user, you might try to write the query like this:

```
SELECT pid FROM photo WHERE owner = $userID
```

However, `owner` is not an indexable field, so the query fails. Instead, you have to use the indexable album ID field, `aid`, in a subquery. Here, we get the photos from albums the user owns:

```
SELECT link FROM photo WHERE aid IN ( SELECT aid FROM album WHERE owner = $userID )
```

Subqueries can also nest other subqueries, as Listing 16.5 demonstrates. This query finds all the photos tagged with application user friends of a particular user. Notice how we reuse the FQL query from Listing 16.2 for getting the friends of a user who are also application users.

Listing 16.5 **Nested Subqueries**

```
SELECT pid FROM photo_tag WHERE subject IN (
  SELECT uid FROM user WHERE uid IN (
    SELECT uid2 FROM friend WHERE uid1 = $userID
  )
  AND is_app_user = 1
)
```

FQL also supports some functions and operators, as shown in Table 16.2.

Table 16.2 **FQL Functions and Operators**

Table Name	Description
`now()`	Returns the current UNIX time.
`rand()`	Returns a random number.
`strlen(string)`	Returns the length of a string.
`concat(string1, ...)`	Returns a concatenation of several strings.
`substr(string, start, length)`	Returns a substring from a start position with a given length. Returns 0 if not found.
`strpos(haystack, needle)`	Returns the index of a needle in the haystack. Returns -1 if not found.
`lower()`	Returns a lowercase string.

Table 16.2 **FQL Functions and Operators**

`upper()`	Returns an uppercase string.
`comparison operators`	FQL supports the following comparison operators: =, >, <, >=, <=
`arithmetic operators`	FQL supports the following arithmetic operators: +, -, *, /
`logical operators`	FQL supports the following logical operators: AND, OR, NOT

Say that you want to retrieve a list, formatted for display, of all a user's friends who have birthdays in the next three months. Listing 16.6 shows how to write that query. We use the FQL `concat()` function to create a formatted string of the user's name and birthday. We use the FQL `substr()` function to get the month from first two characters of the `birthday_date` field, which is always formatted mm/dd/yyyy. We subtract the current month number and constrain our results to when that value is greater than 3.

Listing 16.6 **Accessing Subfields Directly**

```
SELECT concat( name, " - ",birthday ) FROM user WHERE uid IN (
  SELECT uid2 FROM friend WHERE uid1 = $userID
)
AND ( substr( birthday_date, 0, 2 ) - $currentMonthNumber ) >= 3
```

fql.multiquery

One of the problems with the standard FQL query is that that subqueries cannot reference the outer query. This often means that you have to use multiple queries to get the data you need. The `fql.multiquery()` function lets you pass all these queries to be executed in one call, and each query can reference the other. This method takes a JSON-encoded array of queries, each with its own name. Queries use the same format as the normal `fql.query()` method, except you can now reference the results of other queries using their name in the `FROM` clause.

For example, if you want to get both tagged photos and recent links for all app user friends, you can call `fql.multiquery()`, as demonstrated in Listing 16.7. We create a query for the commonly used app user friends query called `appfriends`. This query is used as the pool of UIDs for the other two queries, referencing it like we do here, with the query name preceded by a #:

```
SELECT uid FROM #friends
```

Listing 16.7 **Using `fql.multiquery` to Reference Names Queries**

```
$queries = '{
"appfriends":"SELECT uid FROM user WHERE uid IN (
              SELECT uid2 FROM friend WHERE uid1 = 698700806
             ) AND is_app_user = 1",
"taggedPhotos":"SELECT pid FROM photo_tag WHERE subject IN (
                  SELECT uid FROM #friends
                ) LIMIT 10",
"links":"SELECT link_id FROM link WHERE owner IN (
           SELECT uid FROM #friends
         ) LIMIT 10"}';
$appUsers = $facebook->api_client->fql_multiquery( $queries );
```

The PHP client library's `fql_multiquery()` function returns the result of each query in an array, as shown in Listing 16.8.

Listing 16.8 **PHP Client Library `fql_multiquery()` Results**

```
array
  0 =>
    array
      'name' => string 'appfriends' (length=7)
      'fql_result_set' =>
        array
          0 =>
            array
              'uid' => string '698700806' (length=12)
...
  1 =>
    array
      'name' => string 'links' (length=5)
      'fql_result_set' =>
        array
          0 =>
            array
              'link_id' => string '122217238584' (length=12)
...
```

The `fql.multiquery()` function performs faster than using several individual `fql.query()` calls, even if those calls are batched using the batching API.

Preloading FQL

If your application canvas pages end up using the same queries (or API calls that ultimately call them) each time they are loaded, you can tell Facebook to automatically run those queries before calling your page and pass you the results. Although this doesn't reduce the FQL query time, it does remove the round-trip time those queries take if they are executed via `fql.query()` calls.

> **Note**
>
> This feature is still in beta, but it has been used for a while now by many developers. It was also used for one of the biggest applications on Facebook, Top Friends.

This preloading is achieved through the user of the `admin.setAppProperties()` API function. This function is not called during the normal operation of an application, but as a set up mechanism, much like registering Feed Template bundles. We will set the `preload_fql` property, passing in an array of rules. Each rule is composed of three parts: the name, the pattern, and the query:

- Name is a user-defined name to apply to this rule. This name is used as part of a `POST` variable passed to the application canvas page.
- Pattern is a regular expression that matches the canvas pages to which this should be sent. The entire URL is available, so you can match individual files, entire directories, or the entire site.
- Query is an FQL statement to be executed. It can be parameterized to use the value of any `GET` parameter and can use a special parameter, `{*user*}`, which is the active user.

Let's use our app user friends query as an example. Listing 16.9 shows how to create a rule and pass it to `admin.setAppProperties()`. We set the name to appfriends and our pattern to match all pages. The query is the same one we have been using, except we use the `{*user*}` token for the active user. We use `json_encode()` to make sure that the regular expressions are escaped properly and convert the array to the string format that the API call expects. If we want to use a `GET` parameter called UID instead of the active user for the query, we just replace the curly braces with `{UID}`.

Listing 16.9 **Preloading FQL Using `admin.setAppProperties()`**

```
$rules = json_encode(
         array("appfriends" =>
           array("pattern" => ".*",
                 "query" => "SELECT uid FROM user WHERE uid IN (
                   SELECT uid2 FROM friend WHERE uid1 = {*user*} )
                   AND is_app_user = 1")));

$facebook->api_client->admin_setAppProperties(array("preload_fql" => $rules)));
```

After this code is executed, Facebook changes what it sends to your application in the `POST` variables. This differs between FBML and IFrame canvas pages, so we start with what happens with FBML canvas pages. First, Facebook no longer sends the `fb_sig_friends` variable. If you depend on this list of all the user's friends, you need to add another rule for it, like this:

```
array("friends" =>
  array("pattern" => ".*",
    "query" => "SELECT uid2 FROM friend WHERE uid1 = {*user*}"))
```

The second thing is that Facebook now sends an `fb_sig_appfriends` variable that contains the JSON-encoded results of your query. If there is an error executing the query, this value will be something like the following line, returning the text of the query that Facebook attempted to execute:

```
'appfriends' => string '{"error_query":"SELECT uid FROM ..."}'
```

The third change is that there is a new `fb_sig_preload_fql_timestamp` variable. This is the timestamp for when Facebook started to process your FQL rules. You can compare this to `fb_sig_time`, which is when Facebook finished and called your canvas page, to know if you need to spend time tuning your preload queries.

For IFrame canvas pages, preloading FQL is disabled by default. These canvas pages can either use the Facebook JavaScript Client Library `FB.Facebook.apiClient.preloadFQL_get()` function, passing a callback parameter that receives the preloaded FQL results, or they can turn on preloading for the canvas page using a special rule. This rule has the name `fb_iframe_post`, and the pattern should be set to match those IFrame canvas pages you want to receive the preloaded FQL. No query is needed for this rule. Listing 16.11 shows the addition of this rule for IFrame canvas pages.

Listing 16.10 **Preloading FQL for IFrame Canvas Pages**

```
$rules = json_encode(
          array("appfriends" =>
            array("pattern" => ".*",
                  "query" => "SELECT uid FROM user WHERE uid IN (
                    SELECT uid2 FROM friend WHERE uid1 = {*user*} )
                    AND is_app_user = 1"),
                  "fb_iframe_post" =>
                     array("pattern" => ".*")));

$facebook->api_client->admin_setAppProperties(array("preload_fql" => $rules)));
```

After this rule is added, IFrames canvas pages receive all the POST variables prefixed with `fb_post_sig_` instead of `fb_sig_`. This prevents namespace collisions with the existing Facebook information that IFrame canvas pages already receive as GET parameters prefixed with `fb_sig_`. There is a slight cost to enable preload FQL for IFrames, because Facebook must perform a slight, cached redirect on page access.

Working with Multiple Developers

Developing a Facebook application with multiple developers can be complicated, because it makes it difficult to verify local code changes without pushing to the live server. Generally, developers run a web server on their local machines to test these changes and push them to a live web server only when complete. This section covers a few things that you can do to make this process easier. For our examples, we use the Compliments application with two developers.

Setting Up Port Forwarding for Each Developer

It is likely that multiple developers will be working in the same spot, at least some of the time. Because Facebook applications need to be externally accessible, each developer needs to use a different port for their application, or more specifically, for their local web server to listen on. For example, one developer would get port 81 forwarded to his machine at each location, and the other developer would get port 82 forwarded to his machine at each location. Port 80 is required for some flash testing, so that often rotates between developers as needed. These ports are used in the following steps.

Additionally, if you want to support multiple development locations, create DNS entries for each location, such as *location1.example.com* and *location2.example.com*. In the following examples, we assume that the application deployment server is set to *www.example.com*. We use these values to generate our local callback URLs.

Creating Additional Applications for Each Developer

We already created the main Compliments application in the Facebook Developer application. Now, each developer needs to create his own Compliments application for local testing and debugging. These new applications need to mirror the main application except for the application name, Canvas Page URL, and the Callback URLs. We recommend using a standard naming convention for these, such as the application name followed by the developer's initials. For example, say John creates an application named Compliments-J, with Canvas Page URL set to compliments-j, and all the Callback URLs set to his local server and assigned port.

Developers need to also add each other as developers to the applications, and turn on Sandbox mode to keep their applications from being accessed by other Facebook users and ensure that any messaging these applications publish to Facebook is only visible to their developers. In their local web servers' configuration, they should map their application to the local source directory for Compliments and make sure that the server is listening on their assigned port. Each application will have its own application ID, API key, and Secret key that will be used in the configuration explained in the next step.

Creating a Smart Local Configuration File

The main Compliments application uses a hardcoded `globals.inc` file that contains constants for URLs, paths, API and Secret keys, and template bundle IDs. However, multiple developers need a way to use the correct settings for each developer and location. To do this, we create a configuration file that contains the settings for all the versions of the application. For Compliments, we create a new file called `config.ini` in the `inc` directory and add the contents of Listing 16.11 into it.

This file contains the specific settings for each developer: the application settings, such as name and keys; the database server and schema; the port that is being forwarded; and whether to turn on Sandbox mode. Note that this and any configuration files should never be shown or accessible via the web server; if they were, anyone could access your Secret key, and developers must take appropriate steps to ensure that it stays private.

Listing 16.11 **Preloading FQL for IFrame Canvas Pages**

```
DEV1_FB_APP_KEY        = XXXXXXXXXXXXXXXXXXXXXXXXXXXXXXXX;
DEV1_FB_APP_SECRET     = XXXXXXXXXXXXXXXXXXXXXXXXXXXXXXXX;
DEV1_FB_APP_NAME       = compliments-j;
DEV1_FB_APP_ID         = XXXXXXXXXXX;
DEV1_FB_DB_SERVER      = localhost;
DEV1_FB_DB_SCHEMA      = compliments;
DEV1_PORT              = 81;
DEV1_DEV_MODE          = true;

DEV2_FB_APP_KEY       = YYYYYYYYYYYYYYYYYYYYYYYYYYYYYYYYY;
DEV2_FB_APP_SECRET    = YYYYYYYYYYYYYYYYYYYYYYYYYYYYYYYYY;
DEV2_FB_APP_NAME      = compliments-c;
DEV2_FB_APP_ID        = YYYYYYYYYYYY;
DEV2_FB_DB_SERVER     = localhost;
DEV2_FB_DB_SCHEMA     = compliments;
DEV2_PORT             = 82;
DEV2_DEV_MODE         = true;

WWW_FB_APP_KEY        = ZZZZZZZZZZZZZZZZZZZZZZZZZZZZZZZZ;
WWW_FB_APP_SECRET     = ZZZZZZZZZZZZZZZZZZZZZZZZZZZZZZZZ;
WWW_FB_APP_NAME       = compliments;
WWW_FB_APP_ID         = ZZZZZZZZZZZ;
WWW_DB_SERVER         = maindb.example.com;
WWW_FB_DB_SCHEMA      = compliments;
WWW_DEV_MODE          = false;

PHP_DBG_LOG_EXT        = _log.txt;
VISIBLE_APP_NAME       = Compliments;
```

Listing 16.12 shows a script that parses this configuration file and generates the constants used in the application. For Compliments, we create a new file called `setup.php` in the `config` directory and add the contents of Listing 16.12 into it. This script requires two arguments, the developer's name and the current location, like this:

```
php setup.php dev1 location1
```

The developer's name is put into `$user` and is used to pull the settings prefixed with it, so `dev1` uses all the settings prefixed `DEV1_`. The current location is put into `$location` and used to set the proper subdomain for the callback URLs. The `config.ini` file is then read in, and the values are stored in the `$settings` array and added to `$userConstants` string to be written out. The non-user specific constants are generated and then they are all written out to a file called `constants.inc` in the `inc` directory. Finally, an array of application properties are created to pass to the Facebook `admin.setAppProperties()` API function. In this example, we set the Canvas Callback URL and whether the application is in Sandbox mode. You might add other properties as they fit your application's needs. `admin.setAppProperties()` is called to register these properties, and the script is done.

Listing 16.12 **Script to Generate Constants from Configuration**

```
<?php
  // usage: php setup.php user location
  $user = strtoupper($argv[1]);
  $location = $argv[2];

////////////////////////////////////////////////////////////////////////////////
// Parse the config file
  $settings = parse_ini_file('config.ini');
  // assumption is that we are in a subdirectory of the root, such as config
  chdir('..');
  $settings["MAIN_PATH"]      = str_replace('\\', '/', getcwd() . '/' ) ;
  $settings["FBLIB_PATH"]     = $settings["MAIN_PATH"] . "fblib/";
  $settings["INC_PATH"]       = $settings["MAIN_PATH"] . "inc/";
  $settings["PORT"]           = $settings["{$user}_PORT"];
  $settings["FB_APP_NAME"]    = $settings["{$user}_FB_APP_NAME"];
  $settings["FB_APP_KEY"]     = $settings["{$user}_FB_APP_KEY"];
  $settings["FB_APP_SECRET"]  = $settings["{$user}_FB_APP_SECRET"];
  $settings["DEV_MODE"]       = $settings["{$user}_DEV_MODE"];
  $userConstants = "
    define('FB_APP_KEY',       '".$settings["{$user}_FB_APP_KEY"]."');
    define('FB_APP_SECRET',    '".$settings["{$user}_FB_APP_SECRET"]."');
    define('FB_APP_ID',        '".$settings["{$user}_FB_APP_ID"]."');
    define('FB_APP_NAME',      '".$settings["{$user}_FB_APP_NAME"]."');
    define('FB_DB_SERVER',     '".$settings["{$user}_FB_DB_SERVER"]."');
    define('FB_DB_SCHEMA',     '".$settings["{$user}_FB_DB_SCHEMA"]."');
    define('FB_DBG_OUT_FILE', '".$settings["MAIN_PATH"]."'.
                               '".$settings["{$user}_FB_APP_NAME"]."'.
                               '".$settings["PHP_DBG_LOG_EXT"]."');
  ";
  if(isset($settings["PORT"])) {
      $settings["BASE_URL"] = "http://$location.example.com".
       ":{$settings["PORT"]}/";
  } else {
      $settings["BASE_URL"] = "http://$location.example.com/";
  }

////////////////////////////////////////////////////////////////////////////////
// Output the constants file
  define('DIVIDER', PHP_EOL.'====================================='.PHP_EOL);
  $output = "<?php
  define('MAIN_PATH',          '{$settings["MAIN_PATH"]}');
```

Listing 16.12 **Continued**

```
  define('FBLIB_PATH',         '{$settings["FBLIB_PATH"]}');
  define('INC_PATH',           '{$settings["INC_PATH"]}');
  define('VISIBLE_APP_NAME',   '{$settings["VISIBLE_APP_NAME"]}');

  $userConstants

  //================================
  // FACEBOOK constants
  //================================
  require_once FBLIB_PATH.'facebook.php';

  define('FB_APPS_BASE_URL', strval(Facebook::get_facebook_url('apps')));
  define('FB_APP_URL',       FB_APPS_BASE_URL.'/'.FB_APP_NAME.'/');


  //================================
  // App-specific constants
  //================================
  define('BASE_URL',      '{$settings["BASE_URL"]}');
  define('APP_URL',        BASE_URL.FB_APP_NAME.'/');
  define('IMG_PATH',       APP_URL.'img/');
  ?>";

  echo(DIVIDER.'WRITING CONSTANTS.INI AS:'.DIVIDER);
  print_r($output);

  $path = $settings["MAIN_PATH"].'inc/constants.inc';
  $file = fopen($path, 'w');
  fwrite($file, $output);
  fclose($file);

////////////////////////////////////////////////////////////////////////////////
// Register the  new application settings with Facebook
  define('APP_URL', $settings["BASE_URL"].$settings["FB_APP_NAME"].'/');

  // properties to set via admin.setAppProperties(). Add more settings as needed
  $data = array('dev_mode'                        => $settings["DEV_MODE"],
                'callback_url'                    => APP_URL
                );

  echo(DIVIDER."Setting up for location: $location".DIVIDER);
  echo(DIVIDER.'SETTING APP PROPERTIES TO THE FOLLOWING:'.DIVIDER);
  print_r($data);

  require_once $settings["FBLIB_PATH"].'facebook.php';
  $facebook = new Facebook($settings["FB_APP_KEY"], $settings["FB_APP_SECRET"]);
```

Listing 16.12 **Continued**

```
  define('FB_APP_URL', strval(Facebook::get_facebook_url('apps')).'/'.
                      $settings["FB_APP_NAME"]);

  if(isset($facebook)) {
    $result = $facebook->api_client->admin_setAppProperties($data);

    if($result == TRUE) {
      echo(DIVIDER.'SUCCEEDED!'.DIVIDER);
    } else {
      print_r(DIVIDER.'ERROR\t'.$result.DIVIDER);
    }
  } else {
    echo(DIVIDER."Facebook object error. Cannot set app properties.".DIVIDER);
  }
?>
```

Listing 16.13 shows the output of this script in `constants.inc`.

Listing 16.13 **Script Output in `constants.inc`**

```
<?php
  define('MAIN_PATH',          'D:/src/products/compliments/');
  define('FBLIB_PATH',         'D:/src/compliments/fblib/');
  define('INC_PATH',           'D:/src/compliments/inc/');
  define('VISIBLE_APP_NAME',   'Compliments');

  define('FB_APP_KEY',       'XXXXXXXXXXXXXXXXXXXXXXXXXXXXXXXX');
  define('FB_APP_SECRET',    'XXXXXXXXXXXXXXXXXXXXXXXXXXXXXXXX');
  define('FB_APP_ID',        'XXXXXXXXXXX');
  define('FB_APP_NAME',      'compliments-j');
  define('FB_DB_SERVER',     'localhost');
  define('FB_DB_SCHEMA',     'compliments');
  define('FB_DBG_OUT_FILE', 'D:/src/compliments/'.
                             'compliments-j'.
                             '_log.txt');

  //===============================
  // FACEBOOK constants
  //===============================
  require_once FBLIB_PATH.'facebook.php';

  define('FB_APPS_BASE_URL', strval(Facebook::get_facebook_url('apps')));
  define('FB_APP_URL',       FB_APPS_BASE_URL.'/'.FB_APP_NAME.'/');
```

Listing 16.13 **Continued**

```
  //================================
  // App-specific constants
  //================================
  define('BASE_URL',       'http://location1.example.com:81/');
  define('APP_URL',         BASE_URL.FB_APP_NAME.'/');
  define('IMG_PATH',        APP_URL.'img/');
?>
```

Typically, `config.ini` and `setup.php` are checked in to the project source control, while `constants.inc` is not, because it is generated and specific to each user.

> **Source Control**
>
> If you are not already using a source control system to manage your application project files, consider Subversion *(http://subversion.tigris.org/)* or Git *(http://git-scm.com/)*. Source control is a critical component of any nontrivial software-development effort because it allows multiple developers to work on the same set of files, keeps backups (revisions) of all files, and allows you to roll back to previous versions of files for testing or bug fixes. In most source control systems, every revision of a file is stored with its timestamp and an identifier for the user who made the revision. Different revisions of a file can be compared, and changes made to the same file by multiple users can be merged. This allows every developer to use the same set of source files; moreover, it prevents "...but it works on my machine"-style bugs. No serious software effort should ever be launched without one in place!

The Compliments application includes `constants.inc` instead of `globals.inc`. The `setup.php` script is run on each development machine once to generate the `constants.inc` file, and then again whenever the developer switches locations. It also makes sense to include the functionality from the `register_feed_templates.php` file we created in Chapter 9, "Feed Stories, Feed Forms, and Templates," so that it automatically adds the new template bundle IDs to `constants.inc`.

Summary

This chapter covered the use of the batching API, using FQL, and working with multiple developers. Here are some key points:

- Facebook requires that pages load in 8 seconds or less, so using batching and FQL can be critical for an application's success.

- The batching API can eliminate several round trips between your application and Facebook by sending up to 20 calls at once. These calls can be executed in parallel on the Facebook server, further reducing page load times.
- The `batch.run()` Facebook API function executes all the batched API calls regardless of whether any fail. However, the Facebook PHP client library `end_batch()` function throws an exception at the first error result it encounters, which leaves your application without the ability to know the results of the rest of the calls.
- FQL is a SQL-like language that implements many of the API functions. It offers speed improvements and the ability to eliminate additional API calls because of its flexibility.
- FQL has the constraint of only accessing one table in the FROM clause of the SELECT statement. If you require data from multiple tables, you need to use the `fql.multiquery()` API function while enabling queries to reference other queries.
- Multiple developers can simplify testing and their transition between development environments by using a setup file that automates generating constants and updating the developer settings for their application.

V

Appendices

Appendix A

Resources

This appendix serves as a quick reference for important resources or commonly accessed URLs related to developing for the Facebook Platform. Additionally, the most important beta features Facebook has released are described. Because these lists constantly change, we provide an updated list on our website (*www.essentialfacebook.com*).

Links

These links are grouped into links on Facebook, links related to developer tools outside of Facebook, and other external sites that provide good references for Facebook developers.

Facebook

Facebook provides a lot of documentation on its wiki and other pages, which can make it difficult to find specific items. We believe that these are the URLs that developers will access frequently.

- Application Verification Program. *http://developers.facebook.com/verification.php*
- Client Libraries. *http://wiki.developers.facebook.com/index.php/Client_Libraries*
- Custom Tags Directory. *http://wiki.developers.facebook.com/index.php/Custom_Tags_Directory*
- Developer Application. *www.facebook.com/developers*
- Developer Wiki. *http://wiki.developers.facebook.com/index.php/Main_Page*
- Developer Forum. *http://forum.developers.facebook.com/*
- Developer Test Accounts. *www.facebook.com/developers/become_test_account.php*
- Developer Test Consoles. *http://developers.facebook.com/tools.php*
- Facebook Open Source. *http://developers.facebook.com/opensource.php*
- fbFund. *http://developers.facebook.com/fbFund.php?tab=about*
- Guiding Principles. *http://developers.facebook.com/get_started.php?tab=principles*
- Platform Statistics. *www.facebook.com/press/info.php?statistics*
- Terms of Service. *www.facebook.com/terms.php*

Developer Tools

These websites contain tools that enable or assist with Facebook development that we cover in this book:

- APC. *http://php.net/apc*
- Firebug. *www.getfirebug.com*
- Firebug Lite. *http://getfirebug.com/lite.html*
- Memcached. *www.danga.com/memcached*
- Web Developer Toolbar. *http://chrispederick.com/work/web-developer*
- YSlow. *http://developer.yahoo.com/yslow*
- YUI Library. *http://developer.yahoo.com/yui*

Facebook News

These websites provide news updates for developers and users:

- All Facebook. *http://allfacebook.com*
- Developer News. *http://developers.facebook.com/news.php*
- Facebook News. *http://blog.facebook.com/blog.php*
- Inside Facebook. *www.insidefacebook.com*

Appendix B

Beta Features

Facebook constantly adds new features for developers to use; however, they all must go through a beta period before Facebook releases them or changes the Platform to use them. For some features, the beta period can be long, and some features never make it out of beta. For example, as of this writing, the Data Store application programming interface (API) has been in beta for almost two years. This appendix quickly overviews the most important features that are currently in beta.

Add Page Referrer

Tracking how parts of an application are used is critical, as discussed in Chapter 14, "Measuring Application Success." In that chapter, we went over how Facebook Insights can show which parts of the application are being used and how users respond to its messaging. The Add Page Referrer feature allows developers to track the origins of application installs by adding a new parameter, called `app_ref`, to the end of links that point to the application's authorization page. For example, links in an invitation might have `&app_ref=invite` appended, whereas links on a canvas page might have `&app_ref=canvas`. The results for these tracking parameters are shown in the application's Insights.

Stream

With Facebook's switch to a real-time streaming update model, it realized that it needed to provide developers with a new way to access the Feed. Facebook also wanted to provide developers access to the stream from outside of Facebook, whether it is on an external website, a mobile application, or a desktop application. The new Open Stream API replaces the existing Feed publishing model and allows applications to read content from the stream, publish their own content, and manage comments or ratings for individual Feed stories. This feature is important because it represents the future of developer access to the heart of Facebook's information flow. If you check out any of Facebook's beta features, make it this one.

Custom Tags

Custom tags provide a way for developers to define their own Facebook Markup Language (FBML) tags. These tags can be used within an application to hold common fragments of FBML to reduce bandwidth for the application by sending only the custom tag across the wire. They can also be made public and shared in Facebook's Custom Tags Directory so that any application can use them.

Custom FBML tags can be defined to accept parameterized input, such as most FBML tags, and can include both FBML and Facebook JavaScript (FBJS) code. They even allow for sharing functionality across applications, such as the Family Crest tag, which shows a family crest for a surname, or the iLike tag, which displays a users' favorite songs and playlists.

Data Store API

The Data Store API is an object-based database that's hosted on Facebook's servers with the goal of allowing applications to deploy quickly without having to worry about scaling their own database server. Object Types are like tables in traditional relational databases with the object's properties representing columns. An instance of an Object is like a table row. For small sets of data, the Data Store API is convenient; however, larger amounts of data have caused access times to become increasingly slow. This feature has also been in beta for a long time with minimal updates, so it is not clear if it has a long-term future.

FBJS Local Proxy

When applications make AJAX calls via the FBJS `Ajax` class, the call is routed through a Facebook proxy. This is done so that any FBML returned can be parsed and sanitized. If an application makes AJAX calls that are not returning FBML, it is more efficient to skip the proxy and directly connect the caller to the endpoint.

The FBJS Local Proxy enables this by including a Flash object on the page to serve as a local proxy between the calling FJBS code and the AJAX endpoint. This additionally requires a special file, known as a cross-domain policy file, at the root of the server, and limits the AJAX endpoint URLs to use only port 80. Endpoints will also not receive any session information as part of the call, so this method should not be used if the code at the AJAX endpoint needs it to call Facebook API methods that require it.

Cookies

The Cookies feature enables application-created cookies to be associated with a user's Facebook account so that the data is present across all browsers and machines. For small amounts of data, cookies can provide a convenient and fast data store. Cookies can even be stored for users who have not authorized the application.

FBML Tags

There are several FBML tags currently in the beta phase that are of interest.

<fb:board>

The `<fb:board>` tag adds a discussion board similar to the one on Public and Application Profiles. Facebook provides the full functionality and hosting for the board.

<fb:chat-invite>

The `<fb:chat-invite>` tag renders as a list of the viewer's friends who are currently online and available for Facebook Chat. Clicking an individual user in this list opens a new chat window with that user. The application can provide a precanned chat message, potentially containing a URL, that is displayed automatically in the new window. This could be used inside a game or in any situation where an application has a need for real-time collaboration between users.

<fb:feed>

The `<fb:feed>` tag displays a News Feed containing the latest stories from the application about the viewing user's friends. This can be used only on canvas pages.

<fb:typeahead-input>

The `<fb:typeahead-input>` tag creates a typeahead or autocomplete input control that behaves like the `<fb:friend-selector>` FBML tag or the YUI autocomplete control. The set of completion values are created for a set of `<fb:typeahead-option>` subtags, one for each value.

IFrame URL

Many IFrame applications switch between pages by setting the URL `target` to the IFrame rather than the parent. This can cut down on load times, but the URL in the address bar of the browser might not change, which leaves the user without a way to properly navigate. The beta feature for Facebook Connect provides two methods to enable IFrame applications to set the proper URL in the address bar. The first is the `FB.CanvasClient.syncUrl()` function, which, when called during page load, automatically updates the address bar's URL with the current page using the Quick Transition syntax (see the section, "Quick Transitions"). The other method, used by pages that update their content dynamically, manually calls `FB.CanvasClient.changeUrlSuffix()` when a new "page" has been loaded, passing the new URL identifier. The browser address bar is then updated using the Quick Transition syntax.

Links, Notes, and Status

There are new API methods and Facebook Query Language (FQL) queries to create and retrieve links, notes, and status updates from within an application. To post links to a user's wall, they must grant the `share_item` permission. To create or edit notes, they must grant the `create_note` permission. To set a user's status, they must grant the `status_update` permission. All notes, the most recent status updates, and links set through the application can be retrieved.

LiveMessage

The LiveMessage feature exists in both FBJS and the API, and it allows applications to send messages to a specific user's browser. A message consists of an event name, a recipient user ID, and a JSON-encoded string of the message data. If the targeted recipient is currently interacting with the application on the profile or canvas page, the message can be received by an FBJS callback function registered to accept messages for that event name. This functionality enables real-time updating of application content.

Quick Transitions

Clicking a URL within Facebook previously caused a full page reload, including all of the surrounding Facebook UI (or chrome). Quick Transitions is a technique implemented by Facebook, where clicking a link appends a portion of the new URL onto the old URL, separated by a #. For example, clicking my profile and then the Thought Labs Public Profile results in this URL: *www.facebook.com/home.php#/pages/Thought-Labs/68071669609*. The benefit of this URL system is that Facebook knows that it doesn't need to reload the chrome for the portion after the #, so it just loads the inner content using AJAX, which can speed up page-load times. Applications can enable support for this within their application's settings.

IFrame applications also need to modify how they handle links to other pages or tabs to support Quick Transitions. They can either add onclick handlers for each link to set the correct URL or use the IFrame URL functionality, previously discussed.

Video Upload

The Video Upload feature enables users to upload video to the Facebook video servers from inside an application. Users must grant the application the `video_upload` permission, and they are subject to the same upload limits that they would have if they uploaded directly via the Facebook Video application. These limits can be checked ahead of time through an API call.

Symbols

A

B

G

J

K–L

M

N

O

Q–R

V

W

X–Y–Z

Tap Social Networks to Improve Your Business

The Facebook Era

Clara Shih • ISBN 978-0-13-715222-3

"...A must-read for CEOs and other executives who want to understand Facebook and, more importantly, take the right actions to stay relevant and stay competitive."

—David Mather, President, Hoovers, Inc.

Online social networks are fundamentally changing the way we live, work, and interact. They offer businesses immense opportunities to transform customer relationships for profit: opportunities that touch virtually every business function from sales and marketing to recruiting, collaboration to executive decision-making, and product development to innovation. In *The Facebook Era*, Clara Shih systematically outlines the business promise of social networking and shows how to transform that promise into reality.

Shih is singularly qualified to write this book: One of the world's top business social networking thought leaders and practitioners, she created the first business application on Facebook and leads salesforce.com's partnership with Facebook. Through case studies, examples, and a practical how-to guide, Shih helps individuals, companies, and organizations understand and take advantage of social networks to transform customer relationships for sales and marketing. Shih systematically identifies your best opportunities to use social networks to source new business opportunities, target marketing messages, find the best employees, and engage customers as true partners throughout the innovation cycle. Finally, she presents a detailed action plan for positioning your company to win in today's radically new era—*The Facebook Era*.

For more information and to read sample material, please visit informit.com.

Safari Books Online

This title is also available at safari.informit.com.

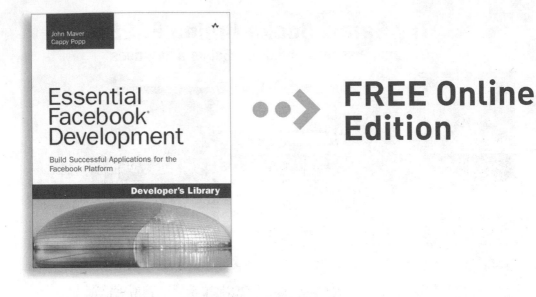